THE BROOKLYN TRILOGY
Three Delvecchio P.I. Novels

OTHER MYSTERIES BY ROBERT J. RANDISI

Hitman with a Soul Trilogy
Upon My Soul
Souls of the Dead
Envy the Dead

The John Headston Series
The Headstone Detective Agency
Headstone's Folly (*)
Blood on a Headstone (*)

The Miles Jacoby Series
Eye in the Ring
The Steinway Collection
Full Contact
Separate Cases
Hard Look
Stand Up

The Nick Delvecchio Series
No Exit from Brooklyn
The Dead of Brooklyn
The End of Brooklyn

The Gil & Claire Hunt Series
Murder is the Deal of the Day
The Masks of Auntie Laveau
Same Time, Same Murder

The Joe Keough Series
Alone with the Dead
In the Shadow of the Arch
Blood on the Arch
East of the Arch
Arch Angels
Back to the Arch

The Dennis McQueen Series
The Turner Journals
Cold-Blooded

The Rat Pack Series
Everybody Kills Somebody Sometime
Luck be a Lady, Don't Die
Hey You, with the Gun in Your Hand
You're Nobody til Somebody Kills You
I'm a Fool to Kill You
Fly Me to the Morgue
It was a Very Bad Year
You Make Me Feel So Dead
The Way You Die Tonight
When Somebody Kills You
I Only Have Lies for You

The Auggie Velez/Nashville Series
The Honky Tonk Big Hoss Boogie
The Last Sweet Song of Hammer Dylan

The Texas Hold'em Series
The Picasso Flop
The Judgment Fold

Stand Alone Crime Novels
The Disappearance of Penny
The Ham Reporter
Curtains of Blood
The Offer
The Bottom of Every Bottle

Collections
Delvecchio's Brooklyn
The Guilt Edge

(*) Coming Soon

ROBERT J. RANDISI

THE BROOKLYN TRILOGY
Three Delvecchio P.I. Novels

Compilation Copyright © 2020 by Robert J. Randisi

All rights reserved. No part of the book may be reproduced in any form or by any electronic or mechanical means, including information storage and retrieval systems, without permission in writing from the publisher, except by a reviewer who may quote brief passages in a review.

Down & Out Books
3959 Van Dyke Road, Suite 265
Lutz, FL 33558
DownAndOutBooks.com

The characters and events in this book are fictitious. Any similarity to real persons, living or dead, is coincidental and not intended by the author.

Cover photography by Axel Taferner
Cover design by Lance Wright

ISBN: 1-64396-139-X
ISBN-13: 978-1-64396-139-2

NO EXIT FROM BROOKLYN
Page 1

THE DEAD OF BROOKLYN
Page 173

THE END OF BROOKLYN
Page 325

NO EXIT FROM BROOKLYN

*To Christopher, and Matthew
and
for the denizens of Brooklyn*

PROLOGUE

The whole thing started—

Let me rephrase that: The *entire* thing started because of boredom and a middle-of-the-night phone call. It sure wasn't because I needed the money. My bank account was pretty healthy at the time, as a matter of fact. I'd just finished a case that would keep me in groceries, rent, and fast food for months, and that was all I ever really needed.

But if there's one thing I hate, it's being bored.

I went into this business of private investigation after an incident that got me pensioned off the police department with one-third of my salary instead of a prison sentence, and I had to find something that would allow me to do the things I was good at. The same "rabbi" who saved me from being railroaded off the job and into prison got me my P.I.'s license, and that was four years ago. Since that time I'd taken a lot of cases in the name of boredom that I shouldn't have, and you'd think I would have learned from that.

Not a chance.

When I get bored, I make the same mistakes all over again.

So the first connection I had with the entire affair was a middle-of-the-night phone call—which I hate almost as much as being bored.

I didn't know how many times the goddamn phone had rung already when I knocked it off its perch and groped about the floor for it.

"Hum, yeah, wha—"

"This Delvecchio?" a man's voice asked.

"Mmm hmm."

"You the private eye?" he asked. I didn't recognize his voice, but then in the middle of the night I probably wouldn't recognize my own father's voice.

"Is this an obscene phone call?"

"Forget the whole thing, pal."

"Fine by me, *pal*."

"No, I mean it, Delvecchio," the guy said. "Forget the whole thing. Got it?"

He stretched out the two words when he said "whole thing," like it really meant something.

"Look, pal," I said, swinging my feet around to the floor, "you woke me up in the middle of the night to tell me to forget the whole thing? Shit, I'd rather get an obscene phone call. At least they make sense."

"Delvecchio, you better wake up and listen to what I'm telling you. If you want to stay healthy, just forget the whole thing."

"Hey," I said amiably, "it's forgotten—" but he had hung up with a loud click.

It was so dark that I couldn't see the phone in my hand, but I knew it was there so I stared at it for a few seconds, then said, "Screw it," left it off the hook, got back under the covers, and went back to sleep.

1

I wasn't really *in* my office the next day, but the same phone line in my one-room office also goes into the adjoining three-room apartment. Summer was knocking on the door, and I was caught trying to decide whether to be bored with the TV, a book, or going down the block to OTB, so I welcomed the interruption.

I answered on the second ring, so real was my dread of boredom.

"Delvecchio."

"Are you the private detective?"

"I'm *a* private detective."

The voice was a girl's, and she didn't sound real sure of herself, so I let my remarks end there and waited. It was up to her to decide if I was *the* private detective she wanted.

"I—I'd like to hire you, but I don't want to come to your office."

"Make a suggestion."

"Can we meet somewhere?"

"Sure. Near you or near me?"

"I live in Bay Ridge, but I don't want to meet there."

"All right. Do you know where the Promenade is?"

"Sure."

"When would you like to meet?"

"In an hour?"

"That's fine with me. Can you tell me your name?"

"Jodi," she said. "I'll meet you in an hour."

She hung up before we could arrange some way for one of us to recognize the other.

Well, at least I had boredom beat for a while.

The official name for it was the Esplanade, but everyone in Brooklyn called it the Promenade. I don't know why, they—we—just do. It's sort of a park without grass that hangs over the Brooklyn-Queens Expressway, and from it Brooklynites and tourists alike can stare out across the East River at the classic skyline of New York City. It was a nice mile walk from my office on Sackett Street.

Of course, it wouldn't be complete without Jake and his hot dog stand.

That was where I saw Jodi Hayworth for the first time, standing by Jake's stand with a handful of hot dog smothered in onions.

I walked over to where she was standing, a girl who was probably about nineteen or twenty with long, straight blonde hair, incredible blue cat's eyes on a tomboy face, and an attitude and demeanor that said, "You can feel the cushions, buster, but you can't sit down." Coincidentally, she reminded me of another Jody—Jodie Foster, the way she looked in a movie called *Carny*. Tomboyish, but sexy as hell.

She was wearing jeans and a tank top, and she didn't have an ounce of excess flesh on her. She had taut breasts, a nonexistent waist, and long, trim legs. On her feet were a pair of calf-high boots with heels that added a couple of inches to her height, which in bare feet I would have put at five-four.

I spotted her because it wasn't noon yet, so the office workers were still at their desks and not having lunch on the Promenade. There was a couple standing at the rail, another sitting on a bench, an elderly woman walking a dog, and this girl. It was either the woman with the dog or the girl.

I opted for the girl.

"Jodi?"

"Are you Nick Delvecchio?" she asked, turning her attention from the hot dog to me.

"That's me."

I looked at the hot dog in her hand and saw that beneath the onions there was no mustard.

"I think I love you," I said.

Her eyes widened and she said, "What?" as if she wasn't sure she heard me right.

"The hot dog," I said, pointing. "No mustard, right?"

"I hate mustard!" she said, with feeling. "I wouldn't put it on my worst enemy."

"I thought I was the only person in the world that felt that way," I said. "This must be love."

"Please," she said, as if she suddenly thought I was running a line.

I don't know. Maybe I was.

"Build me one, will you, Jake?"

"Onions, no mustard," Jake said, shaking his head. "Yer both nuts."

If anyone ever asked me what Brooklyn was, I'd tell them to go and talk to Jake. He was Brooklyn born and bred, ran his little hot dog stand nine months out of the year, and spent the other three months in his condo in

Florida. He was built like a fire hydrant, his seamed face defying you to guess his age. His fingers were almost like sausages themselves, but they were deft as they plucked hot dogs from the water, laid them gently on the bun, and then built it to your specifications. Sometimes I'm almost tempted to order one with everything just to watch his hands fly around.

He handed me mine and I paid him for both.

"Let's go over by the rail," I said. I led the way to the rail, from which we could see the World Trade Center's twin towers. We could hear the traffic whooshing by on the Brooklyn-Queens Expressway beneath us.

"Okay," I said, "I'm Delvecchio, you're Jodi. What can I do for you?"

"I've got a problem I'd like to talk to you about."

"Well, sit down and talk, then."

We sat on a bench, still facing the city. The breeze coming off the water was cool, and strong enough to whip her fine hair about her face. She was carrying a large shoulder bag, and she brought it around so that she could sit with it at her feet. Close up, her eyes were even more startling.

"Why don't we start with your full name."

"It's Hayworth, Jodi Hayworth."

"All right, Miss Hayworth. Why don't you tell me what your problem is."

"Uh, well, I want you to find something for me."

"Something that you lost," I asked, "or something that was taken from you?"

"It's something that's missing—actually, it *is* something that was stolen...from my house."

It was obvious that she didn't have her story straight yet. Oh, she knew what her problem was, all right, but she just wasn't sure how much she wanted to tell me.

I decided to let her go on for a while and see what developed.

"What is it?" I asked, taking a huge bite out of my hot dog.

She made a face and said, "It's what my mother calls an 'object of art,' or something. It's kind of, uh, round with a little, um, hole in the middle—well, actually it's more of a big hole—really, it's more like all hole—ah, shit," she cursed shortly. "I kind of have my own name for the thing."

"Which is?"

"I call it "The hole thing.'"

"The *hole* thing?" I asked, my late-night call coming back to me in a rush. He hadn't said forget the *whole* thing, he'd said forget the *hole* thing!

Suddenly, I wasn't bored at all anymore.

2

"All right, Miss Hayworth," I said, "where was this, 'hole thing' stolen from?"

"I told you, my home."

"Oh, that's right, you did tell me that," I said, shaking my head. "Where do you live?"

"In Bay Ridge. I told you that on the phone."

"With your parents?"

She made a little face before answering, "Yeah."

"Was the house burglarized?"

"Huh? Oh, yeah, the house was robbed."

"What was taken?"

"Oh, just the hole thing," she answered with a shrug. She held her hands apart in an attempt to indicate the size of the item we were discussing. There was still a little less than half a hot dog in her right hand.

"Was it like a statue?"

"Yeah, it's a round thing set on a base. It's kind of a dull gray in color." It was difficult for her to use her hands while holding the hot dog, so she stuffed what was left into her mouth, where it sat half in and half out. As she used her hands it appeared that the thing was about a foot or so high.

"And nothing else was taken?"

"No," she said around the hot dog, then bit and chewed, holding the final small chunk in her hand.

She crossed her legs nervously, and I imagined I could see her leg muscles moving through the tight jeans.

"What did the police say?"

"I, uh, didn't call the police," she said, avoiding my eyes.

"What about your parents?"

"They're...away," she admitted, and the picture started to get a little clearer.

"Your parents are away, someone broke into the house and stole this 'hole' statue, and you didn't call the police. Have I got that right?"

"That's right."

"And nothing else was stolen?"

"That's right," she said again, choosing that moment to examine the remainder of her hot dog.

I put my hands in my lap and regarded her tomboy face in profile for a few moments. I've always hated girls with small noses, but this one was all right.

It was too bad she was a liar.

Well, maybe "liar" was too harsh a word, but at the very least she was feeding me a line of bullshit I was finding hard to digest.

"Miss Hayworth, if you really want to hire me, you're going to have to tell me the truth."

"What—"

"Don't give me that surprised look, young lady, and don't try and con me with that little-girl face. I've been conned by experts."

She lifted one corner of her mouth in the kind of gesture kids use when they realize they're not going to get what they want.

"Come on, Jodi," I said, taking a stab in the dark, "what'd you do, hock the thing?"

Her head jerked up, and she looked at me in obvious surprise.

"How did you—"

"It was just a guess, but I'm generally a good guesser," I said. "Why don't you tell me the truth, now?"

"That is the truth," she said, toying with the strap on her tote bag. "I needed some money, so I hocked the thing."

"Where?"

"Pawnshop on Atlantic Avenue."

"Go on."

"Well, I told the guy I'd be back to claim the damned thing in a couple of days..." she said, trailing off sadly.

"And he sold it out from under you?"

"Yeah, the creep. Said he got too good an offer for it to turn it down."

"How much is the thing worth, Jodi?"

She shrugged and said, "Shit, I don't know."

"How much did you get for it?"

"Two fifty."

"Two hundred and fifty dollars?"

She nodded.

"Do you know what *he* got for it?"

She shrugged.

"Bastard wouldn't tell me. He wouldn't even tell me who he sold it to so I could try to buy it back."

I decided not to ask her where she had gotten the money to try and buy it back. I figured she'd lie again.

"What's going to happen when your parents get back and find it gone?"

She expelled her breath in a disgusted rush and said, "Diane'll have a shit fit."

"Diane?"

"My mother," she said, distaste obvious in her tone.

"And your father?"

"Damn it," she said, "none of this would have happened if—"

"If what?"

"If I didn't need the money," she said, but I had a feeling that hadn't been what she was going to say before.

"When are your parents coming back?"

"That's another problem. They weren't supposed to be back until next month, but I got a telegram saying they're coming back next week."

"You're really in a bind, huh?"

"What do you think?" She turned and looked at me, giving me the full benefit of those blue eyes. "Look, Mr. Delvecchio, couldn't you please try and find it for me? I'll buy it back from whoever bought it."

"Do you have the money?"

"I do now—and I have enough to pay you, if that's what you're worried about," she added. She leaned over to start rummaging about in her bag, but I stopped her.

"Don't worry about my fee, okay?"

She looked up at me from her bent-over position and said, "Then you'll help me?"

"Sure," I said, thinking about boredom, a middle-of-the-night call, and a tomboy face with big cat's eyes.

"Sure," I said again, "why not?"

I found out later why not, but later is always too late.

I asked her where the hockshop was on Atlantic Avenue, and she said she didn't remember the cross streets but she could drive me there. I told her I wanted to go back to my office first so she could sign a contract. She asked if that was necessary, and I said that it was with me. For my own reasons I try to keep my business as up-and-up as possible.

"Where's your car?" I asked.

"Down the block."

"Lead on."

She took the lead and I admired the way her jeans clung to her firm behind. Her waist made me think of those TV commercials about not being able to pinch an inch. On the way out she tossed the rest of her hot dog into a trash barrel.

The car was a black sporty job with no top. Normally you've got to have a lot of balls to park a car like that in downtown Brooklyn, but she'd gotten away with it. There wasn't so much as a cigarette lighter or hubcap missing.

After she'd signed one of my contracts for me, we walked down from the third floor where I lived and worked. I'd forgone a retainer for now, at least until I made sure I could do something for her.

The house where I lived and worked was a converted brownstone on Sackett Street, spitting distance from the Brooklyn Bridge if you're a good spitter, and it stood four stories high. The neighborhood was pretty shitty and nothing like where Jodi lived in Bay Ridge, which, along with Canarsie and Marine Park, was one of the last havens of Brooklyn.

"I like it down here," Jodi said as we walked down the front steps.

"You're crazy."

"Don't you?"

"Sure, but I *know* I'm crazy."

Also, it was good for my business, such as it was. Court Street wasn't very far away, where most of the Brooklyn lawyers had their offices. All of the court buildings were nearby as well, on Adams, Livingston, Schermerhorn, and other streets. Both bridges to—or from—Manhattan were close by, and there were plenty of fast-food places on Fulton Street and in the Albee Mall. This area, Brooklyn Heights, is one of the busiest in all of Brooklyn. My office/apartment sits right on the boundary between the Heights and Red Hook.

Brooklyn has been bad-mouthed in a lot of places. "Only the dead know Brooklyn," Thomas Wolfe said—but I live here, too, so don't say it around me.

She went around to the driver's side, and I hopped over the door on the passenger's side.

"Why'd you hock it?" I asked after she'd gotten us rolling.

She removed a strand of her fine hair that had blown into her mouth and said, "I needed the money."

"For what?"

"Is that important, or are you just nosy?"

"I guess I'm just nosy," I admitted. "If it becomes important, I'll ask you again."

"Okay."

"And you'll answer."

She hesitated, then said, "Okay," with a short nod.

She made a couple of turns, and I was about to tell her that she was headed away from our destination when she said in an exasperated tone, "Where the hell is Atlantic Avenue?"

I laughed and directed her to the Flatbush Avenue Extension. We were traveling south, toward Grand Army Plaza, and I asked her, "Which side of the extension is it on?"

She thought a moment, then said, "I think we have to turn right."

"Okay, we'll try it," I said. "If it's not there, we'll go the other way."

She drove with confidence, but she wasn't a good driver. She seemed to be the kind who felt the road belonged to her and everyone else better get out of the way.

As she approached the place where Flatbush, Atlantic, and Fourth Avenue all come together—a corner where you can get almost anything, from chicken to chicks to a Long Island Railroad train—I said, "Hang a right, Jodi."

She did so, and I added, "Keep your eyes open."

We were halfway between Flatbush and the Brooklyn-Queens Expressway when she cried out, "There it is," and pointed across the street.

"Pull over."

There were no available spots, so she pulled in by a hydrant, in front of a Syrian restaurant.

"There," she said again, pointing.

I saw the place she meant. It was a dingy little hole-in-the-wall that I'd never noticed before, but then hockshops were not among my regular hangouts. There was a sign over the door that said "Antiques, bought and sold."

"Jodi, is this thing valuable?" I asked. "I mean, would this guy know what he was getting?"

"I don't know. He didn't act like it was anything so great. It's just this ugly little, uh, round—"

"Yeah, I know," I interrupted her, "hole thing."

"Right."

"Okay, you wait for me here."

"Can't I come in?"

"I don't want the guy to see you," I said. "When were you in?"

"Uh, last week the first time, and then again a couple of days ago."

"Did you give him a hard time the second time?"

"Oh yeah. I screamed at him, the creep."

"Then let's assume that he'd remember you."

"Hell, yes."

"Okay," I said, hopping out of the car, "wait right here."

"Gonna threaten him?"

"I'm gonna con him," I said, and crossed the street when there was a lull in the traffic.

3

The hockshop stood on Atlantic Avenue, just off of Smith Street, situated between a laundromat and a junk store. In fact, most of the stores along

Atlantic Avenue could be described as junk stores—but then one man's junk is another man's treasure, I guess.

Most of the stores on these blocks were either antique shops or restaurants, but no Burger Kings for Atlantic Avenue, no sir. There were Syrian restaurants, Greek restaurants, pizza places, one legit Italian restaurant, all of this in the ten-block expanse that ran from BQE to Flatbush Avenue. The surprising thing about this stretch is that there were very few bars. There were plenty of those a few blocks over, on Schermerhorn Street and Livingston Street.

When I opened the door to the place, I thought it was going to fall off its hinges, but it held. A small bell over the door announced my arrival.

The place had a thick, musty smell, and it was cluttered with all kinds of stuff hanging from the walls.

"Can I help you?" a voice asked.

I peered around and finally located the source of the voice. He was standing behind a wire-mesh screen. Shit, I thought, this place is right out of *The Pawnbroker*.

"Are you the proprietor?"

"Yes, I'm Mr. Wallach. Can I help you?"

Through the screen I could see a portly, gray-haired man of about fifty-five or so. His hands were dirty, and he had a couple of fingertip smudges on his broad forehead.

I took out one of my business cards and handed it to him beneath the mesh.

"A private detective?" he asked, reading the card. "What do you want to do, Mr. Private Eye, hock your gun?" he then asked, laughing.

"Gun?" I asked. "No, Mr. Wallach, you've got the wrong fella. I don't carry a gun. They scare me."

He looked disappointed and put my card down on the counter.

"What do you want, then?" He had a slight Jewish accent.

"I deal in art objects, Mr. Wallach," I told him. "I'm hired to track down lost and missing ones, that is. A client of mine had one stolen a few weeks ago, and I'm given to understand that it was in your shop as recently as last week."

"I don't deal in stolen goods, mister!" he told me with forced indignation. "*You* got the wrong man."

"Calm down, Mr. Wallach, calm down," I said. "I'm not accusing you of anything, believe me. I'm sure that if the object I'm looking for was indeed in your shop, you came by it quite innocently."

"You can bet I'm innocent," he said, but I would never have taken him up on such a bet.

"I'm also sure you had no idea of the item's true value."

His ears perked up and he craned his neck as he repeated, "True value? What do you mean, true value?"

"The piece I'm talking about is worth quite a lot of money, Mr. Wallach, which is why my client has authorized me to pay a ten percent finder's fee to anyone who can help me locate it."

"Finder's fee?" he asked. "Ten percent? What would that come to?"

"Well, if it's genuine, I suppose ten percent would amount to, oh, five, maybe six thousand dollars. It could even be more."

"Six thousand dollars?" he squeaked. "What kind of item could I have in my shop worth that much?" he asked, looking around at his goods.

"Well, I'll describe the item to you, Mr. Wallach. It was about so high," I said, moving my hands, "and it was round, with a big hole, and it was set on a base—"

"That thing?" he exclaimed, slapping both hands to his face. "That thing?"

"Then you have it."

"Oh, my—I had such a thing only two days ago. It was brought here last week by a blonde girl—"

"A blonde girl, you say?" I asked. "With pretty blue eyes, a pointed nose..."

"That's her. She brought it to me last week, and I bought it from her for two hundred and fifty dollars."

"Two fifty!" I said, looking amazed. "That was quite a bargain, Mr. Wallach. Still, to give her that much, you must have had some idea of its worth."

"I knew it was an art object, and I have some customers who are interested in such things."

"Well, if you can show me where it is, I'm sure I could offer you a little more than ten percent—"

"Oy," he said, covering his face with his hands, leaving more fingertip smudges.

"You do have it, don't you?"

"I had it, I had it!" he cried into his hands.

"You sold it?" I asked, trying to sound disappointed.

He nodded.

"All right, Mr. Wallach, let's not get excited about this. I'm sure we can work something out."

"We could?" he asked, opening his hands and peeking out.

"Sure, Mr.—ah, what's your first name?"

"Sid, Sid is my first name," he said, eager to please.

"Well, all right, Sid. I'm sure you have a record of who you sold it to, don't you?"

He stared at me for a moment, and then his face lit up.

"I have it, yes." Suddenly, though, his face took on a shrewd, crafty look, and I knew the time had come. "I really couldn't give it to you, however," he said. "My records are confidential."

"I realize that, Sid, I really do," I said carefully, "and I would never ask you to compromise yourself, but I'm sure that if we can recover the item, I could get my client to go for more than ten percent. Perhaps even, uh, ten thousand dollars?"

It was a ridiculous figure, but his greed overcame his common sense.

"Ten thousand?"

"That is, unless you can afford to buy the item back yourself. I'm sure the person who bought it knows what they have."

His face fell, and he said, "I—I couldn't afford to buy it back—"

"Ten thousand is still a nice profit from a two-hundred-and-fifty-dollar layout."

"Wait," he told me, holding his hands out, "wait, wait, don't go away."

He disappeared into a back room, and I could hear him rummaging around, talking to himself. Finally he returned with a small, orange card in his hand.

"I have it!" he cried triumphantly. "I have it!"

"Excellent," I said. "Could I see it, please?"

"Of course, of course," he said, pushing it at me from beneath the mesh.

It was neatly typed on a typewriter that was missing a "v" and about to lose a "u," but it was legible.

"Can I take this, Sid?"

"Take it, take it. It has my name and phone number on the back."

"Indeed it does." I tucked the card away in my pocket and said, "Well, Sid, this may be it. I'll check this out, and if we recover the item, you will be quite a few dollars richer." When I left, the old man looked decidedly hopeful.

"Did you get it?"

"I got it," I said, showing her the orange card.

She screamed and threw her arms around me, saying, "You're wonderful."

My mouth was pressed against her bare shoulder and her breasts were pressed against my chest as she showed her appreciation. The flesh of her shoulder was smooth and slightly damp from perspiration, and her hair had that fragrance that only blonde hair does. I started to respond the way a man normally will when a vibrant, healthy young girl throws herself into his lap.

And she noticed.

"Thank you, Nick," she said, staring into my face with her arms around my neck. For a moment her mouth was invitingly close, but before I could decide to take advantage, she was back on her side of the car, behind the wheel.

"Just to show you how much I appreciate this," she said, "I'm going to take you to an early dinner."

"And pay my fee, I hope."

She laughed and said, "That, too."

I checked my watch and it was getting kind of late in the day.

"I guess we can check this address out tomorrow."

"Sure," she agreed. "Getting it was the important part, and I sure hired the right man for that job."

I directed her to a little restaurant I liked on Pacific Street, where it wouldn't matter how we were dressed. We drove there and celebrated over some good Italian food and a couple of bottles of red wine, and by the time I knew it we were in my apartment and my hands were roaming around beneath her tank top...

The next thing I knew it was morning and I was staring at the ceiling above my bed. I didn't have a hangover exactly, but there was a buzzing in my ears, and my tongue had somehow turned into Velcro. My arms were spread straight out to the side so that it didn't take a genius to figure out that I was alone in bed. Jodi was gone who knew how long.

After about ten years I got myself up into a seated position with my feet on the floor. My clothes were strewn about the floor, and there was a dead soldier lying against one wall. I tried to remember how many such bottles we had emptied, but all I could remember was that I seemed to be doing most of the drinking.

That's right, I thought, I did most of the drinking, and who was it kept filling my glass?

No, I thought, don't tell me. She couldn't have been that kind of girl...

I staggered out of bed and retrieved my pants from the floor. My wallet was still in my pocket, and I quickly went through it with a feeling of dread that proved unwarranted. I felt like a heel when I discovered that my cash was still there.

I rubbed my eyes and dropped my arms to my sides, mentally apologizing to Jodi. Maybe a shower would bring me back to life.

I started picking up my clothes, and when I reached my jacket, I remembered that all-important orange card, the reason for the previous night's celebration.

I reached into my jacket pocket and didn't find it. I checked another pocket with the same results. I searched all my pockets and then checked them again and still came up empty. I went through my apartment, my office, and my wallet.

The card was gone, with Jodi.

I didn't see her again for two weeks.

4

The cops found me in the comer laundromat.

Mrs. Goldstein was regaling me with the latest neighborhood gossip when they walked in. They were both in plain clothes, but everything about them said "cop."

Mrs. Goldstein is sort of the neighborhood snoop, for want of a better word. She's a lovable Jewish widow who, since the death of her beloved Abe five years earlier, had sort of taken all of us under her wing. She kept track of the comings and goings in the area, dispensed kindly, well-meant, frequently useless advice, and was always trying to fix me up with one of her nieces.

She's a nice lady, and I like her.

The laundromat doubled as the neighborhood social club. When you're a bachelor and you do your own laundry, you tend to keep meeting the same people around the washers and driers. There was Mr. Quinn, the Greek grocer whose wife never did laundry; there was "Mad Dog" Bolinsky, a huge sanitation worker who lived alone and didn't really like anyone but cats and kids; and there was my neighbor across the hall, the lovely and talented Kit Karson. Well, actually her name was Samantha Karson, but she wrote romance novels under the name Kit. When I asked why she would change her name from something as pretty as Samantha to something as terse as Kit, she said she was saving her real name for her important work. Sam thought that as a private eye, I would sooner or later be the source for that work.

Anyway, I was taking my shorts out of the dryer, listening to Mrs. Goldstein tell me about Mrs. Munchik's boy, the one who couldn't keep a job because of his drinking and womanizing, when the cops walked in and spotted me. Even if they hadn't had "cop" written all over them, I'd have known them for what they were, because I knew one of them by sight. His name was Detective Matucci, and we had managed to go through the academy together without a civil word passing between us. "All right, scumbag," he said, approaching me, "let's go."

"What kind of way is that for a young man to talk?" Mrs. Goldstein asked him immediately.

"Who's this," Matucci asked, "your mother?"

"God forbid I was *your* mother, young man," Mrs. Goldstein replied before I could, "I'd teach you how to talk to decent people."

"Oh, he's got an excuse, Mrs. Goldstein," I explained. "You see, this man is a policeman. He's allowed to talk to people like that, aren't you, Vito?"

"Aye," Matucci said to me, waggling the forefinger of his right hand in my face, "you don't call me by my first name, shitface."

"This is a policeman?" Mrs. Goldstein asked, incredulously.

"That he is, Mrs. Goldstein. One of New York's finest." I would have said "one of New York's finest assholes," but I didn't want to redirect Mrs. Goldstein's ire at that moment. I was enjoying seeing it aimed at Vito Matucci.

Matucci was short for a cop, to his everlasting shame. His father and uncles and brothers were all officers, and all six-footers, while "Little Vito" was barely five-seven. He tried to make up for it with a hard nose and a big mouth, and if his size had been all he had to overcome, he might have made it. Unfortunately for Vito, he was a complete asshole, no matter how you looked at him.

"Who's your friend?" I asked.

"Detective Weinstock," the man said, which immediately put him high on Mrs. Goldstein's list.

"Do you know Moshe Weinstock, from Canarsie?" she asked him.

"I'm sorry, ma'am, no, I don't."

"Polite," she said, smiling triumphantly at Matucci. "You could learn something from your friend."

"They're not friends," I corrected her, "they're partners," and from the look on Weinstock's face I could see I'd hit the nail right on the head.

When you're a complete asshole like Matucci, it's hard to hide it from anyone, least of all your partner.

"Could you come with us please, Mr. Delvecchio?" Weinstock said. "Our boss would like to talk to you."

"How'd you know where to find me?"

"The bitch across the hall told us where you were," Matucci said, further shocking poor Mrs. Goldstein.

I'd have to remember to thank Sam. I'd tell her what Matucci called her. She'd find it interesting.

"Where you boys working out of these days?"

"You don't have to tell him nothing," Matucci said, balling his hands up into fists. I knew he wouldn't swing at me, because the last time he did, I broke his nose for him. "Let's go, Delvecchio."

"Let me get finished with my shorts," I said, transferring the pair in my right hand to my left and reaching into the dryer for the rest.

"Forget about your shorts," Matucci said. "We're leaving—now!"

"Right now?"

"Now."

"Have it your way."

As we headed for the door, Mrs. Goldstein called out, "I'll take care of your laundry, Nicky."

She would, too—all except for the pair of shorts I'd stuffed into my back pocket.

I was grateful for the fact that Matucci drove to the Seventy-eighth Precinct, on Bergen Street. The few times we had ridden in a radio car together, I had discovered that he was such a notoriously poor driver that he couldn't operate the car and talk at the same time. I don't know what Weinstock's excuse was, but he didn't speak either.

When we pulled up in front of the precinct and Matucci had turned off the motor, he turned on his mouth again.

"Okay, skell, out."

"Skell" was a word you learned when you joined the police department. I don't know exactly who coined it, but it generally meant that muck you find "at the bottom of the barrel."

"You still have a way with words, Vito."

"Look, mother—"

"Let's go upstairs, Matucci," Weinstock suggested. "The sooner we turn him over to the boss, the sooner we can be rid of him."

"You've got a point there, Weinstock," Matucci said. "Let's go."

They took me upstairs to the second floor where the squad room was located. The walls of the run-down building were a kind of sickly lime green, complemented by peeling paint and cracks in the wall. In other words, it hadn't changed since I had been a patrolman there.

"Sit down," Weinstock said. "I'll tell the lieutenant you're here."

"Thanks."

Matucci scowled and walked away while Weinstock went into the lieutenant's office. I wondered who was in charge of the squad these days.

"Mr. Delvecchio," Weinstock called. He was waving me over, standing half in and half out of the lieutenant's office.

I got up and walked to the office, with Matucci suddenly behind me. Weinstock stood aside to allow me to enter and Matucci pushed his way between us. Weinstock gave the back of his partner's head an annoyed look.

"This is Lieutenant Wager," Weinstock said, but there was no introduction necessary. Wager and I knew each other.

He was a big, beefy man with red cheeks, and during his years as a desk officer he had been notorious for sending radio cars to restaurants to pick up his complimentary meals—sometimes three or four a tour. From his girth, he looked as if he still did.

I had heard a story once when I first came on the job from an old-timer who had gotten tired of being Wager's gopher. Seems that when he and his partner were sent for coffee, he'd stopped the radio car by an alley, gotten out, pissed in the coffee, and then delivered it to Wager. He didn't know if Wager had drunk it, but that had been the last time he and his partner had made a coffee run for the lieutenant.

"Lieutenant Wager," I said. Although he was in a new position of authority, I was oddly gratified to find that he had not risen in rank.

"Delvecchio and I know each other, Weinstock," Wager said. "You can go and close the door on your way out."

"Yes, sir."

"Sit down, Delvecchio."

I turned to pull a chair over, and Wager suddenly said, "What the hell is that?"

Weinstock and Matucci stopped short, and I turned to look at Wager.

"That," Wager said, pointing behind me.

I reached behind me and pulled the shorts from my pocket. Most of my shorts are solid color, but these had been a gift from an old girlfriend at Valentine's Day, white with red hearts with an arrow through them.

"These are my shorts."

"What the hell are they doing here?"

"When your torrid twosome came for me, I was at the laundromat doing my laundry. They wouldn't let me finish."

Wager threw Matucci a dirty look, as if he knew the asshole was to blame.

"Look, he's just—"

"Shut up and get out, Matucci!"

Matucci's face suffused with blood. He threw me a murderous glare, and then slunk from the room. Weinstock followed, and shut the door behind him.

"Get those things out of sight and sit down!" Wager snapped at me.

I balled them up and tucked them deeper in my back pocket, where they made an uncomfortable bulge.

"You know," I said, taking a seat, "if you wanted to talk over old times, you didn't have to send two of your best to get me. An engraved invitation would have done."

"Shut up," Wager said. "I didn't have you brought here to listen to your lip. I had enough of that when you were a cop here."

"Sure, Lieutenant."

"You know a man named Sid Wallach?"

"Never heard of him."

"That's funny," Wager said. "This was found in his pocket last night."

He held something out to me, and I recognized it as one of my business cards.

"So? I give those things out all the time. I have no control over who ends up with them."

"I see."

"Who was this guy, anyway?" I asked. "Somebody you threw into a drunk tank?"

"No," Wager said, tossing the card on his desk. "Sid Wallach owned a pawnshop on Atlantic Avenue."

"A pawnshop?"

"Does that ring a bell?"

"Actually, it does," I said, thinking of Jodi Hayworth for the first time in a week.

"Care to tell me what?" Wager asked, lacing his fat fingers on the desk top.

"I don't know," I said. "Care to tell me why you're asking?"

"Mr. Sid Wallach was found in his shop last night," Wager said, watching my face carefully.

"Found?"

"Dead."

"Dead?" I repeated.

"And tortured—and he had your business card in his pocket," Wager reminded me. He crossed his pudgy arms across his chest and announced imperiously, "I'm waiting for an explanation."

5

Wager's problem had always been that he expected people to bow to his rank. He never realized that people respect a man, not a rank. Now, sitting with his arms folded, he seemed to think I would fall apart because he was confronting me with a business card.

Well, I didn't, but I think I surprised the shit out of him.

I cooperated.

I run my business by the book as much as I can—which was why I had Jodi Hayworth sign a contract—and it was men like Wager who were the reason. He would have liked nothing better than to have me hold out on him so he could pull my license.

I didn't give him the chance.

I told him exactly what I had been hired to do a week ago by Jodi Hayworth, and I ran it down for him by the numbers, holding nothing back. There was nothing that it would have done me any good *to* hold back, so I didn't mind opening up for him.

"Is that everything?" he asked when I stopped talking.

"That's all I've got, Wager," I said, and he looked downright disappointed.

"You never went back to that hockshop after that?"

"For what reason?"

"And you never saw the girl again?"

"I never even got paid, Wager."

That seemed to cheer him up some, so I didn't bother telling him that I had settled for another form of compensation.

"If you've been straight with me, Delvecchio, you've got nothing to worry about, but if I find out that you held out—"

"I like my license, Lieutenant," I said, cutting him off. "I'm not holding out."

"I'm sure you like your license," Wager said, "considering how you got it."

I let the remark go, because he was trying to get my goat. "Can I go now?"

"Be my guest. Don't think I want to see you any longer than I have to."

"I enjoyed it, too, Lieutenant," I said, standing up. "What are the chances of getting a ride home?"

"What do you think?" he replied, scowling.

"That's okay, I'll get one downstairs."

As I left his office, he was reaching for the phone. I knew he was going to call downstairs to the big front desk—what a friend of mine used to call the B.F.D.—and let them know that nobody was to give me a ride home. Actually, I could have just walked home, but it would do my heart good to get a ride from one of the radio cars.

I went downstairs to see if I had any friends left in the precinct where I had once worked.

I had been a cop in the seven-eight for three years when an incident occurred which changed my outlook on life—and, eventually, my career.

Up to that point I had been a pretty easygoing guy, but I tried to break up a fight one day and suddenly found myself on the receiving end of a beating from *both* parties. It had been a fairly severe pounding, since they had gotten ahold of my nightstick and used it on me. It could have been worse, they told me in the hospital. They could have gotten my gun.

Four months later I was back on the job with a new outlook. Never again would I take a beating like that from *anyone,* no matter what the situation. They told us in the academy that force was to be met by equal force and never by *more* than equal force. In other words, you couldn't use your gun unless the perp had a gun.

Bullshit.

From that point on in my life I used as much force as I needed to use to keep myself in one piece. Never again would I lie in a hospital bed wondering if I'd ever walk or scratch my nose—or fuck—again.

Over the next two years I went before three Internal Affairs Review Boards for excessive violence, and was threatened with three more. I couldn't help it. As soon as I felt I was in danger, I lashed out. I took a couple of suspensions from I.A.D. rulings, but nothing real heavy—until that last time.

I overreacted in that last situation, and I hurt the guy pretty severely. Not as badly as *I* had been hurt, but he went to the hospital. When they called me onto the carpet, they told me I had really fucked up this time. The kid's father was a politician—an upwardly mobile politician—and he wanted my balls.

My only ace was that the kid—who was eighteen, six-three, two hundred pounds—was breaking the law at the time the incident occurred. In fact, he was robbing an old woman and was armed with homemade blackjack. When he turned on me with it, I could have shot him, but I used my nightstick instead. I broke his arm and opened his head for him, and that was that.

Until I.A.D. reared its ugly head with the news that his politician father wanted my ass—and they were going to give it to him.

Or so they thought.

You see, after they gave him my hide, they were going to let him take his "little boy" home—only I wasn't ready to go along with that. I threatened to break the story to the papers, so a compromise had to be made.

I came out of it with a one-third disability pension and a P. I. license.

The politician came out of it with his little boy.

It was now four years later, and I still had my pension and an office on Sackett Street.

All the politician had was a grave, because his son was shot dead six months later by a cop during an attempted armed robbery.

First chance they got, they'd yank my ticket, only I'd never give them the chance. Not even if my business card was found in a dead man's pocket.

* * *

"Hey, Nicky D.!"

I turned and saw Police Officer Neal Citrola bearing down on me. Neal and I had come on the job together.

"Hi, Neal."

"How are you doing, boy?" Neal asked, slapping me on the back.

"Fine, Neal, fine. You coming or going?"

"Just coming on, man. Why?"

"I need a ride."

"Where?"

"Home."

"No sweat. I'll get my unit and take you, right after roll call."

"Uh, I should tell you that Wager called down..."

"You talked to Wager? That asshole!"

"Yeah. I'm sure he called down and left word that I wasn't to be given a ride."

"Well shit, I'll just grab an extra unit and take you right now."

"I don't want to get you into trouble, Neal."

"No trouble, Nicky. I'll just tell the desk sergeant that I'm picking up a sandwich for Wager and I need a car."

"If Wager finds out, he'll have a shit fit."

"Fine with me. I need a complaint this month to fill my quota. Come on, your limo awaits."

"Thanks, Neal."

During the ride we talked about old times and new times, and I found out that there were still ten or twelve guys in the seven-eight who were there when I left, four years before.

"I'm trying to get out myself. I just keep applying for a transfer. Sooner or later I'll get it."

When he dropped me in front of my building, I wished him luck with his transfer and thanked him for the ride.

"Nicky D.," he said, gave me a little salute, and drove off. Most of the people I knew from my old neighborhood still called me Nicky D., and a few of the guys I went through the academy with, like Neal. My father and sister just called me Nicky, while my brother called me Nick. I called him "Father Vinnie." My brother the priest was the pride and joy of my family. Needless to say, I was sort of a black sheep.

When I got upstairs, the phone was ringing. I ran for it, even though I knew that nine times out of ten I picked it up on the last ring and got pissed because there was nobody there. This was the tenth time.

"Nicky."

It was my sister, Maria.

"Hi, sugar."

"How's my big brother?"

"I'm fine."

"Keeping your trench coat clean?"

"All three of them, and my holster is well oiled."

It was an old routine. My sister was actually thrilled that I was a P. I. She was addicted to old movies.

"Nicky, I called to tell you…"

"What, Sis?"

"I'm…going away for a while."

"Going away? Where. For how long?"

"I—a week, I guess. I'm taking a plane today."

"To where?"

"I don't know. I've always wanted to see Greece…"

"Is he going with you?"

"He" was her husband, Peter Geller, who none of us liked for our own reasons. My old man, Vito, hated him because he wasn't Italian. Father Vinnie didn't like him because he wasn't Catholic. I didn't care for him because he was an asshole. I usually referred to him as "Numbnuts," but not so's my sister could hear.

"No, Peter is not coming…" she said, and her voice caught in her throat.

"Sis, what's wrong?"

"I just have to go away for a while, Nicky, and I wanted to let you know."

"Let's talk—"

"Not this time, Nicky," she said. "This time I have to handle it myself and not go running to my big brother."

"Maria—"

"I'll call you."

"Maria!" I said, but she'd hung up. "Damn it!"

She was a big girl, my sister, all of twenty-four, eight years younger than me and ten years younger than Father Vinnie. She was my father's baby, I was sure he'd know something—I just wasn't sure he'd tell me.

6

I dialed my father's number, and he answered on the second ring.

"Pop, it's Nick."

"Nicky, my boy, whatayousay?"

"Pop, what's going on with Maria? I just got a strange call from her."

"That somonabitch!" my father said. When he got his Sicilian up, his Italian accent became thicker and harder for him to handle.

"Are we talking about Peter, Pop?"

He said something in Italian.

"Pop, you know I can't understand you when you do that."

Father Vinnie spoke Italian, but I was never able to get the hang of it beyond a few choice curse words.

"Your sister, she's-a not happy, Nicky. She's-a goin' away to think."

"About what?"

"Her marriage."

"She's only been married a year. What's the matter with her marriage?"

"Who knows?"

"Maybe I should talk to Numbn—uh, Peter—"

"I already talked to him," he said, and I could sense my father trying to calm himself down. He stopped talking like Mamma Leone. "He says he can't make her happy for some reason."

"You knew she was going?"

"She told me yesterday."

"Did she talk to Father Vinnie?"

"You know your brother and sister can't talk, Nicky. They yell."

"Well, shit, Pop, we can't just let her go."

"She's a big girl, Nicky," my father said. "She said she wants to handle this herself."

"What airline?"

"She didn't tell me."

I would never call my father a liar to his face—but then we were on the phone, weren't we?

"Come on, Pop—"

"She made me promise, Nicky."

"Pop—"

"She'll be all right, Nicky. Listen to your father."

I closed my eyes and said, "Okay, Pop."

"So, when you comin' out to have dinner with your old man?"

"Out" was Bensonhurst, where my father still lived. The old neighborhood. My father had lived there ever since he had come to this country from Italy forty years ago and started working on the Brooklyn docks. He'd retired two years ago and now spent his time going to ball games, the race track, and bitching that his kids never came to see him. Hell, he was never home!

"Soon, Pop, soon."

"You get hit onna head lately?"

"No, Pop."

"I don't know why you wanna work on a job where you get hit onna head a lot."

"Pop, you been watching *Rockford Files* reruns again. I'll call you when I'm coming out, maybe later this week."

"Sure, sure, Nicky," he said, "I hold my breath. See ya."

"See ya, Pop."

As I hung up, there was a knock on the door. I must have had a puzzled look on my face because as soon as I opened it, Samantha Karson asked, "What's the matter with you?"

The building was set up so that there were two apartments on each floor, and Sam was my neighbor from the other side of the hall.

Sam's an extremely pretty cornflower blonde with very light eyebrows and eyelids—sort of like Sissy Spacek—and the most startling blue eyes I've ever seen.

To date she'd published three novels and about a half a dozen short stories in the romance field, but she always felt that my occupation might be fodder for that something else, so we talked a lot. We were good friends, had shared a lot of meals and pleasant times but not much else—and I'd be hard put to say why not.

"Why?" I asked in reply to her question.

"You look bemused."

"'Bemused,'" I repeated. "That's a writer's word, isn't it? One that you use when you don't want to say 'puzzled' or 'confused'?"

"They're not all exactly the same. Which *are* you?"

"All three," I said, backing away from the door. "Come on in."

She was wearing a yellow T-shirt which said "Romantic Times" on it, whatever that was or meant. It was tight and tucked into tight jeans and showed off her full breasts very nicely. She was barefoot, which meant she'd come from her apartment and not from outside. I thought briefly of Jodi Hayworth and her tank top. Sam didn't wear tank tops, but my guess was that if she did, she'd stop a lot of traffic.

"What has you in this mood?" she asked.

"I just got off the phone with my sister, and then my father."

"That sweet old man," she said, smiling fondly. Sam and my dad had met on more than one occasion, and they were impressed with each other.

"That sweet old man," I said, "would gladly jump your bones, given half a chance."

"I know," she said, still smiling. "That sweet old man. What did he do to confuse you?"

"He and my sister both. She's flying off somewhere, and he won't tell me when or where."

"She didn't say where?"

"She said something about Greece, but who knows?"

"Your Pop, from what you say. Why wouldn't he tell you, though?"

"Because Maria asked him not to."

"And why would she do that?"

"She said something about wanting to solve her own problems without running to her big brother."

"Well, that's good. From what I know of your sister, it's time she tried that."

Sam had met Maria only once, when we'd gone to my dad's for Thanksgiving. She had met Peter, too, and also thought he was an asshole.

"I don't like it," I said, frowning.

"She's a big girl, Nick. Why don't you concentrate on your business instead of your sister's?"

"I don't have any business right now."

"Nick?"

"Yeah?"

Frowning, she tugged my shorts out of my pocket and held them up like a flag of truce.

"Why is your underwear in your back pocket?"

"Uh, there's a story behind that."

"So, tell it to me? It'll help you stop worrying about your sister."

I took my shorts out of her hand, and said, "You're just trying to pump me again."

"Well, I came over to invite you to dinner, on me," she said, folding her arms over her breasts. "Isn't that worth being pumped?"

"I don't know. What are we eating?"

"Chinese," she said, and then, "Szechuan. I've got it in my apartment, along with the rest of your laundry. Mrs. Goldstein left it off."

"That sweet old lady."

She grinned and said, "That sweet old lady would jump *your* bones if she had half a chance."

"Now, now..."

"Maybe we should introduce her to your father, and they could jump each other's bones?"

"Come on," I said, dropping my shorts back on the couch and grabbing her arm, "I don't like cold Chinese food."

"Will you tell me the story?"

"Does my Chinese food depend on it?"

She nodded and added, "And your underwear."

"Well, in that case," I said, moving her toward the door, "once upon a time there was this hole thing..."

"Wasn't it kind of dumb to leave him your card?" Sam asked.

We'd finished our Chinese food just about the time I finished my story, and were now working on a pot of coffee. Sam didn't cook, but she had mastered what she called "the art of Mr. Coffee."

"I didn't have any phony ones with me." The excuse sounded lame even to my ears. It was dumb to leave the man my real card, but who knew he was going to get killed?

"Well, what do you intend to do now?"

"About what?"

"About the man who got killed."

"Nothing."

"What do you mean, nothing? Aren't you going to try and find out who killed him?"

"What for? It's none of my business."

Her mouth opened once without any sound coming out, and then she tried again.

"Nick, aren't you a suspect?"

"Not really, Sam. Wager knows me well enough to know I wouldn't murder a man after presenting him with my card. Besides, nobody's paying me to find out who killed the old man."

She poured herself another cup of coffee and then said, "This would never work in a book."

"Why not?"

"Fictional private eyes have a code of ethics. They work on cases whether they're being paid or not."

"Why?"

"Why?" she repeated. "Uh, because that's what they do, that's why."

"That's because fictional private eyes don't have to eat."

We'd eaten off her living-room coffee table, sitting on the floor, and my knees cracked as I stood.

"Jesus..." I said, straightening up. "Thanks for dinner, Sam."

"Where are you going now?"

"Not out, if that's what you mean. I'm going into my apartment and put my feet up. I had a good week, but I don't have any cases right now—and I don't need one."

"But here you've got a murder to solve—"

"The police have a murder to solve, Sam," I said, correcting her, "and they wouldn't like me sticking my nose where it doesn't belong."

She walked me to the door, brooding.

"I'm sorry to disappoint you, Sam," I said as I opened the door. "Philip Marlowe I ain't."

"That's okay," she said. "You've got one thing over old Phil."

"What's that?"

"You're alive." She stretched up and kissed me on the cheek. When she did that her left breast pressed firmly against my arm, making me wonder again why I always ended up going back to my own place. "G'night, Nick."

"'Night, Sammy."

She swatted me on the shoulder as I went out the door. She hates it when I call her Sammy.

That is, she *says* she does.

Five days passed and I didn't hear from the cops again. I kept an eye on the papers to see if they'd solved the Hockshop Murder—which was what the newspapers were calling it—but there was nothing.

As for my own business, I picked up one case that took me two days of surveillance to solve. My business brought in enough for a single guy to live on, and since I had no intentions of getting married in the near—or not so near—future, I was satisfied with working one case that week. In fact, four such cases—involving two days of work—at two hundred a day plus expenses—and cheap at the price—were enough to pay my rent and bills and leave some left over to eat and play an occasional exacta at OTB.

Six days after my sister had left town I was sitting in my office going over a *Racing Form*. I still didn't know exactly why she had left or where she had gone, but then I hadn't yet gotten a chance to go out and see my dad. When the phone rang I would never have guessed what news it was bringing me.

"Delvecchio."

"Nick—"

"Father Vinnie, hey!" It only took one word for me to know my brother's voice, especially when that one word was my name. "Whataya say?"

"Nick..." he said again, and this time one word was enough for me to tell that something was wrong.

"What's wrong, Vinnie?" I asked. "Is it Pop?"

"No, it's not Pop," he said. "Nick, it's Maria."

"Maria? What's the matter with Maria?"

"Nick..."

"God damn it, Vinnie!" I said, forgetting that I was talking to a priest. "Stop saying my name and tell me what's going on!"

"I don't know how to put it."

"Just say it, Father."

"Nick, Maria—she's been hijacked!"

7

He'd put it wrong.

It wasn't that Maria had been hijacked, but the *plane* she was on had been. She'd gone to Greece after all, but on the way back her flight had been grabbed by terrorists.

"That's what we got so far from the TV, Nick," my brother said. "They're not even sure yet who the people are who took the plane."

"Are you sure about this, Vinnie? I mean, how do you know she was even on the plane?"

"Pop knew her flight."

"Pop knew a lot more than he was telling."

Vinnie agreed. "He always covered for her."

"Do we know for sure that she was on it? Maybe she missed it."

"We can't be sure either way, Nick," Vinnie said, "not until the authorities release the names, but Pop called her hotel, and they said she checked out."

"That doesn't mean she's on the plane. Where are you calling from?"

"Pop's house."

"I'll be right there, Vin."

I hung up and rushed across the hall to Sam's, hoping she was there. Luckily, she was.

"Sam—"

"What is it, Nick?"

"I need your car."

She knew immediately that whatever was wrong, it was serious.

"Sure, let me get the keys."

She left the door open and I stepped inside, then back outside, feeling numb. I didn't quite know where to stand. She came back with the keys and handed them to me.

"Nick, what's wrong?"

"Maria," I said, "her plane's been hijacked."

She caught her breath and then stared accusingly at her TV, which was off. There was a small dot of light in the center of the screen, though, which indicated that she'd been watching when I knocked.

"You mean, the plane on the news—"

"All I know is what my brother told me on the phone, Sam. I haven't seen the news."

"Where are you going?"

"My father's house."

"Give me the keys," she said, snatching them out of my hand.

"What—"

"I'll fill you in on what I know on the way," she said, grabbing her purse.

"Sam—"

"Besides," she added, "you're in no condition to drive. I can see it in your eyes. You'll probably wrap yourself—and my car—around a tree."

She was right about that. My heart was beating a mile a minute, and my eyes felt hot and dry. I knew that her concern was for me, and not her car.

"Let's go, then."

My father lived on Ovington Avenue, which was also Sixty-eighth Street, between Fourteenth and Fifteenth Avenues. Some people called this section Bensonhurst, but on the map it said Borough Park. His house—the house I'd grown up in—is a one-family wood frame, semiattached on one side. The shingles were the same ugly green they'd been when I was a kid. The houses on the block were basically the same, with a two- or three-family brick thrown in every so often, like cavities. Like so many South Brooklyn blocks, this one was packed with homes, at least fifty-five of them.

I started to feel hemmed in as soon as Sam turned her car into the block. I felt like I had more room to breathe in an apartment on a block of brownstones than on a block like this.

Bad news travels fast. You had only to walk into my father's place to see that.

"What the hell are they doing here?" I asked Vinnie.

He had opened the door before we even reached it. We hadn't seen each other in weeks, but when we clasped hands tightly, it was for more reasons than just that.

"Nick, they all came as soon as they heard," my brother said.

The house was filled with neighbors sitting around as if it was a wake, a good dozen or so of them. I felt myself growing angrier by the minute. My sister had been hijacked—maybe—but, by God, she wasn't dead! They were sitting around like they were waiting for news that she was.

"Nick—" Vinnie said, maintaining his hold on my hand. Sam had noticed the panic in my eyes, and now Vinnie could see the anger.

"Get them out, Vinnie," I said angrily. "Get them out before I throw them out. This is not a damned wake!"

"Nick..." he said again, but then he squeezed my hand and said, "I'll ask them to leave."

"Where's Pop?"

"In his room. Hello, Miss Karson."

"Father. Can I help?"

"Just being here helps," he said. "My father likes you very much, you know."

"Nick, let's go see your father."

I left my brother with the job of emptying the house and led Sam to my father's room. A few people tried to catch my attention, but I marched right past them, ignoring their words, shaking off their touch. I'd never been the neighborly type, and I had no intentions of starting now.

When Vinnie said that Pop was in "his room," he hadn't meant his bedroom, but the sitting room that Pop had added to the back of the house. He'd built it himself when Vinnie and I were kids, before Maria was even born, and from that time on it had been "his room." He had a desk there, and a TV, and a leather recliner, and he was in the recliner watching television when Sam and I entered the room.

"Pop..."

"Shh," he said, holding one hand up. "The news."

We waited and watched with him, but the report didn't say anything more than Sam had told me in the car. Flight 538 had been hijacked soon after takeoff by several terrorists, and as far as anyone knew, no one had been hurt. The plane was still in the air while the terrorists were bargaining for a place to land and refuel. The nationality of the terrorists was either unknown or had simply not yet been disclosed.

When the report ended, Pop lowered the volume with his remote control and then looked at us.

If my eyes had looked anything like his, I was glad Sam'd had the good sense not to let me drive. I didn't even want my father to stand up.

"Pop."

"Nicky."

I walked to the recliner and put my hand on his shoulder.

"I'm sorry, Pop."

He patted my hand and said, "What do we do, Nicky? What do we do?"

"I don't know, Pop. I guess we wait."

He nodded, then looked at Sam.

"Miss Karson."

"Hello, Mr. Delvecchio," she said, coming forward. She crouched down in front of him and took his hand. "I'm so sorry. I'd like to help you."

He touched her face with his other hand and said, "You're so pretty, you help just by being here."

She smiled and said, "You're still a charmer, Mr. Delvecchio," and kissed him on the cheek.

"Ah, if I am such a charmer, then you will call me Vito, eh?"

"Sure, Vito. Whatever you say."

"This is a good girl, Nicky," he said, patting her hand, "a good girl...like my Maria..."

His voice caught in his throat, and I said, "Pop," because I didn't know what else to say. I'd never seen my father cry, not even at my mother's funeral.

"Nick," Sam said, giving me a meaningful look, and I gave her a grateful one. I squeezed my father's shoulder and left the room.

On a table against the wall next to the doorway to Pop's room had always been a statue of the Virgin Mary, ever since we were kids. After Joey had been killed in Vietnam, however, Pop had hung a photo of him above the statue. I was standing there staring at it, maybe even shaking my head, when Father Vinnie came back into the room.

The house was empty and Vinnie was coming in the front door. My brother is taller than I am, six feet or so, and very slender. He is also better-looking than me, which is ironic, since attracting women is not one of his immediate concerns.

"I'm sorry, Vinnie—"

"That's okay, you were actually right...for once."

"Ha! Yeah." Couldn't resist a small dig, even now, huh, Father?

We stood there looking at each other for a few moments, my brother in his dark clothes and white collar that had made my mother so proud. I was wearing jeans and a short-sleeved shirt, and even though it was hot outside, I felt very cold.

"Jesus," I said, shivering suddenly, "is the air conditioner on in here?"

"No, Nick," Vinnie said, "but I know how you feel."

"Yeah, I guess you do," I said, and then I noticed something. "Hey!"

"What?"

"Where is he?"

"Who?"

"Our brother-in-law, Numbnuts, that's who. Where is that sonofabitch?"

"Nick..."

My brother had long ago gotten into the habit of speaking my name and making it sound like a dozen words, all disapproving. I think they had a course in it at the seminary. "Disapproving Tone 101."

"Well, where is he?"

"I don't know. Pop says he hasn't heard from him."

"Anybody call his office?"

Maria's husband worked on Wall Street.

"I don't know the number."

"Well, Pop must have it in his book somewhere. I want that bastard here so I can ask him what he did to make Maria go off like that."

"Nick, don't fight with Peter."

"That's going to be up to him, brother. There's the book," I said, spotting it under an end table on top of a Brooklyn Yellow Pages. I grabbed it up and went through it, looking under "G." The number wasn't there.

"Damn!" I said, slapping the book shut. "He's got their home number, but not Numbnuts's business number."

"Why would Pop want to call…Peter at work?"

"That's a good question. I guess we'll just have to wait for him to hear about it from the news."

"Unless you want to go to his office and tell him."

"I don't know where it is."

"Pop does."

I thought about going to Wall Street to look for my brother-in-law and then said, "Fuck him."

"Nick!"

"Bless me, Father, for I have sinned," I said. My brother gave me a hard stare, and I said, "Okay, I'm sorry. Look, what do we know, so far?"

"Not much. The plane took off from Athens and was on its way to Rome."

"Why would anyone hijack a plane from Greece?"

"It originated from Egypt."

"Do we know who the hijackers are?"

"Not yet."

"You said on the phone that Pop called her hotel. Have you called anyone else?"

"I called the American consulate in Greece, and the State Department here in the United States."

"What did they say?"

"That the names of the passengers would be released at a later date. The State Department said they were inundated with calls and couldn't pick and choose who to keep informed right now."

I hated to admit it, but it sounded fair.

"The consulates in both Egypt and Greece said that they were working on getting a complete passenger list, and that the families of the hijacked passengers would be advised if the situation dragged on."

"Which means?"

"Which means that by the time they get around to calling families, the passengers may be released."

"If history repeats itself, Vinnie, these passengers are going to turn into hostages pretty quick."

"God forbid," he said.

"Damn," I said. "Vinnie, let's go for a walk." I needed some air.

"Where?"

"Up the comer. We'll get an egg cream."

"I haven't had an egg cream in a long time."

"Come on, Vinnie," I said. "It'll be like old times."

"Yeah," Vinnie said, grinning. "I buy, right?"

8

We left the house and walked toward Fourteenth Avenue.

"I wonder how Sam's doing with Pop."

"I'm sure she's doing fine. Pop speaks very highly of her, you know. He says you should marry her."

"Believe me, Vinnie," I said sincerely, "I shouldn't marry anyone."

"You're my last hope, you know."

I knew what he meant. Maria had gone along with Numbnuts and gotten married in a Jewish ceremony. I was Vinnie's last hope of performing the marriage ceremony for a member of his family.

When we reached the comer, we had to cross to get to the luncheonette that Mr. Canizotti used to run when we were kids. The front was so old there was a still a "Breyer's Ice Cream" leaf over the door—faded but readable. Mr. Canizotti had faded, too, about ten years before. I didn't know who was running it now, but I hoped they knew how to make a decent egg cream. Jesus, that was old Brooklyn: egg creams and stick-ball, Coney Island and Nathan's hot dogs and fries.

Right on the comer was an Italian club, and with the front door open we could hear the old Italian music coming from inside. That, too, was part of my childhood. This section of Borough Park was predominantly Italian, which was why there was very little street crime and burglaries. These people wouldn't call the cops, they'd solve the problem themselves. The petty thieves knew this, and wanted no part of the...Italians. If you were "connected," there was almost no need for you to lock your doors.

"Hey, Nicky, Father Vinnie," a voice called from inside the darkened interior of the club.

"Who's that?" Vinnie asked, peering inside.

"Sounds like Mr. Rosetti."

A small white-haired man shuffled through the doorway into the street, and we could see that I was right. Once, old Joseph Rosetti was Joey Rose, a feared man in New York, but that was twenty, thirty years ago. Now he was just old Mr. Rosetti, seventy if he was a day.

"Hello, Mr. Rosetti," I said.

"Hello, boys. We heard about your sister. A terrible thing, terrible."

"Thank you, Mr. Rosetti," Vinnie said.

The old man put a withered hand on my brother's arm.

"Father, you tell Vito that if he needs anything, he should call us, eh?"

"I'll tell him, Mr. Rosetti. He'll appreciate it."

"Old Vito," Mr. Rosetti said, although my father was at least ten years younger than he was. "He'll appreciate it, but he won't call. A proud man, your father. He was much help to us on the docks in the old days."

I didn't particularly want to hear about that. None of my father's old friends—like Joey Rose, Frankie the Arm, and my namesake, Nicky Barracuda—liked it when I joined the police department. They always thought that "Vito's boys" would join them, even though my father was never really in the rackets. When Vinnie went into the seminary, they started to work on me, and maybe that was what pushed me the other way.

Pop did favors for "the boys" sometimes on the docks, because he was real popular with the dockworkers. They respected him and usually did what he asked them to do.

After I left the department, they offered me a job, but I turned them down as nicely as I could. I wanted to work for myself, I said. I'd had enough of working for other people. Maybe, they said, I'd be able to do them a favor or two, once in a while. Sure, I said, and maybe it would work the other way, too. Of course...

"Anyway," Mr. Rosetti said, "you boys know you can call anytime, eh?"

"We know that, Mr. Rosetti," I said.

"Sure, I know you do. Uh, Father..."

"Yes, sir?"

"My Rosa, she not feeling so good lately. Maybe, uh, you could put a good word in? You know, with the boss upstairs?"

"I'll say a prayer, Mr. Rosetti. I'm sure the 'boss' will watch over her."

"You a good boy, Father," the old man said. "You both good boys."

"We're going across the street for an egg cream, Mr. Rosetti," I said. "Would you like to come?"

"I would like to, Nicky, yes, but walking across the street and back would tire me out. Besides, since Canizotti died, the egg creams just ain't the same."

"We'll give it a try anyway," I said.

"Oh, they're still Brooklyn egg creams, Nicky, but Canizotti, he had the touch, eh?"

"He sure did."

"You boys go ahead. Give your father my best, eh?"

"We'll do that, sir."

He turned and shuffled back into the gloomy interior of the club, where he sat and traded war stories and lies with his friends and listened to music from the old country—even though half of them had been born here.

"Can you imagine that old man being one of the most feared hit—"

"I don't want to hear it, Nicky," Vinnie said, cutting me off. "Let's cross."

We crossed over and entered the luncheonette. The woman behind the counter asked us what we'd have. She had white hair, but despite her advanced age her face was virtually unlined.

"Egg creams," I said.

"Vanilla or chocolate?"

Mr. Canizotti would never have asked us that. An egg cream was an egg cream. I was about to lecture her on that when Father Vinnie jumped in ahead of me.

"Chocolate," he said. "Large ones."

We watched her as she made them, and she seemed to do everything right. The seltzer, the chocolate syrup, the milk, everything that old man Canizotti used to do—but no egg.

"Hey, no egg yolk?" I asked.

She stared at me, puzzled, and said, "What egg?"

"Never mind."

When she handed them over and we tasted them, we both made faces.

"Jesus," I said, "where can you get a good egg cream anymore, Vinnie?"

"I don't know, Nicky," he said, apparently taking my use—or misuse—of the Lord's name in stride, for once.

We turned and looked out the dusty plate-glass window at the laundromat across the street. It was filled with old women doing their husbands' laundry, not a decent pair of legs in sight. I almost said as much to my brother, but held my tongue.

"Nicky."

"Yeah?"

"Are you...do you ever see Nicky Barracuda?"

"My godfather?" I said, and I was using the word the way it was originally meant to be used. "Not really. He sends somebody around every so often to...feel me out."

"You don't...work for him, do you?"

"You asking me if I'm Mafia, Vinnie. Outfit, Syndicate, Co-sa No-stra," I said, pronouncing it very deliberately. No real Italian would ever admit that such a thing existed. My father, for instance, wouldn't allow any of those names to be spoken in the house.

"No, I know you're smarter than that. I just don't want you to get in too deeply, that's all."

"I'm not in at all, Father," I said, and putting my half-finished egg-cream facsimile down on the counter, I said, "and I can't drink any more of that."

"Maybe we should have tried vanilla?" Vinnie said, putting his down, too.

"Then it wouldn't have been an egg cream. Come on, let's go back. Maybe Pop heard something on the news."

On the way back I asked, "How are things at the church?" My brother was assigned to the Church of the Holy Family, in Canarsie, and had been since he left the seminary.

"Fine."

"They going to make you pastor yet?"

He shook his head.

"I'm still too young."

Both Father Vinnie and I knew that all he had to do was drop a bug in Nicky Barracuda's ear and he'd be pastor, bishop, or anything he wanted—short of Pope, maybe.

I wondered myself sometimes whether or not Vinnie did favors for Barracuda. The difference between my brother and me was that he wasn't shy about asking. Maybe I was afraid of what the answer would be if I did ask outright.

"Got to have one foot in the grave, huh?"

"Something like that."

"Hey, maybe the Barracuda could—"

"Nick!"

"I'm kidding, Vinnie," I said, hurriedly, "I'm just kidding." We had half a block to go and walked the rest of the way in silence.

My father and Sam were still in his room, watching the TV. There was one difference, though. My father was eating a sandwich, and there was a can of Bud on the floor next to him. When she heard us, Sam turned and looked, held a finger to her lips, and joined us.

"I made some sandwiches and got your father to eat one."

"How'd you do that?" Vinnie asked. "I tried to get him to eat earlier—"

"I charmed him."

"I can believe that," my brother said. It was an uncharacteristic remark. Sam seemed to have conquered all of the Delvecchio men.

"You guys better go into the kitchen and eat."

"Nicky?" my father called.

"Yeah, Pop?"

"Let Father Vinnie go into the kitchen with Miss Karson."

Vinnie looked at me, and I nodded. He and Sam went into the kitchen, and I went and stood by my father's chair.

"We saw Mr. Rosetti today, Pop. He said if you need anything—"

"Nick called."

I knew he was referring to Nicky Barracuda—Dominick Barracondi—his friend, my godfather, and boss of bosses in Brooklyn. I was "Nicky," his son, and his friend was "Nick."

"He says that all I have to do is say the word and he will send a team to get Maria."

"A team?" I said. "Jesus, Pop, you can't let him."

"He says as soon as they land and we know where they are, he can have a crack team—"

"Pop, he'll get her killed. Barracuda's men don't know anything about dealing with terrorists."

"Then you go," my father said, glaring up at me.

"Me?"

"Yeah, you. You the big-a-shot cop, the ace detective," he said, an accent creeping into his speech pattern. "You go anna save you sister's life."

"Pop, that's not fair," I said, feeling like shit.

"Fair! Is what is happening to your sister fair?"

Did he resent me that much for becoming a cop? If so, he'd never shown it before. Was it just his anger talking, or was his anger giving rise to his true feelings?

"Either you go and get her or I will tell Nick to go ahead. We take care of our own, Nicky."

Suddenly, I had the feeling that my father was more involved with the wise guys than I ever thought.

"Pop..."

"If your brother Joey was alive, he'd go."

That was his final shot, and I had neither the inclination or the ammo to fire back.

"Pop, I'll keep in touch."

I didn't know if he'd heard me. His attention was focused on the TV, and he used the remote control to turn the volume up. From what I could see they were simply repeating their report of the incident.

I went into the kitchen and found Father Vinnie eating a sandwich while Sam was drinking coffee.

"Vinnie, are you going to stay around?"

"I don't think he should be alone, do you, Nick?"

"No, I don't, not in his present state of mind. Vinnie," I said, trying to choose my words carefully, "don't let him use the phone."

"Don't let him—Nick, what went on with you and him just now?"

I told him, word for word.

"He threw Joey at you?"

"Yeah."

Sam looked at me, and I shrugged. She knew that Joey, our older brother, had been killed in Vietnam in 1969, when he was nineteen, I was fifteen, and Vinnie was seventeen.

"That's not fair, Nick," Sam said. She got up and came over to me, putting her hand on my arm. "I mean, telling you to go and save her."

"She's right, Nick," Vinnie said, standing up. "You're not thinking of going, are you? You're not going to do anything foolish?"

"Where would I go?" I asked. "To Egypt? Greece? The plane's already gone from there, and it's still in the air. Besides, I don't know anything about terrorists. There are experts for that."

"You're right, Nick," Vinnie said. "I'm glad you're thinking straight."

"Vinnie, Pop's been watching Dan Rather. Why don't you give CBS a call and see if they can't tell you something?"

"Good idea. What are you going to be doing?"

"I have to go see Barracuda."

"Who's Barracuda?" Sam asked.

"Now that's not thinking straight, Nick." Father Vinnie frowned and looked disapproving. "What makes you think you can get in to see him?"

"Oh, I'll get in."

"Who's Barracuda?"

"My godfather."

She looked at me, unsure whether or not I was serious.

"What are you going to say to him, Nick?" Vinnie asked. He looked even more worried now than he did before.

"Save your worrying for Maria, Vinnie, and your prayers. I'm going to ask him to leave the situation alone. The only thing he'll accomplish is to get a lot of innocent people killed—maybe even Maria."

"You're going to tell Nicky Barracuda that we don't want his help?"

Vinnie made it sound like he worked for the only authority higher than Nicky Barracuda. It was a throwback to our childhood, when we really thought that the Barracuda was God.

"Not in those words, but yeah, that's what I'm going to tell him."

Vinnie stared at me, and I thought that he was probably thinking about me what I was thinking about Pop only moments before. He was wondering how I could possibly intend to talk to the Barracuda like that if I wasn't in bed with him.

Well, I wasn't—but maybe I'd have to be in order to get him to lay off.

Maybe that's what he was planning, all along.

9

Sam wanted to come along, but I convinced her to stay. I thought my father would listen to her. She gave me the keys to her car and told me to drive carefully.

I drove to Fourteenth Avenue, made a right, went to Sixty-fifth Street and made another right. I followed Sixty-fifth Street until it met with Avenue P, then took Avenue P to Ocean Avenue. Once I hit Ocean Avenue, it was a straight run south to Sheepshead Bay.

My father's words had stung more than I had realized. When things were back to normal, we were going to have to sit down and talk about it. Was he in deep enough with the boys to have resented it when I enrolled in the police academy? And if so, why hadn't he said anything before, or even after the department and I had come to a parting of the ways?

Yeah, Pop and me were going to have to have a good long talk—after Maria was home.

Sheepshead Bay was a whole different Brooklyn, all the way at the southern tip. It was old homes, small wood-frame houses that used to be summer homes but were now year-round. A lot of them stood below sidewalk level now because they had been built before there was a sidewalk.

The main drag of Sheepshead Bay was Emmons Avenue, which was right on the bay. On one side were the docks, and if you got there later in the day, the boats were all in with their catches, selling fresh fish. The other side was lined with restaurants, most of them seafood places, the best in the city. On weekends there were flea markets in the parking lots, and the streets on both sides of Emmons were lined with street vendors.

This wasn't a weekend, though, and it wasn't late in the day. Kids were in school, people were at work, and Emmons was empty and quiet. The restaurants did a lunch business from nearby business areas. An island ran down the center of Emmons, and on either side of it there was angle parking. At the moment there were plenty of spots, but once it got on toward the dinner hour, there wouldn't be one to be had.

The air smelled of fish, garlic, and, from further down Emmons Avenue, knishes from a fast-food place called Shatzkin's. I parked the car and crossed to the bay side of Emmons, where there was a restaurant called On the Barge, which actually was on a barge. Needless to say, it was a seafood restaurant, but it was an Italian seafood restaurant.

It was also owned by Dominick Barracondi—Nicky the Barracuda.

The inside looked like the inside of a boat, with phony portholes and fishnets hanging from the walls, along with other paraphernalia like harpoons and anchors. The tables and chairs were oak, and so was the bar. Nicky Barracuda did not scrimp when he put together a fine Italian seafood restaurant—and that included the food. I'd eaten there before, and he had excellent chefs and used the best-quality fish and pasta. In fact, he had his own pasta made on the premises. The proof of the pudding was that Barracuda ate there himself, all his meals except breakfast.

They had a good lunch crowd and a maitre d' on duty, and as I entered, the man turned to look at me. He was about eight feet across at the shoulders, dressed in a tux and flashing a diamond pinky ring on each hand. His name was Benvinuto Carbone—Benny the Card—and we knew each other. In fact, we'd gone to high school together.

"Aye, Don Cheech," he said, coming forward with his hand extended. "How's it hanging?"

"Like a noodle, Benny. How you doing?" He had a grip like a duck press.

"Fine, couldn't be better. Whataya think of the outfit?" He turned completely around, modeling his monkey suit.

"The rings are a little blinding, Benny, otherwise it's fine."

"You wanna have some lunch or what?"

"Lunch would be fine, Benny, but right now I've got to talk to Mr. Barracondi."

"I wish I could help you, paisan, but the boss is real busy."

"Would you tell him I'm here, Benny?"

He thought a moment and said, "Well, I guess I could do that."

"I'd really appreciate it."

"Hey, is this about your sister?"

"Yeah."

"Well, why didn't you say so? Geez, I was real sorry to hear about it—"

"Thanks, Benny. Could you, uh, call now?"

"Oh, sure, Nicky, sure." He turned to go to his station to use the phone, but then turned and said, "Hey, if he don't wanna see you, you're gonna have to leave."

"I'll leave."

"Okay, 'cause I wouldn't wanna have to throw you out, you being a paisan and all."

"Okay, fine."

Benny nodded happily and went to his station to use the phone. He dialed three numbers, said something, listened, nodded, and then lumbered over to me. Benny had always had the most unreadable face of all the kids who had ever beat me up in school. I didn't know now whether he was going to hug me or bear-hug me out the door.

"Whataya know?" he said. "The boss says he'll see you. He must like you a lot, Nicky."

"Well, why not? You do, don't you?"

"Not really."

I said we went to school together, but I never claimed that we were friends.

"But you're a paisan. Let's go."

"Lead the way, Benny, lead the way."

Nicky Barracuda was eating lunch at his desk. That meant he must have been pretty busy, which made his seeing me that much more of a favor. Nicky Barracuda dealt heavily in favors. One of his favorite mottos was "Tit for tat."

When I followed Benny into the room, Barracuda looked up from his clams and mussels and pasta and said, "Nicholas, come in, come in. Always good to see you."

"Thank you, Mr. Barracondi." I had always refused to call him "Godfather." It always made me feel like I was in a movie.

"Mr. Barracondi, you hear that, Benny?" Barracondi said. "This boy always did have the proper respect."

Benny didn't know what he was supposed to say to that, so he said, "Yeah."

"Yeah," Barracuda repeated. "That's all, Benny. Go back to work."

"Yes, sir."

Benny gave me a look I couldn't interpret and then backed out of the room, closing the door behind him.

"Sit down, sit down. You want some clams, some pasta?"

"No, nothing. Thanks."

I sat and looked at my godfather. He was in his sixties, a tall, elegant-looking man, almost like an Italian Cesar Romero. He even had the carefully clipped white mustache. As far back as I could remember, he'd always had the mustache.

"When you were a little boy," he said, "you used to call me Godfather. Then as you got older, you started calling me Uncle Dominick...then Uncle Dom. Now I am 'Mr. Barracondi.' I have not seen you for six months, Nicholas. In another six months will we be perfect strangers?"

"I don't think either one of us will ever be perfect, Mr. Barracondi."

He stared at me for a few moments and then said, "How is your father?"

"Not well."

"This hijacking?"

"You know that."

"Why are you here, Nicholas...after six months, why are you here now?"

"To ask you something."

"Ask."

"I want you to stay away from this thing."

"I can help."

"No, you can't help. All you'll do is get somebody killed. Leave it to the experts."

He laughed shortly.

"No one dies when it is left to the experts?"

"True, these things are rarely resolved without someone dying, but they know what they're doing. They've dealt with these people before. You have not."

"I have dealt with much in my lifetime, Nicholas."

"I know that—" I said, and then stopped. I was tired of being careful not to insult him, but I had to admit that I was intimidated by him.

"Mr. Barracondi—" I stopped again, then said, "Godfather, please, leave it alone."

"Ah," he said, raising his eyebrows, "*now* I am 'Godfather.'"

I didn't know what to say to that, but he saved me the trouble of floundering. He put both hands on the desk on either side of his seafood plate and pinned me with a hard stare.

"Let me see if I have this straight. You are asking me for a favor?"

Ah-hah, I thought.

"Yes."

He nodded shortly.

"I just wanted to get that out of the way."

He picked up his fork and twirled some pasta.

"Very well, I will stay out of it as long as I can."

"What does that mean?"

He looked at me quickly and said, "I will let the experts take care of it...until I believe that they *cannot* take care of it."

"That's not good enough..."

He smiled a humorless smile and said, "You are my godson when it suits you, Nicholas. That is not good enough for me." We exchanged stares then, and I backed down.

"All right."

I stood up as he turned his attention to a clam.

"You tell Vito I ask for him, eh?"

"I will."

"And Father Vinnie? How is he?"

"He's fine."

"Still a priest in Canarsie, eh?"

"He seems to like it."

"You tell him to call me when he doesn't like it anymore, eh?"

"Sure, Mr. Barracondi," I said, rising. "I'll tell him."

I left, knowing full well what the visit had just cost me. I knew *what* it had cost me, what I didn't know was when, and how big.

10

I had another stop to make before I went back to my father's house, but I needed a phone first. I left On the Barge, got my car, and drove to a big diner down the road. Brooklyn diners always have breakfast twenty-four hours a day, and pay phones.

I stepped into the entry foyer and found two phones. One had a dial, the other had pushbuttons. Since I had been thinking so much about the past of late, I decided to use the one with the dial. I dialed the number of police headquarters in Manhattan—374-5000—and asked for Deputy Inspector Edward Gorman.

"I'm sorry, sir," the operator said, "the inspector is no longer assigned here."

"Can you tell me where he *is* assigned?"

"I'll connect you to Personnel."

I waited while the connection was made, and then a sweet female voice said, "Personnel, Police Administrative Aide Ingram."

"Miss Ingram, my name is Nicholas Delvecchio, and I'm trying to locate Deputy Inspector Gorman."

"Do you know where he's assigned?"

I bit back the first reply that came to mind and said, "No, all I know is that he used to be assigned to police headquarters."

"How long ago?"

I tried to remember the last time I'd seen Ed Gorman.

"I guess three, four months ago."

"I'll check."

The police department had not invested in Muzak yet, so I was left with a dead line while she did her checking, and it was anybody's guess whether I'd been cut off or was still on hold.

When I joined the department, Gorman had been a lieutenant in the seven-eight precinct. Three years later he was a captain in the two-four, but we kept in touch. When I left the department, he was a deputy inspector. Throughout all of that, he had also been my "rabbi," my connection within the department—if I wanted him to be. Time and time again he had offered to intercede on my behalf, first to get me a promotion, and then to keep me from getting kicked out of the department altogether. He'd had a lot to do with my getting the one-third pension and the P. I. license, although he'd never admit it.

During the four years since I'd left he had risen no higher than D.I., unless something had happened to change that in the past few months. Gorman had always been a man who spoke his mind, and that trait had gotten him to the rank of D.I., but it might also be what was keeping him there. When you have opinions and you voice them, you make enemies—and when one of your enemies rises a little higher and a little faster than you, that can keep you in one place for a long time.

P. A. A. Ingram came back on the line, letting me know that I had not been dropped into Ma Bell limbo.

"Sir?"

"I'm here."

"Deputy Inspector Gorman has been reassigned to the Brooklyn South Area."

I frowned.

"That's in the six-seven building, isn't it?"

"Yes, sir. It's in Flatbush. Snyder Avenue."

"All right, thank you."

"You're welcome, sir."

"Oh, one more thing?"

"Yes?"

"Could you give me the phone number of the six-seven?"

"Of course, sir. That's 469-7300."

"Thank you, Miss Ingram. You've been very helpful."

I hung up, wondering what Ed Gorman had done to get dumped into a shithole like the six-seven precinct.

* * *

The six-seven precinct building used to be on Snyder Avenue between Flatbush and Bedford Avenues, but when it turned one hundred years old, they moved everybody into a new building, still on Snyder but between Rogers and Nostrand Avenues.

Twenty years ago Flatbush Avenue was a shopper's paradise. Sears, Macy's, and dozens of small stores were always packed with shoppers, mostly women and their kids. My mother used to take me, Vinnie, and Joey with her whenever she went shopping, and we'd have lunch in the cafeteria in *Mays*—as opposed to *Macy's*. Mays was gone now, and as I drove down Flatbush Avenue, the decay that the area had fallen into became more and more evident.

Over the years "the wrong element" had taken over the Flatbush area of Brooklyn. The streets were deserted now because people were afraid to walk, let alone shop. Oh sure, the malls had captured a lot of the shoppers who used to frequent the area, but more than that, people didn't want to shop where they had to be afraid they might be mugged, or their children might be threatened. (It was a common ploy for a street thief to approach a woman with an infant in a stroller and threaten the infant if the woman did not give up her purse—and that was if he didn't just knock her down and take it.)

A year before I left the department there had been a massive blackout in New York City, and that had naturally given rise to looting. The Flatbush area had been one of the most heavily hit by looting, and I had been sent there with some others to work the area. It had been like working a combat zone. I mean, under adverse circumstances even the most normal of people could give in to the urge to get something for nothing, but these people weren't normal. Iron gates had been ripped off windows so that they could get into the stores, and more often than not it had taken two or three cracks on the head with my nightstick to bring them down, where one would have normally done the job.

All of which I mention to illustrate what a hellhole the area covered by the men of the six-seven had become.

And D.I. Ed Gorman had been dropped into the middle of this.

Technically speaking, while the six-seven precinct covered the confines of the six-seven itself, the Brooklyn South Area covered all of the Brooklyn South precincts, many of which were not exactly garden spots and one or two of which were just as bad as the six-seven—or worse.

Flatbush Avenue south of Kings Highway was still pretty decent, but north of it—forget it.

I drove on Flatbush Avenue as far as Church Avenue, where Erasmus

High School stood. Erasmus counted among its alumni Neil Diamond and Barbra Streisand, but it hadn't produced talent of that caliber for a long time, and probably never would again.

I turned right on Church, drove three blocks, turned right on Nostrand, drove two blocks, and turned right on Snyder. In the middle of the block the new six-seven building stood, a three-story structure of brick and concrete. I parked in front of a hydrant because summonses were not usually given out on the block of a precinct. There was always the chance that a cop would be ticketing another cop's car—or worse, a boss's.

I entered the precinct building and was approached by a handsome, black female police officer.

"Can I help you, sir?"

"Yes, I'm here to see Inspector Gorman."

"He's in Brooklyn South," she said. "That's on the third floor. Is he expecting you?"

"No," I said. I had called ahead to confirm that he was in, but had not spoken to him.

"I'll have to call upstairs and tell him you're here, then."

"Fine."

She did that, using a phone in an office to our right. When she hung up, she nodded toward the elevator and said, "You can go on up."

"Thank you."

I used the elevator without being decapitated by it and got off at the third floor. A handwritten sign was taped to the wall, with an arrow pointing to the right and the initials "B.S.A." on it—Brooklyn South Area.

I walked into a large room peppered with desks. There were four people in the room, three in civilian clothes and one in uniform. More than likely the ones dressed in civilian clothes *were* civilians. Even before I had joined the department, they had begun hiring civilians to do office jobs, freeing most of the cops for street duty. They called the civilians police administrative aides.

The uniformed cop was the one that approached me. He was a chunky man in his thirties with thinning black hair. His nameplate identified him as Officer Aiello. He had a small, off-duty revolver in a belt holster clipped to his belt on his right hip.

"Can I help you?"

"I'd like to see Inspector Gorman."

"You're..."

"Delvecchio. The desk called ahead."

"Right. Follow me, please."

He led me past the desks and a large Xerox machine to the back of the room, where he knocked on a closed door. A voice from the inside called out, and he opened it.

"Inspector, there's a Mr. Delboccio to see you."

"Delvecchio!" Ed Gorman called out. His booming voice bounced off the walls of the little room. "Get your candy-ass in here!"

11

Ed Gorman had had his nose broken so many times that it seemed to have ceased to exist. In spite of this, his face had a kind of...appeal, I guess, is the word. He looked like the sort of man you could trust. He was in his forties, young for a D.I., but if things went on the way they were going, his age would soon catch up to his rank.

He stood up and came around the desk with his hand outstretched.

"How the hell are you?"

"What the hell are you doing here?" The last time I'd seen him, Gorman was heading up the N.Y.P.D.'s Intelligence Division.

He regarded me for a moment and then said, "Did I ever tell you that I never had a rabbi?"

"You told me."

"I sure could use one now."

I didn't know what I was supposed to say to that.

"Want some coffee?"

"Sure."

He had a coffee machine on top of a filing cabinet. On a table opposite his desk was a color TV Even in a hole like this, rank had certain privileges.

He poured me a cup of coffee in a thick, white mug and handed it to me. He already had one on his desk, only his cup had a captain's shield stenciled on it. His wife had given it to him when he made captain.

"Black, right?"

"Right."

He went back behind his desk and sat down.

"Well, what the fuck are you doing here? I haven't laid eyes on you for three months now."

"You been watching TV?"

"On and off. What else is there to do here? Why?"

"You see the news? About the hijacking?"

"I heard something about it." He frowned. "You handling international cases now?"

I shook my head.

"Inspector, there's a good chance that my sister is on that plane."

"Little...Maria, isn't it?"

"Yes."

He stared at me for a few moments.

"Shit."

"Exactly."

"Shit, Nick, I'm sorry."

"I said she might be on it, Inspector. Nothing's been said on the news about who the passengers are, and I don't know that it will be in the papers yet."

He picked up a pen and began tapping it on the desk. "What are you asking me, Nick—if you're asking me something."

"I am. I'd like you to try and find out for me if she's on the plane."

"How do you suggest I do that?"

I shrugged. "Make some phone calls, ask some questions."

"If I could make those kind of phone calls, Nick, do you think I'd be here?"

"You can't help yourself," I pointed out, "but maybe you can help me."

"You were on the job for five years, Nick. You were on your way to becoming a damned good cop, and I could have helped you, but you never asked me for it."

"I'm asking you now, Ed."

He rubbed his hand over his jaw.

"You're asking for your sister."

"And my father."

"How is the old man?"

"He's not taking this well. If there's a chance that she missed that plane, I'd like him to know about it as soon as possible."

"Nick, have you been out to Sheepshead Bay?"

"I talked to Barracuda, Ed, yeah."

"Did you ask him for his help?"

"I asked him *not* to help."

"I bet he must have appreciated that."

"He considers it a favor," I said, and Gorman gave me a look that said he knew what that meant.

When he began tapping his pen on the desk harder and faster, I knew I had him.

"All right," he said, dropping the pen. "All right, Nick, I'll make some calls and see what I can find out."

"I appreciate it," I said. I stood up and put my coffee cup down on his desk. I grabbed a pad and a pen and wrote down my father's phone number.

"You can call here. If I'm not there, my brother will be."

"Your brother the father?"

"That's right."

I took a sip of the coffee and made a face. "God, your coffee has gotten worse."

"Yeah," he said as I put the cup down on his desk, "I've missed you, too."

I drove back to my father's house and found the situation unchanged. He was still sitting in his chair in front of the television, while Father Vinnie and Sam sat in the living room.

"You've been gone a long time," Sam said as I entered. Vinnie and I both had keys to my father's house. When we suddenly realized that Pop was "elderly," we had insisted on it, and he'd given in just to shut us up.

"Don't worry," I said, "your car is in one piece."

"That's not what I meant, you jerk."

"I know," I said, touching her arm. "How's Pop?" The question was directed more at Vinnie.

"The same, Nick. They're not telling us very much more on TV than before. I guess we'll have to watch the newspapers tomorrow."

"Vinnie, can you stay here?"

We both knew that if one of us stayed, it would have to be him. Pop had always been hard on all of us. Joey had been his favorite, and after Joey died, he was even harder on Vinnie and me. Then after Vinnie became "Father" Vinnie—well, that left me.

"I can stay."

"You might be getting a call from Inspector Gorman." Vinnie had never met Ed, but he knew who he was.

"I asked him to make some calls. He might be able to find out something about Maria."

"What about Barracuda?" Vinnie asked. "How did it go with him?"

"I asked him not to interfere, and he agreed."

"That's it?"

"That's it, Vinnie. Don't worry about Barracuda, just Pop." My brother gave me a look that said I wasn't telling him everything, but then we weren't in the confessional. I was sure that when it came to Barracuda, he didn't tell me everything, either.

"Sam, I better get you home. You probably have some work to do."

I didn't want to see Pop at that moment, nor did I particularly want to talk to my brother. She took the hint and agreed that she did have some work to do.

"Father, if you need anything, please don't hesitate to call me."

"You've been very helpful, Miss Karson. Thank you."

"Nick, will you be by tomorrow?"

"Sure, early. I'll bring some breakfast."

"Fine."

There was a stiffness between my brother and me at the end of the day, and I wasn't sure if it was because of Pop or because of Barracuda. Maybe he felt I should have stayed, but some things had been said that I wanted to think about, and I couldn't do that there.

Sam drove back to Sackett Street and must have sensed that I wanted to think, because she remained silent all the way, right up until the time we reached our floor.

"Do you want some dinner?"

"I've got some frozen dinners in my freezer, Sam. That'll do for me, if you don't mind."

"I don't mind if your stomach doesn't."

"My stomach is used to anything."

"Nick—"

"Thanks for coming along, Sam. It meant a lot to Pop to have you there…and to me."

"Nick, some things were said…your father is very upset…"

"I know that, Sam. Believe me, I know that."

We stood in the hall for a few awkward moments, and then she said, "Thanks, Nick."

"For what?"

"For needing me, today."

And of course she was right. She was my friend, and I'd needed a friend.

I gave her a hug then, probably the most emotional moment that had ever passed between us, and then we went into our own apartments.

12

I was preoccupied with the events of the day as I entered my apartment and didn't become immediately aware that there was somebody there.

"It's about time you got home."

I stopped short and looked up. There were two of them, and one switched on a lamp. They were both big and brawny, almost identical but for the fact that one of them had a smooth complexion while the other's face was scarred with pockmarks. They were both wearing expensive suits, so they weren't just run-of-the-mill knuckledusters. If anything, they were well-paid legbreakers—but paid by who?

"Can I help you fellas?" I asked warily. "These aren't exactly my office hours."

"Well, that's fine with us, friend. This isn't exactly a business call."

"I'd really prefer you call my secretary for an appointment if you want to talk to me."

One of the men frowned and said, "You don't have a secretary."

"Now you've got the idea, friend." I backed up until I felt the door behind me, and then reached for the doorknob. My heart was pounding, because whoever these guys were, they weren't here to just talk, and I had the feeling they wouldn't just walk out when asked.

"I don't think you should open that door, pal," one of them said.

"Why? You want to go out through it? Or would you prefer a window?"

"A tough nut," Smoothie said.

"Tough nuts crack easy," Pockmark replied.

"Not this one," I said. I could feel the panic rising inside of me. I started to sweat profusely, and they misinterpreted that as a sign of weakness.

"Look at him sweat," the smooth-faced one said.

"He's scared."

"What do you want?"

"We want to know where the girl is," Smoothie said. He seemed to be the spokesman.

"What girl?"

"Jodi Hayworth."

"Jodi? I haven't seen her in a couple of weeks."

"Sure, that's when she came to you to hire you to do something for her. To find something for her."

I made no comment.

"You did your job and then she left, but you've seen her since, haven't you?"

"No."

"Look, friend, make this easy on yourself. All we want is the girl. Tell us where she is."

"I've already told you, I only saw her that one day."

"Tough nut," the other man said.

They started to move toward me, and with my back to the door I had nowhere to go.

"Come on, guys," I said. "You don't want to do this."

"You're right, we don't, so why don't you just tell us what we want to know?"

"All right," I said, my mind racing for an out. "All right, I know where she is. She gave me an address."

"What is it?"

"I wrote it down. It's in my desk drawer."

"Where's your desk?"

"In my office. Through that door."

They both turned their heads to look at the door, and I moved. They were standing close enough together that when I charged forward, I was able to hit each of them with one of my shoulders. One of them spun away and fell to the floor, but the other was merely pushed aside.

"Get him!" the man on the floor shouted.

I didn't know exactly what "Get him!" meant at that point. Most leg-breakers didn't use anything more than a fist adorned with some brass knuckles, but I couldn't take the chance that these two might be armed with something more dangerous. If they had guns, they didn't even have to use them, just produce them, and then while one of them kept me covered, the other could administer a beating at his leisure.

I couldn't let that happen.

Not again.

I had a three-foot wooden coffee table set up in front of the couch. It wasn't expensive, and it wasn't real heavy. In fact, with my adrenaline flowing the way it was, it hardly weighed anything.

As the standing man—the smooth-faced one—reached into his jacket, I grabbed the table, lifted it, and threw it at him. It cut through the air neatly and struck him in the stomach. This time he was knocked back and down.

I turned to the other man, who had risen to one knee by now and was reaching into his jacket. I launched a kick that caught him on the butt of the jaw, snapping his head back, and he slumped to the floor like a sack of loose shit.

Next to my couch was a small end table with one drawer. I pulled the drawer open, reached inside, and pulled out the slapper I kept in there. A slapper is a flat jack, carried by a lot of police officers because it is flat and fits better in the pocket than the cylindrical blackjack.

The smooth-faced man pushed the coffee table away from him and rose to his knees, one hand held against his stomach. With the other he began to reach frantically into his jacket. I literally ran across the room, swung the slapper, and caught him right on the forehead. The skin split as he went down onto his back and lay still, blood running down his face.

I sat down on the couch thinking about my gun. I don't carry it, even though I have a license, because I know that in certain violent situations I have a tendency to overreact. I know that about myself. If I *had* been wearing my gun, I might have made a move for it, and somebody might be dead—maybe even me.

There was a banging on the door that may have been going on for a while. I had only just become aware of it.

"Nick, it's Sam," she called out, still banging. "Nick, what's happening? Are you all right?"

I felt very weak and was fighting to catch my breath. I wanted to go to the door and let her in, but there was something else I had to do first—if I could move.

I laid the slapper aside and bent over the man I'd just laid out. I reached into his jacket and came out with a .38. I have a gun something like it, but mine is in a safe in the floor of my office. With certain parties eager for me to take a wrong step, all I had to do was shoot somebody and that would have clinched it.

Of course, I might have clinched it just now.

Holding the gun in my left hand, I checked the man out with my right, looking for a pulse. I found one in his neck, beating strong. His head was bleeding heavily because that's what scalp wounds do, but he was alive.

I moved quickly to the other guy, reached into his jacket, and disarmed him as well. Now if they woke up, they'd be no threat to me.

I moved to the door and unlocked it before Sam could break it down.

"What's going on?" she demanded, looking around. "From across the hall it sounded like a riot."

"Some unexpected guests dropped in," I said, waving an arm at the two men.

"Are you all right?"

"Yes."

I had a gun in each hand and tucked one into my belt.

"What did they want?"

"They wanted the location of a girl who I worked for a couple of weeks ago."

"Do you have it?"

"I have her home address, but I don't think that's what they wanted."

The man with the scalp wound moaned, but he didn't wake up. The other was still lying still, and it occurred to me that I hadn't checked him out, only disarmed him.

"Shut the door," I told her, and went to do it now.

I reached for his neck, felt around for a pulse, then leaned over and pressed my head against his chest. I straightened his head out, but it fell over to the side again real quick.

"Fuck!"

I don't curse often—especially for an ex-cop—but I did it this time with feeling.

"Nick?"

I looked at her and said, "I'm in up to my neck, Sam. This one's got a *broken* neck."

"Is he dead?"

"About as dead as my license."

13

"What are we going to do?" Sam asked.

I looked at her and said, "I appreciate the 'we,' Sam, but you better get back to your own apartment. This is my problem."

"Never mind chasing me away, Nick," she said. "Make use of my fertile writer's mind. Let's figure this out. Do you call the police?"

"There's a lieutenant and some other police department officials, not to mention a politician, who would just love that."

"Why? Two men broke into your apartment, and you defended yourself. What can they make out of that?"

"Whatever they want. I'd rather not give them the chance to interpret this their way rather than mine."

"They'd really take your license away?"

"All they can do is call for a review, but with their recommendation I could very well lose it."

"Well, so what? Can't you go on doing what you do without one?"

"Sure, and so can a doctor, as long as he doesn't get caught either."

"What alternative do you have?"

Smooth-Face chose that particular time to stir, and I looked over at him.

"Maybe just one."

I went over to him and gave him a kick in the side. He moaned and rolled over.

"Come on, you're not hurt that bad."

He pushed himself to a seated position and put his hand to his head.

"I'm bleeding, man."

"You're doing a whole lot better than your partner."

"What?" He looked around and spotted the other man lying on his back. "What happened to him?"

"He got his neck broken."

"You killed him?"

"You could look at it that way."

"Why you—"

He started to get up, but an apparent wave of dizziness had as much to do with arresting the movement as the gun in my hand did.

"You've already made a few mistakes, friend, don't make another. Besides, what was he, your brother or something?"

"No, he wasn't nothing to me," he said, holding his head. "Listen, you ain't calling the cops, are you?"

"What's the matter, pal?" I asked. "Don't you have a license for this?"

"Listen," he said, wiping some blood away with the back of his hand. "You ain't hurt, right? Just let me go before you call the cops. Whataya say?"

"I say you're right."

"What?" he said.

"What?" Sam said.

"Sure, why not?" I said to Sam. "I'm not hurt, so why make him suffer?"

"Yeah, right," the bloody man said.

"Sam, get the man a towel, will you?"

"Sure," she said, giving me a strange look.

She went to the bathroom to get one and I said to Smooth-Face, "All right, come on, get up."

"Sure, pal, sure."

He staggered to his feet and was getting his sea legs under him when Sam came back with a towel. She had dampened it and tossed it to him. He used it to clean some of the blood from his face and then wadded it up and held it to his forehead.

"Can I go?"

"Will you tell me why you were looking for the girl?"

"Hey, man, that puts me in an awkward position, you know? All right, look, we were hired to come here and ask you where the girl is. If you gave us a hard time, we were supposed to put a hurtin' on you. I admit that. If you're gonna let me walk out that door, I can't tell you who hired me. I wouldn't last two hours."

"What if I told you I'll kill you right here and now if you don't tell me?" I said. I raised the gun, pointed it at him, and cocked the hammer back. I felt Sam jump as the hammer clicked.

"Go ahead, man. I'm dead either way."

I had a few choices, then. I could try to beat it out of him, which I was not inclined to do; I could let him walk out; or I could kill him, and further complicate my life.

"Nick, give him to the police," Sam said.

"Hey, no—lady, don't tell him that."

She frowned and said, "I don't understand. You'd let him kill you, but you don't want him to call the police?"

"Lady. I got a record, and if you call the cops, I'll end up back inside for sure. I'd rather be dead than go back inside." He looked at me and said,

"You understand that, don't you?"

"Sure," I said, lowering the gun, "Go on, get lost, but give your boss a message."

"He ain't my boss, we were just doing a job for him, but sure, I'll give him a message."

"Tell him I saw the girl that once, and haven't seen her since. That's on the level."

"I'll tell him," he said, staggering toward the door. "Hey, thanks, man. No hard feelings, huh?"

"Sure, no hard feelings."

As he reached for the doorknob, I said, "Hey, didn't you forget something?"

He frowned at me for a moment, then said, "Oh, yeah, sorry," and tossed down the towel.

"That's not what I meant. Him," I said, pointing at the dead man. "You forgot him."

"But...he's dead."

"And he's all yours."

He stared at me with his mouth open and then got it. "Hey, now wait—"

"Look, pal, either you take him with you or I'll turn you both over to the cops. He doesn't have to worry about going back inside the joint."

"What am I gonna do with him?"

"I don't give a shit what you do with him, I just want the two of you out of here."

He stood there for a few moments, undecided, and I prodded him a little.

"Come on, pal. Shit or get off the pot. Make a move. I can still call the cops."

Luckily, he wasn't that bright, or he might have figured out that I didn't want to call the police any more than he wanted me to.

"Is there a back way out?" he asked.

"I'll show you."

"All right..."

He picked up his dead partner fireman-carry style and started for the door. I opened it, and he preceded me out into the hall.

"Do me a favor," I said to Sam. "Find out if Mrs. Hanratty is home."

"Okay."

Mrs. Hanratty was an elderly lady who lived directly beneath me, and she was the only one who could throw a monkey wrench into the works. If she was home and had heard the commotion...

I stepped quickly into the hall and said to the man with the burden, "This way..."

***

When I got back to my apartment, Sam was inside, waiting.

"How did it go?" she asked.

"Fine. He'll probably drop him in a dumpster somewhere, but I told him to make sure it was at least a mile from here."

"What makes you think he won't drop him on the next block?"

"I told him I could still turn him over to the cops if the body turned up too close."

"Do you know who he is?"

I smiled and took something out of my pocket.

"I'm afraid Mr. Walter Harris is going to have to report his driver's license missing." I'd had him give me his license just before I let him walk away and dump his friend into the car they'd come in. I even played lookout for him to make sure he could do so unseen. He left without saying thank you.

"What about Mrs. Hanratty?"

"I rang her bell and knocked on her door. She's not home."

"Well, that works out fine, then."

I sat down on my sofa, took out both of the guns that had recently come into my possession, and put them into the drawer of the end table along with my slapper.

"Jesus..." I said, dry-washing my face with both hands. Sam came over and sat next to me, putting her arm around my shoulders.

"Jesus, I was scared..." I said.

"You did all right for somebody who was scared."

I started to shake then, and she tightened her arm around me.

"Nick, are you all right?"

"Sure," I said, "sure, Sam, this just happens whenever I kill somebody."

"Oh, my God," she said, taking my hand with her other hand. "I thought..."

"You thought I did that sort of thing all the time, like in books and movies?"

"Nick, I'm sorry..."

"That's all right, Sam," I said, trying to control the shaking, "that's all right. I'm just glad you're here."

She held me tightly, then, and actually began to rock me at one point, holding me until the shakes subsided.

Hell, that's what friends are for, right?

14

On the way to my father's house the next day I stopped at an Italian bakery on Eighteenth Avenue and bought a dozen pastries. Sam had wanted to come along, but I talked her out of it. She insisted I take her car, however, saying she'd be writing most of the day and wouldn't need it.

I let myself in just as Vinnie was coming out of the kitchen. I could smell fresh coffee in the air.

"Just in time," I said, holding up the box of pastries.

"Is that from..."

I nodded and said, "Malzone's."

"All right."

We went into the kitchen together, and he took down three coffee cups while I untied the box.

"Any news?"

"Yup. Last night after you left CBS had a report that the hijackers were Iranians. They routed the plane to Beirut, where they landed to refuel and make their demands."

"Which are?"

He shrugged. "I guess we'll find out sometime today."

"I hope so. Where's Pop?"

"Getting dressed."

"How is he?"

"I finally got him into bed at three, but he insisted on taking the black-and-white portable in his bedroom with him. He fell asleep about three-thirty."

"And he's up now?"

It was almost nine.

"He was up at six-thirty watching what's her name—"

"Joan Lunden?"

"Whatever."

He poured out the coffee, and I had the box open by the time Pop came into the room. I was shocked at how old he looked.

"Pop, pastries," I said.

"I don't want any," he said. He picked up a cup of coffee from the table and said, "I'll be in my room."

"Pop..." I started, but he just walked out as if he hadn't heard me—or hadn't wanted to.

Vinnie was sitting down with a cup of coffee and took a napoleon out of the pastry box.

I sat opposite him and chose a cream puff.

"Vinnie..."

"Yeah?"

"When I went into the police academy, did Pop talk to you?"

"About what?"

"About how he felt about it?"

He thought a moment and then said, "He mentioned something at the time."

"What?"

"Just that he thought you were making a mistake."

"Nothing more...demonstrative?"

"Nick," he said, putting down his pastry, "you're thinking about yesterday, and the things that were said. Pop was upset—"

"What about today? Right now? He didn't even look at me."

"He's upset..." Vinnie said again.

"That excuse can't cover everything, Vinnie."

"Talk to Pop about it, Nick, but after Maria is safe."

"Sure," I said, "sure..."

"What you should do is keep busy," Vinnie said. "I can stay here with Pop, Nick, you've got a living to make."

"Don't you?"

"Our situations are a little different. The church recognizes that I have a personal commitment here, but knows I'm also doing the Lord's work."

I hated it when he talked like that. It made me uncomfortable, and he knew it.

"Besides, if you stay here, all three of us are going to start getting on each other's nerves."

"You mean that I'll start to get on your nerves and Pop's nerves."

"Nick...I don't want to argue..."

"All right, neither do I. Maybe you're right, maybe I should keep busy."

"Do you have any...business at the moment, any cases?"

I almost said no right away, but then I thought about Jodi Hayworth and said, "Maybe I do."

"You don't know?"

"It's kind of up in the air. I haven't exactly been paid..."

"If you haven't been paid, why should you continue on with the case?"

I wondered what my brother the father would have said if I'd told him that killing a man the night before gave me a sort of vested interest?

15

Part of a priest's job was giving out advice, and although I'd gotten very little from that quarter in the past, this time it seemed to make sense.

After another cup of coffee and a second cream puff I told Vinnie I'd keep in touch and left.

In the car, driving to Bay Ridge, I went over that day and night with Jodi in my head. She had never given me her address, but at one point she had talked about living in Bay Ridge all her life, and having gone to Fort Hamilton High School.

I decided to start looking for her there.

Fort Hamilton High is on Shore Parkway in Bay Ridge, and counts among its most famous alumni New York Knick star forward Bernard King.

Jodi hadn't told me when she graduated, but my guess was that it was at least two or three years ago. To get her address, all I had to do was tell the girl who was working in the office that I was throwing an alumni party for those two classes and needed some addresses to complete the guest list. I gave her a half a dozen names, five of which I made up, the sixth of which was Jodi's. To my surprise she came back with two addresses, one for Jodi and one for the nonexistent—or so I thought when I pulled the name out of a hat—Charles Durning. I'd picked the name because I particularly liked Charles Durning the actor—I'd seen him in a Burt Reynolds movie recently—and as it turned out, there was a student by that name among the '84 graduating class.

Once outside the school I discarded the Durning address and looked at Jodi's. It was on Colonial Drive between East Seventy-sixth and Seventy-seventh Streets, about eight blocks away.

The house was a large, wood-frame, three-story, single-family house of the type that would command at least three hundred and fifty grand if it went on the market today.

I parked and went to the front door to ring the bell. My approach was to be very simple. I was looking for Jodi. Period. A girl who looked the way she did had to have a lot of men looking for her.

The door was opened by a woman who was so obviously Jodi's mother it was uncanny, even though she didn't yet look forty. She had the same blonde hair and the same lithe figure, although Jodi's mother was a little bustier than Jodi was. If the mother was any indication of what the daughter would look like later, a man could do worse than hook up with Jodi for the next twenty years or so.

"Yes?" she said.

"Mrs. Hayworth?"

"I'm Mrs. Ponzoni," the woman said, confusing me, but she cleared it up quick enough. "My first husband's name was Hayworth, though."

"Of course, I'm sorry," I said. "My name is Delvecchio and I'm looking for Jodi."

"Jodi?" she said quickly. "Have you seen her? Is she all right?"

"I'm sorry—"

"You see, we recently came back from abroad and we haven't seen Jodi yet."

I was about to explain that I had seen her about two weeks before when a man came up behind the woman. He was tall, dark-haired, broad-shouldered, and I'd seen him before. In fact, when Jodi's mother had introduced herself as Mrs. Ponzoni, I should have guessed.

Jodi's stepfather was "Tony Macaroni," a man who had once worked for Nicky Barracuda, many years ago. They called him "Macaroni" because his name, "Ponzoni," sounded like "Ronzoni," but of course they never called him that to his face.

When I knew him, I was about ten years old, and he was an enforcer on the docks. He probably would have known my father on sight, but he looked right at me without any sign of recognition.

The real test would be when he heard my name, which I had no intention of saying for a second time.

"Darling, this is Mr.—"

"My name is Nick, Mr. Ponzoni, and I'm looking for Jodi."

"She's not here."

"Yes, your wife told me that."

"Is she in trouble again?" he asked. The look on his face made it plain that he wasn't happy with his stepdaughter.

"She may well be, Mr. Ponzoni. May I come in for a moment?"

"I don't see why—"

"Tony," Mrs. Ponzoni said, and Tony Macaroni took a step back.

"Please, come in," she said to me, and also backed away.

I entered, and they led me to the living room. There were small statues everywhere: on the piano, on the mantel of the fireplace, on every end table and coffee table in the room.

"What's your connection with my stepdaughter, Mr.—"

"She hired me," I said, quickly.

"To do what?"

"I'm a private detective, Mr. Ponzoni, and what she hired me for is privileged, I'm afraid."

"I see," he said.

He was well over six feet and had stayed in condition over the years.

There was a hint of a belly, and some gray hairs in the black, but he looked damned good for a guy who had to be almost fifty. The fact that he'd kept his looks had been why I'd been able to recognize him—that and the livid red scar over his left eye. He'd gotten that on the docks, during a strike.

He drew himself up to his full height now, as if it would intimidate me.

"Why are you looking for her, then?"

Here was the first time I really lied—and then again, it wasn't really a lie.

"Well, Mr. Ponzoni, I did the job your daughter hired me for—and believe me, it was nothing very serious, but she did leave without remembering to pay me."

"And you've been looking for her ever since?"

"Not exactly. Today I just seem to be trying to settle some of my old accounts."

"I see. How much did my stepdaughter owe you?"

"One day's work," I said. "Two hundred."

He nodded and was about to say something when his wife tugged on his arm and said, "Pay him, Tony."

"Diane—"

"Would you excuse us for a moment, please?" Mrs. Ponzoni asked, and I nodded cooperatively.

They left the room and had a rather heated, sotto voce discussion outside the door, and then returned with Ponzoni looking none too happy. I had the feeling that the former strong-arm man and enforcer was now a pussy-whipped husband.

As it turned out later, I couldn't have been more wrong. "Mr.—what did you say your name was?"

"Nick," I said, intending to leave it at that, but before he could ask, I added "Delvecchio," watching his eyes very carefully.

There wasn't even the faintest glimmer of recognition—which meant he either didn't remember or he was very, very good.

"Mr. Delvecchio, my wife would like me to hire you to find her daughter."

"Well, I'm already looking, Mr. Ponzoni."

"Yes, but once I pay you what she owes you, you won't have any need to look for her anymore."

That wasn't exactly right. After what had happened in my apartment last night, it had occurred to me that Jodi Hayworth might be in deep trouble way over her head. Although I had no obligation to do so, I found myself wanting to find her and help her.

I didn't tell her stepfather that, though.

"You have a point."

"I will pay you the two hundred she owes you, and a thousand-dollar retainer to keep looking for her."

"That sounds fair."

"There is something else, though."

"What's that?"

"There is also a piece of artwork missing from the house, a statue about so high and shaped like a doughnut."

"A doughnut."

"I would like you to find that, as well. It may or may not be with Jodi, but perhaps if you find her, she can tell you where it is."

"Is it valuable?"

He surprised me by saying, "Yes, it is quite valuable."

"Was the house broken into while you were gone?"

"No indication of that. It's more likely that Jodi has the piece with her."

"Do you think she might have hocked it?"

Diane Ponzoni caught her breath, but her husband seemed to have already considered the possibility.

"Yes, it's possible."

"Have you checked with any pawnshops?"

"We only returned a few days ago," he said as if that explained why he had taken no action yet—if indeed he had not. Tony Macaroni had never really been the kind of man to let grass grow under his feet.

"Will you accept my offer?"

"Sure," I said without hesitation. Let him think I was in it for the money.

"Fine."

I expected him to go somewhere and get a checkbook, but he surprised me by putting a hand in his pocket and coming out with a wad of cash. He peeled off twelve one-hundred-dollar bills and handed them to me.

"I hope those are not too large for you."

"This is the kind of burden I can usually handle pretty well," I said, folding the bills and putting them in my own pocket.

"I will expect you to report to me periodically."

"Of course."

"Thank you for...for saying yes," Diane Ponzoni said.

"I'll find her, Mrs. Ponzoni. Don't worry."

"Thank you."

"I could use some names and addresses, you know, some of her friends?"

"I'll make a list," she said, and went to another room to do so, probably from a phone book of Jodi's.

"Now that we're alone," Ponzoni said, immediately, "I'm really not that concerned about my stepdaughter, Delvecchio. I am, on the other hand, concerned about that piece of art."

"I see."

"Don't judge me," he said without rancor. "That little tramp and I just don't get along, and nothing would suit me better than to have her move out."

"I understand a lot of parents feel that way about their own kids," I said.

"You're right about that. I don't have any of my own, and I don't want any."

"I don't have, either..." I said, and let it trail off as Mrs. Ponzoni came back into the room.

"I've written down the names of her closest friends, and their addresses."

She handed me a sheet of yellow lined paper with five names on it, and I folded it up and tucked it into my shirt pocket.

"I'll get back to you as soon as I have something to report, Mr. Ponzoni."

"Fine, fine," he said, giving me a look that said that we men understood each other. I almost expected him to wink at me over her head.

Outside I got into my car and took out the twelve hundred dollars. Nicky, you dog, you've taken money under false pretenses.

What would Father Vinnie say?

16

It was still early, and I had enough time to check out the names on the list. They were in Bay Ridge except for one, who lived in Manhattan, and they were all female. The four that I managed to squeeze into that one day were all flirtatious young things, and under ordinary circumstances I might have been inclined to make a play. Things were not normal, however, as the female who was occupying most of my mind was my sister, Maria.

It was after dinnertime when I finished with Jodi's four friends, and they had not been able to tell me anything helpful. None of them had seen her in a couple of weeks, and in fact, I'd seen her more recently than they had.

I called my brother from a pay phone to see if he and Pop had eaten, and when he said no, I said I'd bring something home. He said fine, as long as it wasn't Burger King or McDonald's. My brother was not the fast-food enthusiast I was. He did, however, like Chinese, and that was what I stopped and picked up.

When I walked in with the telltale gold-and-red dragon bag, Vinnie looked skyward and said, "My prayers have been answered," with uncharacteristic humor. It was then I realized that he was feeling the pressure as much as Pop or me. We were just all reacting in our own ways.

I carried the bags into the kitchen and deposited them on the table.

"Any news?"

"No, no news."

"Will Pop eat?"

"I'll take it to him."

"Vinnie, do you think we're babying him?"

"What do you mean?"

"I mean all he does is sit in front of the TV We bring him his meals, we put him to bed—all right, you put him to bed, but you see what I mean."

"Nick, Maria's his daughter."

"So, she's our sister, we're functioning, we're coping."

"He's an old man."

"You're making excuses for him."

"Come on. Pop's been through crises before, on the docks, at home—"

"Nothing like this."

"Vinnie—"

"I'll take him some food," Vinnie said, scraping a little from each carton onto a plate—some fried rice, some beef with broccoli, some lemon chicken. He started for the door, then turned.

"What?" I said.

"You're still sore at him for what he said the other day, aren't you?"

I didn't answer, and he left and took Pop the food.

I would have preferred to see Pop on his feet and in the kitchen eating with us rather than sitting on his duff feeling sorry for himself. He always called Maria his baby, and I thought I knew why now. His three boys had disappointed him. Joey went and got killed, Vinnie went and became a priest—which had pleased my mother, anyway, but my father had never been that religious—and me, I became a cop and *then* got kicked off.

Maria married a Jew instead of an Italian. Well, that was all right, she was his baby.

Her marriage was in trouble only a year after she'd said "I do." Well, hey, that was okay, because she was his baby.

Now she'd gone and gotten herself hijacked, and that wasn't her fault, but who was Pop feeling sorry for? Her? Or himself, because they had "his baby"?

Now, all this sounds like I've got something against my sister, and I don't. I love her, but of all the men in her life I was the only one who knew that she wasn't a baby anymore.

I had always thought that I got along with my father, but admittedly I didn't see him that much. Now, since this hijacking thing had thrown us together, we were getting on each other's nerves, and it hadn't taken long. So I knew I had been kidding myself. I stayed away from him because I knew we'd rub each other the wrong way. He called me all the time, but that was just his way of being a father. He never really wanted me to come out and see him.

By all rights this situation should have been affecting one Delvecchio, and the rest of us should have been feeling for her. Well, when Maria was back, there were still going to be things that the men in her life had to deal with.

And speaking of the men in her life...

"What about Numbnuts?" I asked as Vinnie came back into the room.

"Oh, I forgot to tell you. He called."

"He did? When?"

"This morning. He said he saw it on the late news last night when he got home."

"When he got home? How late does a stockbroker get home from Wall Street?"

"I don't know."

"I'll tell you how late. It depends on where else he goes. What was going on between him and Maria, Vinnie?"

Vinnie got two Buds from the refrigerator and then sat down to join me for dinner.

"I don't know," he said, handing me a bottle. "She didn't talk to me like she did to you."

"Well, she didn't talk to me about this. What about Pop?"

Vinnie made a face.

"Don't bother him with that now, Nick."

We were starting to rub each other the wrong way, too. Tragedy has a way of bringing families together...or tearing them apart.

"Is he coming here?"

"I told him there was no need."

"Well, maybe there is."

"Like what?"

"Like maybe I'd like to find out what made Maria leave."

"Nick, don't make one of your sordid divorce cases out of our sister."

"Fat lot you know, pal. I don't handle divorce cases."

"What goes on between a husband and wife is their business."

"Bullshit," I said, and stood up.

"Where you going?"

"A call."

"To who?"

"It's about a case I'm working on."

"What kind?"

"I'm trying to find a girl before someone else does."

"Is she in danger?"

"I think so."

"Can you help her?"

"A lot more than I can help Maria."

I walked to the kitchen phone and dialed the number of the Missing Persons Division of the N.Y.P.D.

"Missing Persons, Detective Siegel."

"Is Detective Reese working tonight, or Detective Hernandez?"

"Reese is here."

"Can I talk to him, please?"

Reese and I had come on the job together, and he had made detective when I was leaving. He was a go-getter—either that or he had a hell of a rabbi. Since I'd gotten my license, he'd done me a favor or two, and he'd introduced me to Hernandez. One of them was usually on duty, and that was helpful.

"Reese."

"It's Nick, John."

"Mr. Private Eye. What can I do for you?"

If there had been a boss around he would have called me "Mr. Nicholas."

"Just do me a favor and check your sheets for a blonde, early twenties—very early twenties—long blonde hair, very taut little body—"

"Taut?"

"Yeah, t-a-u-t, taut."

"Go on."

"About five-five, I guess, one ten or so, no distinguishing marks that I can remember."

"You fucked her and you can't remember?"

"I didn't say I—" I started to answer, and then remembered my brother in the room.

"You said no distinguishing marks that you could remember, you didn't say no marks that you could see. That means you saw it all, and that means you fucked her, and if you can't remember, it means you were drunk."

"Boy," I said, "you should be a detective. Do a thorough check, will you, and call me at this number?" I read off my father's number for him.

"I'll get back to you, Nick."

"Thanks, Reese."

I hung up and went back to the table.

"Do you always describe women like...that?"

"Like what?"

"Like...that," he said, pointing to the phone.

I looked at the phone, and then at him.

"I was talking to a cop, Vinnie, not a priest. I couldn't just say that she was pleasant-looking."

"Was she?"

"Yes, but—"

"Then why couldn't you say that?"

"Because I was talking to a cop."

"I don't understand."

"You never could." Before he could reply I asked, "Did you call CBS yesterday?"

"Yup, CBS, ABC, NBC, and CNN. None of them were very helpful. They suggested I watch their very comprehensive reports."

"Well, Pop's taking care of that, isn't he?"

"Don't start."

"Don't start," I repeated. I looked down at the food on my plate and lost my appetite for it. I wanted Reese to call me back so I could go out and get a quarter-pounder and some fries, maybe even some nuggets. I liked them with the barbecue sauce.

The phone rang.

"Nick?"

"Yeah."

"Nothing on your dolly."

"No blondes at all?"

"Three women, all over forty. Two in the morgue, one in Kings County Hospital."

"Okay."

"Want me to make up a 'Looking For' on her?"

That meant that he'd file her description and if someone matching it did show up, he'd call me.

"Yeah, I'd appreciate it, John. Thanks for trying."

"Sure."

I hung up and turned to look at Vinnie.

"Does all of that mean she's not dead?"

"No," I said, "it means that if she is dead, she's still lying someplace."

He put down the sparerib he had been about to gnaw on.

"Vinnie, I've got to go."

"Where?"

"I've got to find this girl before she does end up dead."

"Are you going to finish eating?"

"No. Save it for Pop's dinner."

"Sure."

"Vinnie..."

"What?"

I hesitated, then said, "Nothing. Forget it. Take care of Pop. I'll call later."
As I started for the door, he called out, "Nick."
"What?"
"Are you going to talk to Peter?"
"Yes," I said, before I even realized that was the answer.
"Why?"
"Because whatever that sonofabitch did to Maria is what put her on that plane."
"Nick..."
"Relax, Father, I'm just going to talk to him."
"What's that in your back pocket?"
I looked down behind me and saw the handle of my slapper protruding just a bit.
"It's nothing—"
"I know it's not a gun because I know what a gun looks like, but I know it's not nothing, either."
"Give me a break."
"Are you wearing a gun?"
"No. Can I go now, Father?"
"Sure, go ahead. And do me a favor."
"What?"
"Don't get killed. As it is, Maria and I don't get along, but if she comes back and finds out that I let her favorite brother get killed, she'd never speak to me again."
He picked up the rib and began gnawing at it.
For want of something better to do, I left.

17

My sister and her husband had a two-family house in a different section of Bay Ridge than the one Jodi Hayworth lived in. Numbnuts had said that a two-family house was a "sound investment," so they bought one on Ninety-second Street between Third and Fourth Avenues. All I had to do was jump on Eighty-sixth Street, drive to Fourth and make a left, then a right on Ninety-second.

After I rang the bell, I started reviewing in my mind what I was going to say to my brother-in-law. I came up with three or four approaches—not the least desirable of which was to grab him by the throat—but I soon realized that he wasn't going to be answering the door.

He wasn't home.

My sister was in some foreign country under the guns of some fucking terrorists, and her husband wasn't home.

Grabbing him by the throat when I *did* find him was looking better and better all the time.

I stopped off on the way home and got a quarter-pounder, some fries, and nine McNuggets. I had the bag in one hand and my keys in the other when I entered my apartment. I didn't know which one to drop in order to go for my slapper, but when I saw who it was on my couch, I didn't have to.

"How did you get in?"

"Through a window," Jodi Hayworth said. "This place is a cracker box."

"Thanks. You hungry?"

"Actually, yes. Being knocked around makes me hungry."

She stood up then, and I got a better look at her face. She still had marvelous cat's eyes, but the skin around them was bruised, as was her bottom lip. Luckily, whoever had worked on her had not broken her wonderful nose.

"Anything broken?"

"Not a chance."

"Can you eat?"

"Of course."

"Well, come into the kitchen, then."

I led the way into the kitchen and turned on the light. I dropped the bag of food onto the table and went to the refrigerator for something to drink—cream soda, as it turned out. Dr. Brown's. By the time I set two bottles on the table, she was already chewing on the quarter-pounder.

"Hope you don't mind."

"That's okay," I said. "I like the nuggets. Can we split the fries?"

"Sure."

We dumped them into the other half of her Styrofoam burger box and covered them with ketchup.

"All right, start talking."

"About what?"

"I don't care what," I said, "as long as it has to do with the hole thing."

So she started talking.

18

The statue had been mailed home by her mother and father from Mexico, where they were "vacationing."

They did this a lot, she said, sent things on home ahead, usually statues of some kind.

Jodi knew that the statues were worth money, and when she found herself in need of money, she decided to hock one.

"What did you need the money for, Jodi?"

"Is that important?"

"No, it's not important," I said, "but I'm the curious type, and I'd like to know. What did you need the money for?"

"I had a chance to make a good buy."

"Are we talking bikinis here, or drugs?"

"Just some coke."

"Uh-huh."

"You gonna lecture me?"

"Not me, I'm not your father. Just continue with your story."

"Well, I knew I was in trouble because this man came to the house a couple of days after I hocked the thing."

"What man?"

"Just a man who said he worked for my stepfather."

"Did he? I mean, did you know him?"

"I recognized him, yeah."

"So what did you tell him?"

"I started to lie to him and he...he grabbed me. He said he wanted that piece."

"Did he scare you?"

"Fucking-a he scared me."

"You told him the truth."

"Yeah."

"And what did he say? Come on, Jodi, don't make me drag this story out of you. I want to help."

"He said that I better get it back before my stepfather came home or we were both in a lot of trouble."

"Why both?"

"He was supposed to pick it up from me earlier, and that would have been before I hocked it."

"So his ass was in a sling with Ponzoni."

"Right. You say his name like you know him," she said, catching an inflection in my voice.

"I knew him once, yeah, a long time ago."

"What's he into—besides these statues, I mean? Is he Mafia?"

"Tell me your story, Jodi."

"Well, since I needed to get it back in a hurry, I decided to hire a detective. That's when I called you."

"Did your father's man—what's his name, anyway?"

"DiVolo. Carmine DiVolo."

I didn't know him.

"Did he agree with you about hiring a detective?"

"No, but fuck him. You got any coffee?"

"I can make some."

"You want that last french fry?"

"No, go ahead."

I got up and put the coffee maker on, then sat back down. "Okay, so you hired me, and I got the address of the guy who bought the piece from the hockshop. We came back here, you popped into my bed, and then left—without paying me, I might add."

"I'm really sorry about that, Nick," she said. "Not about sleeping with you—that was fine. I mean running out on you like that, but I was looking to minimize my complications."

"Minimize your complications."

"Right."

I shook my head and said, "All right, go on."

"Okay," she said, wiping her hand across her mouth, then grabbing a napkin to clean both. "You got me the address, which was in Westchester. I drove up there, but I was too late."

"What do you mean, too late?"

"When I got there, the place looked like it was locked up tight. I broke in and found him."

"Found who?"

"The man who lived there. He was dead."

"How?"

"He'd been shot."

"And the piece, the doughnut?"

"It wasn't anywhere in the house. I looked."

"And left your fingerprints all over the place."

"I suppose."

"Well, where have you been since then? Your mother and stepfather say they haven't seen you since they got back."

"You talked to them?"

"Yes. Your stepfather doesn't seem to like you all that much."

"That's because I wouldn't put out for him."

"He made a pass at you?"

"A pass? He was always touching me and grabbing me. Once he walked in on me while I was in the tub, said that my mother wanted us to be a close-knit family—real close. If she hadn't come home, I think he would have raped me."

"Let's go on with the story."

"Sure. When I left there after searching the house DiVolo was waiting and asked me where the piece was. I told him I didn't know, but he didn't believe me. He dragged me out of the house and into a car with two other gorillas and they took me to a house in Greenpoint."

Greenpoint was a section of Brooklyn that, given a good push, would fall right over into Queens. My impression of Greenpoint has always been that it is a section of warehouses, although I know there are some stores and houses there. There's also a bar called Chambers' Pub where I've been known to have an occasional drink. The owner, Bill Chambers, has lived in Greenpoint all his life, and if I needed to know anything about the area, I'd call him.

"You've been there ever since?"

"Until night before last. DiVolo said they were going to keep me in ice until they found the piece."

"How did you get away?"

"DiVolo decided he wasn't as afraid of my stepfather as he thought and that it was time to fuck me. I had other ideas, so then he decided it was time to knock me around."

"And you had other ideas."

"I hit him on the head with a lamp and got the hell out of there."

"That's why they showed up here yesterday."

"Who?"

"Two men looking for you."

"Two gorillas?"

"That's an apt description, yeah."

"And what happened?"

"I convinced them that I didn't know where you were, and they left."

She looked dubious.

"Just like that?"

"Well, no, not just like that, but the end result is the same."

"So when they lost me, they came after you."

"And I guess they'll keep coming until they find that piece of art."

"I guess so. I'm sorry I got you into this, Nick."

"Well, that's neither here nor there. We're in it, and that's that."

"You mean you're going to help me?"

"Once we agree on just what kind of help it is you need, yeah, I don't see why not."

"Well, I need to get that piece back, that's for sure."

"And do what with it?"

A crafty look came into her eyes then.

"Well, if so many people want it, maybe I can sell it to the highest bidder."

"Like your stepfather?"

"Why not? He owes me for all the times he played grab-ass with me."

"Jodi, what is this piece of art really?"

"I don't know. It's just a round thing—"

"No, no," I said, shaking my head. "It's more than a piece of art. Your stepfather told me that he wasn't worried about you, but he would like to get that piece of art back. Your friend DiVolo wanted it back enough to snatch you, and those two goons last night wanted it enough to knock me around."

"Then what is it?"

"That's what I'm asking you."

"Jesus, all I know about it is that it's this ugly piece of artwork that Diane and Poppa Ponzoni sent back from Mexico just this last trip."

"Mexico," I said. "Was the thing hollow? Could there have been something in it?"

"Like what?"

"I don't know. Like drugs, maybe."

"You mean, I hocked the goddamned thing to buy some coke and maybe it was filled with drugs? Ain't that a kick in the head?"

"Look, Jodi, we've got to get this thing back, that's number one."

"And sell it?"

"I don't know. We'll decide what we're going to do with it when we get it back and find out what it really is."

"Are you saying you're in for a piece of whatever this thing turns out to be?"

She had turned suspicious on me.

"I'm in to keep you—and me—alive long enough to find it. I don't want any part of it once it's found."

That seemed to satisfy her.

"Okay. So, if that's number one, what's number two?"

"Well," I said, "number two may turn out to be number one."

"Which is?"

"We've got to find out who the Westchester police are looking for for this murder of—what's his name?"

"Uh, Berry, James Berry."

"Right, Berry. Anybody see you go in or come out of his house?"

"Not that I know of, except that DiVolo and his apes grabbed me coming out."

"Anybody see that?"

"No. I yelled enough that if somebody saw it, they would have done something."

"Yeah, well, don't count on that."

"Well, if nobody saw me go in, then I'm in the clear, ain't I?"

"Not if you left your fingerprints all over the damn house."

"My prints—"

Of course, even if she had left her prints, they wouldn't do the cops any good unless they were on file somewhere. "Jodi, tell me you've never been arrested."

"I, uh, can't."

"Oh, fine. You were arrested for what? Wait, let me guess, possession of drugs?"

"Just a little bit," she said. "Poppa Ponzoni got me out."

"But you were fingerprinted?"

"Yes...but maybe he got them back. He's got connections, you know."

"You don't know for sure if he got them or not, though, so your prints might very well be on record."

"I suppose."

"Which means that the prints you left in this James Berry's house might be identified."

"Jesus," she said, "you mean the cops might be looking for me right now? For murder?"

"It's possible."

"Well, that's great. Carmine DiVolo's looking for me, my loving stepdaddy is looking for me, the cops are looking for me—"

"Why didn't you go back home after you got away from DiVolo?"

"Because I wasn't all that sure that he wasn't working for Ponzoni, holding me because my stepdaddy told him to."

"What made you think that?"

"I don't know," she said, and for the first time since I met her some of the toughness went out of her. With her black eyes and bruised lip she looked like a sad little girl. "I didn't trust him. I don't know if I can trust anybody."

"Well, you better decide, because if I'm going to help you, you'll have to trust me."

She stared at me, lost control of her lower lip for a moment, then firmed up her jaw and said, "Is that damn coffee ready?"

"Yeah," I said, "the coffee's ready."

I tried to give her the bed, but she insisted that the couch would be fine. I found out later why she wanted me to have the bed.

When she sat on the bed, I rolled over.

"Jodi—"

"I don't want to sleep alone, Nick. In fact," she said, sliding under the sheet with me, "I don't want to sleep at all."

She was naked, and her skin was hot. I was wearing pajama bottoms but no top. The air-conditioning was on and her nipples were hard, scraping my chest.

"Do you?"

I wrapped my arms around her and said, "Hell, no..."

19

We attacked the refrigerator the next morning, and Jodi whipped up some potatoes and eggs, adding some onions that hadn't yet started walking around by themselves. Over breakfast we talked, and I got some more out of her.

"If DiVolo's not with Ponzoni, who's he working for, himself?"

"He's not smart enough."

"What kind of business is your stepfather in?"

"Import and export, or so he says. That's why they make all the trips."

"Did you ever hear him talk to your mother about a competitor?"

She thought a moment.

"Now that you mention it, he used to talk to my mother about a man named Janetti. He often complained that Janetti—I think his first name is Angelo—was trying to put him out of business, or put pressure on him."

That was a surprise to me. I'd been hoping that she was going to say the name Barracondi, or some other name that I'd recognize. Angelo Janetti was a new one on me. And then again, maybe Janetti really was a rival of Ponzoni's in the import-export business, and nothing more.

"Okay, now tell me something else. Has anyone new entered your life recently?"

"New? You mean men?"

"Yes, I mean men."

"Besides you?"

"Jodi..."

"Okay. I started seeing this young guy who lives in Manhattan."

"Has he ever been out to your house?"

"Several times. Why are you interested in who I'm seeing?"

"Well, Berry didn't have the doughnut, and you don't have it. *Somebody* has to."

"You think Terry's got it?"

"Terry?"

"Terry Jacks, that's the guy's name."

"Did Terry ever express any interest in your stepfather's collection?"

She thought a moment and said, "He may have picked up a piece or two to look at. Nick, the hole thing is missing from that house in Westchester now. Whoever killed James Berry must have it."

"You could be right."

"That would be DiVolo, wouldn't it? I mean, why else would he have been there if he hadn't killed him?"

"If he killed him, then he'd have the, uh, thing. Why would he need to grab you?"

"I don't know. What was he doing there, then?"

"Who knows? Maybe he shadowed you. He was probably looking for your doughnut piece of art, and I for one would like to know why."

"So would I."

"DiVolo was outside when you came out?"

"Yes."

"Do you think he was in the house at all?"

"Not then, not before me. He had his two goons hold onto me, and then he went in."

"How long was he in there?"

"Long enough to find out that the man was dead."

"What did he say when he came out?"

"He called me a dumb bitch and told his men to get me into the car. He thought I killed the guy!"

"Silly man."

"Nick, the hole thing must still be in the house in Westchester."

"You looked, Jodi."

"Maybe I didn't look good enough."

"And maybe Berry got rid of it before he was killed. Either that or whoever killed him has it."

"Then we're back to where I started. Whoever killed him has it."

"Guess so."

"Jesus, this is getting confusing."

"We'll figure it out."

She was silent for a moment and then said, "You know, you've never even asked me if I killed him."

"You're my client. I don't take on murderers as clients."

"He was killed *after* you did that job for me."

"Did you kill him?"

"No."

"Okay, fine."

"You believe me, just like that?"

"Yes."

I did, too. As far as I was concerned, Jodi Hayworth was a tough little broad who had gotten in a little over her head, and I was playing lifeguard—only in this case, judging from the visit I'd had the other night, the lifeguard's life might be in just as much danger as hers.

We stared at each other for a few moments, and then she asked, "Well, what are we gonna do first?"

"*You're* going to stay someplace safe. *I've* got to be able to move around and see if I can't find out what happened to the hole thing. I get the feeling we're both in a hole that only that piece of art is going to get us out of."

"You're going to Westchester?"

"That's a possibility."

"To talk to the cops?"

"No, I don't want to talk to the cops out there because I don't want them to know who I am. If they know I'm working for you, a logical move would be to watch this building. No, if I do go out there, it'll just be to take a look around. I'm going to talk to some friends of mine in the police department to see if they can't get me some information from the Westchester cops."

"So where am I going to stay?"

"Across the hall."

"Alone?"

"Sam's home all day, so I don't think you'll be alone. Come on, I'll introduce you."

"Okay."

As she got up, I said, "Oh, by the way."

"Yes?"

"How did you meet Terry Jacks?"

"Through Janet Jackson."

"Janet—that's a friend of yours who lives in Manhattan, isn't it?"

"Yes, how'd you know?"

"Your mother gave me a list of your friends, including Janet Jackson. I talked to all of them except her."

"Can I see the list?"

"Sure."

I retrieved it from the back pocket of the pants I'd worn yesterday and showed it to her.

"How about letting me have that card that we got from the hockshop?"

"Sure."

She reached into her pocket and handed it over. I refrained from telling her that the old man we'd gotten it from was dead. "I don't even see two of these girls anymore."

"What about Janet?"

"She's probably my best friend right now."

"I guess I'll have to talk to her, then."

"About what?"

"About Terry Jacks. Why don't you write his address on the back of that list, too?"

She picked up a pencil and did as I asked.

"Does Janet have a job?"

"Of course. She works in a record store on St. Mark's Place. It's called Sounds."

"Well, you better give me that address, too. What about your friend Terry? Does he work?"

"He's an artist."

Did that answer my question?

"I should find him home, then?"

"Most likely. He paints during the day and goes out in the evening."

"He must have some other source of income than his painting."

"Oh, he's never sold a painting. He lives on an allowance from his father."

I took the piece of paper back from her and looked at what she had written.

"That explains why his address is much further uptown than Janet's."

Janet Jackson lived in an apartment in the West Village, on Horatio Street, while Terry Jacks lived uptown, an address on Eighty-third Street, between York and First.

"Why are you interested in Terry?" she asked, handing the list back to me.

"I'm interested in anyone and anything that came into your life recently. Somebody has this hole thing of yours, and somebody killed James Berry. I'm just looking around, Jodi. That's what a detective does."

"I'd like to help."

"You will, by staying out of sight so I don't have to worry about you."

"Across the hall?"

"Across the hall. Come on, I'll introduce you to Sam."

We started for the door, and I said, "Jodi, one last thing."

"Yes?"

"Is there anything that you haven't told me so far that you'd like to tell me now?"

"Like what?"

"Like something you forgot, or something you're afraid to talk about. Anything at all."

She thought a moment and seemed to honestly be concentrating on the question.

"There's nothing else I can think of."

"All right, then. Let's go."

***

Looking back, I guess it did sound as if I was avoiding mentioning that Sam was a woman. Jodi gave me a look when I introduced them, and then she and Sam gave each other those looks that attractive women do when they meet.

"Jodi, why don't you wait inside," I suggested.

"Sure."

She slid by Sam and went into her apartment.

"How's your father, Nick?"

"Shit," I said, "I didn't call him this morning."

"Well, you must have other things on your mind."

The remark would have sounded catty coming from someone else, but I'd never heard Sam be catty before, and I didn't think she was being so now.

"I'll have to call and talk to Vinnie before I go out. Listen, Sam, Jodi has something to do with those guys that were here the other night."

"She's the girl they were looking for."

"Right."

"Is that how she got beat up?"

"Yes. They had her but she got away, and they're probably still looking for her. I need to stash her someplace safe while I look around."

"For what?"

"I'll have to explain that to you another time."

"All right, I'll keep her here, Nick."

"I appreciate it, Sam."

"But I will get the whole story from you, won't I?"

"Sure—unless you can get it from Jodi. It'll give you two something to talk about."

"Oh, I don't think we'll have any trouble finding something to talk about."

I left, wondering what that meant.

20

I went back into my apartment and dialed my father's number. My brother answered on the second ring.

"Vinnie? How's Pop?"

"The same."

"Any news?"

"The terrorists have made some demands. They want the Israeli government to release Lebanese prisoners."

"What does that have to do with the United States?"

"I guess they want the President to intercede on their behalf."

"Jesus."

"There's something else."

"What?"

"They've released the names of the hostages that are still being held."

"Are *they* calling them hostages now?"

"Yes."

"And?"

"They've released all but twelve people, and Maria is among them."

"What possible reason could they have to keep her?"

"Who knows how they choose, Nick? There's something else going on here, though, now that all of the names have been released."

"What's that?"

"We've been getting telephone calls from *Good Morning America, CBS Morning News,* and from other stations who want Pop to go on TV and talk about this."

"What does Pop say?"

"He says if he goes on television, he'll use up time that could be used to report developments. He wants to stay in front of the TV, Nick, not on it."

"Well, good for him. He won't be part of a media circus."

"But can the same be said for Peter?"

Our brother-in-law was no wallflower. Hell, he'd jump at the chance to be on TV.

"I'll kill him."

"You don't mean that."

"Well, I'll let him have it, then. Take whatever phraseology you prefer."

"Did you see him yesterday?"

"He wasn't home."

"Where was he?"

"I don't know, Vin, but I intend to find out. I'll call you later."

"Wait a minute."

"For what?"

"Your friend Inspector Gorman called."

"What did he have to say?"

"Apparently whatever it is, he wants to say it to you." My brother sounded slightly miffed. "The only message he left was for you to call him as soon as you can."

When I hung up, I thought a moment, then took out my phone book, looked up a number, and dialed it.

"Bogie's," a voice said on the line.

"I'd like to speak to Miles Jacoby, please."

"Hold on, I'll see if he's here."

I could have tried Miles's home number, but he was at Bogie's more than he was at home. Bogie's was a restaurant in Manhattan on West Twenty-sixth Street with a Humphrey Bogart motif—posters, photos, black-bird busts, and "Key Largo" on the jukebox. Jack was a P. I. working out of Manhattan, and I needed him to do me a favor.

"Jacoby."

"Jack, it's Nick Delvecchio."

"Nicky D., how you doing?"

"Pretty good, except I need a favor."

"Well, I've got a few left. What can I do for you?"

"You're not going to like this, Jack, but I'd like you to follow my brother-in-law."

"Your brother-in-law? What's up?"

"Let me give you the whole story," I said, and I told him about the hijacking.

"Jesus, Nick, I'm sorry. Do you know how she is?"

"As far as we know she's fine, but I don't think her husband is as concerned as he should be."

"You think he's stepping out?"

"That might be the reason my sister went away, Nick. Things weren't going too well between them."

"How long have they been married?"

"About a year."

"What kind of fella is he?"

"He hasn't exactly fit in with the Delvecchio menfolk."

"Okay, Nick, you want me to find out if he's got a playmate, and then what?"

"Just let me know. If the bastard sent my sister running off on that flight because he likes to fool around—"

"Nick, easy," Jack said. "I'm not going to finger him for you so you can work him over."

"No, I wouldn't ask you to do that, Jack."

"I'll tail him for you, Nick."

"I'd do it myself, but on top of the thing with my sister I've got a girl's life in my hands."

"No sweat. Just give me the particulars."

I gave him my brother-in-law's name and home address and told him he worked on Wall Street but I wasn't sure where.

"You can pick him up at home tomorrow and go from there—" I started, but Jack cut me off.

"I can find out where he works. If he's fooling around, he might be doing it during business hours. Maybe I can wrap this up for you today."

"I appreciate this, Jack—and listen, make sure you send me a bill."

"Sure, I'll mail it, but you know how the mail service is in New York. When you coming to Manhattan, Nick? You can't hide in Brooklyn forever."

"As a matter of fact, I'll be in Manhattan today for a little while."

"Meet me at Bogie's before you go back to Brooklyn, say at four? That'll give me time to pick your brother-in-law up at work at five and follow him home. If I can't meet you, I'll call you there."

"Okay, fine."

"Just tell Billy Palmer, the owner, or the manager Stuart that you're a friend of mine."

"Will they poison me?"

"Probably, but it'll be the best poison in town. Now let's hang up so we can both get to work."

"Thanks, Jack."

"About your sister, Nick, if there's anything I can do..."

"Thanks again, Jack."

When I hung up, I decided to take his advice and get right to work. That meant going to Manhattan to talk to Janet Jackson and Terry Jacks, or going out to Westchester. The latter was a longer trip, and the possibility of killing a whole day getting out there and back did not appeal to me.

There was an easier way, since I had to call Inspector Ed Gorman anyway.

21

I hate going to Manhattan because it's impossible to take a car into the city without risking insanity, and it's impossible to take the subway without risking death in one form or another. (That might be an exaggeration, but if it is, it's only a slight one.)

I decided to take the easy route and simply walk across the Brooklyn Bridge.

On a good day—like today—the bridge looks like one side or the other is being evacuated. If it's morning, people are walking from Brooklyn into the city, and if it's early evening, they're walking the other way.

Today I was walking to the city with the young executives with their jackets over their arms and their ties and collars loosened, and the young secretaries and women executives in their sundresses or linen suits.

As far as the women went on this day, the view was very pleasant, but my mind kept wandering from Jodi's case to my sister's predicament, back and forth like a goddamned Ping-Pong ball.

If I couldn't locate the hole thing, then Jodi would continue to be in danger.

If my brother-in-law was cheating on my sister, the sonofabitch was in for a hard time from me...

How long would it take for the people who were looking for Jodi to figure that maybe I was the one who took the piece of artwork—and then they'd be after me, if they weren't already. That's what I had meant when I told Jodi that we were both possibly in a hole...

And if I didn't have enough random thoughts flicking through my head to give me a headache, I kept thinking about Maria, my father's baby. She wasn't a baby, though, she was a grown woman with more backbone than my father or my brother gave her credit for.

I wondered how would the terrorists respond to an American woman with backbone?

To try and steady my mind before I got dizzy, I thought about the last call I'd made before leaving my apartment. After hanging up on Jacoby, I'd dialed the Sixty-seventh Precinct number, been cut off by an incompetent civilian on the switchboard, and then finally got through to Gorman.

"Ed, it's Nick."

"I'm glad you called. I thought you'd be interested in knowing that your sister is still alive."

"You know that for a fact?"

"I've got a friend in the State Department. He was able to find out the condition of the remaining hostages. At last report, they were all alive and well."

"Ed, this means a lot to me."

"I'll try and keep an eye on the situation, Nick, and let you know if anything changes, but I can't guarantee anything."

"Whatever you can do, Ed, my family and I will appreciate."

"How's your old man holding up?"

"All right, I guess."

"Why aren't you at his house with your family instead of running around the city?"

"I'm working on something, Ed—and come to think of it," I said, doing my best to sound as if something had just occurred to me, "maybe you can help me with this, too."

"Come to think of it, huh? All right, then, let me have it."

"There was a murder in Westchester about two weeks or so ago, a wealthy man shot in his home."

"Yeah?" His tone was wary.

"I'd like to find out about it."

"What do you want to know?"

"*All* about it. What the cops have found so far, whether or not they're looking for suspects—"

"Any suspect in particular?" he asked. "Like maybe a client?"

"I appreciate all your help, Ed. I'll keep in touch."

I hung up on him while he was still talking. I knew I was taking unfair advantage of his willingness to help, but then I'd never asked for it when I was on the job. Maybe I was entitled. I only hoped that he felt that way too.

22

I tried Janet Jackson's home address first, an old five-story brick on Horatio Street, near Ninth Avenue, but she wasn't there. It was a less then scenic block, filled with aging brick buildings and a park I wouldn't have let a kid near with a suit of armor.

I walked crosstown to St. Mark's Place, and turning into the block between Second and Third—which is also East Eighth Street—was like entering a whole new world, even for Manhattan.

The street was lined with shops and restaurants, many of which had sidewalk service. The people who inhabited that block looked normal...in that they all had two arms, two legs, and a head. Beyond that, they were from another planet.

There were men in turquoise jumpsuits with pink hair on their heads—where there was hair. You haven't lived until you've seen a white dude—or girl—with a pink Mr. T mohawk and a collection of earrings that jingle when they walk. And then there were the leather-clad jerks with punk hairdos, stubble-covered faces and outfits unzipped to their navels revealing hairless chests.

There were hookers on the corner of St. Mark's and Third Avenue who approached cars when they stopped for the red light there. Further down the block was a hotel which was probably where they took the drivers who took their scantily clad bait. There were other gals just waiting on the steps for the johns to make the first move. As I went by, one of them lifted her tank top to expose her breasts to induce me to make that move, but I was less than compelled.

It was fitting that the Second Avenue Theater, just around the corner, was showing *Little Shop of Horrors,* and had been for some time.

When I reached the center of the block, I saw the sign that said "Sounds." A couple in matching jumpsuits came walking out at that point and I really couldn't tell if they were of the same sex, or even which sex they were. The place had huge windows, three of them, with a speaker mounted in each of the end ones. I had to ascend a flight of stone steps to get to the front door, which was made entirely of sheet metal.

Inside, an assortment of St. Mark's Place characters lined the two aisles of record albums, and there were even a couple of young executive types who had probably taken an early lunch to come down and shop.

The counter was way above floor level, probably so the employees could look down on the store, making it easier to spot shoplifters. Behind the counter was a white guy with blonde hair that was cut so close he looked bald, and a stunning black girl with cornrows. She appeared to be in her early twenties, and even for one as easily smitten as I am, she looked like something special.

"Excuse me," I shouted over the music. Some girl singer I didn't recognize was singing about "baad, baad, baad, baad boooys" making her feel "sooo good!"

They both looked at me, and the man asked, "Can I help you?"

"I'm looking for Janet Jackson!"

I didn't know if they could hear me or not, or if lipreading was a requirement of their job, but the girl moved over in front of the guy and said, "I'm Janet."

I was surprised. Jodi had said nothing about Janet Jackson being black.

"Could I talk to you, please?"

"You want to sell some records?"

"No, I want to talk!"

I took out the photostat of my P. I. license and passed it up to her. She read it, frowned, and handed it back. She said something to the young man and then walked to the end of the platform and stepped down. That she was so short was another surprise. She couldn't have been more than five feet tall.

"What's this about?" she asked, putting her lips next to my ear. To do so, she had to press her full breasts tightly against my arm. Her breath was warm and pleasant.

"Jodi Hayworth."

"Is she—" she began, but I overrode her by saying, "Can we go somewhere?"

She nodded and beckoned me to follow her out the front door. When the metal door closed behind us, it became a little quieter.

"There's a bar downstairs," she said in an almost normal voice. That was the first time I realized that she had some kind of an accent, probably Jamaican. "Is that all right?"

"That's fine," I said. "I'll buy."

We walked down the steps, made a sharp right, and walked down five steps to the bar. The front door was plain wood, and there was no name in evidence. As we walked in, the bar was on the left and there was a wooden partition, about chest high, separating it from a group of tables on the right. The crowd inside was a good mix. Apparently the place appealed to the young execs as well as the pink-hairs.

She grabbed a table and said, "You'll have to go to the bar to get the drinks. I'll take a beer. Michelob."

I took the beers back to the table, sat down, and slid hers across the wooden table.

"What about Jodi? Is she in trouble?"

"As a matter of fact, she is. It has to do with a missing art object."

"You mean she did it?" Her skin was a light brown, but her eyes were like dark chocolate.

"Did it?"

"Hocked one of her stepfather's pieces."

"Oh yeah, she did it, all right. Now I'm trying to help her get it back."

"How can I help?"

"You introduced her to Terry Jacks, didn't you?"

"Terry? Why, yes, I did. What does he have to do with this?"

"I'm just interested in anyone Jodi met this month, Miss Jackson—can I call you Janet?"

"I don't even know if I should be talking to you, at all," she replied warily. "How do I know you're really working for Jodi?"

"You could call her."

"Is she home?"

"No, she's at a number I can give you."

"That doesn't sound right. How do I know what number you're giving me?"

"You'll recognize her voice, won't you?"

"Of course."

I took out a pen and wrote down Sam's phone number on a napkin.

"Here. Give her a call and ask her if you should talk to me."

She took the napkin but hesitated, studying me.

"I'll even give you the quarter for the call," I said, handing the coin over.

She smiled and took the quarter, making me feel as if I'd won a small victory.

"There's a pay phone in the back. Wait here."

For a moment I thought maybe she was going to run out on me, but I was able to follow her progress to the back of the place and watch her talking on the phone. The conversation didn't take long, and in a moment she was walking back to the table, a whole line of guys turning their heads and watching her from behind. The view from the front wasn't so bad, either. She was wearing jeans and a pink bodysuit, and her nipples were clearly visible.

"Sorry I was so suspicious," she said, sitting down across from me again. "I don't like talking to cops, and a private detective is sort of a cop...isn't he?"

"I used to be a cop," I said. "I guess the smell is hard to shake."

"Jodi says you're okay, so go ahead and ask your questions—and you can call me Janet."

"Janet, I just want to know what you can tell me about Terry Jacks."

She shrugged and said, "He comes into the store to buy records. That's how we met. He asked me out, we went out a few times, and that was that."

"When did you introduce him to Jodi?"

"At a party that I gave. I invited them both, not particularly to introduce them, but it seemed like a good idea at the time."

"Did you talk to him about her afterward?"

"He came into the store once or twice, but we never discussed Jodi."

"What about Jodi? Did you talk with her about him?"

"Just girl talk, you know?"

"Girl talk."

"Have you ever talked to a guy about a girl he went out with?"

"I think I know what you mean."

"What can you tell me about him personally?"

"He's good-looking, he likes girls very much, all sizes and shapes—and colors." She graced me with an infectious grin. "You like girls in all colors?"

I grinned back and said, "All colors. What else about Jacks?"

"Um, he's got money, he's blonde, fair-skinned, he's fairly good in bed"—she said this last while studying me with raised eyebrows; I didn't rise to the bait—"and he's got a bad temper."

That interested me.

"How bad?"

She hesitated, then said, "I'm only telling you this because you're a friend of Jodi's."

"Okay."

"After we went out a few times, he got rough with me one night."

"Did he hit you?"

"Once, and I kicked him out."

"But you invited him to your parties?"

She shrugged.

"Most of the time he was a nice guy; I just didn't get my kicks the way he got his."

"Did you tell Jodi about this?"

"No. Maybe it was what he wanted to do just with me. I didn't want to...start rumors, you know?"

"I know."

"There's something else I never told her, too."

"What's that?"

"Terry's a switch-hitter."

"You mean, he's bisexual?"

"Yes."

"Are you sure?"

She grimaced and said, "Yeah. Some of my parties get out of hand, you know. I went to use the bathroom at my last one, and Terry was in there in the shower stall. He was getting some action...from a guy!"

"I guess you're sure, then. How long have you known Terry?"

"A couple of months. Ever since he first hit town."

"Where did he hit town from?"

She shrugged and said, "Who knows?"

It might have helped if I did. I made a mental note to remember to ask Jodi.

She hitched up closer to the table and gave me a different kind of look.

"Are you and Jodi...close?"

"I'm just trying to help her."

The bodysuit she was wearing was not particularly low-cut, but it had a rounded neck, and I was able to see the swollen beginning of her deep cleavage. That, combined with the fact that her nipples showed through the thin fabric of the top, made it impossible not to stare. She *saw* me staring and smiled.

"You're kind of cute, you know?" she said. "Why don't you give me your telephone number, and I'll invite you to my next party?"

It was a hell of a tempting offer, but her parties didn't sound as if I would fit in.

I smiled back and said, "I'm afraid I'm not exactly the party type, Janet."

"Well, then, come into the store sometime and buy some records. I'll make you a real good deal."

"I may take you up on that. You want to finish that beer?" I asked, indicating her beer bottle. It was still half full.

"I don't *have* to," she said, pushing her beer away. I left half of mine, also.

We stood up and started for the door, and I put one hand on her rounded shoulder as we reached it.

"Janet, would you do me a favor?"

"Sure, name it."

"Would you mind not calling Terry Jacks to tell him I'm coming to see him?"

She smiled and said, "Don't worry, Nick. We're not that close."

23

I had three choices on how to get uptown. I could walk, and since it was summer that would be a pleasure. On this day, however, I didn't feel like walking from Eighth Street to Eighty-third.

There was the subway, but I've explained how I feel about that.

The third choice was to take a cab, which would get me there the quickest and the safest—safe except for my wallet, of course.

The block and building that Terry Jacks lived in was in sharp contrast to Janet Jackson's. Eighty-third and York was high-priced, and if Jacks's father kept him on an allowance, it was a big one.

The doorman had to call upstairs to get the okay to send me up.

"What shall I say is the nature of your business?"

It never fails to amaze me how putting a uniform on a man whose only job is to hold the door open for you makes him think he's hot shit. This one stared down his nose at me in such a way that he might have simply been examining the tip of it for pimples.

"Tell him the nature of my business is girls."

I figured if he was as much of a pussy hound as Janet intimated, that should get his attention.

"Girls?"

"Yes, girls."

He looked at me, and then some of his icy facade fell away and he said, "That'll do it."

He called upstairs out of earshot, spoke briefly, then hung up.

"You can go up. Six-fifteen."

I took the elevator to the sixth floor, found 615, and knocked.

The man who answered the door was easily recognizable as Terry Jacks. He had blonde hair that fell to his shoulders. He was tall and slender, fair-skinned, and would probably be attractive to some women. Well, a lot of women.

"Terry Jacks?"

"Mr. Delvecchio?"

"That's right."

"Come on in."

He backed up and I entered, passing him. He closed the door behind us.

We were in the living room, which, for an apartment as expensive as this one, was rather sparsely furnished.

It was empty.

Oh, there were canvases and easels, some of them obviously works in progress, and drop cloths on the floor, but other than all of that and a stereo with miniature speakers, the room was bare.

"I live simply," he said, by way of explanation. "My supplies, my stereo, and my bed—speaking of which, you said something about girls?"

He wore an open, good-natured expression.

"One girl in particular."

"Which one is that?"

"Jodi Hayworth."

"Jodi—yeah, I know Jodi. You a friend of hers?"

"Sort of."

He frowned, the good-natured expression slipping slightly. "What does 'sort of' mean?"

"I'm working for her."

"As what?"

"I'm a private investigator."

Now his expression turned wary.

"A private eye? Why would Jodi need a private eye?"

"There's a piece of artwork missing from her house."

"And she thinks I took it?"

"No."

"Then why are you here?"

"Just to talk to you."

"Well, I'm pretty busy—"

"It won't take long."

"Look," he said, "I can't help you. I don't know anything about artwork—"

"Sure you do. You're an artist. You know when a piece of art is worth money."

"So? That doesn't mean I took something from her house. I've only been there once or twice."

"What did you think of her stepfather's collection of art?"

"He's not much of a collector, just some small statues and busts."

"I thought you didn't know anything about art?"

"Like you said, I'm an artist, but I don't know anything about any missing art pieces."

"I never said you did, Terry."

"Then what are you doing here?"

"Let me tell you about detective work, Terry," I said. Calling him by his first name was something they taught you in the academy. Investigators use it to intimidate witnesses and suspects. "All it is is asking questions, some of which don't make any sense."

"Well if that's the case, then you must be doing it right."

I couldn't argue that.

"This place must cost you plenty. You must be doing pretty well with your paintings."

"I've sold one or two."

I walked over to a couple of the canvases, but he quickly moved in front of me.

"I don't like people to look at my work before it's done."

I couldn't blame him for that, either. From what I could see, he was a pretty piss-poor painter.

"Listen, I'm really busy. I'm being honest with you, I don't know anything about a piece of art missing from Jodi's house."

"She says she remembered you picking up a piece or two to examine."

"All right, that's enough," he said, getting angry. "I'd like you to leave before I call the doorman and have him throw you out."

"Do doormen do that?"

He grinned tightly and said, "They do if they want their Christmas envelopes."

"What's your father's name?"

"What's that got to do with anything?"

I shrugged.

"Just one of those questions that doesn't seem to make any sense."

"I'm calling the doorman."

He walked over to a telephone on the floor and picked up the receiver. Seeing him with it made me think back to that first night, when I'd gotten the call warning me to keep away from the "hole thing."

"It's okay, Terry, I'm leaving."

He stopped and stared at me, still holding on to the receiver.

"I might want to talk to you again, though."

When he replied, I listened real close, trying to imagine his voice coming over a phone.

"If you do, you better have a better reason next time, or you won't get past the doorman."

"I'll remember that."

I let myself out, and in the elevator on the way down I thought about what I'd told him about questions that didn't appear to make any sense.

This case was full of them, starting from day one.

Who had called me on the phone, warning me off a case I wasn't even on yet? Had it been Terry Jacks? Or Jodi's captor, Carmine DiVolo? Or somebody else I wasn't even aware of yet?

What was so goddamned important about a doughnut-shaped piece of art?

Why was I worried about this shit when my sister's life was in danger?

Why hadn't I given foxy Janet Jackson my phone number?

24

I got to Bogie's after four o'clock and found Miles Jacoby waiting for me there. He was sitting at the bar with a bottle of St. Pauli Girl in front of him. Jack and I had met when a case took him to Brooklyn and he needed a P. I. who knew the lay of the land. I was recommended to him by another P.I. we both knew, Henry Po. We got along, and he uses me when he needs something done in Brooklyn, and I use him when I need something done in Manhattan.

Seated on a stool next to him was a man with a mustache so bushy that you couldn't see his upper lip. He was in his midthirties, a man of medium height who obviously kept himself physically fit. His name was Billy Palmer, and with his wife, Karen, he owned Bogie's.

Jacoby himself was in pretty good shape, but then he should have been. He was an ex-middleweight and had recently begun working out in karate. At thirty—several years younger than myself—I thought he might have his eye on a comeback of some kind, but meanwhile he had turned himself into a pretty good investigator for someone who had come to it late.

Bogie's bar was separated from the restaurant by a brick wall with two arches. Above the arches, all across the wall, were framed book covers and photos from mystery writers, all signed to Billy and Karen. In the three short years since they opened Bogie's, it had become a true haven for mystery writers, serving as the site for gatherings, awards presentations, and just plain dinner.

Jacoby saw me as soon as I entered and waved me over.

"Elias, get my friend a beer," he said to the bartender, a young, good-looking Hispanic.

The bartender looked at me, and I pointed to the bottle in front of Miles. "The same."

"Nick, you remember Billy."

"Sure, how are you?"

"Fine," Billy said as we shook hands. "Can we get you some dinner while you're here? We've got a new chef who's a hell of a cook. My wife swears by him."

"How is Karen?"

"She's fine, working hard as usual."

His wife was a foxy brunette with more energy than half a dozen normal people.

"In deference to her chef, I have to get back to Brooklyn."

"Brooklyn," Billy said, shaking his head. "The great unknown."

"You've never been there?"

"Once or twice to a friend's house for a party, but we always took a cab. I'd never be able to find my way around by myself."

"Well, I'm not all that fond of Manhattan," I admitted. "For me there's no exit from Brooklyn. I was born there, and I can't imagine living anywhere else."

"Billy," Elias said as he put my beer down, "they want you in the kitchen."

"Excuse me."

Billy left, and I turned my attention to Jacoby.

"Let's get this over with. You've got to get back to Wall Street to follow Numbnuts home."

"Numbnuts?"

"My brother-in-law."

"Well, I don't know whether it's good news or bad news, but there's no need for me to have to follow Numbnuts home."

"There isn't?"

He shook his head.

"He's having it off with a clerk in his office."

"A clerk?"

"A sweet young thing with stars in her eyes, from the looks of it. They go to the Howard Johnson's on Fifty-first and Eighth."

"Howard Johnson's?"

"Your brother-in-law is not much of a high roller, but it apparently doesn't matter to the lady."

"Could this have been a one-time thing?"

"Not from the looks of it, Nick, but I can check it out again tomorrow if you like."

I stared at the green St. Pauli Girl bottle in my hand, which I was holding by the neck. I wished it was my brother-in-law's throat.

"Yeah, all right," I said. "Just find out if they make it again."

"I'll talk to the clerk at the Howard Johnson's and see what he can tell me."

"Fine."

I put the beer down on the bar, still staring at it.

"Say goodbye to Billy for me, will you?"

"Sure. How you holding up, buddy?" he asked, touching my arm.

"Okay, I guess. I'm trying to keep busy."

"Must be a bitch. Let me know if there's anything I can do to help…"

I looked at him and said, "Can you call me tomorrow evening?"

"Sure, no problem. I'll know something by then."

"Thanks, Jack, I appreciate this."

"I'm sorry it turned out this way, Nick. Your sister doesn't need this kind of trouble on top of everything else…"

"He's an asshole, anyway."

"Are you going to tell her?"

"She probably already knows, but I'll decide if—when she comes home." I clapped him on the shoulder and said, "Thanks. See you."

"Take care."

I left Bogie's feeling even worse than before, if that was possible. I think I'd been secretly hoping my brother-in-law was clean and that my sister's and his problems were nothing more serious than socks being left on the floor, or burning his toast in the morning. Those things could be worked out between them.

Now that I knew he was cheating on her, I wished I didn't.

25

Returning to Brooklyn from Manhattan was always the source of great pleasure for me, however I chose to do it. What I had told Billy Palmer about there being no exit from it for me was true. There was no place else in the country—or the world, for that matter—I could ever have imagined living.

I wanted to get back as quickly as possible, so I grabbed a cab from the corner of Twenty-sixth and Seventh, right down the block from Bogie's.

When Sam opened the door of her apartment to my knock, there was a definite chill in the air.

"Sam—"

"Don't ask," Sam said quietly but firmly. "Just come in and get her."

I stepped in and saw Jodi sitting on Sam's couch. When she saw me, she grinned and stood up.

"You're back."

"Yeah."

"Can we…get out of here?"

I frowned, wondering what had gone on while I was away—and then I remembered the last words Sam had said to me that morning before I left.

What *had* they found to talk about that had turned the air so cold?

"Sure, Jodi. Come on. We have to talk."

"Fine." She brushed past Sam on the way out. "Thanks for the use of the hall," she said sarcastically.

She went past me then and out into the hall, where she waited in front of my door.

"Sam, what went on?"

"Remind me to tell you sometime," Sam said, her expression unreadable, then she added, "that is, if she doesn't first."

"I don't—"

"Just watch out for yourself with her, Nick. She's trouble."

Tell me about it, I thought. Already I'd been hauled in by the police and attacked by two bruisers because of my initial association with her, however brief it had been.

"Thanks for your help."

"Sure," she said, "but I don't think it would work again. All right?"

"Yeah, all right. Talk to you later."

I went out into the hall where Jodi was waiting and unlocked my door. When we got inside she whirled on me.

"What did she tell you?"

"Who? Janet?"

"No, your friend, Samantha."

"She didn't tell me anything, why?"

"Nothing. What happened with Janet?"

"I've got to make a call first before we talk. Could you make some coffee?"

"Sure."

While she went into the kitchen, I called Ed Gorman. "Were you able to find out anything for me?"

"How much do you already know about this case, Nick?"

"Nothing."

He heaved a sigh on the other end that almost blew out my eardrum and then started talking.

"The victim is James Berry, male, white, fifty-four, shot in the chest at close range with a .32 caliber revolver, said weapon not recovered."

"Married?"

"No, lives alone."

"Job?"

"He's wealthy—or he was. He made investments from his home." I wondered what Mr. James Berry, who made investments from his home, had been doing down on Atlantic Avenue in a two-bit hockshop, but I couldn't say that to Gorman.

I waited, and when nothing further was forthcoming, I said, "Suspects?"

Another sigh and then, "One."

"Ed, do I have to drag this out of you?"

"I get the feeling I'm walking a one-way street here, Nick. Are you sure you don't know anything about this case?"

"Nothing that would help Westchester find the guy's killer." That was as honest an answer as I could give him.

"All right, it gets a little funny here. A blonde girl was seen going into the house the day Berry was killed. Later she was seen coming out, and then three men grabbed her. One went into the house while the other two stayed outside with the girl. When the first guy came out, they all got into a car and drove away."

"So the cops are looking for all of them?"

"Right."

"Have you got good descriptions of all four?"

"Yes. Sometimes it pays to have a nosy neighbor in the area."

He reeled off the descriptions. Jodi was easy to recognize, as were the two goons who had visited me. The fourth man I didn't know about, but I was sure Jodi would tell me the description fit DiVolo.

"But they're not looking for all four."

"Why not?"

"Delvecchio, you better be being straight with me on this."

"Ed—"

"Never mind. One of the men was found dead the other night."

"How'd that happen?"

"Who knows? He was found in a dumpster with a broken neck."

"A dumpster?"

"In a residential area of Marine Park. Some people rented one because they were tearing down their garage, but they came out one morning and found this guy in it. You want his name?"

"That'd be nice."

"Yeah, well, his name was Lester Wexler, and he had a yellow sheet as long as his arm—his *strong arm.*"

"Who was he working for?"

"He was free-lance. Looks like he finally took one job too many."

"Ah, the tough life of a torpedo."

"God, I haven't heard that expression in years."

"That's what they called them in your day, isn't it?"

"Trying to keep me from asking any questions, aren't you? Like what your interest is in this murder?"

"I'm just...interested. Are these other three people being sought as suspects?"

"Officially, they're wanted for questioning. Only two of them were seen entering and leaving the house, so only two could be called suspects. One of the men and the blonde girl—who sounds just like your type, by the way."

"Not me," I said quickly, "I hate blondes."

"Uh-huh. Listen, Westchester is real interested in why I'm interested."

"What did you tell them?"

"I told them I had a tenuous interest, and would certainly let them know if I came up with anything to help them. That's right, isn't it?"

"That's exactly right, Ed. I couldn't have put it better myself."

"Uh-huh, you eloquent sonofabitch, you. How's your family doing?"

"Hanging in, Ed, thanks."

"I don't have any further news for you. Things seem to be at a standstill over there. The Lebanese government doesn't want to release any prisoners."

"Are they still on the plane?"

"Yeah, but that's subject to change, too."

I felt a chill, suddenly.

"What do you mean?"

"Well, they're asking for a bus."

"They want to take the hostages off the plane?"

"Yeah."

"They can't do that! If that happens, how will we know where they are?"

"We won't."

"Ed, has this been on the news?"

"Not this part of it, no, but they can't keep it from the press for very long. Try and let your father know so he doesn't hear it on TV."

"Yeah. Thanks again, Ed."

"And do me a favor."

"What?"

"Don't get in over your head with this Westchester thing."

"I always manage to keep my head above water, Ed. You know that."

26

When I hung up on Gorman, Jodi came in with the coffee pot and two cups on a tray.

"News about the hostage situation?"

I looked at her.

"Samantha told me about it. I really appreciate your helping me with my problem, Nick, what with your sister...uh, you know..."

"I know. Don't worry about it. Let's talk about your problem."

"Which is?"
"The Westchester police are looking for you."
"Oh."
"That's the bad news."
"What's the good news?"
"They're looking for two men, as well."
"*Two* men? There were three."
"One of them has turned up...dead."
"DiVolo?"
"No, one of the others."
"How did that happen?"
I shrugged as casually as I could.
"They don't know. Somebody broke his neck."
"That makes two people dead, and all because of that hole thing."
"Three."
"What?"
"Three people are dead," I said, and told her about the old man in the hockshop, how he had been tortured for the Westchester address and then killed.

"Jesus, I can't believe this."

I'm afraid I had the hostage situation more in mind than hers when I said, "Yeah, neither can I."

We sat in silence for a moment, and then I shook myself off and addressed myself to the present.

"Jodi, this is the way it sits. The police are looking for a blonde girl and three men, all of whom were seen at that house in Westchester. A man and woman were seen going in and coming out. Anybody with one good eye would be able to match you to the description of the girl."

"And DiVolo to the man's description."

"Right."

"What did you find out from Janet and Terry?"

"Janet cooperated, but Terry was nervous. Do you know who his father is? He wouldn't tell me."

"No, he never told me, either."

"And he never paid an inordinate amount of attention to your stepfather's statues?"

"Not that I noticed."

I sipped my coffee and said, "I'd really like to find out who's paying his bills."

"I could ask him."

"No, I don't want you going near him, or anyone until I can figure this out."

"Ah, the jealous type."

I gave her a sidelong glance and said, "No, not particularly." I drank some more coffee, and then she poured me another cup.

"What happened with you and Sam?"

"Why?"

"I detected a chill in the air when I arrived."

"We didn't really get along."

"You want to leave it at that?"

She thought a moment and then said, "Sure, why not?"

"Fine. You want to get some dinner?"

"Definitely. Where should we go?"

"Nowhere. I've got some menus in the kitchen. We'll order out and have it delivered. Why don't you do the honors?"

"Sure. Where are they?"

"In the drawer next to the stove. Here, you can take this with you, too."

I gulped down some coffee and put the cup down so she could take the tray with her.

While she was in the kitchen studying menus, I went into my office and opened the safe in my floor. I took out the .38 I keep there, well-oiled and as neglected as I could possibly make it. I could count on one hand the times I'd held it since leaving "the job." I took it out of the safe and stuck it in the top drawer of my desk. I hoped it would stay there, but somehow I was more comfortable that it was more accessible.

"Is Italian all right?" she asked as I entered the kitchen. She had the Italian restaurant menu spread out on the counter and was bent over it. She was wearing tight shorts that molded themselves perfectly to her shapely hips.

"Italian's fine."

"What's good?"

"The lasagna and the baked ziti are the best."

"Let's get one of each."

"Fine."

"And some pizza."

"Fine."

She stood up straight and looked at me.

"You're worried."

"Yes."

"About your sister."

"And about us."

"You don't have to go on with this, you know. It really is my problem. I could go to my stepfather—"

"Tony Macaroni."

"What?"

"I knew your stepfather a long time ago, Jodi."

"That's right, you said you knew him. Where was that?"

"A long time ago. I was just a kid, and he was a legbreaker on the docks where my father worked in Brooklyn."

"And they called him Tony Macaroni?"

"That's what they called him."

"I always thought of him as Tony Ronzoni, but I like Macaroni better. Wait a minute."

"What?"

"What's a legbreaker?"

"Just what it sounds like. Somebody who breaks your leg if you don't come across."

"With what?"

"Whatever," I said, shrugging. "If you work for a shylock, it's money."

"Who did Tony Macaroni work for?"

"He free-lanced," I said. "Why don't you call in that order, and then I'll give my brother a call."

"Your brother the priest?"

"You and Sam must have talked a lot, huh?"

"We did...but in the end we didn't get along." She picked up the menu and said, "I'll call this in."

After she called, she went to the bathroom, and I called Father Vinnie. He said that Pop was the same, still sitting in front of the TV. I told Vinnie what Ed Gorman had told me, and he remained silent for a moment.

"You want me to tell Pop?" he finally asked.

"I'll come by in the morning and tell him, Vin."

"Nick—"

I could tell by his voice that something was wrong. "What?"

"When you come—listen, Pop's been talking, you know how he gets—"

"What's he saying now?"

"He's been wondering where you are, why you're not with your family."

I rubbed my forehead, feeling a headache coming on. "Yeah, well, I'll talk to him in the morning, Vinnie."

"He's just talking, Nick—"

"Yeah, yeah, I know how he gets. G'night, Father."

I hung up and sat down on the couch with my face in my hands. I didn't know Jodi was in the room until she put her hands on my shoulders.

I put my right hand over her left—which was on my left shoulder—and asked, "Do you have any money, Jodi?"

"Yeah, why?"

I patted her hand and said, "Because you're the client, and you're paying for dinner, kid."

She gave me a shot behind the head and said good-naturedly, "Bastard!"

It wasn't until she went to the bathroom again after we'd eaten that I realized that I'd missed something earlier.

When she came out, I said, "Let me have it, Jodi."

"Have what?"

"You know what. The coke."

"What coke?"

"Don't bullshit me!"

"You want to do some?" she asked. "Why didn't you say so?"

"I don't want to use it, honey, I want to lose it."

"You're kidding," she said, taking what looked like aluminum foil from her pocket. "This stuff costs money."

"It could also cost me my license if it's found in my apartment."

"Don't be like that—"

"Jodi, if you want my help, you'll give me the rest of that and stay straight until we've solved this thing."

"Nick—"

"Those are the only conditions under which I'll continue working for you."

She stared at me, and then at the wad of foil in her hand. "Self-righteous bastard!" she said, tossing it at me. It bounced off my chest, and I picked it up. "You're so much better than I am, you and your girlfriend next door."

"Sam—"

"Your precious Sam. Why don't you just go next door and bang her tonight, because you're not getting any from me tonight, pal!"

"Sam and I don't have that kind of relationship."

"Oh, now who's bullshitting who, *Nicky?*" If my name had come out with any more sarcasm on it, it would have disintegrated.

"Jodi, we've got enough problems without getting into a fight."

"Fine! We won't fight," she agreed.

She walked over to my modest stereo setup and began looking through my albums.

"Jesus, don't you even have any decent records?"

I consider the small collection of records I have to be decent. Basically, I collect albums by artists who either were born or grew up in Brooklyn. They include Streisand, Neil Diamond, Neil Sedaka, and Billy Joel.

I mean, who doesn't like Billy Joel?

She was pushing me to see how far she could go, and when she realized I wasn't biting, she gave up.

"I'll take the damn couch, and you take the bed, and we'll go to sleep. We've got a big day tomorrow, right?"

"Hopefully."

We stared at each other for a few seconds, and then I said, "Good night, then."

I headed for the bedroom, and she called out, "Hey, Nick?"

"Yeah?"

Indicating the foil in my hand, she asked, "You, uh, you're not gonna flush that, are you?"

I hefted it in my hand and said, "You'll get it back...when our *business* is finished."

So the sleeping arrangements were the same as last night, but with one difference. This time she stayed on the couch.

It was just as well.

27

I woke up to the sound and smell of sizzling bacon. Dressing, I hoped that it meant the fight we'd had last night was behind us. If we were going to make any sense out of this mess, we were going to have to do it together.

I had hidden the coke in a rolled-up sock in one of my dresser drawers and was wondering if I was really going to return it to her or not. Actually, it *was* hers, and who was I to keep it from her once our business was over? I wasn't in the business of reforming cocaine users—or abusers.

When I entered the kitchen, she was scraping some bacon and eggs onto a plate and setting it on the table, where a smaller plate of stacked toast, glasses of juice, and two cups of coffee were already waiting.

"Smells good," I said.

"It's a peace offering," she said, turning away from the stove to face me. She was wearing the same shorts and top she had on the day before, and I realized suddenly that she had no other clothes. "My way of saying I'm sorry I jumped in your face last night."

"That's okay."

"And I'm sorry about...the couch."

"*You* slept on the couch last night."

"I know," she said, "that's what I'm sorry about."

As we sat down to breakfast, I said, "We're going to have to get you some clothes today."

"Does that mean I get to leave here?"

"I could pick them up for you—"

"I'd prefer to do that myself. I usually have to try things on."

"All right," I said, "we'll see what we can work out. I need to go see my father first."

"Any news?"

"None good," I said, and dropped it. She had the good sense not to attempt to pursue the subject further.

After breakfast while she was washing the dishes—and she volunteered to do it—she asked, "Can I come to your father's with you?"

"No."

"Why not?"

"Because things haven't been going well between my family and me during this...crisis. We don't need an audience when we're...bickering."

"I'm used to family strife," she said, drying her hands on a towel.

"Speaking of which, do you want to go back home?"

"Nope."

"Why not?"

"I still don't trust my stepfather. He might be in contact with DiVolo."

"How about calling your mother?"

"Nick, we've gone through this before. I don't trust anybody," she said, and then added, "except you—and even that goes against the grain."

"Well," I said, "that's a start."

I promised to come back and take her shopping after I finished at my father's house.

As I pulled up in front of my father's house in a cab—a *Brooklyn* cab, not one of those crazy Manhattan hacks—I realized that I hadn't even thought about stopping for pastries.

When I entered the house, Vinnie looked up from where he was sitting on the couch. He was wearing his priest's collar, as he had been all along, and I wondered why he had to do that, wear the damn collar in the house all the time. Or did he just put it on when he knew I was coming?

"Vinnie."

"Good morning," he said, standing up. "No pastries today, huh? Well, I'm glad I already had breakfast. Still, you could have brought lunch."

It was only ten o'clock, but that was my brother the father's way of telling me he had expected me earlier.

"Where's Pop?"

"In front of the TV."

"Jesus, can't we get him away from that thing?"

He gave me a look—the one they learn in the seminary in "Stern, Priestly Looks 101"—but I refrained from apologizing. He deserved it for the dig about lunch.

"Where do you want to put him?"

"I don't know. Jesus, we could give him something to do, I guess."

Stern look number two.

"He's got something to do."

"Yeah, sit around and feel sorry for himself."

"You don't think he's got a right to feel sorry for himself?"

"No, I don't," I snapped. "For Maria, maybe, but not for himself."

"Nick—"

"Vinnie, I don't want to fight with you. I've got something to tell you and Pop."

"About Maria?"

"Yeah. Come inside."

We went into my father's room together, and he was sitting in his leather recliner. There was an empty coffee cup lying on its side on the floor at his feet, and his eyes were riveted to the screen. They were showing the earliest pictures they had of the plane and the hijackers.

"Pop, how can you keep watching that stuff again and again?"

He looked up at me, and he looked as if he'd aged five or ten years since I last saw him. Shit, he looked like my grandfather instead of my father.

"Pop—"

"This television," my father said, "is my only connection to your sister, Nicky. You want to take that away from me?"

"Pop, this isn't doing you any good. You can't watch TV all day and all night."

"I want to know everything that's happening."

"Vinnie and I can keep you informed."

"Your brother maybe, but you haven't been around, Nicky. Where've you been while your sister has been in the hands of terrorists?"

"Pop, I've been working—"

"Working?" The disapproval was plain on his face and in his voice.

"Yeah, Pop, it was something I started...before all this happened."

"I don't understand you, Nick. I don't think I've ever understood you—"

I looked at Vinnie, but his face was blank, the way it had always been when Pop was bawling me out.

"Pop, a girl's life—my life—may depend on what I'm doing. I can't just stop—"

"What about your sister's life?" he snapped at me.

"I can't do anything about that!" I was shouting, and it came out before

I could stop it.

"Your brother Joey—"

"Joey's dead, Pop."

This time my words were soft, but they had more impact. He looked stunned, as if it was the first time he was hearing that bit of news.

"Nick—" Vinnie said, grabbing for my arm, but I shook him off.

"Look, Pop, we went through all of this years ago, let's not dredge it up now. I've got some news about Maria."

"What news?"

"There's been some talk that the terrorists might take the hostages off the plane."

"But if they do that, how will they know where they are?" my father asked.

"Pop—"

"No, you're wrong, Nick," he said, shaking his head. "If you're gonna bring me that kind of news, then don't even come around."

"Pop—"

He turned away from me and fixed his eyes on the television again. He was dry-washing his hands in his lap, over and over and over again, and finally clasped them so tightly together that the knuckles of his thick, red dockworker's hands turned white.

"Pop, you've got to face the truth—"

"Nick," Vinnie said, taking my arm. "Come on, let's go inside."

I allowed my brother to draw me into the living room, because talking to my father was like talking to a deaf man.

"Why'd you tell him that?" Vinnie demanded.

"Because I didn't want him to hear about it on television."

"No, I mean where did you get it from?"

"Inspector Gorman. He got it from a contact of his in the State Department."

"How does a cop have contacts in the State Department?" There was an unspoken "mere" in front of the word "cop," the way my brother said it. I've never been able to understand how or why a priest should have such a low opinion of cops.

"He wasn't always just a cop, Vinnie."

I don't know if that satisfied him, but he let the subject drop.

"What you said in there."

"About what?"

"About your life, and a girl's..."

"Vinnie, try to understand. I can't do anything about Maria, but maybe I can keep this girl alive."

"Yeah," Vinnie said. "Well, while you're keeping her alive, don't forget about yourself."

"Yeah, sure."

Moments like that were few and far between for us, and it was awkward.

"Have you heard from...from Peter?"

"No, he hasn't called. Have you seen him?"

"No, I haven't." Briefly I considered telling him what Jacoby had told me, but I decided against it. I'd handle that part myself.

"I'll call, Vinnie. Try and make Pop understand what might happen, all right? So he's not surprised by it?"

"I'll talk to him."

"And do me a favor, will you?"

"What?"

"When I come over tomorrow...lose the collar?"

28

I took Jodi over to Fulton Street, where we shopped in Abraham & Straus and then went over to the Albee Square Mall to eat in their food court.

Years ago Fulton Street—like Flatbush Avenue—was packed with shoppers every day of the week except Sunday. (That was back when stores actually closed on Sundays.) In addition to A & S there used to be a Korvettes there, a Mays, a McCrory's, and dozens of smaller shops. About five or six years ago they decided to close the street and make an open-air mall out of it, and then they opened the Albee Mall right on Fulton, which was a smaller, closed mall with shops and a food court.

Malls had given birth to the food court, and as a fast-food fiend I was all in favor of them. This one, on the second floor, had a chicken place, a hot-dog stand, Chinese food, Greek food, a McDonald's, a pizza place, a pretzel stand, and an ice cream parlor.

Jodi waded her way through some chicken, Chinese, and pizza while I settled for chicken and fries. Afterward we tried the ice cream place, where I had a simple cone while she had a banana-boat surprise.

During the course of the day much of the toughness left her, and she relaxed more. I believe she really had a good time with me, as I did with her—in spite of the fact that I was carrying all of the packages. She did her shopping with a credit card that she wielded like a double-edged sword, cutting a swath through large department store and small clothing shop alike. She said she'd left her oversized bag behind when she escaped from DiVolo, but she didn't keep her credit card in there, anyway.

Over the ice cream she said, "Thanks, Nick."

"For what?"

"For this. You could have taken me out, let me buy some jeans and a top, and dragged me back to your place."

"You're going to be cooped up some until this is over, Jodi," I said. "Don't let this fool you, but I did want to give you some time out."

"And now it's over?"

"I'm afraid so. I'll have to take you back and then get to work."

"What happened at your father's?"

The question surprised me, and I decided to answer her.

"My father blames me for not going over to Beirut and getting my sister back."

"But that's crazy!"

"I know it...but he's got to get mad at somebody, and I'm an easy target. It's always been easy for him to get mad at me."

"I know how that feels, but what about your brother?"

"How do you get mad and pop off at a priest? We'd better get back."

"Are you going to leave me with Sam again?"

"I don't think so. I get the feeling you two will never be the best of friends."

"Well, we're both blondes."

"What's that got to do with it?"

She shrugged and said, "We just started off on the wrong foot, that's all."

"Well, I've got someplace else to take you, and we can go there from here."

As we stood up, I stopped suddenly, and she said, "What's the matter?"

"I just thought of something."

"What?"

"Where's your car?"

She even had to stop and think, but then she said what I had been afraid she was going to say.

"It's out in Westchester."

"Great," I said. "I guess I'll be going out to Westchester, after all."

29

"Who lives here?" she asked.

We were in front of a three-story building at Eighth Street and Seventh Avenue in Park Slope, a better than decent neighborhood that was not only residential, but had a lot of doctors' offices in the area. In fact, Methodist Hospital was only a couple of blocks away.

"A friend of mine, a computer nut who goes by the name of Hacker."

"A guy?"

"A guy I trust, so don't be thinking that he'll make any moves on you just because you're in the same apartment. He rarely comes out of his computer room."

We went up to the door, and I rang Hacker's bell.

"Who?" his voice squawked from the box.

"Nick."

"Hey, Nicky D. Come on up!"

"I've got a lady with me, Hacker, so clean up."

"That would take a month," his tinny voice called back, "but I'll give it my best shot."

He buzzed the door open, and we went in.

While we were walking to the third floor, she asked, "Why do you call him Hacker?"

"It's some kind of a computer term that he can explain to you better than I can, but in addition to that he hates his real name."

"What is it?"

"Wild horses couldn't tear it out of me. He'd tap into an IRS computer and have me audited every year for the rest of my life."

When we got to the door, it was ajar. I knocked, and we walked right in.

"Jesus," Jodi said.

The apartment was a mass of literature: stacks and stacks of magazines, literally rows of them, and all of them computer magazines. Most of the stacks were six feet high or less, but every so often there was one that was floor to ceiling, and these were usually made up of smaller stacks that were tied together.

"This would be the living room, if you could see it," I said. "Kitchen's over there, bedroom there, and that's Hacker's room over there. He's got a daybed in there, so you'll be using the bedroom."

"You know this place pretty well, don't you?"

"We shared it for a while," I said. What I didn't tell her was that Hacker took me in after I had to leave the department, because I couldn't pay my rent. I lived with him for four months until I found the place on Sackett Street.

"I'll get him."

I put down Jodi's packages and walked to the door of his room to pound on it with the flat of my hand.

"Hacker! Come on, man, you've got company."

The door opened almost immediately, and Hacker stepped out. I knew that on the other side of the door was a collection of computer parts—pieces from different systems—that he had set up into one of the most elaborate computer systems privately owned.

"Hacker, this is Jodi."

"Hello."

"Hi."

Hacker was about my age, but he was what was commonly known when we were in school as a nerd. All that meant was that he was one of the smarter kids in school who always had something on his mind and consequently gave little thought to things like his appearance.

He was tall, dark-haired, sallow-skinned, and painfully thin. He wore dark-framed glasses and a quick, contagious smile. He was a sweetheart of a guy, and I loved him like a brother.

"What's up?"

"She needs a safe place to stay, Hack."

"My friend," he said to Jodi, pointing to me. "Every time a woman needs a 'safe' place to stay he brings her to me. Tell me, do I look that harmless?"

"You look like a pussycat."

"I like this girl, Nicky."

"I thought you would."

I turned to Jodi and said, "Do whatever Hacker tells you to do. You can trust him like you trust me."

"Ha!" Hacker said, but he tempered it with a wink in her direction.

"You keep your hands on your keyboard, Hacker."

"Can she cook?"

"She made me breakfast."

"Then you're most welcome, ma'am. I'm real tired of eating out of boxes and bags."

"I'll see what I can do."

Such was the degree of our friendship that I didn't have to do any explaining to Hacker.

"Walk me to the door," I said to Jodi.

At the door she said, "Nick, he looks like a nerd."

"He doesn't happen to think that's something he should apologize for, Jodi. He's a good guy, and he'd go to hell and back for a friend."

"How many friends does he have?"

"Me," I said, "and if you play your cards right, you."

"When will you be back?"

"Later today."

"And then we'll go back to your place?"

"I don't know, maybe we'll just all stay here. We'll talk about it later."

"You're going to Westchester?"

"Yes, and that reminds me. Give me the keys to your car." She reached into her new jeans and handed them over. "Hacker," I said over her shoulder, "I need your car."

"Treat it gentle," he said, tossing me his keys.

"Or it'll fall apart," I added. I looked at Jodi and said, "The man drives a '77 Grand Prix that's got a hundred thousand plus on it."

"If you treat her nice, she runs fine."

"I'll treat her so nice she won't want to come back to you. Do me a favor while I'm gone."

"Like what?"

"Entertain this young lady. Show her some of your little toys."

"Sure thing."

"See you later, Jodi."

When I left, Hacker was telling her he was going to show her a computer no bigger than her purse—if she'd had a purse.

30

It took a lot of driving around, asking directions, and wrong turns, but I finally found Jodi's car parked down the block from James Berry's house. Actually, it was more than a house and just a little less than an estate. The grounds were enclosed by a black wrought-iron fence, and the house appeared to be two stories, with a Victorian slant to it. The front door still had a police department crime-scene seal on it.

I made a circuit of the block to see if anyone was watching Jodi's car, then parked Hacker's green Grand Prix a few hundred feet behind it because I didn't want the Prix and Jodi's sporty job seen together.

After leaving Hacker's house, I had driven to a pay phone and made a call to a man named Plummer. Plummer is not a friend, but he is somebody I use to do odd jobs for me. Over the phone I gave him the address out in Westchester and told him to meet me there. The reason I needed Plummer was because I was one man and could not drive two cars.

I got out of the Grand Prix and walked back up to Jodi's car. I looked around, but there was no sign of Plummer, and it was then I got the idea of going into the house.

Or maybe I'd intended to all along.

Anyway, I found a likely stretch of fence that was covered by trees and made my climb. Happily, James Berry had not been paranoid enough to go in for an electrified model. When I dropped down to the other side, I waited to see what would happen—alarms, dogs, whatever—but apparently Mr. Berry hadn't had a paranoid bone in his body. When nothing did happen, I started moving.

I reached the house without incident and circled it carefully, looking for an easy way in. The best way appeared to be a pair of French doors. I peered inside and guessed that this was Berry's study. There was a desk which must have been where he was found.

I was wondering how I was going to get inside when the door I was leaning against swung inward. A quick look at the lock told me that I wasn't the only one wanting to get inside. Someone had been here ahead of me, picked the lock, and left the door open on their way out. Then I remembered what Jodi had said about breaking in, and wondered if this was her work.

There were two other possibilities.

One, somebody else—DiVolo, Terry Jacks, maybe Tony Macaroni himself, but *somebody*—had been there ahead of me looking for the art piece.

Two, the house had simply been burglarized, maybe by someone who watched the obits.

Whichever way it went, there didn't seem to be any good reason to go inside and look around, but I was there, so I went in.

It occurred to me to safeguard my prints, but the place had already been dusted. I started with Berry's desk, the blotter of which had a very large bloodstain on it. I went through the drawers and found a lot of papers and reports which, if I had seen them earlier and had the money to invest initially, could have ended up making me a lot.

I was about to replace the folder I was holding when something jumped out at me through the closed cover. It was as if I had seen it, passed over it, and was suddenly seeing it again. I opened the folder again for a second look, and sure enough, the reports in this particular folder had been prepared by the investment firm of Fielding & Wilder.

That was the company my brother-in-law worked for on Wall Street.

Shit.

I replaced the folder and slowly closed the drawer. I moved out of the study to look through the rest of the house, pushing all thoughts of my brother-in-law to the back of my mind for the time being.

I checked drawers and cabinets, but it was obvious that they had been gone through before by somebody who knew what he was doing. Upstairs there were four bedrooms, but only one looked like it had been lived in. I went through Berry's dresser drawers and found nothing. Either anything to be found had already been found by someone else, or there *was* nothing to be found.

The house was filled with art: paintings, sculptures, several pieces to a room rather than all collected in one room. From what I could see, his pieces were far superior to what Tony Macaroni had in his house, but then I knew next to nothing about art.

I left the house, thinking about the deceased James Berry.

There was a possibility here that I didn't remember considering—but then my mind wasn't one hundred percent on this case. Whether I had thought about it before or not, I was thinking about it now.

What if James Berry's murder had nothing to do with Jodi's doughnut? True, the doughnut statue was not in the house, but Berry could have bought it and then sold it himself. He could have been killed for an entirely different, totally unconnected reason.

Which would really fuck things up.

I wondered if whoever did have the piece knew what they had, because I sure as hell didn't.

Outside, after retracing my steps, I found Plummer standing by the Grand Prix, which was the car I had described to him.

Plummer was forty-five or so, with thinning hair the color of a gray mouse and skin to match. He was an extremely un-healthy-looking individual, and would probably outlive me because he was also one of the luckiest people I knew.

"Plummer."

He whirled around, eyes wide, and then relaxed when he saw me. He was wearing jeans and a yellow T-shirt that said "Canal Hi Fi" on it. It also had some Chinese writing on it, which might have also said "Canal Hi Fi." I didn't know, and I didn't ask.

"Delvecchio, you scared the shit out of me, man." He tapped the hood of the Prix and asked, "Is this the rust bucket you want me to drive back to Brooklyn?"

"This is it," I said, handing him the key. "Treat it gentle. I promised the owner I would."

"Be gentle with it? The kindest thing to do would be to take it out and shoot it. Hey, I tried to get ahold of you the other day. Why don't you get a secretary, or an answering machine?"

"They both cost money. What did you want?"

"I had a good exacta for you."

"Did it come in?"

"Of course it came in. The top horse paid twenty, but the exacta only paid ninety. They're playing games out there, I'm telling you."

"Nothing we can do about it, Plum."

"Yeah, I know. Uh, by the way, what are you payin' me for this ride?"

"Walking-around money."

"Forty?"

"Twenty."

He looked like I had just scalded him with hot water, and screeched. "That's all?"

"Look at it this way. You can put it on another exacta and turn it into nine hundred."

"Sure, sure. Can I get started? I been standing here for twenty minutes. It don't look good. Somebody's bound to call the cops."

"Look how far back from the street the houses are, Plum, and how much space is between them. How could someone see you standing here, unless they were looking for you?"

"I just get antsy being in one place for too long. Can I split?"

I had always suspected Plummer of having been a hippie in the Sixties, because every so often his speech pattern would fall into that time period.

"Yeah, okay, get going, Plum. Here's the address." I handed him a slip of paper with Hacker's address. "Just park the car as close to it as possible and leave the keys in the glove compartment." I reached into my shirt pocket and pulled out the twenty I had put there for him.

"Here's the twenty. Get going."

"You got it."

He got in the car, started it up, and peeled out, leaving some rubber behind. For a guy who didn't want to be noticed, he was a lousy driver.

I walked up the road to Jodi's car, climbed in, and fit the key into the ignition. I didn't turn it on because it was then that my brother-in-law's name finally came back to the forefront of my somewhat addled and confused brain. I hadn't wanted to stop and think about him while I was in the house. Shit, I never wanted to think about him, but I did now.

Fielding & Wilder was a big enough company, even though they were no E.F. Hutton. It shouldn't be any great surprise to find that a man of Berry's wealth was one of their clients.

The surprise had come at the top of one of the F & W statements, the box where it said, "Your Account Executive is"—and then it said, "Peter Geller."

Numbnuts.

31

I used it as an excuse to go see him. I drove to my sister's house in Bay Ridge, and used my key to get in. It was a key Maria had given me when she first got married, and Numbnuts didn't know anything about it.

When I got inside, something I'd often suspected about my brother-in-law was confirmed.

The man was a pig!

I mean, I'm not the world's greatest housekeeper myself, but this dude was the pits.

The kitchen was a mass of take-out cartons and bags, and filled-to-the-brim garbage bags. Out of respect for my sister, I cleaned up the mess while I waited for Peter to get home.

I was looking out the front window when he showed up, walking at a brisk pace. Today seemed to be a day that he came straight home from work, but then it was Friday. Who knew what plans he had for the evening.

Whatever they were, I was going to change them.

I saw him pause when he saw the pile of plastic garbage bags in front of the house. He looked at the house with a strange expression on his face, and it was then I realized that he thought Maria was home.

The man did not look pleased.

He started up the walk slowly, and for a second I thought he was going to stop and turn around. I went to the front door and opened it, staring at him through the screen door.

"Come on in, Petey. We have a lot to talk about."

"What the hell—" he said.

I opened the screen door for him, and he came up the steps slowly.

"How the hell did you get in?"

Did I mention that my brother-in-law doesn't like me any more than I like him?

"I used my key."

He walked past me, then turned and said, "She gave you a key?"

"That's right."

"I expressly forbade her to give you a key." He said, "For Bad."

"Tough shit."

"What do you want?"

"I want to talk."

"I've got nothing to say to you."

He threw his briefcase on the couch and took off his jacket. He tossed it toward a chair and it missed, landing on the floor.

Every time I had ever seen him he was the very picture of the successful young businessman: tall, about six-one, and physically fit. With his blonde hair, blue eyes, and fair skin, he didn't look at all Jewish. I always suspected that he bleached his hair.

It was his looks that first attracted my sister to him, but for the life of me I couldn't understand what hooked her beyond that.

"Do your clients know what a slob you really are?"

"Look, Nick, I'd like you to leave before I throw you out. You have no right here."

"Go ahead," I said, feeling like Clint Eastwood, "throw me out." Yeah, I almost said, "Make my day."

His muscles tensed, and I could see him considering it. My violent past may have had something to do with his decision to back off, but I'd like to think he was just a coward.

"Where've you been, Peter? You haven't been to see my father."

"Why should I go and see the old man? We hate each other."

"Out of respect."

"Respect," he said, making the word sound dirty.

"You don't seem all broken up about Maria being on that plane."

"There's nothing I can do about it."

"Sure there is," I said, "again in the name of respect. You could stop seeing your dollies."

"My what?"

On the way to the house I had stopped and called Jacoby at Bogie's. He said that the clerk at Howard Johnson's confirmed that my brother-in-law was there at least three times a week with his little girlfriend—and he said that she wasn't the first.

"Your girlfriend, Petey, the little girl in your office you fuck during lunch."

His eyes narrowed as he thought it over.

"Did Maria ask you to follow me?"

"She's in Beirut, you asshole."

"I mean before she left. Was it you—"

"I didn't know anything about it until yesterday. Did she know? Is that why she went away?"

"Why she left is our business, not yours."

"Wrong," I said, taking a step toward him. "I'm making it my business. If she dies over there, Peter, I want you to know that I hold you responsible, and I'll make your life a living hell."

"You—you can't threaten me."

"Open your eyes, fuckhead. I just did."

But he didn't give up that easy.

"You can't talk to me like I was one of your...your..."

"Scumbags. That's the word you're looking for, Peter, like one of the scumbags I deal with on the street, and you're wrong. I will talk to you like a scumbag because that's what you are to me. I've put up with your shit because of Maria, but Maria's not here now. You're not family, Peter, no matter what it says on your marriage certificate."

I took two more steps and planted a rigid forefinger right into his breastbone, hard! He flinched and took a backward step.

"I'm going to tell you a few things now, and you're going to listen. Number one, while my sister is in the hands of the terrorists, you're going to carry on like a worried, loving husband. You'll keep in touch with my father and brother, and you'll come straight home from work every night and stay home. Number two, you won't be spending any more lunch hours at Howard Johnson's—or at any hotel—banging little girl clerks. You got that?"

"I don't know who you think you are—"

I hit him a short one in the stomach, hard enough to drive the air out of him. He doubled up, hugging himself, and I bent over so he could hear me real good.

"As far as you're concerned, motherfucker, I'm God. You'll do what I say, just as if I had passed some commandments down to you. You got that, scumbag?"

He glared at me through teary eyes and nodded. I decided to play on my violent history.

"I'd just as soon kill you as look at you, you bastard, but out of respect for my sister I'm going to leave you alive at least until she comes back. After that it's up to her."

I could tell by the way he was looking at me that he wasn't sure whether to believe me or not.

"Straighten up, now," I said, moving away from him. "I didn't hit you that hard."

He made a try at straightening, gasped, and then tried again and succeeded. He stood there rubbing his stomach.

"I always thought you were crazy, Nick, but now I know it."

"Careful," I said, wagging a finger at him, "you might make me mad. Do you understand all the conditions I just gave you?"

"Yeah, I understand. Now you can get the hell out of here."

"Speaking of here," I said, "when my sister comes home I want this house to be spotless. I don't care if you do it yourself or have somebody come in, but it better be done."

"Are you through playing tough guy?"

"Almost. Do you know a man named James Berry?"

"James Ber—what's he got to do with Maria?"

"Nothing. This is something else. Do you know him?"

"He's a client."

"He's also dead. What do you know about that?"

"Dead? What?" The look of confusion on his face could only be genuine.

"You don't read the papers?"

Looking dumbstruck, he shook his head.

"He was shot to death in his house. You wouldn't know anything about that, would you, Peter?"

"How would I know something like that?"

"Listen, haven't the cops been to see you?"

"No—the cops, why?"

"Well, there are financial reports on his desk with your name on them."

"My name?"

"I'm surprised they didn't see it, but then again, it could always be brought to their attention—"

"Nick, wait, I don't want to talk to the police—"

"Why not? Have you got something to hide?"

"No, of course not."

"Then why not?"

He was still rubbing his stomach, as if in a bid for sympathy. It was the wrong tack to take with the guy who had hit him in the first place.

"Well, you of all people should know that I don't like cops."

"Oh, really? And I thought it was just ex-cops named Delvecchio."

"No, look, see—"

"Nolooksee? Is that the way young upwardly mobile executives are talking these days?"

"Nick, let me finish—"

"You are finished, friend. I won't give the police your name if you'll do something for me."

His face brightened, and he even forgot about rubbing his stomach.

"What?"

"I want to know whatever you can find out about James Berry."

"Like what?"

"Like was he in financial trouble, was he seeing somebody's wife, what was he into that might have got him killed? Oh, and did he collect art?"

"Well, he did collect art, I can tell you that. He haunted antique shops and hockshops, hoping to find something he could buy cheap and sell at a profit."

"That's the kind of stuff I want to know."

"Well—"

"But not now. Gather it up, and I'll give you a call. I'm hoping I won't need it, but if I do, I want to be able to reach you, so make sure you're always by a phone. Give me your business number."

He reached into his pocket, came out with a small gold case, and handed me one of his business cards.

"How many hot little numbers have you given this to?"

"None. I've never given out my home number."
"Sure, you're a real homebody."
"No, I'm not, but then neither is your sister."
"What?"
"Nothing..."
"No, no, never mind 'nothing.' You started to say something, now finish it."
"You'll hit me again."
"I won't."
He looked at me dubiously.
"I won't!" I insisted.
"Well...I wasn't the first one in this marriage to be unfaithful."
"What?" I asked, as if I hadn't heard him the first time.
"Your sister, Maria," he said carefully, "was fucking around first."
I hit him.

32

"You said you wouldn't hit me!"
He was sitting on the floor with a bloody mouth, and I couldn't hit him again unless I picked him up.
"Don't hit me again," he said as I hauled him to his feet.
"You're a liar, man!"
"I'm not!" he said. "Four months after we were married she was having an affair with a guy down the street. A month after that it was her aerobics instructor, and a month after that the mechanic who works on our car."
"And you stayed with her?"
He shrugged.
"The head of my firm likes to promote married account executives."
"Which is why you married Maria in the first place."
"Yes."
"And when she found out about it, she began having affairs."
"Well...yes."
"So it still all falls in your lap, shithead. We're back to square one." I pushed him away from me, and he staggered against a table. "The marriage is falling apart because it never should have happened."
He had the good sense to look embarrassed, and I hated to think that he might not be all bad.
"Look," I said, pointing a finger at him. "I'm not kidding, Peter. You stay clean until Maria gets back and we can clear this up."

"Do you think she's coming back?" His tone clearly implied that he didn't.
"She'll be back, and I don't want to hear different, understand?"
"Sure, sure..."
"Now you stay by a phone at all times until you hear from me."
"What about lunch?"
"Have it at your desk."
"I have meetings—"
"Leave a number where you can be reached—and if I find out it's a hotel—"
"It won't be a hotel," he said wearily.

He wiped a smear of blood away from his mouth with the back of his hand, then looked around for someplace to wipe that.

"I'm sorry I hit you the second time," I said, "but don't think I won't break your fucking head if—"

"There's no need for your garbage mouth," he said. "I understand."

I stared at him, wondering what would happen if anyone ever said "fuck" within the hallowed halls of the office he worked at.

"Okay, but remember this, too. If Maria doesn't come back, it's going to be the saddest day of your life—for all the wrong reasons."

He stared at me, then wiped his hand across his mouth again, nervously.

"Later, Pete."

I started for the door, then turned around and faced him again.

"Oh, one more thing."

"What?"

"I'd better not see your face on *Good Morning America* or anything."

"How did you know—"

"I don't want you cashing in on my sister's situation, Peter. It would be a very bad idea to try and do that, believe me."

I left him standing in the middle of the living room looking at the blood on the back of his hand.

I walked to Jodi's car and climbed in. For the second time that day I was trying not to think about my brother-in-law, this time what he'd had to say about my sister.

I looked at myself in the rear-view mirror, slapped my own face, and said mockingly, "You garbage mouth, you."

It was getting late when I drove away from my sister's house and I had two choices: either go to my father's and call Jodi on the phone at Hacker's, or go to Hacker's and call my brother.

I decided to go to Hacker's. My father and brother might not have been happy at the moment, but they were quite safe from any sort of physical harm.

The same could not be said for Jodi Hayworth.

The set-to with my brother-in-law had only served to overburden my mind further. I could not quite reconcile myself to the picture he'd painted of my sister as the cheating wife. Oh, not that she wasn't attractive. There had been a time, however, where she had been an almost perfect Catholic. The first crack in that perfection had been marrying Peter Geller, and now, if my brother-in-law was to be believed, the second was adultery.

I hoped that wherever she was, she had not forgotten how to pray.

33

I found a parking spot for Jodi's car at one end of the block, then located Hacker's Grand Prix at the other end and removed the keys from the glove compartment. Then I walked to his house and rang his bell.

"Who is it?"

"It's Nick," I said into the intercom.

"Go away," Hacker said, "we're fornicating."

"That's okay, I only want to watch."

"In that case, come on up."

When I got to the third floor, the door was open, and cooking smells were wafting out into the hall.

"What's cooking?" I bellowed as I entered.

"Beef stew," Jodi shouted from Hacker's kitchen. "My own recipe."

I entered the kitchen and looked into the pot from over her shoulder. It looked delicious. The table was set with three places. There was a bowl of salad in the center, and a basket of Italian bread.

"Wait a minute," I said, knowing how well stocked Hacker kept his cupboard. "Where did all this stuff come from?"

"We went out and got it."

"I told you to stay inside."

"You told me," she said slowly, "to do what Hacker told me to do."

"And he told you to go out?"

"He told me to cook him a meal the likes of which he had never seen before, and that's what I'm doing. Besides, he went with me."

I stepped back and pretended to take a long look at her. She was wearing an apron that said "Computers Do It Better."

"Is this the tough little girl who came to see me a couple of weeks ago?"

"So I'm tough," she said, lifting her chin. "That doesn't mean I can't cook."

"Of course not. Where's the genius?"

"In his room. Tell him that dinner will be ready in five minutes."

"I'll tell him."

I went to the door of Hacker's room and knocked.

"That you, dear?" he called out.

"Yes, it's me."

"Come on in."

Every time I entered his room I felt privileged, because I knew he never let anyone else in there.

He was seated at an elaborate console, looking at a green screen with green print on it.

"How can you stare at that day after day and not go blind?"

"What?" he asked, turning to face me. He was doing something he used to do when we were in school together. He had rolled his eyes all the way up so that only the whites were showing.

"Very funny. Jodi says dinner will be ready in five minutes."

"She's a gem, that one."

"Why'd you take her out?"

"I was hungry."

"Hacker—"

"We only went to the comer, Nick, and nobody knows she's here, right? What's the harm—and smell that cooking!"

I inhaled and couldn't argue with that logic.

"Just don't do it again, huh?"

"Sure."

"We'd better go and eat."

"Nick—" he said, grabbing my arm.

"Yeah?"

"We haven't talked—I mean, about Maria…"

"We don't have to, Hack," I said, putting my hand on his arm. "We're friends. I know how you feel, so why embarrass both of us by trying to put it into words. You know how hopeless you are with words."

"Wait," he said. He turned to the console, cleared it, and punched up some keys. On the screen these words appeared: IF THERE IS ANYTHING I CAN DO TO HELP…

"I know, Wilbur," I said, "I know."

He hit another key and these words appeared: DON'T…CALL…ME…WILBUR!

"Nobody likes a wise guy, Wil—Hacker."

***

After dinner—enough of which we all consumed to stuff six normal people, and *still* there was some left over—Hacker stood up and said, "I've got some work to do in my room now, and then I'll turn in. Jodi, that was a wonderful dinner, and I can't thank you enough."

"I'll put the rest away in the refrigerator for you, Hacker."

"What a good girl." He punched me on the arm and said, "Nicky D., you spending the night?"

"I don't think so, Hack. I'll see you in the morning. Make sure you lock your door, I don't want this lovely young lady to be tempted."

"If she only could…" he said, wistfully. "Good night." After he left, I helped Jodi clear the table and put everything away.

"Are you leaving now?" she asked.

"After I make a call, which I should have made before we ate."

"Your father?"

"Yes."

"I wish there was something I could do to help, Nick…"

"You've got enough problems of your own to worry about, Jodi."

"Yeah, well, so do you, but you're taking time to help me with mine."

"It's my job."

"Sure."

I went to the kitchen wall phone and dialed my father's number.

"Vinnie—" I said when my brother answered, but he cut me off before I could say another word.

"Where the hell have you been, Nick? I've been calling everywhere!"

"Did something happen to Maria?"

"Not Maria," he said. "Pop."

"What's the matter with Pop?"

"He collapsed, Nick. He's at Maimonides Hospital."

34

Maimonides Hospital was on Fort Hamilton Parkway in the forties. I convinced Jodi to stay at Hacker's, and she convinced me to take her car. I had borrowed more cars during these past few days…

Vinnie had gotten back there ahead of me, and I was surprised to see Sam there as well.

"What are you doing here?"

"Father Vincent called my apartment looking for you. When he told me what happened, I came right over."

"I'm glad you're here." I looked at Vinnie and asked, "What does the doctor say?"

"Pop'll be all right."

"What happened to him?"

"He's worn himself out, Nick, with worry, not keeping up his strength—"

"I thought you were seeing to it that he ate."

I hadn't meant it to sound like an accusation, but he responded as if it was.

"What do you expect me to do, force-feed him?"

"I didn't mean that—"

"Don't start arguing," Sam said, "not here in the hospital."

We both looked at her and then at each other.

"I didn't mean to accuse you."

"That's all right."

"Is Dr. Leary here?"

"Leary retired last year," Vinnie said. "Pop's doctor is Dr. Resner now."

"Resner? I don't know him."

"I recommended him to Pop. He's not Catholic, but he lives in my parish."

"When can Pop go home?"

"I've explained the situation to Dr. Resner, about Maria. He thinks we leave Pop here until the crisis is over so they can keep an eye on him."

"Good idea."

"Will your father go for that?" Sam asked.

Vinnie and I exchanged glances, and then I said, "He doesn't have to. We'll go for it."

"Here comes the doctor," Vinnie said.

Dr. Resner was a large man with a round, protruding belly that seemed as hard as a boulder, and a balding head. He appeared to be in his early forties.

"Doctor, this is my brother, Nicholas."

"Nice to meet you," Resner said, and we shook hands.

"How's my father, Doc?"

"He's resting. I've given him a sedative that will help him sleep tonight."

"Can I see him?"

"I don't think so. He's asleep already, and he needs his rest. Perhaps by tomorrow morning this terrible ordeal will be over."

"I doubt it," Vinnie said.

"Why?" I asked.

"Pop was watching television, Nick. It was when they announced that the hostages had been removed from the plane that he collapsed."

I kept quiet, not being the type to say "I told you so," but my brother could read my face pretty well.

"I see," the doctor said. "Well, I still think the best thing for him is to stay here where someone can keep an eye on him at all times."

"All right, Doctor," Vinnie said.

"He'll be yelling for a television in the morning," I said.

"Well, he'll have to pay to get one. Are you leaving him any money?"

"I haven't got any money, have you?" I asked Vinnie.

"Not a cent," my brother the father lied.

"Then he'll have to wait until one of you boys gets here and pays for it."

"Thank you, Doctor," Vinnie said, extending his hand.

"My pleasure, Father. I like your father very much and I'd like to help him through this."

"We appreciate it," I said.

He nodded, said good night to Sam, and walked away.

"Vinnie, where will you be?"

"I'll stay at the house, Nick, just in case we get some kind of call."

"All right. I'm going home."

"Can you give me a ride?" Sam asked. "I had to take a cab. Somebody forgot to fill my car with gas."

"Jesus, I'm sorry, Sam—"

"Never mind. Just give me a ride home."

"Sure."

We started for the front entrance, and then I froze.

"What is it?" Vinnie asked.

He looked where I was looking and saw the same thing I was seeing. Dominick Barracondi—Nicky Barracuda—walking in the front door...alone.

"Nick, Father Vincent. I came as soon as I heard." His tone was solicitous.

"Who called you?" I asked.

"I still have friends on your father's block, Nick."

That meant that somebody called him when they saw Pop being carted out to the ambulance.

"Pop's asleep, Mr. Barracondi," Vinnie said.

"That's all right, Father. I just want to talk to his doctor."

"About what?" I asked.

He looked at me and smiled, his teeth impossibly white for a man his age. They had to be capped.

"Your family has enough to worry about as it is, Nick, without having to be concerned with a hospital bill. I intend to take care of that."

"Is this another favor?" For a moment, as his eyes flashed and his smile slipped, I thought that maybe I had gone too far.

"This is something I want to do, Nick, for an old friend and his family. Allow me that privilege."

"Mr. Barracondi—" Vinnie started, but I cut him off.

"Whatever you say...Uncle Dominick."

He smiled without revealing his teeth, and for a moment he looked old, like one of the old men in the Italian club, drinking wine and reliving their pasts.

"Thank you, Nicholas."

He walked past us then, and I didn't know if he was thanking me for letting him foot the bill or for calling him Uncle.

Shit, I don't even know why I *did* call him that. Maybe I believed he was sincere in what he said.

He was still smooth, after all these years.

"What a charming man," Sam said. "Nick, was that really—"

"Yeah," I said, cutting her off and taking her by the arm, "that was my godfather."

We all walked out together, and then we walked Vinnie to his car before going to Jodi's.

"Nice car," Sam said, getting in. "Is it hers?"

"Yes."

"Is she at your place?"

"No, she's somewhere safe."

"And you? Are you going to stay somewhere safe?"

"I'm staying in my apartment."

"Well, that's smart." Needless to say, she was being sarcastic.

"If they come for me again, Sam, I'll be ready, this time."

"Good," she said, "maybe this time you'll kill both of them, or all three, or however many they send."

"I won't kill anyone, I'll just find out what the hell is going on."

"You still don't know? She hasn't told you?" "She" came out like a dirty word.

"What do you mean?"

"Just what I said, are you sure she's telling you the truth?"

"I think so."

"You think so."

I looked at her and saw that her jaw was firmly set. "What's wrong?"

"You're letting that girl take you for a ride, Nick."

"What did she say to you?"

"Oh, nothing about the case. She just wanted to let me know in no uncertain terms that you were sleeping together."

"We're not...sleeping together."

"Oh? You didn't have sex with her?"

"Once," I said, and then immediately realized I'd made a mistake. I said, "Well, twice," and then realized saying that was a mistake, too.

"Well..." she said, and fell silent.

When we got to our building, we walked up to our floor. "Well" had been the last thing either one of us said.

"Sam, thanks for being at the hospital."

"Sure," she said, fishing in her bag for her key.

"About Jodi—"

"You don't have to explain anything to me, Nick. You're a big boy. I'm sure you can take care of yourself."

"Well..." I said, but she opened her door and went through, shutting it behind her without saying good night.

What was she so pissed at?

I unlocked my door, reached in and flicked on the light switch, and then went in quickly.

Empty.

I locked the door behind me, went into my office, and sat at my desk. I rubbed my face a couple of times with both hands, then took my gun out of the drawer and put it on top of the desk. It would be a good idea from now on if I kept it on me.

The last thing I remember before falling asleep at my desk was thinking that I had a holster in my desk somewhere.

35

It was morning, and somebody was trying to knock down the door to my office, which woke me—for which I was thankful. I'd been having a nightmare to end all nightmares, all about my sister and my father and Jodi and Sam and Hacker and a band of terrorists who were going to kill them if I didn't give them each a doughnut—and Father Vinnie wouldn't give me the money to buy doughnuts.

I sat up straight in my chair and caught myself reaching for my gun. I almost took it with me to the door, but some sixth sense told me to put it away in my desk. I opened a drawer other than the one it had been in before, and there was the holster that went with it. I fitted it into the holster, a clip-on belt type, and closed the drawer.

I went to the door and opened it. It occurred to me that if there was somebody on the other side who meant me harm, they wouldn't be knocking.

I was almost wrong.

"Matucci," I said, taking a step back. "What do you want?"

"Your ass, scumbag," he said. He moved into the room and his partner, Weinstock, came in behind him, looking embarrassed as always.

"I didn't know you went that way."

"I don't, dickhead, but you're going my way. Come on, let's go."

He reached for my arm, and I yanked it away from him.

"I just woke up, Matucci, and I haven't had my oatmeal yet. Can't this wait?"

"Murder don't wait, Delvecchio."

"Murder? Whose murder?"

Weinstock finally deigned to speak.

"We've received some information that you might be involved with a murder that went down in Westchester a couple of weeks ago. We'd like you to come with us to the precinct to answer a few questions, please."

"Now you see," I said to Matucci, "his mother taught him manners—but then, his mother also allowed him in the house."

"Cut the crap and let's go, Delvecchio."

Looking over Matucci's head—which pissed him off because it was so easy to do—I said to Weinstock, "Would you and your partner mind waiting for me in the hall while I freshen up? I answer questions a lot better when I'm not feeling so grungy."

"When is a private dick not grungy?" Matucci wanted to know.

"Private dick," I said to Weinstock. "He's been watching George Raft movies again."

"Come on, partner," Weinstock said, plucking Matucci's sleeve. "Let's wait in the hall while the man washes up."

"Sure," Matucci said, "and he goes out the other door."

"What's he gonna run for? All we want is to ask a few questions. So we'll watch the other door, too."

"Look, Weinstock—"

"Excuse me, fellas, but can you take this show on the road? I'll be right out, I promise."

"Don't fuck around!" Matucci said.

"Oh, no sir, detective, I wouldn't think of it."

They went out into the hall, and I closed the door behind them.

I had no intentions of trying to run away. Weinstock was right, all I had to do was answer their questions—that is, Lieutenant Wager's questions—and then I'd walk.

I went into the bathroom, removed my shirt, and started to wash up.

Of course, it didn't escape my notice that they had received a tip—and probably an anonymous one, at that—that I had some information about a murder in Westchester.

And who could have made such a call, I asked myself as I dried off.

Why, Numbnuts himself, my brother-in-law.

That asshole.

I got a fresh shirt out of my bedroom and slipped into it.

He was so reluctant to talk to the cops, what made him think that I wouldn't turn around and give the cops his name?

I mean, I wouldn't, but what made him think so?

That was easy.

He didn't know.

He'd simply made a dumb play that wasn't going to pan out—and when I finished with Wager, I'd let him know in no uncertain terms.

Feeling slightly less grungy, I went to my office door and opened it. I stepped into the hall next to Weinstock and asked, "Where's Matucci?"

Weinstock inclined his head to where Matucci was standing, further down the hall, in front of my apartment door.

"Oh you," I said, chastising him. "You just have no faith in anyone, do you?"

Looking disappointed that I hadn't tried to get away, giving him a chance to shoot me in the leg or someplace equally painful, he came slinking down the hall.

"Come on, come on..." he said, passing us.

I fixed Weinstock with a stern look and said, "Well, come on, come on!"

Wager was waiting impatiently in his cubicle.

"Sit down, Delvecchio."

"I want to commend these boys on their manner and class, Lieutenant," I said, taking a seat. "The little one there, the one who was too busy running his mouth to stand in line when God was giving out height, he didn't call me but three or four four-letter words all the way over here."

"Listen, you smart-mouthed fuck—" Matucci started.

"Ah, you ruined it!" I scolded him. Looking at Wager, I grinned and said, "That's five."

Wager fixed Matucci with a glare and said, "Get out."

"Yes sir."

Weinstock, ever the smart one, left with him without being told.

"What can I do for you, Lieutenant?"

"What do you know about a murder in Westchester?"

"I don't know anything about murder, Lieutenant."

"We got a call that said otherwise."

"Oh? And who called?"

"That's not for you to know."

"Oh, anonymous, huh? You guys putting credence in those kinds of calls now?"

Looking annoyed, Wager said, "We're just checking it out, giving Westchester a hand."

"Do they need one?"

"They're not getting very far—" he started to say, then seemed to realize who he was talking to. "Never mind. You sure you don't know anything about it?"

"If you'd fill me in on some details—"

"Never mind," he said. "I've got enough work of my own without filling you in on the details of a two-week-old murder case that wasn't mine to begin with. Go on, get your ass out of here."

"Sure," I said, getting up and heading for the door, "and you're welcome."

"For what?"

"I thought I heard you say something like…'Thanks for coming.'"

"Get out."

I shrugged and said, "Close enough."

36

I went back home, entered by the office door to be on the safe side, and took a shower. Dripping, with a towel around my waist, I called my brother-in-law's office.

He came on the line and said, "Geller."

"Hello, Numbnuts."

"Nick? W-where are you calling from?"

"Not from the slammer, if that's what you expected."

"Why would I—"

"Can the crap, Petey. You called the cops—my old precinct, too—and left an anonymous tip that I knew something about a murder in Westchester. Lucky for both of us the message was taken by an incompetent and overworked lieutenant."

"Nick, I didn't—"

"You were so anxious that I not give your name to the cops yesterday, Petey, didn't it occur to you that I might throw you to them today?"

There was a long silent period, and then he said, "I didn't think…"

"Well, don't try. Just sit tight by a phone and wait for me to call you—and get to work on what I told you."

"All right, Nick, all right."

"Pop's in the hospital," I said before I hung up. "Maimonides. Send him a card."

"All right."

"Make it a Hallmark."
"Yes."
"A big one."
"All right."

I hung up on the obliging bastard, went into the bathroom, and sat on the commode, drying my hair. My next move was not crystal clear. Somebody had that doughnut, and somebody else—DiVolo or somebody he was working for—wanted it.

The big question for me was not who had it, or who wanted it, but why?

There was only one person who could tell me that.

I still had Jodi's car, but I couldn't use it to get where I was going, so I took a car service. I had the driver stop a few doors away from Jodi's house and wait and then walked the remainder of the way.

Jodi's mother answered the door.

"Oh, Mr. Delvecchio. Have you found my daughter?"

"Not yet, Mrs. Ponzoni. I have some more questions, however, which may help me. Is your husband home?"

"Uh, no, he isn't. Is there something I can do?"

"Possibly. May I come in?"

"Please."

She stepped aside, allowed me to enter, and then closed the door.

"Shall we talk in the living room?"

"Why not?"

On the way she asked, "Can I offer you a drink?"

"I don't think so. I won't be here very long."

"Well then, what was it you wanted to ask my husband?"

"I had some questions about the art pieces you and he own."

"He owns them, really. He had a small collection when we were married that he's continued to build up."

"Are they valuable?"

"Not really. It's more of a hobby than an investment."

"What about the missing piece?"

"What about it?"

"Is it valuable?"

"It is to him."

"Then why does he want it back so badly?"

"Mr. Delvecchio, do you collect anything?"

I thought briefly of my record albums by Brooklyn singers, but said, "No, not really."

"Then you don't know what it feels like to have a part of a collection missing. You want very much to get it back."

"I don't know that I understand him wanting the object back more than he wants your daughter."

"Well, she is *my* daughter and not his."

"I see."

It didn't seem to bother her that Ponzoni didn't want Jodi back. It obviously was not news to her.

"I guess that's it, unless your husband is coming back soon?"

"Not very soon, I'm afraid. In fact, I don't know when he'll be back."

"Has he gone out of town?"

"No, nothing like that, but sometimes his business keeps him out until all hours."

"I see," I said again. "Well then, I'll be going."

On the way to the door she said, "I'm sorry I couldn't be of more help to you."

"That's all right. I'll try to get your husband another time." She let me out and closed the door behind me immediately. It's been my experience that when you let someone out of your house, you watch them walk away, just out of habit. That she didn't do this made me stop and think.

When I got back in my waiting car, the driver said, "Where to, pal?"

"Nowhere, for the moment. Let's just wait a few minutes and see what happens."

"You ain't a cop, are you?"

He was a middle-aged Hispanic with a wart on his left cheek and not much of an accent. His hack license on the seat back in front of me said that he was Fernando Velasquez.

"No."

"But in a few minutes, if somebody comes out of that house, you gonna tell me to 'follow that car.' Right?"

"Right."

"I was afraid of that. You a private eye?"

"Yeah, I'm a private eye."

"I'm keeping the meter running."

Since he was a private-car-service driver, he had no meter in his car, but I understood what he was saying.

"I wouldn't have it any other way, Fernando."

37

"She's heading for Staten Island."

"How do you know?" I asked him.

We were on the Belt Parkway moving toward Manhattan, which of course meant we were also heading for the Verrazano Narrows Bridge, but right now it was a toss-up as to which borough she was going for.

"Educated guess," the driver said. "She your girlfriend?"

"My girlfriend's mother."

"And you followin' her to see if she's gettin' a little onna side, right?"

"Right."

"Well, if she's gettin' a little, my bet is she's headin' for Staten Island."

"Care to speculate a little further?"

"Sure. There's a Holiday Inn on Richmond Avenue. I've taken plenty of, uh, newlyweds there."

"Care to make a wager?"

"Sure. What's the bet?"

"Whatever I owe you."

"Double or nothin'?"

"Yep."

"You're on."

That was just to add some spice to the ride.

She hadn't wasted any time after I left.

She came walking down the front walk twenty minutes later and got into a small car with a Mercedes emblem.

"I know," my driver had said, "follow that car," and we had.

She had gone first to a ladies' lingerie shop on Eighteenth Avenue, one that specialized in sexy lingerie, and then had jumped on the Belt Parkway. Her choice of stores was what made me first think that she was—as Fernando also put it—steppin' out.

As we approached the entrance to the bridge and the Fourth Avenue exit, she moved into the right lane. She was either getting on the bridge to go to Staten Island or getting off at Fourth Avenue to go home.

When the time came, she got on the bridge.

"You lose."

"I thought the bet was the Holiday Inn."

"Geez, mister—"

"Not so sure now, huh, Fernando?"

Now it was his turn to add a little spice to the ride.

"Ah, what the fuck. You're on!"

We went over the bridge onto the Staten Island Expressway, past the exit for Hylan Boulevard, which has its share of motels and inns. This reinforced Femando's theory about the Holiday Inn—unless she was going to Jersey.

"Jersey," I said.

"What?"

"Maybe she's going to Jersey."

"If she's screwin' around, she ain't goin' to Jersey, pal. She woulda gone to the Golden Gate Inn in Brooklyn, or she's headin' for the Holiday Inn. Now from Manhattan, when they step out, they go to Jersey, but not from Brooklyn."

He sounded like the voice of years of experience.

"Where do they go when they step out from Long Island, Fernando?" I asked, just out of curiosity.

"Those people are crazy, man," he said, shaking his head. "They do it in their own *houses*. Don't shit where you live, that's my motto."

"And a good motto it is, too."

"See," he said suddenly, "she's gettin' off at Richmond Avenue. See the Holiday Inn?"

"Big as life."

We got off the exit right behind her, circled around, and came out heading south on Richmond Avenue.

"And there she goes," Fernando said, pulling over to the curb underneath the overpass. "Momma is definitely fuckin' around."

Mrs. Ponzoni had turned on her left signal, waited for traffic to allow it, and then turned left into the Holiday Inn parking lot.

"You win, Fernando."

We settled up, and then he said, "Want me to wait?"

I thought about it for a moment, then decided against it. If she was there to have it off with someone, then she would be inside for a while.

I didn't think I could afford Femando's prices.

I crossed the street after the car pulled away and then ran over to the hotel. I entered the lobby, shivering as a blast of cold air-conditioning struck my moist arms.

Diane Ponzoni was standing at the counter, checking in. I stepped off to one side and tried to be inconspicuous.

The clerk was all smiles and never even asked her if she had any luggage. That would have been the tip-off even if she hadn't paid him in advance. She'd been there before.

I wondered if the object of her affections was already there, and then chided myself.

Grow up, Delvecchio. If the male half of this tandem was already there, she wouldn't have to be checking in.

After she had taken her keys and walked quickly into an elevator, I strolled up to the counter slowly, taking the time to watch the floor indicator. It stopped at four, and then started back down.

"Good afternoon, sir," the desk clerk greeted me cheerily. Sure, I'd be cheery too if I had a fresh new twenty in my pocket.

"Has Mr. Ben Franklin checked in yet?"

"Sir?"

"Yeah, I know, he gets kidded about it all the time. Has he checked in?"

"Franklin. I'll check, sir."

He did his checking in his computer and then came back to me shaking his head.

"I'm sorry, sir, but we have no Ben Franklin registered."

"That's okay. I'll just sit and wait for him."

"Of course, sir."

I sat in one of the lobby chairs with my back to the wall. Somebody walking in would have to look way to his left to see me, which wasn't likely since the front desk would be ahead of them and to their right.

It only took fifteen minutes for somebody I knew to arrive, and since I was a firm disbeliever in coincidence, he had to be there to meet Diane Ponzoni. Feeling surprised and confused, I watched him as he walked straight to the elevator, waited for it with his back to me, and then got in. He might have seen me just before the doors closed, but appeared to have something else on his mind. I watched the floor indicator stop at four—which was really pushing coincidence—and then the car started back down.

I sat there, wondering what my next move should be—that is, besides wondering what Diane Ponzoni was doing having an afternoon rendezvous in Staten Island with Terry Jacks.

38

I took the bus back to Brooklyn, figuring the ride would give me time to think. But things were no clearer when I finally arrived at home.

I spent the bus ride trying to figure out the connection between Terry Jacks, Jodi Hayworth, and Diane Ponzoni. Janet Jackson had introduced Jodi to Terry. Had Diane met him through Jodi, or did she meet him before her daughter did?

And what was Terry Jacks's game in seeing both? Was he turned on by screwing a mother and daughter without one or the other knowing about it?

Or did he have something else in mind?

When I entered my apartment, I found a bottle of Dos Equis in the fridge and took it into my office. At my desk I took out a lined yellow pad and began to make a list, using all capital letters, as if that would somehow make what I wrote easier to understand.

- ✓ JODI HOCKS THE "HOLE THING."
- ✓ THE OLD MAN AT THE HOCKSHOP SELLS IT, PRESUMABLY TO JAMES BERRY. JODI HIRES ME TO GET IT BACK.
- ✓ SHE SETTLES FOR THE ADDRESS OF THE MAN WHO BOUGHT IT, AND DISAPPEARS.
- ✓ I'M VISITED BY TWO LEGBREAKERS LOOKING FOR JODI.
- ✓ JODI SHOWS UP AT MY APARTMENT AND TELLS ME ABOUT JAMES BERRY'S MURDER.
- ✓ THIS DAMN LIST IS TOO LONG.

I tore off the sheet of paper and started anew, listing only the most pertinent facts.

- ✓ THE "HOLE THING" IS MISSING.
- ✓ PONZONI WANTS IT, AND SO DOES DIVOLO, WHO IS SUPPOSED TO BE WORKING FOR YONY MACARONI. WHO IS DIVOLO WORKING FOR?
- ✓ SOMEBODY HAS IT, AND PROBABLY KILLED JAMES BERRY TO GET IT.
- ✓ TONY MACARONI, PONZONI AND DIVOLO WOULD BE SUSPECTS, BUT SEE # 2.
- ✓ TERRY JACKS—

I put the pen down abruptly. Obviously most of the questions that needed answering had to do with Terry Jacks, so he deserved his own list.

I started a new page.

- ✓ TERRY JACKS WAS SEEING JODI, AND HAD BEEN TO HER HOUSE.
- ✓ TERRY JACKS IS SCREWING DIANE PONZONI. (WHERE DID THEY MEET? AT THE HOUSE?)
- ✓ TERRY JACKS IS A SUSPECT—BUT WHY WOULD HE WANT THE STATUE, AND WHAT'S HE DONE WITH IT? IF HE STILL HAS IT, WHY WAS HE STILL HANGING AROUND? WHAT ELSE COULD HE BE PLANNING?
- ✓ WHO IS TERRY JACKS?

I put the pen down again. Terry's page was turning into an essay. I went back to the second list and added a question.

- ✓ WHAT IS IT ABOUT THE STATUE THAT MAKES EVERYONE WANT IT?

I got up from my desk, walked around it, then stopped and leaned over to grab the pad again. I wrote one more question down.

✓ WHO CALLED ME THAT FIRST NIGHT AND WARNED ME OFF—BEFORE I HAD EVEN MET JODI HAYWORTH?

I took all three pages into my apartment with me and sat on the couch. I spread them out on the coffee table and read them all.

Question number seven from the second list could very easily have gone to the head of the first list, because as far as my involvement went, it had happened before anything else. I tore it off the bottom of list number two and put it at the top of list number one.

When I was in Terry Jacks's apartment, I hadn't been able to determine whether his voice was the one on the phone. It could have been him, disguising his voice. Or it could have been Carmine DiVolo, whose voice I had never heard.

If it had been Tony Macaroni disguising *his* voice, then that would mean he remembered me, and he had given no indication of that at his house. I was willing to disregard him as the man who had warned me off.

That left DiVolo and Terry Jacks.

I didn't think DiVolo was the man who had killed James Berry. For one thing he was still looking for the statue, and for another he wouldn't have had to go into the house after he grabbed Jodi.

I was willing to disregard him as the killer.

That left Terry Jacks—or someone totally unrelated to the statue.

I pulled the phone from the end table onto the coffee table and started making calls.

39

First I called my brother to see how Pop was. Vinnie wasn't home, so I assumed he was at the hospital. I knew I'd have to go over there later.

Next I called Jodi, at Hacker's apartment.

"Are you fornicating again?" I asked when Hacker answered.

"I've tried, but the girl won't have any. How's your dad?"

"Can't get Vinnie at home. I'll have to check in at the hospital later. What's Jodi up to?"

"She's cooking. I'll get her."

When she came on, she said, "Hi, how's your father?"

I told her the same thing I told Hacker.

"I need some information, Jodi."

"About what?"

"About Terry Jacks."

"What about him?"

"Where does he come from?"

"He didn't tell me—"

"Think for a moment. Maybe he said something during a conversation that would give us a clue."

She took a moment and then said, "We only went out for a couple of weeks, a half a dozen times, maybe—wait a minute. I remember something."

"What?"

"He mentioned something about Cambridge once."

"Cambridge? In Boston?"

"I guess. He said something about Brooklyn reminding him of Cambridge, where he grew up."

"Boston," I said, half to myself. "I'll have him checked out."

"How?"

"I know somebody in Boston who can do it for me."

"What is it about Terry, Nick? Is he the one who killed Berry and took the hole thing?"

"The hole thing..." I repeated, this time low enough for her to be unsure that I was talking to her.

"What? What did you say?"

"Jodi, who else besides me knows that you call the thing a 'hole thing'?"

"I don't know—"

"Come on, think. Who'd you mention it to?"

"Well...Janet, when I told her I was going to hock it, and..."

"Terry?"

She was silent, and then she said, "Yes. Once when he was at the house and he picked it up. He asked me what it was and I told him."

"All right!"

"What is it?"

"That night before we met, I got a call warning me off. The voice said 'forget the hole thing.' Who else would have referred to it that way? That's what you call it, nobody else."

"And I told Teny. So it was Terry who killed James Berry."

"That's a conclusion we can't jump to. All I feel I know now is that Terry called me and warned me off. Did you tell him you were going to hire me?"

"Yes. He called me and wanted me to go out with him, but I told him I had to meet with you."

"You specifically mentioned me by name?"

"No, I said I was seeing a private detective, and he asked me your name.

I didn't think anything of it at the time, so I told him. But I told DiVolo that, too."

"Yes, but he never heard you refer to the statue as the hole thing. No, Terry called me." And Terry's sleeping with your mother, I added to myself. Did that mean she was involved? "Jodi, did your mother—or Ponzoni—ever meet Terry?"

"No, I started going out with him while they were away." Then how the hell had they met? I asked myself, not that it really mattered.

"All right. I've got some other calls to make. I'll talk to you later."

"All right—"

"Wait. One more thing."

"Yes?"

"Where in Greenpoint were you held? Do you remember the address?"

"Not exactly. It was on Franklin Avenue, near Greenpoint Avenue."

"Near the piers?"

"There were some piers there, yeah. I just kept walking away from the piers until I found a cab."

"Is there anything about the building that sticks in your mind?"

"Let me think. There was some writing...if I can only remember...Wait, it said 'Imports,' that's why I remember, because Stepdaddy is in the import business. The writing said...'J&D Imports.'"

"All right, good girl. Put Hacker back on."

"What's up?" he asked a moment later.

"I need you and your computer. Jodi will tell you everything she just told me. I'd like you to try and find out who owns the building."

"I can try," he said. "If I can't use the computer, I can always use the phone."

"All right. Give it your best shot. I'll call you back later." I hung up and stared at my television set. With a start I realized that I hadn't thought about my sister all day. Would there be anything on the news about the hijacking?

No, I was actually better off not knowing, *not* thinking about her.

She'd be home soon.

I picked up the phone again.

40

I dialed Miles Jacoby's home number, hoping that he'd be there and not at Bogie's. I lucked out.

We went through the amenities about my father and sister, and then I asked him if he knew a P.I. in Boston. I knew he had a phone book that was filled just with phone numbers of P.I.s across the country. He'd inherited it from Eddie Waters, the man who taught him the business. Every once in a while he let me pirate a number from him, and I in turn put it in a book of my own.

He gave me the phone number of a man named John Francis Cuddy. Using Jacoby as a reference, I asked Cuddy if he could check up on a man named Terry Jacks, and gave him all the particulars. I even mentioned that he might have grown up in Cambridge. Cuddy said he'd be happy to run a check, and I asked him if he could do it as soon as possible.

After I hung up on Cuddy, I dialed my brother-in-law at home. He was there.

"What have you got for me on James Berry?" I said without preamble. What was I supposed to say? "How's it going, Numbnuts?" After all, I was turning the screws on my dear brother-in-law.

"I've made some notes...I'll get them..."

He sounded nervous, as if he was worried about pleasing me. I didn't feel sorry for the bastard.

He got his notes and started reading things off. A lot of them were inane and useless—he was left-handed, he liked soap operas, he had never been married—but then he said two things that interested me.

"He's gay, which somebody here told me. I never knew. Oh, and he collected art—"

"I knew that," I said, thinking of the things I'd seen in his house. Statues, paintings—

"He's gay, you said?"

"That's right."

"All right, Peter. Thanks."

"Does this help?"

"I'll let you know." I was not inclined to take him off the hook just yet.

"Oh, I went to see your father, today."

"How is he?"

"He wants out of the hospital, but the doctor says he has to stay. Father Vincent was there, too."

"All right. You're doing good, Petey. Stay available."

I hung up without giving him a chance to answer.

There were two things about James Berry that interested me now. One was that he collected art—and Terry Jacks was an artist. The other was that he was gay—and Janet had told me that Terry swung both ways.

Of course, there are a lot of gay men and a lot of art collectors, but this was a possible connection—James Berry and Terry Jacks—and Terry was looking better and better, for taking the statue and for the murder. There was nothing the police could act on, but I had enough to confront good old Terry with.

I called Ed Gorman and asked him what he knew about Tony "Macaroni" Ponzoni's business.

"He broke away from your godfather Barracondi years ago, Nick, and went out on his own. Ostensibly he's in the import business, but Intelligence feels he's using that as a cover for smuggling."

"Of course."

"What?"

"Nothing, Ed. Who's Ponzoni's right-hand man?"

"Fella named DiVolo. He's connected, but talk is he's out for himself, now."

"Did they have a falling out?"

"Not that I know of. Ponzoni's out of the country a lot, and we hear that DiVolo's been making deals on his own. I think he's just trying to get ahead."

"That's an admirable trait in a cheap hood. Who's Ponzoni's main competitor?"

"An operator named Angelo Janetti. He's an out-of-towner who opened up shop here about five years ago."

"Does Mr. Janetti have someone here handling his business?"

"No. He comes to town to handle things himself. He uses the shuttle."

"From where?"

"Boston."

"Boston?"

"That's right. What's the matter with Boston?"

"Nothing, Ed. Nothing at all. Does he have an office here?"

"Warehouse out in Greenpoint. He might have an office there."

"On Franklin Avenue?" I knew I sounded anxious.

"I don't know exactly where. Do you want me to try to find out?"

"No, that's okay."

"Nick, is this the same case you've been working on? If you've got something on Ponzoni or Janetti, maybe you should talk to Intelligence—"

"If I get something on either one of them, Ed, you'll be the first to know."

I hung up, figuring that if Ed had all that information, he must still be in touch with his old office.

I also was thinking about Boston and Greenpoint. Terry Jacks was from Boston, and so was Ponzoni's competitor Angelo Janetti, who had a warehouse in Greenpoint.

Could Terry be working for Janetti? Had Janetti sent him to New York to use Jodi—or her mother—to get into Ponzoni's house? And if so, why was Terry still popping Diane? Could it be that they really had something together? Diane Ponzoni was certainly an attractive woman, but she had to be almost fifteen years older than him.

And what about Carmine DiVolo? If he'd had Jodi held in a warehouse belonging to Janetti, that meant that he'd changed sides—but wouldn't that mean that he and Terry were on the same side? If Terry had the statue, why was DiVolo still looking for it?

I took a pen from the end table and started writing on the backs of the lists I had. I wrote down a bunch of names, again using caps.

PEOPLE CONNECTED TO TERRY JACKS JODI (DEFINITELY)
DIANE PONZONI (DEFINITELY)
JAMES BERRY (POSSIBLY)
ANGELO JANETTI (POSSIBLY)
CARMINE DIVOLO (POSSIBLY, IF THEY BOTH WORK FOR JANETTI)

Terry Jacks had to be my man, but why was he still hanging around? Was he looking for a buyer for the piece? If so, had he offered to sell it back to Ponzoni?

My stomach told me it was dinnertime, and I went into the kitchen to feed the furnace. I had some frozen dinners—Hungry-Man style—and put two of them in the oven. I had just done that when Hacker called.

"I've got a name for you."

"Angelo Janetti."

"So, if you already know this shit, why are you bothering me with it?"

"I was just guessing. Anyway, that's what the 'J' stands for. You can tell me what the 'D' stands for."

"DiVolo."

After that he said something else that I didn't hear. "What? I'm sorry..."

"I said do those names mean anything?"

"They mean a lot."

"Yeah, Jodi said they might."

"When did they buy the building?"

"Two months ago."

Hadn't Janet Jackson told me she'd met Terry right after he came to town...two months ago?

"Okay, thanks, Hacker."

"Talk to you later."

I hung up and shook my head, which was buzzing. Angelo Janetti and Carmine DiVolo were partners in J&D Imports. That put DiVolo in direct competition with his "boss," Ponzoni. All I needed to do was connect Terry Jacks with Janetti for sure, and I would really be confused. If Terry worked for Janetti, why wasn't he working for DiVolo?

The answer was fairly simple.

Terry Jacks had decided to go into business for himself. Maybe that's why he was still making it with Diane Ponzoni.

A half hour later I had my yellow sheets on the kitchen table, and had gotten fried-chicken grease on the corners from my frozen dinners. I was moving them around when the phone rang again.

It was Cuddy.

"That was fast," I said.

"Surprised me, too. I ran the customary checks—DMV, utilities—and then I called a contact with the police department and had them check for a yellow sheet on Terry Jacks."

"And he had one?"

"A long one, for drugs, both using and peddling. And by the way, Jacks is not his real name."

"What is?"

"He's the son of a big mob guy here in Boston. His name is Janetti, Terry Janetti."

I hung up, but the phone didn't give me time to think about what I'd just learned. I hadn't even taken my hand off the receiver when it rang again. I pulled my hand away as if it had been scalded, then picked it up.

"Mr. Delvecchio?"

"That's right."

I didn't recognize the voice at first, but it wasn't the one that had called me way back when and warned me off.

"This is Anthony Ponzoni…Jodi's stepfather?"

"Yes, Mr. Ponzoni. What can I do for you?"

"I'd, uh, wonder if you'd be able to come out here now."

"To your house?"

"Yes."

"It is rather late, Mr. Ponzoni," I said, and I had a lot to think about, too.

"It's about Jodi."

"Really? Do you know where she is?"

"Well, it's not about Jodi, actually. It's more about the missing sculpture and a boy Jodi knows."

"Mr. Ponzoni, I'm getting confused—"

"Jodi was seeing a boy named Terry Jacks, who lives in Manhattan. I just received a call from that boy."

Uh-oh, I thought, a man answered, and Jacks was too dumb to hang up.

"And?"

"He said that he has my art piece and is willing to sell it back to me."

Bingo.

"I see."

"I'd like you to make the buy for me, Delvecchio."

"You're going to pay?"

"Of course. I have to have that sculpture back."

"Why?"

"Could you come here so we can discuss the details?"

I looked at my watch, which is something I do when I'm thinking. Sometimes I don't even see it, it's just a habit.

"All right, Mr. Ponzoni. I'll be there as soon as I can."

"Good," he said, and hung up.

You're welcome.

41

This time I took Jodi's car, not worried about whether Ponzoni saw it or not. I had a feeling we were coming up on come clean time.

I pulled up in front of the house at eleven P.M. and rang the bell.

"I'm glad you could come," Ponzoni said, admitting me. "Let's go into my study." He either didn't notice the car or didn't show that he did.

On the way to the study we passed the living room and the kitchen, and Diane Ponzoni wasn't in either room.

"Is Mrs. Ponzoni asleep?"

"My wife is out," he said, and didn't elaborate. I had visions of her lying in bed next to Terry Jacks when he called her old man and offered to sell the sculpture back to him.

He closed the door to his study and said, "Can I get you a drink?"

"I don't think so," I said. "It's late, and I'd like to get this cleared up."

He regarded me for a moment, then went around behind his desk. It was made of oak, and dwarfed the room, which was rather small but well furnished. Expensive rug, small portable bar, well-crafted bookshelves, everything the successful suburban businessman could want.

"All right, then," he said, lacing his fingers together, "let's get it all cleared up, shall we?"

I sat down and said, "Fine."

"I remember you, Delvecchio."

"Good, I remember you, too."

If he did recollect me, it had come to him after our first meeting. I was sure he hadn't placed me then.

"Actually, I remember your father from the docks. He was a hardnose. Are you a hardnose?"

"It's probably the only thing I inherited from him."

"Good. It's an admirable trait."

"You should know."

"You're right, I should. It got me where I am today."

"Which is where?"

He stared at me for a few seconds and then said, "Fair enough. If you're going to work for me, you should know a little bit about what I do."

"You're in the import-export business."

"Import is a nice way of putting it," he said. "I smuggle."

"What?"

"Anything I can. Drugs, artifacts, precious gems. You name it."

"And what's the story behind this 'hole thing'?"

"Hole thing?" he asked, looking puzzled.

"That's what Jodi calls it."

"Oh, I see. Yeah, I guess that's as good a name as any."

"What's in the doughnut, Mr. Ponzoni?"

"Doughnut—oh, the hole thing. Well, I don't think I'll tell you that, Delvecchio—can I call you Nicky?"

"Only if I can call you Tony Macaroni." His jaw tensed at the sound of his old nickname, and I said, "I prefer Nick."

"All right...Nick. I'm not going to tell you what's in the thing, because finding out will be added incentive for you to get it back. Am I right? You're curious about what's in it?"

"There is something in it, then?"

"More than you'd think."

"What's that mean?"

"It's not the only thing missing from the house."

"What else is missing?"

"A list, from my desk."

"What kind of list?"

"It's a list of names, new contact points, that I'll use in my business."

"Terry Jacks has that, too?"

"He doesn't know it."

"How's that?"

"The list is in the base. I put it in there before I sent it back here from Mexico."

"You don't have a duplicate?"

He shook his head.

"Can't you get one?"

"It would embarrass me to have to call Mexico and ask for it. I think you can see that."

He was right, I could see that. The people he was working with wouldn't think much of him if they found out that he had...misplaced this list so soon after they had given it to him. "It also wouldn't do you any good if Janetti got that list."

"Janetti?" he said, frowning. "What's that bastard got to do with this?"

Was it possible that he didn't know?

"I assumed you knew that Terry Jacks was Janetti's son."

"What?"

He exploded out of his chair, standing straight up and staring at me as if I had just told him his pecker was on fire. "His son?"

"Yes."

"That bastard sicced his son on me—on my stepdaughter?"

If you only knew the whole of it, I thought.

"It makes sense," he said. "He used Jodi to get into the house and then grabbed the piece."

"How did he know what piece to take?"

"That's a good question."

"I think I may have the answer."

"What?"

He started to sit, and I stopped him.

"You might jump out of your seat again."

"Why?"

"Carmine DiVolo."

"I knew it!" he said, crashing his fist down on the table. "I knew that prick was up to something."

I told him about the warehouse in Greenpoint, and he just stood there, nodding his head.

"Carmine's a fool. Janetti will use him and throw him away."

"So DiVolo knew what was in the piece, passed it on to Janetti, who passed it on to his son."

"But what's the kid doing offering to sell it back to me?"

"He's gone into business for himself. Trying to get out from under Poppa's thumb."

He sat down, considering that.

"I guess you're right. You've done pretty well with all this, haven't you?"

I shrugged.

"I stumbled onto a lot of it. How much does the kid want?"

"A hundred grand."

I whistled.

"Have you got that kind of scratch?"

"I will tomorrow night. That's when he wants it."

"You want me to pick it up and pay him."

"Actually, no..." he said, "the kid is the one who asked for you."

That surprised me.

"We've only spoken once."

"If I didn't believe that, I wouldn't have called you. We discussed some go-betweens, and he's the one who brought you up."

"Why doesn't he want you to bring it?"

"My guess is he's afraid of me...or maybe he's just real cautious."

"How do you want me to handle this?"

"You'll do it?"

"I'd like to see this through to the end, yeah—but when it's over, we have to talk about Jodi."

"What about her?"

"When it's over."

"All right, fine. I'll get the money together tomorrow afternoon. You be here at eight to pick it up. He's going to call us with the exchange point."

"My guess is it will be either Greenpoint or Manhattan. I'd prefer Manhattan. Greenpoint's too deserted."

"We'll find out tomorrow."

I stood up and said, "Just let me get this straight so I know what I'm doing. You want me to pay him and pick up the piece?"

"I don't expect you to whack him out," Ponzoni said. "I know you wouldn't do that, but if you could get the piece back without paying him...well, that'd be worth ten percent of what you save me. Understand?"

"I understand, Mr. Ponzoni." I walked to the door and said, "I'll see you at eight tomorrow."

"Bring your hard nose, Delvecchio," he called out after me. "You might need it."

The fucker picked Greenpoint.

I think I know why.

One, he had a key.

Two, by using his father's warehouse, he was thumbing his nose at his old man.

Kids feel like doing that, sometimes. I know...

I returned to Ponzoni's house that night after lying to a lot of people.

I lied to Jodi, telling her that I had a lot of checking to do that day and couldn't stop in to see her.

I lied to Sam when she caught me going out. I told her I was going to see Jodi, which didn't seem to sit well with her, but if I had told either one of them the truth, they'd have wanted to go with me, for their own reasons.

I lied to Father Vinnie, telling him I couldn't come by to see Pop that night because I had something to do. Well, it wasn't a real lie, just a lie of omission—but maybe when you tell a lie like that to a priest, it's real. I don't know...who cared, at that point.

So I told a bunch of lies and showed up at Ponzoni's at eight. Not only did I bring my hard nose, but I brought my snub-nose as well. Actually, my .38 wasn't a snub-nose, but I couldn't resist the pun...

The attaché case was chock full of money, more money than I had ever seen in one place at one time...in one lifetime!

Ponzoni let me look at it for a few moments, then slapped the case shut.

The phone rang.

"Yes," Ponzoni said into the receiver. Then "Yes, I have it." He listened again and then replied, "I believe he knows where it is."

I mouthed "Greenpoint," and he nodded.

"Midnight," Ponzoni said, and I grimaced. Greenpoint at midnight was not my favorite place in the world. "All right, he'll be there, just make sure you show up with—hello? Damn it, hello?"

He slammed the receiver down and said, "The little shit." I agreed wordlessly. "You heard."

"Yes. Greenpoint, midnight. I assume it's the warehouse?" "Yes. I have a good mind to call his father..."

"Would he believe you?"

A small smile formed on his lips, and he said, "No. We've been business rivals of one sort or another for too long."

"Do you have anything to eat in the house?" I asked. "I haven't had dinner."

He stared at me for a few moments, then understood. It was ten after eight and the meeting wasn't until midnight, and I had no intentions of wandering around with a hundred thousand dollars in an attaché case until then.

"I'll have Diane fix something for both of us."

Asking for something to eat was also my way of finding out if Diane Ponzoni was home or not without actually asking. Obviously, she was, and I hoped to be able to make sure that she stayed home, one way or another.

He started around the desk, and I said, "What about the money?"

"Bring it," he said. "You might as well get used to carrying it now."

I picked it up and didn't know how to react to the weight, since I didn't know what I'd expected. It was neither too heavy nor too light.

He left the room and I followed, carrying a hundred grand of Tony Macaroni's hard-earned money.

42

I took Jodi's car to Greenpoint. I figured I was sacrificing it in a good cause.

The breeze off the East River was cool and damp, but it had nothing to do with the chills I was feeling. I was about to walk into a dark, empty warehouse with a hundred thousand dollars in my hand and a gun on my hip. For some strange reason, my mind was not at rest.

The dockside door of the warehouse was open, as promised, and I stepped inside. My muscles were tense, and I knew that if I was alive tomorrow, my back was going to hurt because of it.

I pulled the door shut behind me and thought about the last thing I had said to Ponzoni as he showed me out the door.

"Do me a favor, Tony."

He'd started a bit at my use of his first name, but then said, "What?"

"Keep your wife home tonight."

"My wife? What do you mean?"

"Let's talk about it when this is over, but in the meantime, try to keep her home. Okay?"

Frowning, he said, "She doesn't have any plans to go out that I know of."

"Good, try and keep it that way."

I'd left him on his doorstep, still frowning. Maybe he'd gone inside and asked her about it, and her affair with young Terry Jacks—ne Janetti—was out in the open.

I didn't delude myself about why I was in that warehouse. Sure, there was Ponzoni's promise of ten percent of a hundred grand, but I was there to get the answers to a lot of questions.

I hoped Terry Jacks was in the mood to answer them.

Apparently, young Terry was not intending to keep me waiting so as to make me nervous and testy, because no sooner had I shut the door behind me than the lights went on.

Brightly.

I squinted and raised one hand to shade my eyes, in an attempt both to spot him and to save my eyesight.

"Do you have a gun?"

"Yes."

"Throw it away from you, where I can see it."

I did as he asked, and the gun clattered and slid across the floor.

"Do you have a gun?" I asked.

"Yes, and it's pointed right at you."

"This would be a lot easier if I could see you," I said. My eyes were adjusting to the light, but I still could not locate him.

"I'm up on a catwalk above you," his disembodied voice called out. "Is the money in that attaché case?"

"It is."

"Open it."

"How do I know you have—"

There was a shot, a loud one that reverberated through the empty warehouse—and it was totally empty. Either it was between shipments, or it was simply a dummy.

"Now you know. Open the case."

"I am opening the case." The shot gave me no choice.

I set it down on the floor, flipped the catches, and opened it so he could see the contents.

"Dump it out on the floor."

I dumped it. It made a nice-looking pile on the floor.

Something struck me on the shoulder lightly, and I jumped back. It was a canvas sack, sort of like a mailbag, and it was dangling from the end of a rope.

"Fill it up."

Beyond giving orders, Terry was not being very talkative. One thing was happening, though. Because of the disembodied quality of his voice—like a voice on the phone—I was starting to identify him as the man who had called me that first night and warned me off.

Question number one had been answered.

I picked the money up off the floor a couple of bundles at a time and filled the canvas sack.

"Okay," I said when I was done, "it's full."

He started to haul it up, but I held tight to it.

"Where's the sculpture?"

"I have it with me. Let the money go, and I'll give it to you."

"Send it down—"

"I've got to haul the rope up in order to send it down. I don't have another rope."

I held on to the bag.

"That's the only way it's going to be done, Delvecchio. Let go of the rope!"

Well, there went my ten percent—I only hoped that he would actually send the hole thing down. I mean, why would he keep it?

I released the rope and the bag went straight up. I thought I could see him on the catwalk, but there were shadows toward the ceiling and I couldn't be sure.

"Okay, Delvecchio," he called out, "here comes the hole thing. Enjoy it."

Suddenly something was falling toward me, and I jumped out of the way just in time to avoid it. It struck the floor and broke into dozens—hundreds?—of pieces.

The lights went out at that point, and I was in the dark with my gun somewhere on the floor, and the only part of the sculpture that hadn't been smashed to smithereens was the hole.

I moved quickly after that.

It was easy for me to find the door I had come in by, and I left it open behind me while I went to get Jodi's car, which—surprise, surprise—was still there. I didn't have a flashlight, so I did the next best thing. I drove the car up onto the dock and stopped it with the headlights shining on the doorway. I got out of the car and went into the warehouse, and the headlights gave me enough light to see.

I found my gun, and the attaché case, and the pieces of the statue. I gathered up as many pieces as I could and dropped them into the attaché case. I found out that there was another part that had not been smashed, and that was the base, which was solid and survived the fall with only a couple of chips to show for it. It was fairly heavy, and I put it in the case with the rest of the pieces.

If there had ever been anything hidden in that hole thing, it sure as hell wasn't there when it hit the floor.

I ran out of the warehouse then, got into Jodi's car, gunned it, and headed for Manhattan.

Would Terry Jacks be dumb enough to go back to his apartment?

I was going to find out.

During the ride across the Fifty-ninth Street Bridge something became increasingly evident to me as I passed a car stuck in the right lane.

Terry had not been alone in that warehouse.

He couldn't have been up on the catwalk and at the main light switch at the same time, so he had an accomplice.

I wondered if Tony Macaroni had been able to keep his wife home, after all?

***

The doorman at Terry Jacks's apartment house was very cooperative—as would most people be, confronted by a twenty-dollar bill.

I was carrying the attaché case with me when I reached his door. Maybe I thought I'd really get the money back, or maybe I just didn't want to take a chance on losing the hole thing now that I had finally found it.

I tried the doorknob right off and found the door unlocked. I started to take my gun out of its holster, then pulled my hand away as if the thing was hot. I didn't want to take it out unless I had to, and I was fervently hoping I wouldn't have to.

I opened the door and stepped into the apartment. It was as it had been the last time I was there, stereo equipment and a lot of easels; otherwise it was empty. If Jacks hadn't come back here, then he was holed up somewhere with his money, and I didn't know how I was going to find him—unless I could find out from Diane Ponzoni...and that was only if *she* wasn't gone, as well.

I found the phone and called Tony Macaroni.

"Did you get it?"

"I got it," I said, not bothering to tell him the shape it was in. "Is your wife home?"

"Of course she's home. I don't appreciate these insinuations you're making about my wife, Delvecchio."

"That's tough. Go and check and see if she's home."

He started to protest, then told me to hold on.

When he came back he said, "She's in bed, reading. What's this all about?"

"Later," I said, and hung up.

I put the attaché case down on the floor and opened it. I took out the base and fiddled with it until the very bottom of it slid away and a piece of paper fell to the ground. It was an 8½-by-11-inch piece that had been folded several times, and when I unfolded it, I saw that it was covered with typewritten names and addresses, as well as some numbers I didn't understand. I refolded it and put it in my pocket, then threw the base back into the case and closed it. I picked it up and was about to leave when I remembered Jacks's bedroom. I figured I might as well check and see if he'd left anything behind.

As it turned out, he hadn't left anything behind—*he* had been left behind. Dead.

43

"Let's go into your study," I said when Ponzoni opened the front door of his house.

"Fine," he said. "We have some things to get settled." More than you know, I thought.

In his study I asked, "Is your wife still upstairs?"

"Yes, asleep. What's—"

"And she never left?"

"Delvecchio, what the fuck are you trying to say about my wife?"

"Tony, Terry Jacks is dead."

"What? I thought you said you wouldn't—"

"I didn't, but somebody did."

"Suppose you just tell me what happened?"

I did, starting from the point where I entered the warehouse. I altered things very little. For one thing, I told him I had gotten the hole thing back, but I didn't mention its condition. I also told him that I hurried to Jacks's Manhattan apartment to try and get his money back for him.

"What made you think he'd be there?"

"I didn't, but where else could I have looked?"

"Who killed him?"

"If I knew that, I'd know who was in the warehouse with him."

"Wait a minute, wait a minute..."

I gave him a moment to gather his thoughts. Go ahead, Tony, I thought, put it together. You're a bright boy.

"Is that why you've been asking about my wife? You thought she was Jacks's accomplice?"

"I don't know about being his accomplice, Tony, but I know she was his mistress."

"His mistress?"

"All right, 'mistress' is a very genteel word for it. They were fucking."

When he swung, I was ready, and he was only half serious, anyway. It was as if he felt obligated to give it a shot, and in his legbreaking days it probably wouldn't have mattered that I was ready. He was much better then. As it was now, I moved aside and the force of his punch threw him off balance, causing him to stagger past me.

"Come on, Tony, cut the crap. I'm not making this up to piss you off. All you've got to do is tell her he's dead and then ask her."

He righted himself, and I waited to see if he was going to throw another punch.

Instead he said, "All right, it makes sense. Janetti sent his son in here to romance my stepdaughter, and somehow the kid decided to do the same with my wife. That makes me a cuckold, and I'll live with it. Did you get the piece?"

"Pieces," I said. I set the attaché case on the desk, opened it, and said, "I got the pieces."

"Jesus," he said, staring at the rubble in the case. "Where's the—"

He stopped and picked up the base.

"Where's the what, Tony?"

"The paper, where's the piece of paper?" That wasn't what he was going to say originally.

He pried the bottom off the base, stared, and then dropped it back into the case.

"Have you got it?" he asked, turning to face me with his hand out.

I thought about holding out on him, but decided against it. I took it out of my pocket and gave it to him.

He took it, went around his desk, sat down, pulled out a checkbook, wrote me a check, and handed it to me. It was for considerably less than ten percent of a hundred grand, but I'm no dummy. I took it, but not without opening my mouth. "This is all you want from me?"

"You did your job."

"What about your wife?"

"That's between me and her."

"And what about whatever else was in that thing?" I said, pointing to the case.

"Who said there was anything else in it? Did you see anything in it when it shattered?"

"No, it had already been taken out by then."

"What had?"

"Whatever was in it!"

"I'm getting tired of playing charades, Delvecchio. It's time for you to leave."

"What about the hundred grand?"

"For all I know, you killed Jacks and have the money."

"That's crazy."

"Maybe, but the money's gone, and I'm not going to worry about it. It's a business write-off." He stood up and said, "I'll show you to the door."

"You expect me to buy this act? You don't care that your wife cheated on you, helped her lover get a hundred grand out of you—"

"He's dead, isn't he?"

"He is, and I'd like to know who killed him."

"Well, I wouldn't, so when you find out, don't tell me."

In that moment I wondered if maybe Ponzoni hadn't had somebody waiting at Terry's apartment when he returned. Somebody to kill him and relieve him of the money and whatever else he had that belonged to Tony Macaroni.

"I'll find my own way out."

"Do that."

"Oh, one more thing."

"What's that?"

"Jodi."

He waved a hand negligently and said, "Tell the little bitch to come back or stay away, it's her choice."

I went to the front door, folding the check he'd given me and putting it into my pocket.

Money's money, and he was right. I'd earned it.

It was getting light when I left Ponzoni's house.

On the way back to my apartment I tried to figure my next move.

Other than the killer, I knew of two people who knew that Jacks was dead, Ponzoni Macaroni and me. Even if Ponzoni didn't know when I called him, both of us knew that I had been in the apartment—and the doorman had to be added to that list. That meant that I had to make a call to the cops about the body or risk the possibility of losing my license. That was why I had called them and waited for them to arrive at Jacks's apartment.

When the cops arrived, I had given them the bare bones of what I had been doing there—without naming my client—and then invoked the name of Inspector Gorman to get away from them early. It had also taken a promise that I would reveal my client's name (a) only after clearing it with him, or (b) if my license depended on it. There is no legal client confidentiality between a P. I. and his client. That only works for lawyers.

Before leaving Ponzoni's, I decided not to tell him about the cops and my promise to them. My intention had been to tell him to have his lawyer draw me a check so I could claim confidentiality when the time came, but his attitude had changed my mind.

Fuck him.

What was my next move? Finding Jacks's killer? That was the police's job. So was finding James Berry's killer, although they hadn't been doing very well. Jacks might have been good for that, and now they'd probably never know.

All along, my job had been to find the hole thing and fix it so that Jodi didn't have to worry about Stepdaddy getting mad. That was done.

I had also been interested in what was inside the sculpture that made it so valuable, but that was just curiosity. I'd survive without the answer.

By all rights, I was through with the whole episode.

When I got to my apartment, I called Hacker's number and talked first to him, then to Jodi.

"Jesus, Nick, it's seven o'clock in the morning," Hacker groused.

"I know. I've been up all night. Has Jodi been there all night, Hacker?"

"Sure she has. She's still asleep."

"The phone didn't wake her?"

"Phones are off except in my room. She couldn't hear it. What's up?"

"I'm about to cut her loose. Put her on."

"Jeez, she's asleep, Nick."

"Wake her up, Hack."

He sighed and said, "Hold on."

I waited while he plugged in one of his other phones, and then Jodi came on the line sounding half asleep.

"Nick, what's wrong?"

"Nothing at all. You can go home now."

"What? Home?"

"Go home or stay away, your choice, little girl, but take my advice."

"What?"

"Get a job and a place of your own. Things are going to be a lot different at home."

"What do you mean?"

"You'll find out. If you want my advice, go home only long enough to collect your things."

"When will I see you—"

"I'll call."

I hung up before she could say anything else.

File this one under closed cases.

I had just about decided to give my brother a call before getting some sleep when somebody started banging on my door. It sounded uncomfortably like Detective Matucci's knock, but the voice that called out with it wasn't Matucci's. "Nick, come on, open up!"

It was Sam.

I opened the door, and she said, "Where the hell have you been?"

"I've been working all night, Sam, and I just got home. Can this wait?"

"No, it can't—"

"I was just about to call Vinnie and find out how Pop is—"

"Your father's home."

"Home? They let him out of the hospital?"

"Yesterday—"

"Why?"

"If you'd let me tell you," she snapped, putting her hand over my mouth.

"What?"

Her face split into a beautiful, wide smile, and she said, "They've released the hostages. Your sister's coming home!"

44

Two days later Father Vinnie, Pop, and I picked up Maria at Kennedy and brought her home. This time when the neighbors came, I didn't have Vinnie kick them out. In fact, we had a hell of a party, with neighbors, family, and friends.

The house was packed, and we had catered food and a well-stocked bar, and music, and it all drove Maria into the backyard for some privacy.

"Hi," I said, coming up behind her.

She turned and looked at me, and I saw a different Maria than I had ever seen before. There was a haunted look to her eyes. The horrifying experiences that she had been through had changed her, and I had the feeling that my little sister had finally grown up.

"Would you mind giving me a hug?" she asked.

"Hey," I said, opening my arms, "what are brothers for?"

She put her head on my chest and said, "Pop looks bad."

"He'll be okay, now that you're back."

"You all fought, didn't you?"

"Like cats and dogs," I said, "but people react differently in bad situations, kid. That's how we got through it. How did you get through it?"

"Well, after we were released, at our debriefing we were told by an expert that we might need some help readjusting to normal life after the experience we'd been through. This expert even suggested that some of us might need professional help."

"A psychiatrist?"

"Yes, but I don't think I need that, Nicky."

"Why not?"

"Because the whole time I was there, waiting to die, I kept one thought in mind."

"What was that?"

She looked up at me and said, "I knew that if I got out of there alive, I was going to divorce Peter."

I squeezed her and said, "Good for you."

"Shall we go inside and drink to it?"

"Let's go."

I decided I'd never ask her about her affairs, or Numbnuts's affairs, or who had whose first. I didn't care. She was alive, she was back, and she had just taken a huge step toward making her life better.

Later, a huge bouquet of flowers arrived for Maria, who excitedly opened the card. I was hoping they weren't from Numbnuts, trying to make points now that she was home. They weren't.

"Who are they from?" Father Vinnie asked.

She looked at Vinnie and then at me.

"Uncle Dominick."

There was a moment of silence at the mention of the Barracuda's name, and then I said, "Well, put them in some water."

Pop pushed his way to Maria and, putting an arm around her, led her away saying, "Aye, old Dominick was gonna send in a team to get you..."

At another point I found myself in close proximity to my father, who was having a ball now that Maria was home.

"Nicky, my boy," he said, putting his right arm around my shoulder. He had a drink in his other hand, and some of it sloshed over onto the floor.

"How you doing, Pop?"

"Great, just great. Isn't it great?"

"It's great, Pop."

I found myself wanting to get away from him. In his present condition he had totally forgotten the harsh words that had passed between us, but I hadn't.

He laughed and said, "We're a family again, huh, Nicky?"

"That's right, Pop. Just one big happy family." I eased out from under his arm and said, "I'd better check and see how the food's holding out."

I left him standing there with his arm out and a puzzled look on his face.

As I left the room, I came face to face with the stern Father Vinnie, who had obviously heard the exchange.

"Nick, come on. You can't hold the things he said against him. Maria's home, and everything is back to normal."

"You're wrong, Vinnie. Nothing's normal, and we're all going to have to deal with that, sooner or later. You'll see."

He shook his head and stepped aside to let me by.

Maybe he'd never see.

***

Once or twice during that welcome-home party, or victory party, or whatever you wanted to call it, I could have sworn that I saw faces of people I didn't know, but I didn't care. *Everybody* was welcome that night.

Well, almost everyone.

I was standing at the food table, having finally decided to have something to eat, when someone came up behind me. I'd started to turn when I felt something hard poke me in the small of the back.

"Just stand easy, Delvecchio."

I didn't know the voice, but I knew that poke in the back.

"What do you want?"

"You and I are leaving this party."

"For how long?"

"Maybe for good."

"I don't know who you are," I said, "but I'm not leaving—"

"You want this welcome-home party to turn into a funeral?" he asked, jabbing the barrel of the gun deeper into my back.

"All right, look, you want to talk, let's talk," I said. "We'll go for a walk."

"No," he said, changing his mind suddenly about taking me away. "We'll go out into the backyard, where we can be alone but where I'll still have access to these nice people with this." He drove the gun hard against my back again to bring his point home.

I was torn between staying at the house and trying to force him to take me somewhere else. While we were close to the house, there was a chance that someone else could get hurt, but if I let him take me away from the crowd, there was a good chance I could end up dead.

"Okay," I said, "the backyard."

I turned away from the table, which had been set up in the dining room, led the man through my father's room—which had been made off limits during the party—and into the backyard. With a gun in your back a thirty- or forty-foot walk can be like thirty or forty miles, and all the way I was trying to figure out who this dude was.

I could only come up with one answer.

When we got to the backyard, he said, "You can turn around now."

I turned to face a tall, dark-haired, rather oily-looking man who was holding a gun in his right hand.

"Carmine DiVolo, I presume?"

"Good guess."

"I don't remember inviting you to this bash."

"I saw on the news that your sister was one of the released hostages, and I figured you might be having some kind of a full house. If it was my sister, I would."

"I'm touched."

He made sure I knew he still had the gun in his hand by pointing it at me.

"Why don't you hold that a little higher so everyone can see it? That's just what this party needs, a bunch of cops."

He frowned, then lowered the gun to waist level, keeping it more or less pointed my way.

"Okay, tell me what you want so I can go back to the party."

"What I want is what was in that sculpture."

"What?"

To be honest, ever since I had heard the news about the release of the hostages, I hadn't thought much about Jodi Hayworth or the sculpture. I hadn't even heard from Jodi and didn't know if she had taken my advice or not, but then I'd been out of my apartment more than in.

"That piece of sculpture you bought back from the kid for Ponzoni."

"What about it?"

"I want what was in it!"

"I don't even know what was in it, let alone have it."

"You got it from the kid."

"I got a million pieces from Terry Jacks, DiVolo. There was nothing in that piece of crap when he dropped it from the catwalk in that warehouse." Then it hit me. "Wait a minute. You must have been there. You must be the one who hit the lights."

"I was there, and we were supposed to meet at his apartment to divvy up the money except my goddamned car died on the Fifty-ninth Street Bridge."

I remembered the car I had passed on the bridge that night, stuck in the right lane.

"Jeez, if I had known that was you, I would have stopped and picked you up."

"I didn't need you to pick me up. I got to Terry's building just as you were leaving...after you killed him and took the money and what was in that sculpture."

"He was dead when I got there, DiVolo. How do I know you didn't kill him?"

"I didn't—wait a minute. Let's don't turn this around."

"I think that's what's happened, DiVolo. Things have gotten turned around—on you."

"What do you mean?"

"Well, let's see if we can figure this out. You and Jacks conceived this plan to rip off Ponzoni."

"No, no, that was Janetti's idea. He sent the kid here to romance Ponzoni's wife's kid, Jodi, and to get his hands on what was in that sculpture."

"How did you come into it, then? I thought you worked for Ponzoni."

"I did, but the kid offered me a lot of money to help him show his dad something, and I agreed. I was getting ready to split from Ponzoni anyway, so I figured I might as well do it for a hundred grand."

"A hundred grand? Terry was going to give you the entire hundred grand?"

"That was the deal, but now you've got the money, which is what I wanted, and you've got the...whatever was in that statue thing, which is what the kid wanted."

"Wait a minute, let me get this straight," I said. "*You* don't even know what was in it?"

"He never told me."

"DiVolo, believe me, I don't have your money, and when Terry Jacks, or Janetti, dropped that statue on me, it broke into a million pieces. There was nothing in it."

"I know that," DiVolo said irritably. "Terry took it out before he dropped the thing on you, but you—or somebody—killed him and took it out of his apartment."

Well, that was a load off my mind, anyway. By saying that me or "somebody" had killed Terry, he was saying that maybe he was starting to believe that I hadn't done it.

"Look, DiVolo, put the gun away and come inside and have something to eat. I think we've both been taken in this thing. I delivered a hundred grand for a worthless statue, and you've been cheated out of the same hundred grand."

He studied me for a few moments, then said, "Ah, shit!" and put the gun away. "I believe you."

"Then come inside and eat."

"Nah, I've got to find out who took my money—besides, I already ate. Can I get out of here without going through the house?"

"There's a gate over on this side."

DiVolo nodded.

"Uh, look, sorry to interrupt your party. I'm glad your sister's okay."

This was crazy. We were parting like a couple of buddies, me inviting him inside, and him telling me how happy he was for me.

"Good luck," I said, because I couldn't think of anything else, and he just nodded and started around the side of the house.

"Hey, Delvecchio," he called from out of the darkness on the side of the house.

"Yeah?"

"Watch out for the old man."

"Yeah, sure..."

As I started back for the house, I suddenly realized that maybe he hadn't been talking about my old man, but Terry Jacks's father.

Was he warning me to watch out for Angelo Janetti?

After the party we decided that Maria would spend the night at Pop's and then in the morning would go with Father Vinnie to her house to collect her things. Both Maria and Vinnie wanted to keep me away from Peter, just in case he was there. As much as Vinnie didn't like him, he certainly wouldn't get into a fight with him. Needless to say, Numbnuts hadn't been invited to the party, and he'd had the good sense not to try and crash it.

Sam, on the other hand, had been invited. I had come with her to the party, and we drove back home together in her car. Apparently, any differences we'd had over the past week or so had faded away in the light of Maria's return.

"Your father looked very happy tonight."

"He was drunk."

"Maybe he had a right to get drunk."

"Maybe."

She was driving, keeping her eyes on the road ahead, and I stared out the passenger window. I was thinking about Jodi's hole thing again, since the subject had forced its way back into my mind at gunpoint.

"Nick, you're not going to let what passed between you and your father affect your relationship, are you?"

"My relationship? I don't even know what kind of relationship I have with my father."

"Some things were said under the worst of conditions—"

"Let's just forget about it, Sam."

"None of my business, huh?"

"Mmm."

"What's on your mind tonight, Nick? As the night went on, you got quieter and quieter."

"Murder."

"What?"

"Murder is on my mind."

"What murder?"

"Actually, it's two murders."

"What two murders?"

I started talking, then, telling her about James Berry, about Terry Jacks, and about Jodi's "hole thing." It was the first time I had laid the entire thing out for her—or anyone.

"A McGuffin."

"Not now, I'm not hungry."

"No, not a McMuffin, silly," she said, "a McGuffin. Don't you know what a McGuffin is?"

"No."

"Alfred Hitchcock coined the phrase. It's what everyone in his movies is looking for."

"What is?"

"The McGuffin."

"But what is it?"

"That's the beauty of it. It doesn't matter what it is, it's a McGuffin."

"And that's what this sculpture was?"

"Right."

"That's real helpful, Sam."

"What are you going to do?"

"The problem is I shouldn't do anything. It's up to the cops to catch the killers."

"But you feel a responsibility to find the murderers?"

"No, Sam, that's in your books. I'm just curious."

"About what in particular?"

"Well, Berry doesn't bother me so much. I'm pretty sure Terry killed him, but who killed Terry and took the money and the...McGuffin, well, that bothers me."

"So find out."

"That'd be like working for nothing, though, and that also only happens in your books."

"You wouldn't be working for nothing if you found that hundred thousand dollars."

She had a point there. Oh, not that I'd keep the entire amount, but maybe Ponzoni's offer of ten percent would still be available.

"Well, then, all I've got to do is figure out who killed Terry Jacks."

"Wouldn't it have to be someone who was in on it from the beginning?"

"Sure."

"Somebody who knew all of the principals involved?"

"Uh, sure. Well, at least somebody who could have introduced...Jodi and Terry..."

"Do you know anyone who fits that bill?"

After a moment I said, "You know, I think I do."

EPILOGUE

I waited for her outside of where she worked and then followed her home.

It was no easy task, waiting on that street, trying to look inconspicuous. I finally settled for a table at a sidewalk cafe down the block, from where I was still able to see the front steps of the store.

Finally she came out, and I stood up and followed her.

I had spent the day wondering if this was the right thing to do or not. Of course, Sam said it was, but that was because it made me fit into the mold of her fictional heroes, Marlowe and Archer and the rest.

I finally decided to do it because if I didn't, the curiosity would eat at me for a very long time, wondering if she had done it.

When she turned into Horatio Street, I knew she was going straight home, and I was glad. I would have hated to have to tail her around the city as she hit all of her favorite watering holes, or whatever. This way I could brace her in her apartment, where she just might have everything hidden—if she was the amateur I thought she was. I was willing to give her the benefit of the doubt on that count.

After she used her key to enter the building, I hotfooted it up the front steps and managed to catch the door before it eased closed. I allowed it to close, but just didn't let it close enough to lock. Through the dirty glass I could see her walking down a long corridor and then up a flight of stairs. She never once looked back.

I checked the mailboxes and saw that her apartment was on the second floor. I opened the door and started quietly down the hall. I had reached the foot of the steps when I heard a door close from upstairs. I went up the steps quickly, found her door and knocked. I didn't want her to be able to catch her breath.

When she opened the door, the surprise on her face was obvious.

"Oh, hi."

"Remember me?"

"Sure, you're Jodi's detective. Still working on her case?"

"More or less. Mind if I come in?"

"No, not at all," she said, swinging the door open. "Come on in."

I entered and found myself in a small kitchen. There was one other room beside the bathroom, and it held a bed, a couch, a TV, and some stereo equipment.

She closed the door, and I turned to face her. She was still very sexy, with her comrows and her bodysuit—different color this time, but same effect. Still very attractive, even if I did think she was a killer.

"Tell me about it, Janet."

"About what?"

"About killing Terry and taking the hundred thousand dollars out of his apartment."

"I don't know—"

"The thing I really want to know is how you got past the doorman without him seeing you. The rest I can figure out for myself."

Actually, that part wasn't really important. The fire escape to Terry's apartment was one possibility. However she did it, my whole case began with the assumption that she had, one way or another.

She folded her arms beneath her very fine, very firm breasts and said, "So go figure."

"I think Terry came to town and met you and got you to meet Jodi and then introduce her to him. If I ask Jodi, I'll bet I find out that she met you after Terry hit town."

"I've already admitted I introduced them. So what?"

"So I think you did more. I think when Terry got the idea to cross his father, he got you to go along with it. Who else did he know in town? DiVolo? Carmine was just a stooge, hardly the kind of guy that Angelo Janetti's son would want to partner up with. You, on the other hand, were dynamite in bed and real sharp, weren't you? A hundred grand would take you a long way."

"Don't you wish you could find out how good I am in bed, white boy?"

I ignored the remark.

"You introduced him to Jodi, and through Jodi he met her mother. Why did he ever start an affair with her, I wonder?"

"He dug her." The look on her face plainly said that she couldn't understand it. "No, really, he was into older women. He said he liked to fuck somebody's mother every once in a while."

"How did you feel about that?"

She shrugged.

"I didn't care."

"But you were there when he wanted you, weren't you? And when he needed somebody to hook him into Jodi Hayworth? He used DiVolo for the scut work—like grabbing Jodi, trying to scare me off, and going to the warehouse with him—but he probably wanted to save you for the real important stuff, like holding the money for him?"

"You're telling it."

"You got into his apartment, and you were waiting for him to come back from the warehouse with the money. I think when you saw it, you decided that instead of playing house you deserved an even split. All that money got to you, didn't it, Janet? You asked him for half, and maybe he laughed, maybe he said that you were along for the ride for as long as he wanted you, and that's all. How close am I?"

"So he dumped me," she said, shrugging again. "I been dumped before. That don't mean I shot him."

"What?"

"I said that don't mean I—" She stopped short as if she had just realized that she was the first person to bring up the fact that he had been shot. The papers had said that Terry Jacks—also known as Janetti—had been killed, but the cops had deliberately left out the manner in which he had been killed. They wanted to sit on that for a while, at least until the phony confessions had stopped coming in. They had found drugs in Terry's apartment, and some sexual paraphernalia that indicated that Terry went both ways, and when sex and drugs were involved, the weirdos came out of the woodwork and started confessing to everything.

"How'd you know he had been shot?" I asked, feeling like I was in a bad TV show. Rockford or Harry O., entrapping the killer through the slip of a tongue.

Hey, sometimes it happens that way in real life, too.

She was smart enough to know, however, that she didn't have to admit anything. After all, there was only her and me there. Unlike Rockford or Harry Orwell, I had not thought to bring along a police friend to stand just outside the door and listen for the confession.

"You're still telling it."

"I'm almost done. From the beginning, then. I think that Terry had DiVolo find out from a helpless old man in a hockshop who had bought the statue after Jodi hocked it. Terry found out that the buyer was a homosexual and used that to get into the man's house. I think he killed him and stole the statue. I think he took whatever was in the statue out and then offered to sell the statue back to Jodi's stepfather. He probably wanted to make Jodi part of that deal, but she got away. He tried locating her, then went ahead with the sale, anyway, suggesting that I act as middleman. The sale went down, except I got stiffed, and then when he tried to stiff you, you shot him. The gun was probably his own, which you found in the apartment and used. Come on, Janet, I'm running out of breath. It's time for you to help me out here. Tell me it was an accident and that you didn't plan to rip him off and kill him all along."

"You been watching too much TV, Jim. This here girl ain't saying nothing to nobody that she don't have to. You can't prove a thing!"

She was cool, too cool to be the amateur I had originally thought she was. She was a barracuda, and had probably had an eye on ripping Terry off the whole time. He was trying to prove to his father what a top operator he was, and he got taken off by a sweet, young, black barracuda.

"You're right about that," I said, "I can't prove a thing, but there is something I can do."

"What's that?"

I stepped past her and opened the door.

"First I can plant a bug in Tony Ponzoni's ear about where his money is."

"You would—"

"And second, I'm sure Angelo Janetti would like to know who killed his son."

"You can't do that—"

"It's up to you, babe. Turn yourself in by tomorrow, or buy a plane ticket to take you a long way from here. You won't get away, but you might last a few months. These men play dirty pool like you've never seen played uptown."

I left her standing there with her fists clenched. Somewhere in her apartment was a hundred thousand dollars and what Sam called a "McGuffin." Sam was right about one thing. It really didn't matter what the McGuffin was.

I walked across the Brooklyn Bridge, once again experiencing that relieved sensation of coming home to Brooklyn.

My curiosity about who killed Terry and took the money was assuaged. The lady had not protested enough, and had been just too cool about everything. I was satisfied that I had constructed the sequence of events from Jodi's hocking of the hole thing to Terry Jacks's death in the proper order. I'd check with Gorman tomorrow to see if she had turned herself in. If she had, I'd find out just how right or wrong I was. If she hadn't, I'd have to see if I really wanted to throw her to Ponzoni and Janetti or tell the cops what I knew. I'd also have to give them DiVolo's name as the man I thought killed the old man in the hockshop, and Terry Jacks's for killing James Berry.

Then again, I could just forget it and let DiVolo and Janet Jackson get away with murder.

My choice.

Sam was going to love it. She'd say it was the way these kinds of books are supposed to end.

THE DEAD OF BROOKLYN

To Alyssa & Nolan, the new generation.

1

It was what I call one of my "Brooklyn Blues" days. I was thirty-two, a bachelor, doing my own laundry in the neighborhood Laundromat. On top of that, I hadn't had a case for a couple of weeks and money was getting tight. Did I say tight? It was damn well cutting off my circulation. The last five hundred dollars I had made had not gone very far.

I have done laundry in Laundromats when being there was a bachelor's delight. In fact, up until about six months ago there were these three girls who were roommates living in the neighborhood and they used to take turns doing the laundry. In the summer those girls would come in dressed in shorts and halter tops of bathing suits, and in the winter—when they took off their coats—they'd be wearing tight jeans and leg warmers. I mean, all during that time I looked forward to my time in the Laundromat, but they only lived in the neighborhood for a few months and then moved, and laundry went back to being a chore.

As a whole, the regular people who used this Laundromat were pretty nice, but they were no great shakes to look at. Mrs. Goldstein is a woman in her late fifties who sort of adopted me—telling me which detergent to use, and which fabric softener, and "Oy, boychick, don't wash those in cold water!"—but she kind of resembled the south end of a battleship going north; Big "Mad Dog" Bolinsky, a bruiser who worked for the Department of Sanitation, looked like the whole ship; Mr. Quinn, the Greek grocer, was in his late fifties also, and don't think Mrs. Goldstein didn't know he was a widower, just as she was a widow.

And then there was Sam. Her real name was Samantha Karson, but she wrote her romance novels under the name "Kit Karson"—when she sold them, that is. I think she has sold three, so far, huge tomes with lurid covers showing big breasts on the women and bare chests on the men. Sam lives across the hall from me and takes time out from her computer from time to time to take in a movie with me, or to do her laundry. She's not the neatest person in the world, but she's pretty and easy to get along with. We're very good buddies, and we've never slept together.

So it was on one of my Brooklyn Blues days, when I was feeling slightly sorry for myself, when Linda Kellogg walked in.

She had never been there before and naturally became the center of attention right away—with me because of her good looks, and with Mrs. Goldstein because she's the neighborhood busybody.

Nobody spoke to her beyond saying hello because that wasn't the way things were done. If she came back again, indicating that she might become a regular, then everyone would make an effort to get to know her. I would have made an effort right off the bat, but as she took the machine right next to mine I noticed that she was wearing a wedding ring.

I noticed a few other things too. She had a bruise alongside her left eye, and as she was putting her clothes into the machine I noticed a blouse with blood on it. When she turned my way at one point, I saw that her lip was split and puffed on one side. The lip and the bruise looked to be about five or six days old. Three days ago she would have looked a lot worse. This could all have been the result of anything from a mugging to a family dispute, and I really didn't give it a second thought after leaving the Laundromat that day.

The second time she came around I found out her name—from Mrs. Goldstein, of course—and during the course of the next couple of weeks she came in every Tuesday and Friday—Friday being my regular day—and Mrs. Goldstein, who was at the Laundromat three days a week, busied herself getting all the dope. (Mrs. Goldstein was a widow who lived alone, so you know she didn't *have to* go to the Laundromat three times a week just to do her *laundry*.)

Linda usually had a small bruise here or there when she came—she *could* have just been clumsy—but finally one Friday I noticed her talking to Mrs. Goldstein and crying, and that was when nice Mrs. Goldstein dragged her over to me.

"This quiet fella is Nick Delvecchio, Linda. He's a nice enough boy to be Jewish." That was the highest praise Mrs. Goldstein could have given me. "He's also the best private detective in Brooklyn." A dubious distinction at best.

Of course, Mrs. Goldstein is addicted to mystery novels that feature private eyes. She was always trying to get Sam to write one instead of those "meshugge" romance novels. At that very moment she had a paperback copy of something called *Jackpot* by Bill Pronzini in her voluminous purse.

"Hello," Linda said meekly.

"We've met in passing," I said. I was starting to get a picture I didn't like.

"Linda has a problem, Nick," Mrs. Goldstein said, "and I told her you could help her."

"Is that a fact? What kind of a problem?" I asked, noticing the mouse she had beneath her right eye. The first day I had laid eyes on her was one of my Brooklyn Blues days, and I had the feeling this was going to turn into one, too.

I hate domestic cases. Nobody ever wins. What was worse, I couldn't very well turn this one down with the rent coming due, and with Mrs. Goldstein looking at me the way she was. Besides, I had already turned down a case recently, for personal reasons. I couldn't afford to take any more high moral stands, not at this point.

"Tell him, dearie," Mrs. Goldstein was urging Linda Kellogg.

Linda looked from Mrs. Goldstein to me a couple of times and I said, "Mrs. Goldstein, isn't your machine finished?"

"What?" the older woman said, looking behind her. Her wash was still being swirled inside her machine, but never let it be said that Mrs. Goldstein couldn't take a hint.

"Hmm," she said, giving me the eye. "You help her, Nick. She's a nice girl."

"We'll see, Mrs. Goldstein."

"Hmm," she said again, and left us to go back to her machine and her book.

"She's a nice old busybody," I said.

"I like her."

"Do you want to tell me about it, or do you want to let her think you're telling me about it?"

"I think I'll talk to you, Mr. Delvecchio. Even if you can't help me, it might do me some good."

"All right," I said. "You don't mind if I fold my shirts and...other things while we talk, do you?"

"Oh," she said, as if the thought of a man folding his own belongings surprised her, "I'll do that."

She walked to my pile of laundry and began to talk and fold at the same time. I hoped she was using some sort of universal fold, and that I wouldn't have to refold my things so they'd fit in my drawer.

Put succinctly—which she did not do—it seemed that over the past few months, since even before they moved to this neighborhood, her husband had taken to beating her up on occasion. That was what she said, "On occasion." I asked her to define "occasion." She said that sometimes he would come home from work angry and hit her, even if she had cooked him his favorite dinner.

"Is it always after work?" I asked.

"Yes."

"But you can never predict it?"

"No," she said. "Most nights he's fine, very loving, and other nights the slightest thing will set him off. I can't understand it."

"How long have you been married?"

"Two years."

"Do you have any children?"

"No."

"Have you ever been pregnant?"

She frowned and said, "No, I said we never had any children."

That wasn't exactly what she'd said, but I let it pass. I figured there was no point in bringing up the question of miscarriages. I'd known men who beat their pregnant wives into miscarriages, but that didn't seem to apply here.

"And this is only a recent development in your marriage?"

"Yes."

"Had he ever struck you before these incidents?"

"No, never." She answered all the questions without looking at me, but looking at the laundry she was folding.

"Linda...do you think he might have a girlfriend?" I was fairly sure that would be what was uppermost in her mind. I was wrong. She looked at me with shock written all over her face. I couldn't believe that the thought had never occurred to her.

"I *never* thought of that."

Was she on the level? Could she really be that innocent? Or was I just too much of a cynic?

Probably a little of both.

"Linda, what about drugs?"

"No," she said firmly, "never."

I shrugged to myself. She may have been sure that he had no girlfriend and no involvement with drugs, but to me they were very real possibilities for the cause of the problem she was describing.

"Linda, what is it you would like me to do?"

"I—I would want you to find out what is making him so angry," he said, folding a pair of my boxer shorts. "You see, if he didn't come home so angry, then it wouldn't happen. He wouldn't have any reason to hit me. Do you see that?"

No, I didn't see that. I didn't believe in men hitting women for any reason. I felt that men who beat their wives shouldn't have gotten married in the first place, but then what did I know? I'd never been married, I'd never even lived with a woman.

"Have you ever thought about leaving him?"

That shocked her as much as the question about a possible girlfriend. In fact, it shocked her into looking at me.

"And go where? I have no family. I barely have any friends. I wouldn't have anyplace to go, Mr. Delvecchio. Besides, I love my husband. Will you help me? I can pay you."

I almost told her not to worry about that, but since I was so short of money, I kept my mouth shut. Maybe I would just charge her one month's rent and be done with it. I'd snoop around some, see if her husband had a girlfriend, or a nose-candy habit, see what was making him so mad. If I didn't find something out in a day or two...well, that would be that.

She had finished folding my laundry and was just staring at me, waiting for my answer.

Helpless before the so completely innocent look in her eyes, I said, "I'll try and find out what makes him so angry."

She put her hand on my arm and said, "Thank you, Mr. Delvecchio, thank you."

I smiled halfheartedly and said, "Call me Nick."

2

Linda Kellogg's husband's name was Dan, and he worked as a dispatcher for a trucking firm with an office in the Greenpoint section of Brooklyn. According to Linda, the position was a promotion for him, and the raise in salary was what had enabled them to move to a better neighborhood. My block of Sackett Street wasn't quite in Park Slope and was almost in south Brooklyn. The bodega on the corner had a sign in the window that said, "No selling drugs on the street in front of the store." That was because they probably sold drugs *inside* the store and didn't want the competition. If the Kelloggs considered this a better neighborhood, I hated to think where they'd been living before.

I had followed Dan Kellogg to and from work for a week, and so far I had discovered two things: I didn't know what was making him so angry, and he didn't seem to have a girlfriend—which, for all I knew, might have been what was making him so angry.

I spoke to Linda after the week was up and she told me that Dan hadn't laid a finger on her since she hired me. I asked if she thought he knew about me and she said she was sure he didn't. She asked me to please stay on the case for a little while longer and I agreed. Once again she assured me that she could pay me. I wondered where she was going to get the money, and how she would explain its disappearance to her husband without getting beaten up again.

After two weeks total there was still no indication that *anything* was bothering Dan Kellogg, and there was still no sign of a girlfriend. In fact, he hardly ever went out for lunch. Maybe the problem had resolved itself.

I felt guilty taking a fee from Linda, and when she asked me how much she owed me I charged her for one week instead of two without telling her. It was five days' work, since Kellogg didn't work on the weekends. I managed to come out of it with a month's rent, plus some grocery money. We severed our business relationship in the same place where it had started, at the Laundromat, and after Linda left, Mrs. Goldstein came over.

"Did you help her, Nicky?"

"I tried, Mrs. Goldstein, but I couldn't find out anything."

"No girlfriend?"

"No girlfriend."

"So," Mrs. Goldstein said, "that's something. You put her mind to rest about that."

"Yeah," I said, "that's something." I didn't bother telling her that I was the one who had put the idea into Linda's head in the first place. "I think maybe this problem may have solved itself, Mrs. Goldstein."

Looking doubtful, she said, "Mark my words, boy-chick. Problems very rarely solve themselves. Somebody usually has to solve them."

"I'll remember that, ma'am," I said, and left with my clean laundry. I hoped that in this particular case, she was wrong.

3

The following week I walked into the Laundromat and got from Mrs. Goldstein the dirtiest look she could muster.

"So, Mister Smart-Guy?" she asked, folding her arms across her ample chest.

"So what, Mrs. Goldstein?"

"What have you got to say for yourself?"

"About what?"

"About what," she repeated. "About Linda Kellogg."

"Mrs. Goldstein," I said, still puzzled but becoming a little annoyed, "could we stop playing Twenty Questions and just get down to the nitty-gritty?"

"Sure, tough-guy-private-eye talk you can do," she said accusingly—sounding uncomfortably like my father—"but when it comes to helping a little girl whose husband beats her up and puts her in the hospital—"

"Wait a minute," I said, interrupting her. "Are you telling me that Linda is in the hospital?"

"That's what I said."

"What hospital?" I put my laundry basket down on her machine.

"That one near Atlantic Avenue."

"Long Island College Hospital?"

"That's the one."

"Mrs. Goldstein, will you do my laundry and hold it for me?"

"Are you going to the hospital to try and help her?"

"Yes."

"Then I'll do your laundry, Mister Private Eye. You go and do what you should have done before, give that brute what for."

I wasn't about to give Dan Kellogg "what for," but I did want to talk to Linda Kellogg. I wasn't feeling very good about her at the moment.

Linda Kellogg was sharing a room with three other women, but I pulled the curtain all the way around her bed so we could have some privacy. I was glad not to find her husband there.

"He's at work," she said. "With his new job he can't take that much time off. He said he'd be coming up later on."

"Tell me what happened."

She didn't look too bad, although her face was bruised and swollen so that she had to speak out of one corner of her mouth. Most of the damage had been done to the rib area; he had cracked two of her ribs.

"He came home, and he was angry," she said in a puzzled voice. "I thought he was all over that. I tried to talk to him, but suddenly he was hitting me and telling me to shut up and leave him alone. I couldn't believe it!"

I didn't think that she should have been all that surprised, but I kept that opinion to myself.

"Who called for an ambulance?"

"Dan did."

"And the police?"

"No police," she said, shaking her head.

"Linda, he could have killed you this time—"

"I want to hire you again," she said, interrupting me. "Find out what's making him so angry, Nick...please!"

"I'll find out, all right, but I've already been paid and I didn't do the job. This time it's on the house."

She closed her eyes and said, "Thank you." Her last jolt of painkiller was kicking in.

When I left she looked like she was asleep. I wondered idly what she had told the doctors about how she'd received her injuries. I stopped at the nurse's station to ask for Linda's doctor. His name was Geary, and he wasn't available. The nurse said that he'd be making rounds that evening.

As I left the hospital I figured there was only one way I was going to find out what was making Dan Kellogg so angry, and that was to ask the son of a bitch!

4

Dan Kellogg's place of business was on Metropolitan Avenue, in an industrial area of Greenpoint, and I cabbed it there from the hospital.

Greenpoint is a funny section of Brooklyn, because from some parts of the borough, in order to get there, you've got to go into *Queens* and then come back into Brooklyn. My driver, however, simply jumped onto the BQE—the Brooklyn Queens Expressway—and got off at McGuinness Boulevard, which left us just a few blocks from our destination.

Greenpoint is largely industrial, with some neighborhoods made up of single and multiple dwellings. If you're looking for a nice one-family house with a driveway, a yard, a garage, and a picket fence, though, Greenpoint is not the place for you.

When I got to Kellogg's building, there was a sign on the front that said MUELLER BROS. TRUCKING. I went inside and asked someone where I could find Dan Kellogg and they directed me to the dispatcher's booth.

The man in the booth was a burly guy of about thirty, with thick brown hair and a full mustache. It was the first time I had been closer than across the street from Dan Kellogg.

"Kellogg?" I said, leaning my head in the window of the booth.

"Just a sec," he said. He held a short conversation with someone over the radio, then swiveled around to face me and asked, "Can I help you?"

"I'd like to talk to you in private, if you can get relieved."

"Relieved?" he said, laughing. "Mister, you know how many trucks I'm juggling? I can't get just anybody to relieve me, you know. What's it about?"

"It's about your wife, Mr. Kellogg."

"Linda?" he asked, frowning. "You from the hospital?"

"No."

"The cops? What?"

"I'm investigating her...accident." There was an implied lie there, but I figured to let him think I was a cop just long enough to get him out of the booth.

His eyes widened and then he licked his lips, wondering if his wife had sicced the cops on him.

"There's a lounge down the hall," he said then. "Wait for me there, will you?"

"Sure."

There was another man in the lounge, but as I entered he got up and left. It took Kellogg five minutes to find "just anybody" to relieve him.

"Why are the police interested in my wife's...accident?" he asked, sitting next to me on a worn leather sofa. Even though we were alone in the room, he spoke softly. "Did somebody say something…"

"About what, Mr. Kellogg?" I asked, prodding him.

"Nothing," he muttered. "What is it you want to know?"

"I want to know exactly how your wife received her injuries."

"Didn't the hospital tell you?"

"I want you to tell me."

"She fell…while changing a light bulb."

"Really?"

"Yes…really," he said haltingly. "That's what happened."

I stared at him for a few minutes, letting him stew.

"Look…" he said nervously, "that's how it happened. Did anybody say different?"

"Can I see your Lands, Mr. Kellogg?"

"What for?" he asked, burying his hands in his lap.

"I'm curious," I said. "Humor me."

"Look," he said, standing up and keeping his hands behind him, "I don't know what you're after, but I think I want to see your badge and identification."

"That won't be necessary, Mr. Kellogg," I said, standing up. He was about my height, but he had me by a good twenty pounds across his shoulders and chest. Still, I was pretty sure I could handle him. Men who beat up on women can rarely handle another man. "I'm not a policeman. I never said I was."

"What?" His face turned red. He forgot about his hands and allowed them to come into sight. I could see that he had a couple of skinned knuckles. "Just who the hell are you, mister?"

"Somebody who'd like to know what kind of man would take his anger out on a woman, with his hands," I said, and then added, "and not just any woman, but his own wife."

His hands closed into fists, but he held them at his sides. "Get out of here!"

"You beat up your wife, Mr. Kellogg," I said, taking out one of my business cards, "you've done it before, only this time you put her in the hospital. You know it and I know it." I tucked one card into his shirt pocket. "I'm going to prove it, and I'm going to find out why—unless you want to tell me that right now. What is it that makes you so angry that you've got to beat up your wife to get rid of the anger?"

"I ain't telling you shit," he said. "I don't have to tell you nothing!"

"You're right about that," I said. "You don't have to tell me anything, so I'll tell you something, Danny. If you touch that girl again, I'm going to personally break you in half."

"You think you can?" he asked, puffing up his chest, but his fists stayed at his sides.

I smiled at him. "I know I can."

He snorted and said, "What are you, her boyfriend?"

"No, Danny boy," I said, quelling the urge to deck him. "Your wife loves you, although God only knows why. She doesn't have a boyfriend, but I wish she did. She needs someone to protect her from you."

"And you're volunteering for the job?"

"That's right, Danny," I said, poking his chest with my right forefinger, "I'm volunteering. You want to talk to me now?"

"I got nothing to say to you! Get out of here before I throw you out."

I laughed in his face, hoping that he would take a swing at me.

"That's a laugh," I said. "In case you haven't noticed, I'm not a woman, so don't waste your threats on me. Just remember what I said, and if you want to talk to me, just give me a call."

He stood there shaking with impotent rage, and when I was dead sure he wasn't going to swing I left, feeling more than vague disappointment.

5

Two nights later I was returning home, dragging my ass. I had been tailing Kellogg again for the past two days—I decided I'd even try watching him on the weekend—and had still come up empty. I was tired, and very frustrated. I had stopped off for a beer on the way home at Aldretti's, a neighborhood bar, and the one beer had stretched into two during a conversation about horse racing, and then into a third during an argument about which was the better horse, Easy Goer or Sunday Silence, both of which had been recently retired by injuries.

After talking to Kellogg that afternoon two days ago, I had returned to the hospital. I couldn't speak with Linda because she was asleep, but I was able to speak with her doctor.

"In my opinion," Dr. Geary said, "her injuries are not consistent with her story about falling off of a chair while changing a light bulb."

"Are you required to make a report to the police?" I asked. "I mean, this is not a knife or gunshot wound, I know, but you do suspect violence."

"I didn't say that, Mr. Delvecchio." Dr. Geary was a white-haired, distinguished-looking man in his sixties. He was soft-spoken and had, I suspected, a pleasing bedside manner. He was probably very popular with his patients.

"I do suspect violence," he went on, "but as you say, this is very different from a gunshot wound. I *suspect* violence, but I can't prove it, and I certainly can't prove it was her husband." I hadn't mentioned *domestic* violence. "That is what *you* suspect, isn't it?"

"Yes."

"Well," he said, "I can't help you, Mr. Delvecchio, but I am glad that you are helping her."

"Yeah, well," I said, "I'm doing the best I can, Doctor." Unfortunately, the best I could do had landed her in the hospital.

One room of my four-room apartment is set up as an office, and it has its own entrance from the hall. There was only one other apartment on my floor, the third, and that was Samantha Karson's. I entered through the office door, and my new friend was winking at me from my desk, a red light going on and off, on and off several times. I switched on the light and walked to the desk. I'd only had the telephone answering machine for about a month. It had been a gift from Sam on my birthday. She had bought it secondhand, which was the only way she could have afforded it, but I appreciated the thought. She also thought I should have a computer. I said I couldn't afford one, and she said it would streamline my operation. I laughed. If my "operation" got any more streamlined, the "patient" would die.

I stared at the red light and contemplated not checking the messages until the next morning, but I finally pressed the "play" button and propped my hip on my desk to listen. I didn't care who was on the machine, I wasn't leaving my apartment again tonight. I was going to pop a frozen dinner into the oven and watch a ball game.

The first message was from my father: "You know I hate these machines. I want to talk to someone with a pulse. I want you to come to dinner tomorrow night. Your brother will be here and your sister will be doing the cooking. Call me. I hate these fucking—"

The second message was from Walter Koenig, Salvatore Cabretta's attorney. It had been a month since I turned them down, and I'd forgotten about them.

"Mr. Delvecchio, this is Walter Koenig. My number is two-five-seven-three-one-four-two, please call me at your earliest convenience. It is very important that we speak. It would be to our mutual advantage."

Yeah, sure...

The third message was from my brother, Father Vinnie.

"Nick, it's Vinnie. No matter what time you get this, call me at the Rectory. It's urgent. The number is two-five-one, three-nine-one-six."

I frowned at the urgency that was present in my brother's voice. Usually, I was the only one who could get him that rattled. Vinnie, two years older than me, was very disapproving of my way of life, and of the way I treated my family. I, on the other hand, was proud of my older brother, the priest—but I'd be damned if I'd ever tell him that.

I picked up the phone and dialed the Rectory number of the Church of the Holy Family in Canarsie. It rang once and was picked up.

"Nick?"

Jesus, I thought, what was he doing, sitting on the phone?

"Vinnie?"

"Wait." He covered the phone with his hand but I heard him say, "No, Monsignor, I have it." Then he came back on the line. "Nick?"

"Vinnie, what's going on—"

"I can't tell you now, Nick, not on the phone. Are you coming to Pop's for dinner tomorrow?"

"Vinnie—"

"I really need to talk to you, Nick," Vinnie said. "It's important!"

It wasn't what he said, but how he was saying it. His voice was actually shaking.

"All right, Vinnie," I said. "I'll see you at Pop's tomorrow."

"Great!" he said. "Nick...thanks for this."

"Sure, Vin. See you tomorrow."

He hung up without saying good night, or even a "God bless you."

Man, something was *wrong!*

I waited until the next morning to call my father to tell him that I would be over for dinner.

My father reacted in what was becoming typical Vito Delvecchio fashion.

"It's about fuckin' time."

6

When I reached my father's house, Maria was already there, but Vinnie hadn't arrived yet. I had tailed Dan Kellogg home and then hopped the subway and come straight to Pop's house.

I got a hug and a kiss and a "Why haven't you called" from my pretty sister. I ducked the last one. My sister, since her divorce, lived near my father in a small apartment. Even she couldn't live *with* him, though, not at this stage of his life.

I wasn't being biased when I referred to my sister as pretty. She had always been pretty, and the boys had started chasing her at an early age. She had always worn her brown hair long, and it was beautiful hair, like my mother's had been when she was young. Of course, Maria's older brothers had always been very protective of her, and she both loved and hated us for it.

In retirement, my father had regressed to the point where he was more little boy than I or my brothers had ever been. He wasn't senile, he just wanted what he wanted, and he couldn't have it, so he reacted by cursing and drinking beer...

What my old man wanted more than anything else, even seventeen years after the fact, was my older brother Joey back. Private First Class Joseph Delvecchio was killed in Vietnam when he was nineteen. A soldier walking next to him stepped on a mine, and it killed both of them.

At least there had been enough left of Joey to send home. The funeral had been a phenomenon to me. Eight hundred people, touched by Joey in his nineteen years of life, came to the funeral parlor over a three-day period, to the amazement of everyone concerned.

At the time Vinnie was seventeen and I was fifteen. Maria had been five, and she stuck close to me throughout the wake and funeral. She claimed she could still remember the whole thing vividly. She remembered Joey, too, and I was glad of that. Everybody who knew Joey remembered him, but unlike my father, we had all let him go to his rest.

Pop had Joey's picture on the wall, above a statue of the Virgin Mother, like a little shrine to his memory. I hated the damned thing. I didn't need a shrine to remember my brother. I loved him—and still love him—but I hated what his death had done to my father. It had turned him bitter, more bitter even than the death of my mother, who died of cancer the year before Joey. Maybe it was a combination of the two. Who knew? At least he hadn't erected a shrine to my mother. He had let her go to her rest; why couldn't he do the same thing for Joey?

I wanted my father to get on with his life. There was life after retirement from the docks, but try to tell him that.

"Where's Father Vinnie?" I asked Maria.

"He's coming, Nick." She squeezed my hand and said, "I'm so glad you're here."

I put my other hand over hers and said, "What's the matter, Maria? Some boy bothering you? You want me to beat him up?"

She laughed and said, "I'm well beyond that, Nicky. No, I'm worried about Father Vinnie."

"Why?"

"I don't know, but something feels wrong."

"Woman's intuition?"

"It hasn't done me much good to this point, has it?" The irony was plain in her voice.

My sister was twenty-two, and had made a few mistakes in her life. One was her marriage, which had broken up last year, right after she and all the other passengers had been rescued from a hijacked plane. That time was the most helpless I'd ever felt in my life, but I'll say one thing for the experience. She seemed to have grown as a result of it. The rest of us just "aged," but bless her heart, she'd grown—and she had proved it by getting rid of her husband, "Numbnuts," otherwise known as Peter Geller.

Of course, Father Vinnie had not been happy when she married out of "our faith," but even he was happy when she divorced Geller—although Vinnie would never let the Church know that. His happiness for her was that of a brother for his sister. Of course, as a priest he could not condone divorce.

"Has he said anything to you?"

"No," she said, "but he sounded funny when I talked to him yesterday. Have you talked to him lately?"

"No," I lied. I decided to keep Vinnie's late-night phone call to myself. I sniffed the air and changed the subject. "The sauce smells good. Yours?"

"Uh-huh," she said. "I'm making lasagna and veal parmigiana."

"Umm," I said, licking my lips. The only thing I liked better was spaghetti with garlic and olive oil.

"Speaking of which," she said, sliding her hand from mine, "I'd better get to it. You want a beer?"

"Sure. Where's Pop?"

"In his room."

Pop's "room" was a room that he had added on to the house himself when we were kids. He had a desk, a recliner, and a TV in there, and that's where he used to go to hide from all of us.

Maria handed me a Bud and I carried it into my father's room.

"Hello, Pop."

He was seated in his recliner, watching the news on TV.

"Humph," he said, "big-shot private eye made time for his old man, huh?"

"Pop—"

"Okay, never mind," he said, "you're here; I guess I should be grateful."

"You want a beer, Pop?" I asked.

He raised his left hand and there was a half-consumed bottle of Bud already in it.

"I'm gonna see if Maria needs any help."

"Your sister takes after your mother in the kitchen," Pop said, "she don't need your help. Sit down."

I went and sat behind his desk. It was the only other place to sit in the room.

He hadn't shaved, and his stubble was gray. I always lose track of his birthdays, but I'm pretty sure he is sixty or better. Maria knows all our birthdays, and she never forgets them. We don't celebrate Joey's, but she always lets us know when it's here.

My father had put on weight since his retirement. He could have worked until he was sixty-two, but his back had started to give him trouble when he got into his late forties, and had finally driven him to a disability retirement at fifty-five or so. His belly hung over his belt, a testament to all the beer he'd consumed since retiring, but his biceps were still hard, even though there was some loosening of the skin around them. I frowned. It was the first time I had noticed the loose skin. I stared at my father and wondered when he had started to look so old.

His face was naturally red, his hair—worn in a Mickey Spillane crew cut—was totally gray, and his eyes were unnaturally red. I wondered what time he'd started drinking today.

"Got a girl yet?" he asked.

"No, Pop."

"Making money?"

"No, Pop."

"Ready to try some other line of work?"

"No, Pop."

Pop hadn't liked it when I became a cop. The Irish became cops, he'd said, Italians became priests—or wise guys. When I left the cops and got a PI's license, he had liked that even less.

He shook his head wearily and said, "If Joey was alive..."

"I'm glad we had this little talk, Pop," I said, rising quickly, "but I think I hear Vinnie." I rushed from the room and went into the kitchen to join Maria.

"Nick?" she said, eyeing me.

"He started that 'If Joey was alive' stuff," I said. "I had to get out of there."

"Be patient, Nick."

"Maria, baby sister..." I started, but we both heard the front door open and close.

"Father Vinnie," she said.

"I'll get him," I said. "Gimme another beer."

I went into the living room and found my brother in front of the Virgin, looking up at the picture of Joey. He wasn't wearing his priest's collar tonight. He had an odd look on his face, one I didn't remember ever having seen before. When you grow up with someone, you eventually see every facial expression that person has—happy, sad, mad, scared—sure, I'd seen my brother scared before, but this was different.

This was naked fear.

"Vinnie?"

Without looking at me he said, "You ever wonder what he'd be doing if he was alive today?"

"Same thing we do," I said, "try to avoid coming to see Pop too often."

Normally, that would have drawn a disapproving look, or a verbal scolding from Father Vinnie, but he let it go right by.

Oh boy, I thought, something was wrong.

"The monsignor catch you whacking off in the confessional or something?" I wanted to ask, but bit my tongue. If this was serious, he was going to have to get to it in his own time.

"If he was here," I said, "we could all go out and tie one on together."

"Yeah," Vinnie said, and he smiled. I knew what he was remembering—the first time the three of us had gotten into a bottle of Pop's bourbon. We'd gotten so sick that Pop hadn't even pounded us. I think that was why I hardly ever drank anything but beer.

"You guys," I said, moving next to him, "you almost got me killed that time."

"It was your idea."

"Hell it was," I said. "I was the baby, remember?"

"Some baby," Vinnie said, "you thought of things Joey and I would never had thought of."

I looked up at the picture of my brother Joey. It was taken just before he'd gone to 'Nam.

"You think he'd be a priest now too?" I asked.

"Him?" Vinnie said. "He'd be a bishop by now."

"Or a cardinal."

We looked at each other and we both said, "Or Pope." That got a chuckle from him, but it didn't go a long way. My brother was taller than me, six-two, and better-looking. If I had his looks I wouldn't have become a priest, I would have terrorized the female population of New York—and they would have loved every minute of it.

"Here," I said, handing him the other beer. As he took it I said, "You want to talk, Vinnie?"

He looked beyond me, toward the kitchen, toward Pop's room.

"After dinner, Nick, when we're alone, okay?"

"Whenever you're ready, big brother."

Maria entered the room at that point, said, "Father Vinnie," and gave him the same hug, kiss, and question she'd given me.

Pretty, my sister Maria, but not a lot of imagination.

7

My father's house was a one-family brick house on Ovington Avenue. If you looked at a map of Brooklyn you'd see the area marked "Borough Park," but we always called it Bensonhurst. What you call it depends on when and where you were brought up.

Most of the conversation at dinner was between Maria and my father. I chimed in once in a while, but Father Vinnie was silent the whole time, pushing his food around his plate.

"Aye," my father said at one point, "Father, what'samatta, they feed you this good in the Rectory every day?"

"No, Pop," Vinnie said, "the only time I get food this good is when you or Maria cook."

"So what'samatta, you're not eating?"

"I guess I'm just not hungry."

"Well, pass your plate over here, then," Pop said. "I ain't about to let good food go to waste."

Maria stood up and started to clear the table.

"I'll help..." Father Vinnie started, but Maria cut him off and showed me that she was more on the ball than I gave her credit for.

"Never mind, Vinnie," she said. "You'll just get in the way. Why don't you and Nicky go for a walk? By the time you get back I'll have coffee ready."

Vinnie looked at me and I said, "It sounds like a good idea to me. Come on, Vin."

The house was between Fourteenth and Fifteenth Avenues, and when we left the house we started walking toward Fifteenth, just strolling.

"What's going on, man?" I asked my brother. "I've never seen you like this."

He rubbed his hand over his face and said, "I don't know where to start."

"It's a cliché, Vin, but start at the beginning, why don't you?"

"Yeah," Vinnie said, "the beginning. That was this past Saturday."

This was Monday.

"What happened Saturday?"

"The police came to church Saturday," he said, looking down at the ground while we walked.

"Is that a first for the Church of the Holy Family?"

"It is for me," Vinnie said. "I was hearing confessions and they took me right out of the confessional. Monsignor Genovese had to finish up for me."

"Why? I mean, why'd they pull you out of church?"

"They took me to the precinct, Nick."

"What for?"

"It seems one of my parishioners was killed Thursday night."

"So? What's that got to do with you?"

He looked at me then and I saw the fear in his eyes. "They think I killed her."

I grabbed his arm and turned him around to face me. There was fear in his eyes, and something else. Pain.

"What? Say that again?"

"They think I killed her, Nick."

"That's crazy. Did they say that?"

"No, not in so many words."

I took my hand off his arm and we started walking again.

"So? Talk to me, Vinnie? What'd they ask you?"

"They asked me how well I knew her," Vinnie said. "They asked me if I ever saw her outside of church. Nicky, they think I was her...lover, or something."

"Wait a minute, Vinnie, this is getting screwier by the second." I grabbed his arm again and stopped him. "Why didn't you call me?"

"I wasn't under arrest or anything," Vinnie said. "They just said they wanted to talk to me. They didn't tell me what it was about until we got to the precinct."

"The six-nine?" The Sixty-ninth Precinct was the local precinct in Canarsie, where the church was located.

"Yes. When we got there they told me that Gloria—that was her name, Gloria Mancuso—that she was dead, and asked me what I knew about her and her husband. Then they started asking me the other questions...the...the suggestive ones."

"Wait a minute. She was married, and they think she was having an affair with you, a priest?"

"That's the impression I got from their questions," Vinnie said. "God, Nick, I'm scared. I wasn't so scared then, but the more I think about it, the more scared I get. What's the monsignor going to think?"

"What does he know, so far?"

"Just that one of our parishioners was killed, and that the police asked me questions about her. He wanted to complain to the police about the detectives pulling me out of confession, but I stopped him."

"Why?"

"I don't want him to know what they're thinking until it's absolutely necessary."

I put my hand on his shoulder and said, "Vinnie, I'm your brother, but I gotta ask you. You weren't seeing her, were you?"

When he didn't answer right away I got a cold feeling in the pit of my stomach.

"Vinnie..."

He moved away from me then, turned his back and walked to the curb.

"Come on, Vinnie!"

He looked at me over his shoulder. He had the same look he had on his face when, at six and eight years of age, we had broken one of Mom's favorite lamps by playing ball in the house.

"I think I wanted to, Nick."

"But did you?"

"I never slept with her, if that's what you're thinking," he said, "but...I did...I did see her outside of church a few times."

"Why, Vinnie?"

"She was an attractive woman, Nick," Vinnie said. "I mean, she was beautiful, and she was always...flirting with me. One night she called me and asked me to meet her. I thought she was in trouble."

"And?"

"I met her at a diner, and we had some coffee. She told me then that she was...attracted to me."

I could understand that. After all, my brother was a good-looking guy, even if he was a priest.

"What did you do?"

He laughed humorlessly and said, "I ran. God, I got out of that diner fast. The following Sunday she was laughing at me in church."

"And after that?"

He turned and faced me.

"Nick, I swear to God, I only saw her two more times after that."

"Where?"

"She invited me to a party at her house."

"And you went?"

"The monsignor wanted me to go. Her husband is well off, and he donates time and money to the parish. Monsignor Genovese wanted to keep him happy."

Church politics, I thought.

"And what happened?"

"I only intended to stay a short time, but somehow she managed to get me alone, even though I was avoiding her."

"This broad sounds like she had all the moves." Naturally, my brother would never know how to handle a sharp cookie like Gloria Mancuso.

"She said she...she wanted to have sex with me. I tried to talk her out of it, but she said it was no use. She wanted me, and she was going to have me."

Every man's dream—unless he was wearing a priest's collar.

"Nick," he said helplessly, "I didn't know what to do. I don't have any...experience dealing with that kind of woman."

"And the other time you saw her?"

He composed himself and continued.

"She called one night and asked me to come to that Holiday Inn in Staten Island."

"Staten Island? And you went?"

"She—she said she'd kill herself if I didn't meet her."

"Jesus, Vinnie..." I started, then decided that was too harsh. I composed *myself* and then said, "Vinnie, this broad sounds crazy. You, uh, went?"

"I went," he said, shaking his head. "Nick, I couldn't take the chance... She had taken a room and I...sneaked up. God," he said, looking at the sky. "I felt so...dirty, like I was doing something wrong."

"You weren't, you know," I said. "She was."

"Yeah," he said, putting his hand to his forehead, "I know, Nick."

"What happened?"

"She let me into the room. She was wearing a nightgown, and some kind of perfume...Nick, she was beautiful, and I *am* a man, after all."

"Vinnie..."

"She took off the nightgown and taunted me, standing there naked and...and so beautiful. Oh, Nick," he said in an anguished tone, "I wanted to...I wanted to so badly..."

"But...you didn't."

"I told her no, I couldn't break my vows."

"What did she say?"

He bit his lip and I could see that his hands were shaking.

"She...pressed her body against me. I...I couldn't move. I felt as if my feet had taken root. My body was...betraying me."

I knew what he meant. Just listening to him tell it, my body was betraying me.

"She said if I didn't make...love to her, she would tell her husband that...that I raped her."

"Jesus, what did you do?"

"I told her I forgave her," Vinnie said, "and I left. She was screaming something about making sure I would pay, but I didn't listen...I left."

"And she never told her husband the lie?"

"I guess not."

"When was the last time you saw her, Vinnie?"

He looked at the ground, scuffing his shoes.

"Vinnie?"

"That was Thursday night, Nick."

It was getting worse.

"Vinnie, you saw her that Thursday night, and after you saw her, someone killed her?"

"Yes."

"Where?"

"In that motel."

"Jesus...Did you tell the police you were with her?"

He stared at me, tears forming in his eyes, and said, "God forgive me, no, I didn't, Nick. I didn't...I lied..."

"You didn't lie, Vinnie," I said, "you just didn't tell them you were there. Did they ask you if you were there?"

"No, not specifically—"

"Then you didn't lie."

"It's like a lie, Nick," Vinnie said, "don't try to convince me otherwise."

"Vinnie," I said, "why aren't you wearing your collar?" His hand went to his throat, as if he'd forgotten he wasn't wearing it.

"I—I can't—" he stammered, "I don't deserve—"

"Vinnie," I said, moving closer to him, "what do you want me to do?"

He stared at me, naked fear in his eyes, and said, "I want you to help me, Nick...Oh, God, I want you to help me..."

For the first time since I can remember I put my arms around my brother.

"That's just what I'm gonna do, Vinnie, don't worry. That's what I'm gonna do."

8

On the way back to the house we decided to keep this from the rest of the family as long as possible. Maria kept giving me looks over coffee. She assumed that I had found out what was troubling Vinnie during our walk, and she expected me to tell her. Her assumption was, of course, correct, but her expectations were denied her when I was the first to leave. I told them I had some late work to do on a case, and Vinnie walked me to the door so that Maria wouldn't.

"I'll call you tomorrow, Nick," Maria said firmly. That was fine with me. I had the answering machine. At the door I told Vinnie, "Don't say anything to anyone until we talk again. Understand?"

"I understand," Vinnie said. "What are you going to do?"

"I'm gonna check into this," I said. "What were the detectives' names?"

"Uh, Devlin and O'Neal."

I didn't know them.

"I'll talk to them first, and then go out to Staten Island and see what I can find out."

"Nick," Vinnie said urgently, "if I get arrested—"

"If you get arrested—" I started, and then stopped. I had been about to tell him not to worry about it, but that was wrong. We had to deal with the possibility that he might be arrested.

"Let's step outside," I said, and we did, closing the door behind us. "I'm going to talk to the cops tomorrow. After that, if I think you need a lawyer, I'll get you one. Did they read you your rights?"

"No, but—"

"That's right, you weren't under arrest. Look, just don't go anywhere tomorrow. I'll come by the Rectory. Okay?"

"What time?"

"I don't know," I said, "after I see the detectives. First I've got to find somebody who knows them, so that they'll talk to me. Just wait for me."

"All right," he said. "I may not be in the Rectory, but I'll be on the church and school grounds."

"Okay, okay," I said. "I'll see you tomorrow."

"Nick," he said, "uh...thanks."

"Don't be an ass."

When I got home I went into my office and sat behind my desk. My head was still spinning from what my brother had told me. How could anyone think that Vinnie, a priest, would kill someone? That was a dumb question even for me to ask myself. Anyone was capable of murder. As far as the cops were concerned, Vinnie was just a man, just another suspect. Jesus, I thought, this Gloria must have been really something to have my brother going around in circles. I had always thought that Father Vinnie was immune to women. That showed that I didn't know my brother as well as I thought I did. Maybe that came from not spending enough time with him.

Jesus, now I was starting to sound like my father.

I had to put my house in order before I could work on my brother's case. I needed someone to follow Dan Kellogg for me. I thought of a couple of amateurs I could have asked. There was my friend Hacker, a computer genius who lived in Park Slope, but if I took him out from behind his computer, he would probably get lost. I dismissed a couple of other choices, too, and decided to ask another PI.

I picked up the phone and dialed Miles Jacoby's number. Jack lived in Manhattan, but I didn't think he'd mind coming across the river for a favor.

"Jacoby."

"Hello, Jack. It's Nick Delvecchio."

"How're you doing, Nick?"

"I could be better," I said. "I need a favor."

"Shoot."

I told him about the Kellogg case, from beginning to end.

"Sounds pretty straightforward," he said. "What are you working on?"

"Something personal," I said, "real personal. I can't get into it right now, but if you're not busy—"

"Say no more, buddy," Jack said, cutting me off, "I'll pick Kellogg up at his house in the morning."

"That'll be pretty early, Jack," I said, trying to make it easier on him. "Why not pick him up at work?"

"If he stops off somewhere on the way to work and tears off a piece, and you miss it, you're gonna kick yourself, Nick."

I knew that.

"Besides, I'm up early for roadwork, anyway."

Jack used to box pro.

"You gettin' back into it?" I asked.

"No, just keepin' in shape. I'll report in to you tomorrow night. Okay?"

"I appreciate this, Jack," I said. "I'll just turn the fee around to you and—"

"We can talk about that later," he said. "Good luck with your personal thing. If I can help, let me know."

"You are helping. Thanks, Jack."

So, that took care of Dan Kellogg. I looked at my watch. It was too late for me to call the cop I wanted to call. I'd have to try and get him early in the morning. If anyone could help me in getting Detectives Devlin and O'Neal to talk to me, he could.

I shut the desk lamp and left the office. As I was making coffee, I thought, jeez, Devlin and O'Neal. Just like Pop said. The Irish became cops.

9

I had been to the Sixty-ninth Precinct before, but not for years. When I was still in uniform—or "in the bag," as cops say—I was loaned out to them once or twice. When I entered, though, I didn't see anyone I knew. There was such a turnover of personnel at police precincts, that being out of the job for almost five years just about put me out of touch.

I approached the front desk and told the sergeant there that I would like to see Detective Devlin and/or Detective O'Neal.

"What's it about?" he asked without looking at me.

"Homicide."

"Old or new?"

"What?"

He looked at me now.

"An old case, or a new one?"

"Uh, a current one."

"You a witness?"

I took out my ID and passed it to him. He looked at it, then passed it back to me.

"Wait a second."

He picked up the phone, punched a few buttons, and waited.

"Yeah, Devlin or O'Neal…Yeah, I got a PI down here named Delvecchio. Wants to see one of you about a current homicide case…uh-huh…okay, sure." He hung up and said, "Upstairs to the second floor."

"Thanks."

He didn't reply.

I took the stairs to the second floor and when I reached the top there was a man waiting for me there. He was tall, with narrow shoulders and a burgeoning girth, graying hair and long legs. He looked like a twenty-year man. He was wearing a white shirt with an open collar, gold-colored pants, and he had both hands in his pocket. "Delvecchio?"

"That's right."

"Follow me," he said curtly. No handshake, no introduction. I didn't even know if he was Devlin or O'Neal.

I followed him to a door with a sign on the wall that said "P.D.U." It stood for Precinct Detective Unit.

Inside were a number of desks, half full and half empty. At the back of the room was a holding pen. The walls were painted a drab green. He led me to two desks in the back of the room that were butted up against one another. There was a man sitting at one desk holding a Styrofoam cup of coffee. There was another cup on the empty desk. The seated man was sandy-haired and overweight. Another twenty-year man. Two old war horses paired off with each other. This wasn't going to be easy.

"Mr. Delvecchio, this is my partner, Detective O'Neal." This was said by the man who had waited for me by the stairs.

"I guess that makes you Detective Devlin."

"Hey," Devlin said, "you *are* a detective."

Nope, I thought, not going to be easy at all.

Devlin sat down and picked up his coffee.

"So?" he said.

I was a little off balance. This wasn't exactly the reception I had expected, I guess.

"I'm here about the Gloria Mancuso case."

Devlin looked across the expanse of both desks at his partner and said, "Mancuso?"

"Not our case."

Devlin looked at me and said, "Not our case. Sorry."

"Look, I know it's not your case," I said. "I know she was killed in Staten Island, but—"

"Then why don't you go to Staten Island and harass them?" Devlin asked.

"Hey, I'm not harassing anybody," I said, wondering what was going on. "I'm just trying to get some information."

"About what?" Devlin asked.

"Look, you guys pulled my brother in here on Sunday and questioned him. I want to know if he's a suspect."

"Your brother?" Devlin said.

"The priest," O'Neal said. "His brother is the priest."

"Oh," Devlin said. "That's nice, your brother's a priest."

"Yeah," I said, starting to heat up, "he's a priest and I used to be a cop. All I'm asking for here is some cooperation."

"You used to be on the job, huh?" Devlin said.

"That's right."

"What happened?"

"I busted one too many heads," I said. "What's your problem, Devlin?"

"Since you ask," Devlin said, setting the coffee down on the desk, "I'll tell you what my problem is. I don't like getting called into my CO's office and being told that I got to cooperate with some two-bit PI who used to be on the job, when the ex-cop PI don't have enough sense to come right to me with his request."

"Oh," I said, "I see."

"Yeah," Devlin said. He picked his coffee up, sat back in his chair, and stared at me.

"I fucked up."

"Royally," O'Neal said.

I had called an old colleague of mine, Deputy Inspector Ed Gorman, who had been my "rabbi" when I was on the job. It was he who had worked out the deal for me where I could retire on a one-third disability instead of facing criminal charges. I figured if anyone would know these two detectives, he might. He said he'd take care of it. Obviously he didn't know them, but he had called their CO and asked for cooperation. When they in turn had been called in by their captain, they had been "told" to cooperate, not "asked."

"Okay," I said, "I fucked up, I'm sorry. Obviously, what I wanted to happen did not."

"And it ain't gonna," Devlin said. "We were told to cooperate and we will. We will talk to you about any of our cases you want to hear about. We can't talk to you about a case that isn't ours."

"Look," I said, "give me a chance to clear this up. I didn't know you fellas, so I called a friend of mine and asked if he did. He said he'd help."

"A friend?" Devlin asked.

"A DI."

He mugged and looked at his friend.

"I wish I had a friend who was a deputy inspector." He looked at me again and asked, "Why couldn't he help you out with your, uh, departmental difficulties?"

"He did," I said. "He kept me out of jail."

That surprised them, and they exchanged a glance that they had probably been exchanging for years.

"Sounds like a nice man to have on your side," Devlin said carefully.

I smelled a deal in the air, but I figured they wanted me to approach them with it.

"Okay," I said, "my rabbi is your rabbi. What have you got?"

They exchanged a glance again, and O'Neal nodded.

"Okay," Devlin said, looking around quickly. "We got a call from a Detective Lacy at the one-two-two in Staten Island. They had a homicide at a Holiday Inn on Richmond Avenue. A broad was killed in one of the rooms."

"How?"

"She was strangled."

"Okay, go ahead."

"They wanted us to pick up a priest named..." Here he looked at his partner.

"He knows his name," O'Neal said, "it's his fuckin' brother, for Chrissake."

"Right," Devlin said. "They wanted us to pick up your brother and question him."

"They weren't at the, uh, interview?"

"No," Devlin said, "they said they would talk to him later."

"They wanted you to soften him up first. Scare him a little."

"Put the fear of God into him, they said," O'Neal said, chuckling. When he saw I wasn't laughing he stopped and said, "Well, they thought it was funny."

"So you pulled him out of church right in the middle of confession, hauled him back here, and questioned him."

"Right."

"And some of the questions were...suggestive."

"Huh?"

"You made him believe that you thought he was sleeping with the woman."

"Right," Devlin said. "Personally, I didn't like doing it. I mean, Jesus Christ, the guy's a priest!"

I looked at O'Neal but he didn't comment. I guess he didn't mind doing it. No Catholic guilt there.

"Do they have anything solid on my brother?"

They looked at each other again.

"We really don't know," Devlin said. "We were just cooperating, you know? Precinct to precinct?"

"Yeah," I said, "I know, but if you had to guess..." I looked at Devlin, and then at O'Neal. It was O'Neal who answered.

"If I had to guess," he said, "I'd tell you to get your brother a good lawyer."

10

A very attractive woman in her twenties answered the door at the Rectory. I had only been there once or twice, so I didn't know if she was regular help or volunteer. She had short brown hair, pretty eyes, and a nice mouth. She was wearing a blouse and skirt, and she had nice, trim legs that would have been shown off better if she hadn't been wearing sensible shoes.

The precinct was located on Rockaway Parkway and Foster Avenue. The Church of the Holy Family was located on Rockaway Parkway and Flatlands Avenue. The distance was about four long blocks, and I'd walked it.

"Can I help you?" she asked.

"Yes, I'd like to see Father Vin—uh, Father Delvecchio."

"Are you a parishoner?"

"No, ma'am, I'm his brother."

She smiled and said, "Oh. Well, Father is in the school gymnasium. The regular gym teacher is ill, and Father is taking his class."

"Thank you, ma'am."

"Sister," she said, "Sister Olivia."

"Really?" I said. Boy, you can't tell these days, when they don't have to wear habits.

"Thank you...Sister."

"You're very welcome."

She closed the door and I stood there shaking my head. They shouldn't allow nuns to look like that. Sister Olivia looked nothing like my seventh-grade teacher, Sister Manassa Mauler.

The School of the Holy Family was across the courtyard from the church. I knew from the other times I had been there that the best entrance for the gym was on the Conklin Avenue side. I walked through the courtyard to that side of the building and entered. Once inside I had only to follow the sounds of the whistle and the slapping feet.

As I entered the gym I saw Vinnie. He was wearing a T-shirt with the school insignia on his chest, which precluded him from wearing his collar. The kids running back and forth with a basketball looked like eleven- or twelve-year-old boys and girls. The school was a boys-and-girls parochial school, grades kindergarten to eight.

I caught myself watching one of the girls who was running up and down the floor. She had long, flowing blonde hair, beautiful skin, strong legs and thighs, and she needed some sort of athletic bra. The boys her age, running with her, were more interested in her bouncing boobs than the bouncing ball. Some of the other girls were pretty, too, and somewhat advanced physically, but the blonde was a total knockout.

Jesus, I thought, they didn't have nuns or students like this when I was in parochial school.

Vinnie saw me and held up five fingers, indicating that there was five minutes left in the class. I spent the five minutes watching that blonde girl run up and down the floor and trying not to feel guilty about it.

Vinnie finally blew the whistle and told the boys and girls to go and get dressed. The filed out through a door at the opposite end of the gym.

"Hi, Nick." He was wiping his hands on a white towel he'd had around his neck.

"Sister Olivia told me you were over here. How come they didn't have nuns like her when we were kids?"

"They have changed, haven't they?"

"So have the kids," I said, "especially the girls."

"You noticed Lisa."

"The blonde? I couldn't help it. What grade is she in, anyway?"

"Eighth," Vinnie said. "She's thirteen."

"My God," I said. "Her mother ought to talk to her about a sports bra before she starts high school."

"She can't," he said, wiping his dripping face with the towel. "Her mother was Gloria Mancuso."

"Oh." I wasn't sure what to say. "At least that explains her looks."

"Oh, she's got her mother's looks, all right," he said, "and her attitude as well. She's gonna be a terror in high school."

I could just imagine how many teenage boys would be walking the halls of her high school with swollen balls.

"Let me just check on the kids," he said, "and then you can walk me to the Rectory. I've got to take a shower. That was the only gym class I had to take. The others are covered."

I thought how ironic it was that he'd had to take the class that Gloria Mancuso's daughter was in.

"I'm surprised she's in school," I commented.

"First day back since her mother...died."

"When are they burying her?"

"I'm not sure."

He used his key to open a side door of the Rectory, and I followed him up a flight of back stairs to his room. I'd seen my brother's room only once before, and it hadn't changed. It was still a spare, neat room with a desk, a bed, a chair, and an end table with a lamp. There was also a small bookcase, filled with paperbacks.

"I'll take a quick shower," he said, "and then we'll talk."

When I was a kid I served as an altar boy, so I had seen the inside of a Rectory then. I remember thinking what a hardship it must have been for all the priests to have to share a bathroom. My brother did not have that hardship. He had a bathroom adjoining his room.

I heard the shower go on and checked out the books in the bookcase. There were some fiction and nonfiction best-sellers, some Andrew Greeley books, some of the Harry Kemelman Rabbi books, and some books by William X. Kienzle. The Greeley, Kemelman, and Kienzle books were all mysteries with a clerical detective. I hadn't know that my brother was into mysteries. I moved some of them around and found a book set crosswise atop them. When I took it out I was surprised to find one of Samantha's Kit Karson romances. The lurid cover had been torn off and discarded.

Vinnie reentered the room, wearing a pair of jockey shorts and drying his hair. He stopped when he saw me in front of the bookcase.

"Sam will be flattered," I said, holding her book up. "What happened to the cover?"

"I bought it in a used-books store like that," he said. "She's a good writer."

"I'll tell her you said so."

"Anything happening with you and her?"

I put her book back where I'd gotten it from and said, "We're friends, Vinnie."

"She was real helpful last year, when Maria was...in trouble."

"She's a helpful gal."

"Pop liked her a lot," he said. "I thought maybe you two—"

"Vinnie."

"Okay," he said, "sorry." He went back into the bathroom and came out without the towel. He pulled on a pair of black pants, and then sat on his bed to pull on a pair of black loafers.

"So tell me," he said, "did you talk to the detectives? Do I need a lawyer?"

"Yes, I spoke with them, but I don't know yet if you need a lawyer."

"What do you mean? What did they say?"

"They said they were just assisting the Staten Island detectives with their case. They have no facts themselves, because it's not their case. They were simply asked to question you and...shake you up a bit."

"Well, they did that." He stood up, crossed the room and took a white T-shirt from a dresser drawer. He rolled it up, pulled it over his head, and rolled it down.

"The Staten Island detectives will probably be talking to you," I said. "Before that happens, I'll talk to them, but I think I'll find you a lawyer, anyway. I don't know if you need him, but I think you should call him whenever they approach you to speak with you."

He took a new white shirt out of another drawer, stripped the wrapper, and started removing the pins. "Can't that be avoided for a while?"

"What? Calling the attorney?"

"As soon as I notify the Diocese that I need an attorney, the whole story will have to come out."

"No, it won't."

"The Church will have to foot the bill," Vinnie said. "I'll have to tell them why."

"You tell them you can't talk to them until you speak to your lawyer."

"That's a Catch Twenty-two, Nick," he said, gesturing with the shirt. "I can't tell them why I need a lawyer until I have a lawyer, and they won't hire a lawyer until I tell them why I need one."

"If the Church won't hire you a lawyer," I said, "I'll foot the bill."

"Nick—"

"I'll go with you."

"What?"

"We'll go and talk to whoever we have to talk to together."

"We'll have to go to the office of the Diocese in downtown Brooklyn," he said, "but eventually we're going to have to talk with Manhattan."

"O'Malley himself?" I asked. Cardinal O'Malley was a famous man. He had a fabulous physical presence, which came across well on TV. He always said Midnight Mass on television on Christmas Eve.

"He's going to have to be told."

"Let's take one step at a time," I said. "I'll go to Staten Island to talk to the detective, then I'll get the lawyer and we'll have dinner together. After that, we do what he tells us."

"I can't pay a lawyer—"

"I doubt that we'll have to front any money."

"Look, Nick, it's bad enough that I'm asking you for favors, but to ask your friends—"

"Don't worry about it, Vinnie."

He stared at me for a few moments, then slipped into the shirt. He tucked it into his pants, then grabbed a black jacket and went to the door. He opened it, but I pressed my palm to the door and closed it again.

"What?" he said.

"Where's your collar, Vinnie?"

"My collar?"

"Your collar."

"Why do you want my collar?"

"Don't play games with me, Father," I said. "I don't want your collar."

"Then why did you ask me for it?"

"Where is it?"

"It's in my jacket pocket."

"Take it out and put it on."

"Nick..." he said, starting to open the door, but I kept my palm pressed to it.

"Nick..."

"We're going to keep this thing between us as long as we can," I said. "Maybe we'll be able to straighten it out, and maybe we won't, I don't know, but you're going to wear your collar."

He took it out of his pocket and looked at it.

"I don't deserve to."

"Bunk!"

"What?"

"I can't say what I wanted to say, I'm in the presence of a priest."

"I'm not worthy of—"

"Bull dooky!"

"Nick!"

"I'm gonna run out of substitutes pretty soon."

"This is silly—"

"Put the damn collar on!"

"Don't curse in here."

"Then put it on."

My brother stared at me for a few heartbeats and then put the collar on. "Can I go to work now?" he asked.

I opened the door for him and said, "We'll both go to work now."

11

I played it differently with the Staten Island detectives. Instead of asking Inspector Gorman to call them, I asked Devlin if he would. He did, and Detective Lacy and his partner, Detective Giambone, were expecting me. Before I left the six-nine, O'Neal made a point of reminding me of our little deal. I gave them each one of my business cards and told them that if they ever needed anything to call me. What was implied there was that they should not call Deputy Inspector Gorman directly. Devlin gave me a conspiratorial wink before I left, as if to let me know that we were now all on the same side—theirs!

I borrowed Hacker's 1976 Grand Prix for the ride out to Staten Island. Since he rarely left his computer consoles, it was very unlikely he'd miss it. I decided to stop in and see the detectives before I went by the Holiday Inn, as a courtesy. I'd learned my lesson from fucking up with the six-nine detectives. I wasn't going to make the same mistake with the one-two-two dicks.

I entered the new-looking one-two-two building on Hylan Boulevard. The damned thing looked more like a catering hall than a precinct. I approached the front desk as I had in Brooklyn, and asked for Detectives Lacy and Giambone. The location was changed, but the personnel almost seemed interchangeable. The desk officer called upstairs, announced me, and then told me to go ahead up.

No one was waiting for me at the stairs when I got to the second floor, but I managed to locate the squad room and ask for Lacy and Giambone. I was pointed in Lacy's direction, and told that Giambone was out.

I approached Detective Lacy's desk and he stood up and extended his hand. He looked to be about thirty, nattily attired in a powder-blue suit, his styled hair perfectly in place. I wondered what Devlin and O'Neal would think if they saw Lacy. The new breed of detective.

There were an "out" box and an "in" box on Lacy's desk. His "in" box was empty. His "out" box had a *Wall Street Journal* folded on top of a bunch of blue DD 5s. Apparently, Detective Lacy kept well up on his Detective Follow-Up Reports.

"Thanks for agreeing to talk to me," I said, sitting next to his desk.

"Coffee?"

"Sure."

He got up to pour me a cup and handed it to me. "You were on the job, right?"

"That's right."

"The coffee hasn't changed."

I sipped it and said, "Brings back memories."

"Did you make detective?"

"No," I said, "I went out a patrolman."

"Tough break."

I didn't know if he meant never making detective, or the way my career in law enforcement ended.

"Speaking of tough breaks…" I said.

"Yeah," Lacy said, "this Mancuso thing. Whew, what a looker. How anyone could kill a woman as fine as that is beyond me."

"You know that Vincent Delvecchio is my brother, right?"

He nodded. "Devlin mentioned it. So, your brother's a priest, huh?"

"That's right," I said. "Father Delvecchio. What have you got on him?"

Lacy sat forward and said, "I'm going to try my best to be helpful here, Mr. Delvecchio, but I hope you understand I can't give you my case." He touched his hair lightly, verifying that it was still in place. "I assume you're going to hire a lawyer for your brother?"

"That's right."

"Well, if your brother is arrested, his lawyer will benefit from his right to disclosure, and he will see all the evidence."

Helpful Detective Lacy sounded more like a lawyer than a cop. I was willing to bet that he was going to law school at night.

"Just between you, me, and the lamppost, Detective," I said, leaning toward him, "how close are you to an actual arrest?"

"We still have some investigating to do, Mr. Delvecchio, before we present our case to the DA. In fact, my partner is out at this very moment, continuing to do preliminaries."

"When will you be getting around to talking to my brother?" He didn't answer right away and I said, "I want to be able to get him a lawyer in time."

"I tell you what," Lacy said. "Get him a lawyer, and have them both come in to see me."

"I think I can arrange that."

"How about Thursday morning?" he suggested. "Ten o'clock?"

I nodded.

"Well, good," Lacy said, standing up abruptly. He put his hand out and said, "I'm glad we had this little talk, Mr. Delvecchio. I'm always happy to cooperate."

Lacy struck me as the kind of man who never wanted to get anyone mad at him, just in case he ever needed him for something.

But I was thinking, what talk? I hadn't found out a damned thing and he was already giving me the bum's rush—albeit it a very polite one.

I stood up and took his hand, but I didn't let him push me out the door.

"How about throwing me a bone?"

"What do you mean?"

"How'd you get onto my brother?"

He frowned, then gave a little shrug. "Why not? We had a witness who saw him drive up and enter the hotel. It struck us odd, a priest going to a Holiday Inn, *and* he didn't stop at the desk. He went straight up. They got his plate number, and we ran it. Once we knew what church he was, uh, assigned to, we realized it was the victim's parish. It wasn't hard to ID your brother from his description."

"If he had gone there to kill her," I said, "he wouldn't have used a parish car, he wouldn't have worn his collar, and he certainly wouldn't have used the front door."

"True," Lacy said, without missing a beat, "but we're not saying he went there to kill her."

Point to him.

"Is it all right with you if I go and look around the motel?"

"The Holiday Inn? Sure, sure." His tone was magnanimous. "It's a public place. The room where she was killed is still sealed, though." The last was said with a warning in his voice, as if he were talking to a small child.

"I don't have to get inside the room," I said. "I just want to snoop around outside."

"Snoop to your heart's content." He waved his right hand in a go-right-ahead gesture, and then while it was out there used it to check his hair again.

I didn't like the man. I had the feeling that he had been laughing at me from the moment I entered the room. No, not laughing...*amused* by me.

"Tell me something," I said before leaving, "are you attending law school?"

"Why, yes," he said, smiling. "You really are a detective, aren't you?"

"So I've been told."

12

It was ironic to me that Gloria Mancuso should have picked the Holiday Inn in Staten Island to die in. Just last year I had tailed another faithless wife to the very same hotel. That woman hadn't died as a result of it, but someone had. A cabbie told me that time that when Brooklyn spouses stepped out on their better halves, this Holiday Inn was a popular spot for it. I'd had my doubts then, but I guess he was right.

I drove Hacker's Grand Prix from the precinct to the hotel and parked in their parking lot. I'd forgotten to ask Vinnie how he got to Staten Island. If he had taken one of the Church vehicles, someone might have gotten a license plate. If he had taken a cab, the cabbie could probably ID him. Either way he was fu—um, in trouble.

I went inside and approached the desk clerk. I couldn't remember if he was the one I had spoken to last year. He was wearing the Holiday Inn green jacket and looked to be about college age. He watched me as I approached, appraising me.

"Can I help you?" he asked.

"Yes," I said. "I'm investigating the murder that occurred here Thursday night."

I held my breath, waiting for him to ask me if I was a cop.

"I talked to the other detectives already," he said. "Twice."

"Well, maybe you wouldn't mind going over it again for me, just one more time." I dredged up my cop smile from my past, pasted it on and said, "Please?"

"Look," he said, sighing, "all I saw was the priest come into the lobby. He looked kind of on edge, you know? If he hadn't been a priest, I would have thought he was just some guy meetin' his dolly, you know?"

"What'd he do?"

"He went into the elevator."

"Did you notice what floor he went to?"

"No," the clerk said. "I told the other cops, I didn't see what floor he went to, and I never saw him leave."

"Is there another way he could have gotten out without passing you?"

"If he really wanted to," the clerk said, "there was plenty."

I hadn't asked Vinnie how he left the hotel. There were probably a lot of things I hadn't asked him that I might have asked him if he weren't my brother. Maybe I should keep that in mind next time we talked.

"All right." I took out a five and handed it to him. "Thanks."

I started to walk out, but he called out to me before I reached the door.

"Hey!"

I turned and he beckoned to me. I walked back to the desk.

"The other cops didn't give me nothin'," he said. "Maybe that's why I didn't remember to tell them somethin' else I noticed."

"Like what?"

"Well, the broad, the one who was killed? Man, she was some looker. She had legs that wouldn't quit, and a tight ass—"

"I know all that," I said, cutting him off.

"Yeah, well, there's somethin' you don't know." "What?"

"She didn't come here alone."

"What?"

"Naw," the kid said, "somebody dropped her off."

"Who?"

"Man, I don't know that. I don't even know what kind of car, only that it was shiny blue."

"What about the doorman who was on duty that night? Would he remember?"

"We don't use a doorman at night all the time," the kid said. "We ain't all that busy, except for…well, you know."

"And you didn't have a doorman that night?"

"No."

"How'd you know the car was shiny blue? And how did you know she was dropped off?"

"Well, there ain't much to do here at night, and when a car pulls in you can see the headlights. When I saw the lights I looked out the door. When she opened the passenger door the inside light went on, and I saw her step out. I mean, I saw her legs first. Man, they were—"

"The car."

"Yeah, the light from inside was enough for me to see the color of the car. Shiny blue."

"Did you see the driver?"

"No."

"Man? Woman?"

"Couldn't tell. Hey, I was lookin' at the blonde, ya know?"

"Yeah, right." I took out another five and held it out to him.

"Hey, man, I wasn't hintin'—"

"Forget that," I said. "You earned it."

"Thanks."

I started away, but this time something occurred to me and I turned back.

"One more question."

"Shoot."

"Did she check in?"

"Did she—no, now that you mention it, she went right into the elevator, like she already had a room key. Hey," he said, snapping his fingers, "that means somebody else checked her in, huh?"

"That's what it means," I said. "Listen, can you check something for me?"

"What?"

"I want to know how many keys were given out for that room, and how many you got back. Can you do that for me?"

"I'd have to look it up," he said, "and I can't do it right now."

"That's okay," I said. "If you can do it by tonight, though, I'd appreciate it." I took out another five and gave it to him.

"Where do I call you?"

Now I had to admit I wasn't a cop, because I couldn't have him calling the precinct.

"Look," I said, taking out one of my business cards, "I'm not really a cop..."

He took the card and said, "You never said you were, man. I'll give you a call tonight."

"Thanks. If I'm not in, just leave the information on my machine. When I get it, I'll drop a twenty in the mail to you. Okay?"

"Sure, man," he said enthusiastically.

I noted his name on his jacket—"Riley"—so I could mark the envelope to his attention.

"When did you know I wasn't a cop?" I asked him before leaving.

He grinned and said, "When you laid that first five on me, man."

13

I drove Hacker's car back over the Verrazano Bridge to Brooklyn, dropped it off by his apartment, and took a cab to my place. I could have walked it, but I was in a hurry to get back. I had to line up a lawyer for Vinnie. I knew plenty of lawyers. I had *worked* for plenty of them, but I had to get one that I would trust with my brother's life. My problem was I didn't know one who fit the bill. I did know, however, that Miles Jacoby had a friend who was a lawyer, a man he thought very highly of. His name was Hector Delgado, and he had his office in Manhattan.

I pulled out a Manhattan phone book and looked up his number. I would have preferred to wait for Jack, so that he could introduce us, but I didn't have time. Jack wouldn't be calling in until after five, and Delgado would not have office hours then. Since I had promised that Vinnie and his lawyer would stop in to see Detective Lacy and his partner at 10 A.M. Thursday morning, I had to get Vinnie together with a lawyer as soon as possible.

I dialed Delgado's number and his secretary answered. I asked for Hector Delgado, and she told me that he was in court.

"Listen," I said, "it's very important that I talk to him. My name is Nick

Delvecchio; I'm a PI out of Brooklyn."

There was a pause and then she asked, "Are you Miles Jacoby's friend?"

"That's right."

"He's mentioned you," she said. "I'm Missy. I'll have Mr. Delgado call you back as soon as he gets in, Mr. Delvecchio."

"My name is Nick, Missy," I said. "I'm gonna wait right here until he does call me back. Thanks."

"Okay, Nick," she said, her tone friendly, and we hung up.

I remembered Missy. She had worked for Jacoby's mentor, Eddie Waters, before Waters was killed. Jacoby found Waters' killer, and Missy later went to work for Hector Delgado.

I was glad Missy recognized my name. That meant Delgado might, but if he didn't, she'd tell him. I felt fairly confident that I would hear from him today.

Next I called Vinnie at the Rectory, but he wasn't there. I left a message with Sister Olivia for him to call me back.

I checked my watch. It was four o'clock and I was hungry, but I couldn't leave until I got my calls. I went out into the hall and knocked on Sam's door. I left the door to my office open, so I'd hear the phone if it rang.

Sam answered, and I knew she'd been working. Her hair was tousled, as if she had been running her hands through it between paragraphs, and the tart, pleasant scent of girl sweat made its way to my nostrils. She says that even in an air-conditioned room, when she's writing she sweats. I told her women don't sweat, they glow.

A while back I used to be able to tell if she was working just by listening at her door. That was back when she had a typewriter, and, later, one of those noisy printers. These days, you couldn't hear the printers unless you were in the same room with them.

Sam doesn't look like Sissy Spacek, but she's got the same hair and eyebrows. However, the resemblance stopped there. From the neck down Sam looked more like a playboy centerfold. Right now she was wearing a T-shirt which did nothing to hide the fact that her firm breasts were unfettered.

"Nick, hi."

"You got anything to eat?"

"What?"

"I'm hungry," I said, "and I can't leave the building. I'm waiting for some important calls."

She leaned against the doorjamb and folded her arms beneath her breasts.

"Did you break that answering machine already?"

"No, the machine works fine, it's just that I have to be here to get those messages personally."

"Well, I'm very sorry," she said, "but my cupboard is bare."

"Great," I said. "Why couldn't I get a neighbor who can cook?"

"Sorry, friend," she said wryly, "but you got one with looks."

I suddenly realized what a bore I was being, so I smiled and said, "I sure did. You know, with your build, you shouldn't wear T-shirts. It's too dangerous."

"For who?"

"For the male population of Brooklyn."

"Well," she said, "when I'm working, I like to be comfortable."

"I can see that," I said. "Look, I'm sorry I bothered you. I'll send out for a pizza."

"Get it with pepperoni," she said, raising her eyebrows, "and I'll split it with you."

"You got a deal," I said. "I'll call you when it's here."

"Fine," she said, "and while we're eating it, you can tell me what's the matter with you."

"Does it show?"

She smiled and said, "It does to me, Nicky."

I made a face at her and she closed the door. She knows I hate it when anyone outside my family calls me that.

I went back into my office and called for a pizza from a nearby pizzeria. I ordered it with *half* pepperoni.

14

Over pizza and beer in my kitchen—I always have beer in the fridge—I told Sam what was going on. I even told her about Vinnie. Sam is probably my best friend, and she's as level-headed as they come—or as level-headed as someone who is trying to write for a living can be.

"Your brother is no killer, Nick," she said when I was through.

"I know that."

"And he'd never break his vows."

"I know that, too," I said, then squinted at her suspiciously and asked, "How do *you* know that?"

"I've met your brother."

"Yeah, but...you never made a pass at my brother, did you?"

"Well, no...but he is real good-looking, you know?"

"I know, I know," I said. "He looks like an actor."

"Or a model."

"So you've got a thing for my brother?" I asked. "Is that it?"

She grinned at me and took a big bite from a slice of pizza. A big glob of cheese slid off and fell onto her chest.

"Serves you right," I said, while she tried to wipe up the mess with a napkin.

"So," she said, "what are you gonna do?"

"I've got to get my brother together with the lawyer, so the lawyer can tell us what to do."

"Why are you rushing this?"

"Lacy was too smug," I said. "I think he wants to arrest my brother."

"On what evidence?"

"He was there," I said, "and I can't have him deny that. Once they arrest him, if he tells them anything about his three meetings with Gloria Mancuso, he's gonna look even more guilty."

"Will he tell them?"

"I guess that'll be up to the lawyer."

"Who's the lawyer?"

"Hector Delgado," I said, "a friend of Miles Jacoby's."

"Jacoby's that PI from the city?"

"Yeah," I said, "the one who's watching Dan Kellogg for me."

"How are you gonna keep working for Linda Kellogg when your own brother needs your help?"

"I don't know," I said. "Maybe I should just drop her case—"

"You can't do that!" Sam said. "Her husband's a brute. She needs somebody to protect—"

"She needs *somebody*," I said, "that's the key word. It doesn't have to be me. Maybe I'll just turn the whole thing over to Jacoby, if he wants it."

"And if he doesn't?"

"There are other PIs who could use the work."

I saw a look come into her eyes and she eased forward in her chair.

"What?" I said.

She picked up a napkin and wiped pizza oil from her hands so she could use them when she spoke. If I didn't know better, I would have sworn the girl was Italian. "Let me do it."

"Sam—"

"No, no," she said, waving her hands, "I can do it. Let me follow him."

"You can't."

"Why not?"

"You're not trained."

"Nick, anybody can follow somebody—"

"Hell no," I said, "you have to be trained for surveillance work—"

"Nick," she said, "I've read so many books—"

"Reading about it and doing it are two different things, Sam."

She stared at me and then said, "What's the real reason you don't want me to do it?"

"The real reason?"

"Yeah."

"Your tits are too big."

"What?"

"There's no way you could follow someone and go unnoticed," I said. "Also, your hair is too blonde."

"Am I supposed to take this as a compliment?" she asked. "My hair's too blonde, my tits are too big...I tell you what. I'll wear a hat and tuck my hair up underneath, and I'll wear a big, floppy sweatshirt." Her hands were gesticulating wildly.

"A floppy sweatshirt?" I asked. "Sam, it's Indian summer." The temperature that day had hit 85 degrees.

"So," she said, wiggling her pale eyebrows at me, "I won't wear anything underneath."

I was having visions of that when the phone rang. "Hold that thought."

I went into my office to take the call. It was Miles Jacoby.

"He was clean today, Nick," he said. "In and out. He didn't even go out to lunch."

"Par for the course, Jack."

"You want me to take him again tomorrow?"

I hesitated, then said, "No, I may have that covered. There is something you can do for me, though."

"Name it."

"Well, actually," I said a bit sheepishly, "I've already used your name."

"What are you talking about?"

"Let me explain."

I went on to tell him about the trouble Vinnie was in, and about having called Hector Delgado.

"Heck can do the job for you, Nick," Jack said. "I'll give him a call right now."

"I don't want this to be a favor, Jack," I said. "We'll pay his fee."

Jack laughed and said, "Heck won't have any problem with that, Nick. Let me get off. He might be trying to call you, and I'll try to call him. Talk to you later."

"Thanks, Jack."

I hung up and went back into the apartment. Sam had taken the opportunity to get a piece ahead of me.

"You shouldn't eat so much pizza," I said, sitting down opposite her again.

"Why not?"

I picked up a slice and said, "You're gonna have to be light on your feet when you're tailing Dan Kellogg tomorrow."

15

Sam had gone back to her apartment to work when the phone rang again. This time it was Heck Delgado.

"Mr. Delvecchio?"

"Speaking."

"Hector Delgado here. I understand you wanted to talk to me."

Delgado had a definite Ricardo Montalban accent that probably served him well in court, especially with female jurors.

"Have you spoken to Miles Jacoby yet?"

"Not this evening. Why? Is Miles involved in this?"

"Only to the extent that I called you because of what I've heard about you from him."

"Well, I'm glad Miles has spoken highly of me. Suppose you tell me what the problem is?"

I did, from beginning to end. He asked some relevant questions along the way, but otherwise listened in complete silence. The only thing I left out for the moment was the fact that I had made an appointment for him and Vinnie to be in the 122nd Precinct on Thursday, at 10 A.M.

"Well," he said when I was finished, "this sounds very interesting."

"Does that mean you'll represent my brother?"

"When may I speak with him?"

"As soon as possible. Well, there is something I didn't mention," I said, and told him about the appointment.

"Well, I don't like that," he said, "but perhaps we can work with it. I will have to speak to your brother first, though. May I see him tonight?"

"I'll arrange it."

"Where?"

I took a moment to think. We couldn't go to the Rectory, because we didn't want anyone there to know about this yet. The same was true of my father's house. "Would a restaurant, or a diner, be okay?"

"I would rather talk somewhere more quiet. I can understand why you wouldn't want me to go to the Rectory at this point. What about your apartment?"

"That's fine with me," I said. "I'll set it up."

"Would eight P.M. be convenient?"

"Sure."

"Very well," he said, "all I would need now from you is directions. Would you give them to my secretary for me?"

"No problem," I said. "I appreciate this, Mr. Delgado."

"Not at all," he said. "Please hold on."

I held for less than a minute and then Missy came on and took down the directions. She said that Delgado would be driving, so I simply gave him directions from the Brooklyn Bridge on.

I hung up the phone and it rang almost immediately. It was Vinnie.

"Can you get out tonight?"

"Of course," he said, "I'm not a prisoner here, Nick."

"Well, be here by seven-thirty," I said. "I've got a lawyer coming at eight."

"Who is it?"

"His name is Hector Delgado. He was recommended by a friend."

"Can't we do this tomorrow?"

"No," I said, and told him why.

"Nick, you think they're gonna arrest me?"

"Vinnie," I said, "let's talk about it when you get here, okay?"

"All right," he said. "I'll be there soon."

"You remember where it is?"

"I remember."

"Okay, see you soon."

I hung up and went and checked the refrigerator. I had enough beer, so I didn't have to go out. I was wondering if I should make some coffee when there was a knock on the door to my office. I opened it and Sam was standing there.

"I heard your phone, and my curiosity got the better of me."

"Would you like to make some coffee?" I asked quickly.

"Well...sure."

"Come on in..."

16

Vinnie arrived well before Delgado, which pleased me. We'd have a chance to talk. When Vinnie entered and saw Sam he smiled.

"Miss Karson," he said.

"I thought we settled that last time, Father," she said, kissing him on the cheek. "Call me Sam."

"It's good to see you again, Sam," he said. "That's not my brother's coffee I smell."

"No," she said, smiling, "he was smart enough to ask me to make the coffee."

Not only had she made the coffee, but she had gone out and picked up some doughnuts for us. The only place that was open was the bodega with the sign in the window about drugs. She'd managed to find a box of Hostess doughnuts with a current expiration date. She had set them out nicely on a plate and covered them with a paper towel.

"The coffee is all ready," she said, "and I have to get back to work."

"Must you leave me with him?" Vinnie asked, jerking his thumb at me.

"I'm sorry, Father, but I must."

"I'll walk you to your apartment."

"Just walk me to the door, Nick."

I did that, and opened it for her. I put my arm around her waist and said, "Thanks, Sam."

"Thank you," she said. "I'll pick Dan Kellogg up at home in the morning and stay on him all day."

"Look," I said, squeezing her, "be careful, all right? If he sees you, break it off."

"He won't see me," she said, smiling broadly. "I have the perfect disguise."

"You gonna dye your eyebrows and eyelashes?"

She elbowed me in the ribs and said, "I'll talk to you tomorrow evening."

I watched her enter her apartment, and then closed the door to mine.

"She's prettier than I remembered," my brother said.

I almost made a comment about her having the hots for him, but then I remembered why we were there.

"Want a cup of coffee while we wait?" I asked.

"Sure."

We went into the kitchen and sat at the table. Sam had prepared a twelve-cup pot in the coffee maker, so it wasn't going to hurt for us to have two while we waited for Delgado to arrive.

"Tell me what happened in Staten Island," Vinnie said.

I laid it out for him, including what I had found out at the Holiday Inn.

"But...who could have brought her there?" he asked when I was done.

"I don't know, Vinnie. Do you know what kind of car her family has?"

"No."

"I'll check into that."

"You think her husband took her there? That's crazy, Nick."

"I don't know what to think, Vinnie," I said. "One thing I'm gonna have to do is find out how their marriage was doing."

"I don't know, but if she was happy, would she have approached me?"

"One has nothing to do with the other, brother," I said. "There are plenty of women who are happy with their husbands who still fool around, and vice versa."

"I guess I just don't understand today's morality," Vinnie said, shaking his head.

"Vinnie," I said, "how did you leave the Holiday Inn that night?"

He averted his eyes and said, "I used the side exit."

"Why?"

"I...didn't want to be seen."

"But you went in through the front door, and you were seen."

"When I went there, I managed to convince myself that I was doing so for a noble cause. I don't know if I really believed that she intended to kill herself, but I couldn't take the chance."

"And later?"

"Later," he said, looking into his coffee cup, "I was just running. I was ashamed, and I didn't want anyone to see me."

"Vinnie, what did *you* have to be ashamed of?"

"Nick." He looked at me and I could see the anguish in his eyes. "I failed her."

I couldn't believe what I had just heard.

"What?"

"She needed me, and I failed her."

"She needed you, all right, in her bed."

"No, I don't mean that," he said, "I mean she needed me to save her soul."

"You can't save the world, Vinnie."

"This wasn't the world, Nick," he said, "this was one disturbed, misguided woman."

"Vin—" I said, but there was a knock on the door. I looked at my watch. Delgado was fifteen minutes early.

"Vinnie," I said, standing up, "it's important that you talk openly to Delgado. If he's going to represent you, he's gonna have to know everything."

"He's not going to represent me," Vinnie said, "or know anything unless you let him in."

I went to let him in.

17

Heck Delgado looked just the way I expected him to look. He was tall, well-groomed, in excellent shape, maybe a little younger than I had expected. I didn't think he was yet forty, or if he was, he had just made it. Between him and my brother, I felt like the sad sack of the three. I was glad Sam hadn't seen Delgado. He *wasn't* a priest, and I may not have been able to get her to leave.

Delgado and I shook hands at the door. He had a firm handshake. In his left hand he was holding what looked like an alligator-hide attaché case. The watch on his wrist wasn't a Rolex, but it still had to cost a bundle.

"I spoke to Miles before I came," he said. "He has a very high opinion of you."

"I feel the same about him." What else would we say about each other? "My brother is in the kitchen. This way."

"I understand you used to be a police officer."

"That's right," I said, "but not for about five years." In the kitchen I introduced Vinnie to him as Father Vincent Delvecchio.

"Father, a pleasure," Delgado said.

"Mr. Delgado."

"Coffee?" I asked.

"Yes, that would be nice," Delgado said, sitting at the table.

I brought him a cup of coffee and then uncovered the doughnuts. He opened his attaché case and took out a normal yellow ruled pad. I don't know what I expected to come out of that alligator-hide case. Maybe a pad in gold leaf. He had a silver and a gold Cross pen in his shirt pocket. He chose the silver.

"I haven't had a chance to eat dinner," Delgado said, and took one of the doughnuts. He looked at us and said, "Gentlemen, for the next half hour or so, you are going to talk and I am going to listen. I want to know everything that you can tell me about this case, down to the smallest detail. Father, why don't you start?"

Vinnie told Delgado how he had first met the Mancusos, Anthony and Gloria. It was several years earlier, when they transferred their daughter into the school. At first he only saw them in church, and at church functions. After a year or so Vinnie became involved with the PTA, and Gloria Mancuso was also active there. A year after that she became president of the PTA, and they worked even more closely together.

"You never noticed an attraction to you?" Delgado asked. He had started on his second doughnut, and I freshened his coffee. He had been taking notes the entire time. He had a rather large, flowing handwriting that I found difficult to read upside down.

"Mr. Delgado," my brother said slowly, "when you are a young priest, there is a tendency for some mothers to...to flirt with you."

"Is there a tendency to flirt back?" he asked.

"No," Vinnie said, growing tense.

"Father," Delgado said, putting his Cross pen down carefully on top of the pad. "I am not your enemy. If I agree to represent you, I will want you to consider me your only friend in the world. Please don't take offense at anything I ask you. I have good reasons for all my questions."

"I'm sorry," Vinnie said. "I've thought about this a lot. I never considered myself a…a flirt, but I have become…more relaxed with some mothers than others. Gloria may have been one of those mothers. But I never intended…"

"No, of course you didn't," Delgado said. "Please, continue."

Now we got to the part where Gloria Mancuso had first approached Vinnie about her feelings for him.

"Can I say something here?"

Delgado looked at me and said, "Please."

"I don't think we should consider that the dead woman had…feelings for my brother. I don't think we should consider that she was in love with him to any degree. I think this was a woman who saw men as a challenge, and she saw my brother as her greatest challenge."

"Was she loose?" Delgado asked. "In general, I mean. Did she have a reputation for playing around?"

"I have no way of knowing that," Vinnie said.

"Well, we'll have to find out," Delgado said.

I assumed that by "we" Delgado meant him and me. Later, I would find out differently.

"Please," Delgado said, picking up his pen, "continue."

I poured him more coffee, but he did not take another doughnut. I hadn't had any yet, so I took a powdered one. He had eaten two plain ones. There were also some that were chocolate-covered. Vinnie hadn't had any.

Vinnie went on and told Delgado everything he had told me. He didn't leave anything out, even though I knew it was difficult for him to discuss it with a stranger.

"Is that all of it?" Delgado asked after Vinnie had stopped talking.

"That's it," Vinnie said. "She was alive when I left her."

"Did you see anyone at the hotel that you knew?"

"No."

"Did you see any vehicles you might have recognized in the parking lot?"

"No."

"You drove there in a car owned by the Church?"

"Yes."

Delgado turned his attention to me.

"I assume you've spoken to the police?"

"Yes."

"Please," he said, "tell me everything you've been told, or learned on your own."

I relayed everything to him that I had learned from Devlin and O'Neal at the six-nine, and from Lacy at the one-two-two. I then told him everything I had found out from the desk clerk.

"Has he called yet about the keys?" he asked, writing furiously on his pad.

"Not yet."

"I'll want to know what he says as soon as you learn it," he said "and as soon as you find out anything about that blue car. I will leave you my home phone."

"You'll represent me?" Vinnie asked.

"Yes," Delgado said, "if you want me to."

"Yes," Vinnie said, "yes, I do." I could see that Vinnie was impressed with Delgado's thoroughness.

"Good," Delgado said, capping his pen and sliding it into his pocket. "What is the protocol for this, as regards the Church?"

"Uh, well," Vinnie said, "I'm not altogether sure. We'll have to go to the office of the Diocese, here in downtown Brooklyn. It's on Joraleman Street. Nick said he would go with me."

"You and I will go to the Diocese together," Delgado said. "There is no need for your brother to go."

I almost objected, but decided not to.

"I'll start checking on Gloria Mancuso's marriage," I said.

Delgado looked at me and said, "You've done a fine job up until now, Nick, but I have my own investigators. I'm sure you understand."

I did, but I didn't like it. I opened my mouth to protest, but Vinnie got there before me.

"Mr. Delgado, I want Nick to work on this."

"Father," Delgado said, "I can appreciate how you feel, but—"

"Mr. Delgado," Vinnie said, cutting the man off, "there's no way I can know for sure whether or not you, or any of your investigators, will believe that I did not kill Gloria Mancuso. I do know, however, that my brother believes me. I need that."

"Father—"

"Also," Vinnie continued quickly, "no one will work as hard for me as my brother will, no matter how much you pay them. He's my brother."

Good for you, brother, I thought, and watched Delgado. After a moment, Delgado smiled at both of us.

"I can't argue with that," he said.

Vinnie extended his hand and Delgado took it.

"Thank you," my brother said.

Delgado looked at me and said, "May I have another cup of coffee? We still have some talking to do."

18

Delgado left before Vinnie. He shook hands with both of us. He and Vinnie were going to meet downtown in the morning and go to the Diocese together. Meanwhile, he had mapped out a strategy for me to follow, which would put us ahead of the game in the event they arrested Father Vinnie over the weekend.

"We're meeting with the police Thursday morning," he'd said. "There is a chance that they will arrest you right there and then, but I doubt it. If it comes, it will probably come after the weekend. Still, we must be prepared for anything."

We agreed that Heck—he had asked us both to call him that—would call me after he and Vinnie had spoken to the Diocese.

After Heck left, Vinnie came back into the kitchen with me.

"More coffee?" I asked him.

"No."

He sat down and toyed with a doughnut.

"How about a glass of milk?" I asked.

"Sure."

I gave him a glass of milk and sat opposite him. He sipped the milk and gnawed at a chocolate-covered doughnut.

"What do you think?" I asked.

"I like him," Vinnie said. "He impressed me. I think I can have confidence in him."

"Good."

He looked at me and said, "I'm scared, Nick."

"You wouldn't be human if you weren't, Vinnie," I said, "and priest or no priest, you are human, you know."

"I know," he said, "but once we go to the Diocese tomorrow, I may not be a priest for very much longer."

"Don't you expect the Church to stand behind you on this?"

"Yes," he said, "of course." He sounded less than convinced.

"They can't...fire you for getting arrested...can they?"

He started shaking his head and then said, "I don't know what they'll do, Nick. I just don't know. I mean, we know that I didn't kill her, but they're also going to be concerned with why I went there that night. There's been a lot in the media lately about fallen priests, you know? The whole Covenant House thing, and that fiasco down south with that woman who slept not only with a priest, but a bishop. God," he said, covering his eyes, "the press will have a field day with this, especially since it's the New York press."

"So," I said, "you might be in a no-win situation."

"I know..."

"But that doesn't mean you're not gonna fight...right?"

"Fight for what?" he said. "If I'm not a priest, what will I be?"

I looked at him and said, "You'll be out of jail, free, and alive...by the grace of God."

He looked at me sharply. I knew why. The last line of my statement surprised even myself.

"Yes," he said, seeming oddly calm suddenly, "by the grace of God."

After Father Vinnie left to go back to the Rectory I rinsed off whatever glasses and dishes had to be rinsed off, then decided to have a beer. I still had two bottles of Dos Equis and two St. Pauli Girls among the Meister Braus in my refrigerator from the last time I had the money to buy imported beer. I chose Mexican over German and took a Dos Equis into the living room with me so I could go over the day.

First, I wasn't sure I had done the right thing in letting Sam tail Dan Kellogg the next day. She wasn't a pro, but then neither was Kellogg, so where was the real danger? What were the chances that he'd notice her, especially now, when she would be the third person to tail him in three days? Even if he looked behind him, he wouldn't see the same person. On the other hand, he hadn't looked behind him the entire time I was tailing him. Well, maybe I'd let her tail him one day, and then I could get somebody else.

Wait a minute! I don't know why I didn't think of it before. I knew another Brooklyn PI who, coincidentally, lived in Greenpoint, and owned a bar there. And for good measure, he was Italian. Right, so in the morning I'd call Sal Carlucci and line him up for the next day, and as many days after that, that he could handle. Carlucci was in his fifties, sort of semi-retired, and he had a gimpy leg from when he was a cop, but I was sure he could handle this.

If need be, I could probably rotate Jacoby, Carlucci, and Sam. That way I would be taking up a minimum of their time and still be covering Kellogg full-time.

I looked at my watch. It was too late to call Linda Kellogg at the hospital. I'd call her in the morning, and assure her that I was still on the job.

The Kellogg matter handled, I settled down to think about my brother's problem.

Tomorrow, while he and Heck went to the Diocese, I was going to have to start checking up on Gloria Mancuso. According to Heck, if Vinnie was arrested and went as far as going to trial, all we had to do was raise some reasonable doubt, and finding a passel of boyfriends would certainly do that. Vinnie told me that I could pick up a list of the PTA people in the morning from Sister Olivia, and I could start with them. Once again, as I had done at the Holiday Inn, I'd simply present myself as "investigating" Gloria Mancuso's murder, and let the people assume that I was a cop. In the event they asked for ID, I'd give it to them, and then try to get them to talk to me anyway.

Under normal circumstances, I wouldn't have gone anywhere near an active homicide investigation. That was the fastest way to get my license lifted. This was different, however. This was my brother.

Something that Vinnie and I hadn't yet talked about was how and when we were going to tell Pop and Maria that he was in this jam. It would have to come straight from Vinnie, and he should probably tell both of them at the same time, simply so he wouldn't have to go through it twice.

When we talked tomorrow, I'd broach that subject with him. We could probably wait until we knew whether or not he was going to be arrested. My feeling—and Heck agreed—was that if and when they decided to arrest him, in light of the cooperation we were giving them, they'd probably just call Heck and ask him to have his client give himself up.

Jesus, I thought, how would Vinnie react to being in jail? I squeezed the bottle in my hand and hoped that Father Vinnie's faith in God was strong enough to see him through this.

19

I got to the Rectory nice and early, but still after school started. Sister Olivia answered the door again and smiled at me. I was struck once again at how pretty she was.

"Hello, Mr. Delvecchio," she said, "come in."

"Thank you, Sister."

I entered the foyer and she closed the door behind us.

"This way, please."

I followed her to a small office off to the side. The Rectory smelled just like the Rectory I knew when I was a kid.

"Father left just a little while ago," she said, "but he asked me to give you this."

She handed me an 8 ½-by-11 sheet of paper. It was a Xerox of a list of the parents in the PTA. Next to their names was their position. Right at the top of the list it said "Gloria Mancuso, President."

"Thank you, Sister."

"Are you, uh, investigating our PTA?" she asked. Before I could answer she said, "Forgive me, but I'm very curious. I, uh, read mysteries, and books about private eyes are my favorites."

"Not Greeley, or Kemelman?"

"No," she said, smiling, "Jeremiah Healy and Sue Grafton."

I tried a shot in the dark.

"Bill Pronzini?"

"Oh, yes," she said, "ever since I was...younger."

I was running into a lot of people lately who read mysteries, including my own brother.

"Well, Sister," I said, lowering my voice dramatically, "I really am not at liberty to say, right now."

"Oh," she said, lowering her voice, "client confidentiality, right?"

"That's right." We were staring at each other and I couldn't stop myself, so I asked her, "How could somebody so pretty become a nun?"

She flushed and was about to answer when a distinguished white-haired man walked in, and we both straightened up as if we had been doing something we should feel guilty about.

"Monsignor!" she said.

"Sister," the man said, nodding to me, "have you seen Father Delvecchio?"

"He, uh, left a little while ago, Monsignor."

"Left? To go where?"

"I don't know, Monsignor."

"He didn't say?"

"No, sir," Sister Olivia said. I was edging toward the door when she added, "but this is Father Delvecchio's brother. Perhaps he can help you."

Monsignor Genovese looked at me and raised his white eyebrows. He had a ruddy complexion and light-blue eyes. He would charm the pants—well, he'd charm all the older ladies in the parish.

Weren't there any ugly priests or nuns these days?

"Father Delvecchio's brother?" he said. "How nice." He extended his hand and I shook it.

"Nick Delvecchio, Monsignor. It's a pleasure to meet you. I have to be going—"

"Would you know where your brother went this morning, Mr. Delvecchio?"

"Uh, well..." My Catholic background somehow kept me from lying immediately, but I finally got it out. "No, sir, I don't. I really have to go—"

"Would you be able to come into my office with me for a few moments, Mr. Delvecchio?" he asked then. "There's something I want to talk to you about."

"In your office?"

"Just for a few minutes, please."

"Well...sure..."

"This way, please."

Monsignor left the small office, and I looked at Sister Olivia, who looked distressed. I smiled so she wouldn't feel bad about giving away my identity, and then followed the monsignor.

The monsignor's office was impressive. It was almost big enough to hold the oakwood desk he moved around to sit behind.

"Take a seat, please."

"Monsignor—"

"Please sit!"

I felt like an altar boy again. I sat.

"Mr. Delvecchio, I would like to know what is going on."

"Monsignor?"

"Please," he said, holding his hands up to me, palms out, "don't lie. You did it badly before. You hesitated. I would think that a private investigator would know how to lie better."

"I do," I said, "it's this place."

"Were you ever an altar boy?"

"Yes."

"When was the last time you were in church?"

"Um—"

"Or to confession?"

"Uh—"

"What is going on, Mr. Delvecchio? I know it has something to do with the police taking your brother out of confession on Saturday. It must also have something to do with the death of one of our parishioners, Mrs. Mancuso, eh? Now, if I put two and two together, I *will* come up with four, but perhaps you would like to save me the effort?"

I stared at him for a few moments, and then decided that I couldn't tell him anything, Catholic guilt or not.

"I'm sorry, Monsignor, there's nothing I can tell you. I think you should wait for Vinnie—that is, Father Delvecchio, to return, and then talk to him about it."

He was frowning mightily as I spoke.

"Mr. Delvecchio," he said, "I am not a happy man."

"I understand that, sir."

"Is Vincent in trouble?"

"Again, Monsignor, that's going to be up to him to tell you. I hope you can understand that."

"Your brother had better have a good explanation for me when he returns."

"I think he will, sir," I said. "I also think he's going to need some understanding from you."

"Mr. Delvecchio—Nick," the monsignor said, folding his hands on his desk, "I am a very understanding man, but my understanding, and my patience, both have limits."

"I understand, sir."

He stared at me for a few moments, then nodded and said, "You may go."

"Thank you, sir."

I stopped by Sister Olivia on my way out. She had her legs curled under the chair she was sitting on, and I noticed that she had nice calves. Firm, strong runner's calves. "Marathoner?" I asked.

"What?" she asked, looking up in surprise.

"I said, are you a marathoner?"

She smiled and said, "I run, but the most I've done is half marathons. How did you know?"

"I, uh…" I hesitated, then said, "I noticed your, uh, legs."

She looked down at her legs, then blushed and said, "Oh."

"Do you ever wear your habit?"

"For formal functions," she said, then smiled again and added, "but never when I run."

I opened my mouth to say something, and then shut it. I realized what I was doing. I was flirting with a nun. Sure, she was a young, attractive female… with nice legs…but she was still a nun.

"Sister, what can you tell me about Gloria Mancuso?" The smile, and good-natured expression, left her face at the mention of the dead woman.

"Mr. Delvecchio—"

"Please call me Nick."

"Nick…you're asking me an impossible question," she said. "I really can't speak ill of the dead."

"I take it then that you didn't think highly of her." She compressed her lips for a moment, then looked around.

"She was fine with the children, Nick," she said, "which is why she was a good PTA president."

"She wasn't so good with the adults?"

Sister Olivia stared at me.

"Oh, I think I see," I said. "She got along better with the fathers than the mothers?"

"She was well liked," Sister Olivia said, "by both…but for different reasons."

"Sister," I said, touching her arm, "I understand what you're saying."

"Please," she said, "the monsignor—"

"Don't worry, Sister." I was still touching her, so I removed my hand. "I won't say anything to the monsignor."

"Mr. Delvecchio—Nick...is Father Vincent in trouble?"

"He might be, Sister," I said, "he might be. In any event, we both appreciate your help."

"If I can really be of any help, please let me know."

"I sure will, Sister."

She got up and walked me to the front door. I started out the door when she opened it, then stopped.

"Sister, excuse me for asking, but...have you taken your final vows yet?"

"Oh, yes," she said, "two years ago."

"I see."

"Why?"

"Never mind," I said, shaking my head. "I was just curious."

20

The list Sister Olivia had given me had names, addresses, and phone numbers of all the officers of the PTA. All I could do was go and see the people, and see if they would talk to me.

Given what Sister Olivia had indicated to me about Gloria Mancuso, I thought I'd be getting different reactions from the women than from the men. As early as it was, I'd probably only be finding some of the wives home, and most of the husbands would be at work. There would probably be exceptions, but I prepared a story that I could use on the ladies. After all, most of the PTA positions were held by mothers.

I spent most of the day doing interviews with PTA members and got a variety of responses from them.

The vice president of the PTA was Harriet Dean who, I assumed, would now move up into the presidency. Did that give her a motive? People have been killed for less, but it seemed pretty farfetched.

Harriet Dean was in her thirties, trying hard to look younger. She wore tons of makeup that gave her face a brittle look, and tight clothes that bulged in all the wrong places.

What did she think of Gloria Mancuso?

"Gloria was a go-getter," Mrs. Dean said, "and what she usually went and got was men."

"Did her husband know about this?" I asked.

"Well," Mrs. Dean said, "if we did, I assume he did, also."

"What do you mean when you say 'we' did?"

She batted her mascara-laden eyes at me and said, "Why, everyone."

"Well, how did he feel about it?"

"To tell you the truth," she said, "I don't think he cared all that much."

"Why not?"

"Well, he was a busy man. He had other things on his mind," she said, and then used her forefinger to bend her little nose over and added, "if you know what I mean?" To some people, all Italians are Mafia.

Georgia Taylor was the PTA treasurer. She was younger than both Gloria Mancuso and Harriet Dean, probably just in her mid-twenties.

"I've only been in the PTA a year," she said. "I got the treasurer's job because I was willing to give my time, and because Gloria pushed for me to get it."

"Pushed?"

"She...what's the word...politicked for me. I really appreciated her help."

"Some of the other women have indicated to me that Gloria may not have been the most faithful wife in the world."

"Did you show me your badge?"

The head of the Hospitality Committee was a very attractive, well-dressed woman in her early thirties named Beverly Smith, whom I caught on her way out. Mrs. Smith struck me as something of a snob.

"I really don't have time to talk with you, officer," she said.

"But I was only after a few words from you about Gloria Mancuso's death."

"I'll give you a few words," she said, pausing as she opened the door of her beemer, "it couldn't have happened to a nicer bitch."

After a while the names and titles ran together. There was a group of women who spoke quite cattily about Gloria, painting her as a hard worker, but also a hard player. They didn't approve of her attitude toward their husbands. This group was definitely not made up of her friends.

"Was this attitude only directed toward the husbands?" I asked one lady.

"Mister," one young, sweet-faced, very Catholic-looking mother named Molly McBain said, "she tried to fuck anything with a zipper. I wouldn't be surprised if she nailed a priest in the confessional. That would be the kind of challenge Gloria would have liked."

"Any particular priest?"

"Well, the best-looking one was Father Delvecchio," she said, "but as long as he had a zipper, he was fair game. I told all of this to the other police detectives."

"I'm just backtracking a bit..." I said.

I wondered which detective she had told that to, and if she had mentioned Vinnie's name.

The other group, her friends—including Harriet Dean and Georgia Taylor—seemed to have put her up on a pedestal, all of them thrilled with her alleged sexual exploits. None of them, however, could come up with any names for the men she had on a string. All of them, quite obviously, got their kicks vicariously through her and her stories.

I asked one woman, "Do you mean she bragged about having other men?"

"Darling," the woman told me, "what's the point of having them if you can't brag about them?"

I found several husbands home. Since many mothers worked these days, it made sense I'd find some men home. It only took one of the men to sum up their opinion of Gloria Mancuso, though.

"She was a cock tease," the man said, with a four-year-old clinging to his leg, "but what a looker, man."

"Did she ever come across?"

"Well, man," the fella said, "I don't exactly kiss and tell, you know?"

Especially when you've got nothing to kiss and tell about, I thought.

By 5 P.M. I was talked out, and I had a pretty good picture of Gloria Mancuso. She was a hard worker for the PTA, and for the kids, but she didn't let that stop her from having her fun. She was certainly a flirt and a tease, and she had friend and foe alike convinced that she slept around, but no one could give me any specific names. Only one man's name had been mentioned, and that was Vinnie's, but the person who mentioned it certainly didn't know anything definite.

Still, if she had mentioned his name to a detective, it could be very damaging—especially if that detective lacked imagination.

Having spoken to three of the four detective who were involved with the case so far, I thought that was pretty likely.

21

I took a cab home and got there by six-thirty. There was one message on the machine. It was from Sam. She just wanted to tell me that it was 3 P.M. and everything had gone all right so far. She said she'd talk to me tonight. She sounded both pleased and excited.

I made a quick call to Sal Carlucci in Greenpoint. He said he couldn't help me tomorrow and was tied up on the weekend, but he'd be free on Monday, if I still needed him. I told him I'd let him know by Sunday.

I was disappointed not to find a message from Vinnie. I had thought about stopping by the Rectory on my way home, but I didn't want to run into Monsignor Genovese again. I was also a little ashamed of the way I'd flirted with Sister Olivia. Her manner could be called flirtatious, although I was sure she didn't mean it to be, and I wondered if that was the kind of thing Vinnie had meant when he mentioned that he was more "relaxed" with some mothers than with others. I was sure that Sister Olivia had flirted back quite innocently, not meaning anything by it.

Was that how it had started with Gloria and Vinnie? And had it led to disaster?

I went across the hall and knocked on Sam's door.

When she didn't answer I started to worry. Kellogg usually made it home by six or so and by routine, stayed there. Sam should have been at home by now. I decided to give her half an hour more before I really started to worry.

As soon as I reentered my apartment, the phone started to ring. I went into the office and picked it up on the third ring. The machine answers on the fourth.

"Delvecchio," I said.

"Nick, this is Heck."

"Heck, how'd it go?"

"We spent quite a bit of time at the Diocese office. As it turned out, we talked with some of their legal advisers. I managed to convince them that I did not need a Father Shannon as an assistant on this."

"Father Shannon?"

"Apparently the Church sent Father Shannon to law school, and he *is* a lawyer, but I doubt that he's ever been involved in anything like this."

"How did they react?"

"At first they were shocked and dismayed. That quickly degenerated into worry and panic. I only wish I could say they were worried about your brother."

"What *were* they worried about?"

"The image of the Church," Heck said. "Did I tell you that I am a lapsed Catholic?"

"Is that different than being a non-practicing Catholic, like me?"

"Yes," Heck said, "if you call yourself a non-practicing Catholic, that means that you either admit that there is a chance you'll go back, or you have a brother who is a priest."

"One out of two."

"With me, there is no chance I could go back. The reasons are very personal and go back many years, but seeing their reaction to Father Vincent's predicament, I am even more convinced that I made the right decision."

"Heck," I said with concern, "are they gonna back Vinnie on this?"

There was a long silence, and then he said, "They said they will."

"You don't believe them?"

"Like anyone else," Heck said, "what the Catholic Church says and does can be two different things."

"What happens now?"

"With the Church? They want Vincent to go to Manhattan."

"To see the cardinal?"

"We will find out who he is to see when we get there."

"When will that be?"

"Friday."

"Are you still on for the one-two-two tomorrow?"

"We will be there," he said. "How did your day go?"

"Well, in the morning I was called in by Vinnie's monsignor. He's no dope," I said, and filled him in on our conversation.

"Your brother will have to handle that this evening," Heck said. "He probably only just got back to the Rectory a little while ago. What else happened? What did you get on Gloria Mancuso?"

"What I figured to get," I said, "not that it helps us a lot. A lot of hearsay and rumors." I told him what the other mothers and fathers thought of Gloria, and he took it all in in silence.

When I was finished there were a few moments of silence. I assumed he was taking notes. After a few moments he spoke.

"What you need...to do..." he said, and he spoke as if he were still writing, speaking with divided attention, "...is find her best friend."

"Well, I certainly didn't do that today. It's possible that whoever it is is not involved in the PTA."

"Yes, of course," he said, "by all means go outside the PTA. Is there someone there who might be able to help you with that?"

"Yes," I said, thinking of Sister Olivia, "there might be."

"Good, good," he said. "All right. We'll speak again tomorrow, after your brother and I talk to the detectives assigned to the case."

"All right, Heck," I said. "Thanks for calling."

I hung up and thought about Sister Olivia again. She probably wouldn't want to talk to me in the Rectory, where the monsignor might see us.

I wondered if nuns accepted invitations to lunch.

22

I kept the door to my apartment open until I heard Sam coming down the hall. I looked at my watch and saw that it was after nine. I catapulted off the sofa and ran to the door as she was putting her key in the lock.

"Where the hell have you been?" I demanded.

She jumped at least a foot and placed her hand over her heart.

"Jesus, you scared the shit out of me!"

"And you scared the shit out of me," I countered. "And what are you doing dressed like that?"

She was wearing a black dress so tight it was hard to imagine how she had gotten it on. It covered her to her neck, but she still looked naked because her breasts were plainly and perfectly outlined. You could even see her nipples. It also had no sleeves and shoulders, and her pale skin stood out starkly against the black. At the other end it was so short that I could see the tops of her net black stockings. On her feet she was wearing black boots with high heels. Her usually pale eyelashes were covered with dark mascara, and she was wearing more makeup than I had ever seen her wear.

"That's your idea of going unnoticed when you're tailing someone?" I demanded.

"Look, Nick, let me change and then I'll explain."

"The hell with changing," I said, grabbing her arm, "explain now, dammit!"

"Don't yell at me," she said, pulling on her arm to get it away from me, but I wasn't letting go. I pulled her right into my apartment and shut the door, *then* I let her go.

"Friends don't yell at each other," she told me belligerently.

"No, but employers yell at employees, and you were supposed to be working for me today, not going out on a date."

"I *was* working for you today. If you'll shut up long enough, I'll tell you about it."

"All right," I said, folding my arms across my chest, "talk."

"I picked Kellogg up at his home this morning and followed him to work."

"Dressed like that?"

"No, I wasn't dressed like this," she shot back. "Are you gonna let me tell it?"

"Tell it," I said tightly.

"I stayed with him, but he never even left his place for lunch. After work he didn't go straight home."

"What?" I unfolded my arms. "That's a break in pattern."

"I know."

"Where'd he go?"

"Aldretti's."

Aldretti's was only a few blocks from our building. "What was he doing there?"

"Well, I looked in the window and he sat in a booth, not at the bar. If he had sat at the bar I might have figured he was there for a quick drink, but since he took a booth I thought he'd be there awhile. That's when I got the idea."

"What idea?"

"I ran home and got out my fuck-me dress," she said, doing a slow pirouette. Jesus, I could see the cleft between her buttocks.

"Sam—"

"Nick," she said, "we wanted to find out if he was a chaser, right? What better way than to dangle some bait in front of him?"

"I didn't send you out there to be bait!"

"I know, I know, but I decided to use some initiative. Isn't that what a good detective does?"

"I guess I wouldn't know," I said. "Go on. What happened when you got back to the bar?"

Suddenly her face fell.

"I don't think he ever looked at me."

"Well, that makes him either blind, dead, or…gay?"

"If he was gay, there are other places for him to go than Aldretti's."

"Okay, so if he didn't come on to you, what did he do?"

"He met a guy."

"A guy?"

"He must have been waiting for him, because the guy came in and sat right down with him. He didn't even have to look for him, just walked right to the booth."

"What happened then?"

"They argued. I couldn't hear what they were saying because I was sitting at the bar, too far away, and I was fending off every other guy in the bar."

"You don't frequent Aldretti's, do you?"

"I don't hang out in bars, Nick," she said. "At least, not bars like Aldretti's."

"My point is, no one there knew you."

"No," she said, "but they all wanted to."

"I can't say I blame them."

"What?"

"What else happened?"

"Nothing. They had a beer each, argued for a while, and then Kellogg calmed down and the other man talked to him for a long time."

"Did Kellogg look like he might be afraid of this other guy?"

"I don't see why he would be," she said. "The other guy was a lot smaller, a real skinny, frail-looking guy."

"Fear doesn't have to be something physical, Sam. Maybe the guy's got something on Kellogg."

"What?"

"I don't know."

"You think he's a got a past he doesn't want anyone to know about?"

"Could be. I'll have to have it checked out."

"I could do it."

"You?" I said in disbelief.

"Why not?"

"Sam, you are not a detective, and you proved that today."

"I thought I did pretty well today."

"You did, until you got this crazy idea to dress up. Look at you."

She looked down at herself, then at me.

"What's the matter with the way I look?"

"Well, it's a little cheap, isn't it?"

"Cheap?"

"Sam, you look dangerous," I said. "Walking around like that you could start fights, cause traffic accidents."

She peered at me suspiciously and said, "Are you complimenting me?"

"I'm scolding you, dammit!" I said. "Don't you know when you're being yelled at?"

"For what? I found out he wasn't interested in other women."

"You found out that he wasn't interested in *you*," I said, "not today, anyway. You also drew a lot of attention to yourself, when you were supposed to be running surveillance *without* drawing attention. Whether you think so or not, he must have seen you, which means I can't use you anymore."

"But—"

"No buts," I said. "I have someone lined up to take him on Monday."

"What about Thursday and Friday? And the weekend? If he's got a girlfriend, won't he try to see her on the weekend?"

"I don't think he's got a girlfriend," I said. "I think there's something else making him so mad."

"What?"

"I don't know," I said, "and I don't have the time to try and find out myself. I'm going to have to go and see Linda and tell her that I'm turning the case over to someone else."

"Who?"

"Whoever wants it. Jacoby, Carlucci, Henry Po. If they don't want it, maybe they can recommend someone who will."

"Linda Kellogg is counting on you, Nick."

I rubbed my hand over my face and said, "I know, but so is my brother."

23

"What's happening with your brother?" Sam asked.

"Let's finish this up first," I said, "and then I'll tell you."

"There's nothing to finish up. He left Aldretti's and I followed him home."

"Wait a minute," I said, slowing her down. "Who left first, him or the other guy?"

"He did."

"Did the other guy see you?"

"I...think so. He looked over at the bar a couple of times. He could have been looking at me."

"Bet on it. I don't want you going near Aldretti's anymore."

"I told you," she said, "I don't hang out at neighborhood bars...although there were a couple of good-looking guys with interesting offers. You know what one of them wanted to do with whipped cream?"

"I don't want to know," I said quickly. "You're off the case, Karson, and you've got a book to write."

"Oh, shit," she said. "I forgot about that."

"Better get to work."

"What about Linda Kellogg?"

"She's safe in the hospital, Sam," I said. "Go on, go back to work."

"First tell me what happened with your brother."

I gave her the short version, telling her that we really wouldn't know much until after he and Heck Delgado had met with the detectives.

"Well, keep me informed, all right?"

"Sure."

"What about your family?"

"They don't know yet."

"Are you going to tell them?"

"I think Vinnie should do that."

"You're probably right."

She headed for the door, opened it, and then turned and said, "What do you really think of this dress?"

I took a moment to look at her. Sam's not really tall, but I think she'd qualify as a big, healthy woman. She looked fabulous in the dress, especially with her shoulders and arms showing. Sam works out, and you can tell she does from the wonderful muscle tone in her arms and shoulders. She lifts weights, and has said on occasion that she might have done so seriously if her tits weren't too big.

Her pale skin and blonde hair really played well off the black dress. I had that rare thought about why we were just friends—good friends, granted, but why just friends?

"Sam," I said, "you don't need a fuck-me dress to attract attention."

It was the only harmless thing I could think of saying. I couldn't tell her that seeing her dressed that way, with her nipples so plainly pressing against the material of the dress, made my heart rise up into my throat. That's not the kind of thing one friend says to another.

She thought about that for a moment, and said, "I think I'll take that as a compliment."

"It was meant that way."

"Now tell me why you were so mad at me."

"That's easy," I said. "I was worried about you."

"Really?"

"Really."

She walked back to me and kissed me on the cheek. I could smell the fresh scent of her hair. I loved the way her hair smelled.

"You're sweet," she said. "Thanks for giving me the chance."

"You're welcome," I said, and as she walked back to the door I said, "As a detective, you weren't exactly a total fuck-up."

"Now that," she said, with the doorknob in her hand, "I *will* take as a compliment."

Once she was out of the apartment and out of my sight in that dress, I sat down and waited for my breathing to return to normal.

I was thinking about Riley, the clerk at the Holiday Inn, when the phone rang. He was supposed to call me back about the room keys, and I was hoping this was he.

I couldn't have been more wrong.

"Nicholas?"

There was only one man I knew who called me Nicholas.

"Hello..." When speaking to Dominick Barracondi, I always had a problem with what to call him. Nicky "Barracuda" had been a friend of my father's for years, even before he rose to be the Godfather of Brooklyn. My problem was that he was also *my* godfather, and I could never bring myself to call him that. It always summoned up visions of Marlon Brando with his mouth stuffed with cotton.

I didn't approve of my godfather, but I always treated him with respect.

"How are you?" he asked.
"Just fine."
"And your father?"
"He's fine, too."
"Please give Vito my best, and your lovely sister, too."
"I will, sir."
"Nicholas, I was wondering if you would come and see me tomorrow."
"About what?"
"I...would prefer to discuss that when you are here—if you would be kind enough to come?"

That was the closest I'd ever heard Nicky Barracuda come to saying "please."

I frowned, wondering what he wanted.

"Well...all right." Curiosity kept me from saying no.

"Come for lunch?"

"Yes."

"Excellent! It has been some time since we have talked."

"Is that all you want to do," I asked, "talk? Pass the time?"

"Uh, no, no, I have something very specific in mind. I will see you at one, eh?"

"One is fine."

"Good, good. See you then, Nicholas."

I hung up, puzzled, and then a dim light dawned. He had asked about everyone in my family except Vinnie. He always asked about "Father Vinnie." Why not this time? Did he know Vinnie was in trouble? Was that what he wanted to see me about?

If he did know, how?

The answer was simple.

He was, after all, Nicky "Barracuda."

24

About eight the next morning I was at the Rectory again. And once again I was driving Hacker's Grand Prix. I had called ahead to make sure Vinnie would be there to see me. I knew that he'd be leaving for Staten Island at about eight-fifteen, to meet Heck at the one-two-two.

A woman who wasn't Sister Olivia answered the door. She was a hard-looking forty-five, squat and gray-haired, wearing wire-rimmed glasses.

"Good morning, Sister."

"I'm not a nun," she said. "My name is Mrs. Graf. I'm staff. Can I help you?"

"I'm sorry," he said. "Without the habit it's hard to tell."

If she sympathized with my predicament, it didn't show on her face.

"My name is Nick Delvecchio," I said. "Father Delvecchio is my brother. I'd like to see him, please."

"Step in and wait, please."

I stepped inside. She closed the door and went off into the bowels of the Rectory. While I was waiting in a sort of waiting room, the monsignor came by.

"Good morning, Monsignor."

"I don't know if I should speak to you, Mr. Delvecchio," the monsignor said.

"Monsignor—"

"I am certainly more angry at Father Delvecchio for not having enough faith in me to confide in me before he went to the Diocese," he said, "but I have enough anger left over for you, too."

"I hope you have enough forgiveness for both of us, Monsignor."

The older man pointed his forefinger at me and said, "Don't patronize me, young man."

"I'm not, Monsignor," I said. "I'm serious, more for my brother than for me. He was unsure of what to do and came to me for help. I know you can understand that."

"Of course," he said reluctantly. "You *are* his brother."

"Yes, sir, I am," I said, "and once he did come to me, he had to do what I told him to do. It was I who told him not to tell anyone until after we spoke with a lawyer. My father and sister don't even know about this yet."

"I suspect your father might be even angrier than I am." He started out of the room, then turned at the door and said, "Maybe."

His footstep had just echoed out when I heard those of Mrs. Graf returning.

"Father will be right down," she said, sticking her head in the door.

"Thank you."

Five minutes later my brother appeared.

"Come on," he said, "walk me out."

Outside, I asked, "How are you?"

"Okay."

"No," I said, "really, Vinnie."

He took a deep, shuddering breath and said, "Right now I'm more nervous than scared. I'll know better later on today."

I walked with him toward the parking lot, which was on East Ninety-eighth Street.

"But you know something?" he said as we walked. "I feel better, somehow. Dealing with it, and dealing with it effectively, has made me feel better, and I have you to thank. Heck, too, but mostly you."

I didn't know how to react to that, so I just put my hand on his shoulder for a moment.

"How was it with the monsignor?"

"He was a little disappointed, and hurt, that I hadn't come to him. He covered it up with anger."

"I know, I got some of that."

"He said he's behind me, though. He knows I'd never break my vows. He also knows what Gloria Mancuso was like."

"Vinnie," I said after a pause, "maybe we should go and see Pop tonight?"

He thought about it for a moment, then said, "Yes, I think so. Will you call him, and Maria, for me?"

"Sure."

We reached the parking lot and stood next to the late-model Ford that he'd be driving.

"Before you go," I said, "uh, you haven't spoken to Dominick about this, have you?"

"Dominick?"

We both knew whom I was talking about. In my family, Nicky Barracuda had always been "Dominick." For a while he was even "Uncle Dominick," but that changed as we got older. Even in my own mind I referred to him now as Barracondi.

"Why would I do that?"

"I was just wondering."

"You wouldn't ask me that without a good reason, Nick," he said, turning to face me.

I put my hand on his shoulder again and said, "Go to Staten Island, Vinnie. We'll talk tonight."

"Nick—"

"Go," I said, giving him a push. "Good luck."

As he started to walk to get into the car I called out, "Hey, where's Sister Olivia today?"

"She's not working in the Rectory today," he said. "Try the Convent."

I nodded, waited for him to pull out of the parking lot, then waved and started toward the Convent.

I rang the bell at the Convent, remembering the times as a boy in the midgrades I'd been sent to the Convent to help Sister Michaela Tyson carry something to the school. The nuns I had in grammar school were stronger than most men I knew. Why is it that the things we remember most about the nuns we had in school are the right crosses and left hooks, the rulers across the knuckles, the time Sister Sugar Ray made one of the kids take off his pointed shoes—the ones with the illegal taps—and wear paper bags on his feet the rest of the day?

I couldn't imagine Sister Olivia striking a child, or even striking fear into a child's heart. That's what I remembered most about the nuns I had in school, being afraid of them.

Maybe the nuns didn't hit the parochial kids of today. Lucky kids. I was still flinching years after I graduated from parochial school.

The door was opened by a nun in a habit. She was neither as pretty as Sister Olivia, nor as hard-looking as most of the nuns I remember. She had a remarkably smooth-skinned face, which made it very difficult to approximate her age.

"Yes?"

"Hi," I said, "I'd like to see Sister Olivia please?"

She regarded me benignly and asked, "Is there something I can help you with?"

"Uh, no, it's, uh, something, uh, personal." I was stammering. Were nuns allowed to have something personal?

"And your name?"

"Delvecchio, Nick Delvecchio."

Recognition lit up her eyes, and at that moment I'd have guessed her in her late twenties.

"Father Delvecchio's brother?" she said excitedly. "The private eye?"

"Uh, yep, that's me."

"Oh, come in, come in," she said, backing away from the door.

The farthest I had ever gotten into the Convent when I was a kid was a room just to the left of the front door. The Rectory and Convent were places of mystery when I was a kid.

"Wait here," she said, clasping her hands together in front of her. "I think Sister has just returned from her run."

She ran off into the dark recesses of the Rectory and I sat in a chair by the door and waited.

I could hear voices from inside the Convent, and three times different heads poked out and took a look at me.

My goodness, could it be I was the first private eye ever to enter this Convent?

"I'm sorry I kept you waiting," Sister Olivia said, entering the entry foyer. "I had to finish my cooling-down exercises."

I was staring, I knew I was staring, but I couldn't do anything about it. She was wearing light-blue running shorts and a dark-blue running top and—

Jesus—she had a sports bra on underneath it. I remember as kids we used to wonder: *Do nuns wear bras? Do nuns have breasts? Do they have...nipples?* What was the one Jerry O'Brien had asked? Oh, yeah: *Do nuns shave their legs?*

Looking at Sister Olivia, I knew that the answer to all those things was Yes. The great mystery was solved. Jerry O'Brien had been my best friend in seventh and eighth grades. I wondered where he was now.

She had a towel around her neck, and there were some sweat spots on the top, making it stick to her skin. The ends of her hair were wet, plastered to her forehead and neck. I could smell her sweat. There was a big sweat spot right between her breasts. *She smells just like a woman, Jerry,* I thought.

Okay, enough of that...

"Nick?"

"Hi," I said. "Remember what you said about wanting to help more if you could?"

"Yes, I remember."

"Do you still want to help?"

"Of course."

"Have lunch with me, Sister," I said. "I have to talk to you."

"Lunch?" She said it in a low voice, and then looked around as if to see if anyone had heard my invitation.

"This is on the up and up, Sister," I assured her. "I need your help in order to help Father Vinnie."

"Father Vinnie?" she said, and then giggled. "No one here calls him that. They call him Father Vincent, or Father Delvecchio. Father Vinnie...I like it."

"Sister? Lunch?"

She studied me for a moment—maybe she was trying to figure out if I was harmless or not—and then said, "Sure, I'll have lunch with you."

"Great!" I said, maybe with too much enthusiasm.

"I have to shower and change, and I have some errands to run."

"That's all right," I said. "We have time. I'll, uh, come back and get you at twelve o'clock."

"All right."

"I'll, uh, let myself out."

She smiled at me as I opened the door and stepped outside. It was quiet outside, but compared to the latent silence inside the Convent, it sounded positively loud. I could clearly hear the sound of children's voices coming from the school.

25

Once outside, I realized that I had three hours to kill. I found a pay phone across Rockaway Parkway and dialed the number for Long Island College Hospital. When the phone was answered, I asked for Linda Kellogg's room.

"Linda?" I said when she answered. "It's Nick Delvecchio."

"Oh...hi."

I don't have to be hit over the head with the obvious. The hesitation in her voice told me all I needed to know. "Is he there?"

"Yes."

"When are you getting out?"

"Friday."

"That's good," I said. "I hope you're feeling better."

"Yes...much."

"All right," I said, "I won't keep you. I just want you to know that I'm still on the job."

"That's good."

"I'll talk to you soon."

"Fine. Good-bye."

Well, that killed all of five minutes. I was wondering if I should go and re-interview some of the PTA people when I realized that there was still one person I hadn't interviewed about Gloria Mancuso.

Monsignor Genovese.

I dialed the Rectory number. I knew the monsignor was in, but that didn't mean he'd have the time to see me or take the time.

When Mrs. Graf answered I asked for the monsignor. "Who is calling?"

"Nick Delvecchio."

There was a long pause and then she said, "Weren't you just here?"

"Yes, I was."

There was another long pause and then she said, "Hold on."

"Mrs. Graf?"

"Y-yes?"

"Would you simply ask the monsignor if he could spare me some time this morning?"

"Of course," she said. "When may I tell him you would like to see him?"

"Oh...in about five minutes?"

Another puzzled pause and then: "I'll check. Please hold."

I held for a couple of minutes and then Mrs. Graf came back on.

"You may come over anytime, Mr. Delvecchio. The monsignor can spare you some time."

"Thank you, Mrs. Graf."

I hung up and quickly crossed the street. As I walked toward the Rectory I saw that there was a florist's shop across the street. I hesitated a moment, then went across and bought a bunch of mixed flowers for Mrs. Graf. The poor woman probably thought Vinnie had been cursed with a deranged brother.

When she answered my knock I handed the flowers to her.

"For you."

"Oh…my," she said, accepting them. I could swear there were tears in her eyes. I guess Mr. Graf hadn't given her any flowers lately.

"Please come in," she said. "Monsignor is waiting for you."

She led me to the monsignor's office, the door of which was open.

"Monsignor? Mr. Delvecchio is here."

As I sidled on past her into the room I said, "You'd better get those into water."

"Yes…right away."

"Bribing my staff?" Monsignor asked.

"I confused the poor woman so much, I thought it was the least I could do."

"Frankly," he said, "I'm in somewhat the same state. What is it you want to say to me now that you could not have said earlier?"

"I had to make sure I spoke to my brother earlier, before he left. May I close the door?"

"Of course," he said, waving a hand negligently. "I don't have a lot of time, though. I have a meeting in…twenty minutes."

"I'll be brief, then," I promised, "and to the point. What can you tell me about Gloria Mancuso?"

His distaste showed on his face, but I didn't know if it was for the woman, or simply the subject.

"The woman is dead. What would you like me to tell you about her?"

I sat opposite him and said, "Anything you can tell me."

"I afraid I don't—"

"Let me ask you some questions, then. Were you aware of her flirtatious nature?"

"Mr. Delvecchio," he said, closing his eyes, "are you asking me if I knew Mrs. Mancuso was a tramp?"

"Monsignor!" I said, only half feigning shock. "That's a harsh word."

"People are what they are, Mr. Delvecchio," he said. "By not speaking of it, we don't change that. Yes, I knew what kind of woman Mrs. Mancuso was. Yes, I am aware that she has had affairs with some of the men whose children are in the school."

"Monsignor," I said, trying to hide my excitement, "could you give me any names?"

"No, I couldn't."

"Why not?" I asked. "This is to help my brother, Monsignor. If you could give me names—"

"I can't give you names because of where I got my information, Mr. Delvecchio."

"And where was that, Monsignor?"

"The confessional."

I stared at him for a moment, and then said, "Oh."

"Is there anything else I can do for you?"

I thought suddenly of the old talk-show host—was it Mike Douglas?—who, when one of his guests started telling a story about someone he or she couldn't name, would ask, "Could you give us the initials?" I didn't think that would work with the monsignor.

"It was not my intention to strike you dumb, Mr. Delvecchio."

"Nevertheless, Monsignor..." I said.

There was a knock at a door, a different door than the one through which I had entered, and it opened. A priest stepped into the room. He was tall and husky and looked to be about thirty-five or so, with curly dark hair.

"Oh, I'm sorry, Monsignor..."

"That's all right, Father," Monsignor said. "Father Kelleher? This is Nick Delvecchio."

"Ah, Father Delvecchio's brother," Father Kelleher said. He did not approach me, nor did he offer to shake hands. "A pleasure. Monsignor, you have a meeting in ten minutes."

"I know, Father, thank you."

Father Kelleher nodded, said, "Nice to have met you," to me, and left the same way he'd entered.

"Is there anything else, Mr. Delvecchio?"

"Yes, Monsignor," I said. "Do you think my brother was...indiscreet with Gloria Mancuso?"

"No, I do not," he said. "I have the highest respect for your brother, Mr. Delvecchio. I think that someday he will make a fine priest."

I couldn't help myself. I felt there was something unspoken in his reply.

"Just a fine priest?"

Monsignor stood up, preparing to leave. He picked up what looked like a ledger book and tucked it beneath his arm.

"I don't know that he will ever progress further than that, Mr. Delvecchio. His handling of this...affair, for want of a better word, left much to be desired. Oh, I know how Mrs. Mancuso could bedevil men, and the Lord knows we're all just men, but I still feel he could have handled it...better. Now, if you will excuse me." He started for the side door Father Kelleher had used.

"One more thing, Monsignor."

"Mr. Delvecchio," he said in exasperation, "I've tried to be patient—"

"Has Mrs. Mancuso ever made sexual advances toward any other priest?"

"No!" he said, much too quickly and loudly. "If she had, I assure you I would know about it. None of my other priests has the same low regard for me that your brother obviously has. Now good day, sir!"

Without waiting for me to leave, he went out that side door.

Whoa, I thought. The monsignor was really prickly on the subject, and he was bitter as hell—pardon—at my brother for not having come to him. Maybe the monsignor felt that Vinnie had made him look bad to the Diocese by going over his head to them.

I had one brief moment where I was thinking about searching the monsignor's desk, then shook my head and got out of there.

26

"Mrs. Graf?" I said, poking my head into her office. The flowers were in a vase on her desk.

"Oh!" she said. "You startled me."

"I'm sorry. I wonder if you could help me."

She frowned, but said, "I'll try."

"How many priests are there here at the Church of the Holy Family?"

"Um, let me see...Father Kelleher...Father Macklin...um, Father Delvecchio, of course...Father Delbert—"

"Delbert?"

Mrs. Graf smiled for the first time since I'd met her, and shrugged.

"...There's Father Sullivan and...Father Scanlon." It struck me then that the Church and the Police Department had a lot in common. Many of their employees were Irish and Italian. Pop wasn't so right, after all.

"Are they all here now? I mean, for the past week, have they all been here?"

"Well, no," she said. "Father Scanlon is on retreat still, and Father Delbert had to go to Our Lady of Perpetual Faith—they are short-handed—um, I think that's it. The others have been here."

"Are either Father Macklin or Father Sullivan as young as Father Kelleher, or my brother?"

"Oh, no," she said, "Father Sullivan has been here for years, he's well into his seventies, and Father Macklin is about sixty, I believe."

"What about Father Delbert and Father Scanlon? How old are they?"

"Well, Father Delbert is in his forties, and Father Scanlon—that's hard to say. He's had a beard for so long, and there's some gray in it...and he is developing a bald spot...I suppose he's in his late forties."

"Thank you for your help, Mrs. Graf. I hope you have a very pleasant day."

"Why...thank you."

I went outside, juggling all of the priests' names and ages in my head. Certainly the monsignor, Father Macklin, and Father Sullivan were beyond Gloria Mancuso's range. That left Fathers Kelleher, Scanlon, and Delbert as...what? Say it, Nick. As suspects!

Just because my brother was true to his vows didn't mean all priests were.

A block away I found a McDonald's and bought myself a cup of coffee. There was a pay phone right outside, and I used it to call Pop and Maria to arrange dinner at Pop's house.

"What'samatta?" Pop asked. "You invitin' yourself to dinner now?"

"I want to talk to you about something, Pop," I said. "Father Vinnie will be there, too."

"Fine," he said, "bring some Italian pastries..."

"Nick, you poop," my sister said. That's as close as she got to cursing these days. "You ran out the other night without telling me what's wrong with Father Vinnie."

I told her to be at Pop's tonight, and she'd hear it all. She wanted me to tell her on the phone, but I said no and hung up before she could think of something stronger to say to me.

I killed the rest of the time drinking coffee and juggling names...

I sat on the bottom two steps of the Rectory to wait the last ten minutes, watching kids play in the parking lot, which apparently also doubled as a playground. On the way there I had remembered that I was supposed to have lunch with Dominick Barracondi. I also wanted to talk with Sister Olivia about who Gloria Mancuso's best friends were. So I decided to kill the proverbial two birds.

Wait until the Godfather found out whom I was bringing to lunch.

***

She took about twenty minutes, which was okay. I wasn't supposed to meet with Barracondi until 1 P.M. We could walk along Sheepshead Bay for a while and look at whatever fishing boats hadn't gone out yet.

When the door opened I stood up and turned around. I almost didn't recognize her because it was the first time I had seen her wearing her habit. It looked odd to me to see her in full dress uniform, with the headdress—or hood, or whatever they called it—the big white collar, the silver crucifix hanging around her neck, and the long string of brown rosary beads at her side.

She came down the steps and we stood staring at each other for a few moments. I thought she looked rather sad.

I finally realized that she was trying to send me a message—and I got it. I wasn't to forget who she was.

"Okay," I said, finally finding my voice, "let's go."

"Where are we going to eat?"

"Sheepshead Bay."

"Sheepshead Bay?" she asked, surprised. "Why all the way over there?"

"Because," I said, "I'm going to introduce you to a real gangster."

"They don't really call them gangsters anymore, do they?"

Emmons Avenue is the real Sheepshead Bay. It's lined with restaurants and coffee shops, bait-and-tackle shops, fast-food restaurants, small grocery stores. When you reach the halfway point you see the docks, with all the fishing boats. It was afternoon now. The morning boats were returning, picking up the afternoon fishermen. Sometimes there were fishermen just fishing off the docks.

I had parked the car near Dominick Barracondi's restaurant, The Barge, and we were walking along the docks now. Right across the street were the seafood restaurants, pizza shops, sidewalk cafes, and ice-cream shops. When the weather was nice enough for walking, there were sidewalk flea markets set up. When the weather was really nice, in the spring and fall, there were people walking at all times of the day and night. In the summer, people walked at night.

Behind all the stores and shops were the bungalows. Once, this had been a beautiful place to live, right near the beach. Now families were living in tiny bungalows because they couldn't sell them. There were rows of them behind the stores and the main streets, some of them separated only by small walkways with grandiose names.

But to the question of gangsters.

"There are so many different names, and they change all the time," I said. "Now they call them wise guys."

"Wise guys? Why?"

"Because somebody decided it was a likely name."

"Isn't that a TV show?"

"You have TV in the Convent?"

"Of course," she said. "What do you think, we're in the Middle Ages?"

A nun walking along Emmons Avenue was not an everyday occurrence. We were drawing looks. I checked my watch.

"Let's start back," I said. "By the time we reach the restaurant, it'll be time to go in."

"This man, Dominick..."

"Barracondi," I said. "When he was younger, they called him Nicky Barracuda."

"He's actually your godfather?"

"Yes."

"Were you named after him?"

"No," I said, "he's Dominick, and I'm Nicholas. He and my father were friends, but my mother didn't like him, so they compromised. They named him my godfather, but didn't name me after him."

"But you're both called Nick, or Nicky?"

"Nobody calls him Nicky Barracuda anymore," I said. "Remember that."

"And you?" she asked playfully. "Who calls you Nicky?"

"Only my family," I said. "My father and my sister."

"Not Father?"

"No."

"Can I call you Nicky?"

I hesitated, then said, "No."

We were a few blocks from the restaurant when I said, "Sister, I've got to ask you some questions you might not want to answer."

"Shoot."

I gave her a look and she smiled.

"First, I need to know who Gloria Mancuso's best friends were."

"Friends?" she said. "Gloria didn't have friends. She had admirers. Men admired her because she was beautiful, and women admired her because she... well, because they wished they could be like her. Of course, at the same time they hated her for what she was."

"A tramp."

She looked at me and said, "Who told you that?"

"Monsignor."

"Really?" She was shocked. I decided not to tell her what he'd said about the confessional. Somehow, I didn't think his mentioning it to me was...kosher.

"Sister, what about the other priests?"

"What about them?"

"Do you think Gloria ever made...sexual advances to them?"

She smiled and for a moment I thought she might laugh out loud.

"What?"

"I was just thinking of Gloria Mancuso chasing Father Sullivan or Father Macklin."

"What about the others? Father Delbert?"

"No," she said with assurance.

"Why not?"

"He's a dear man, but he's also the homeliest man I've ever met. No, I think Gloria, if she had approached a priest, would have chosen your brother, or Father Kelleher. The Sisters generally consider your brother the best-looking priest in the Diocese."

It was my turn to be surprised.

"You...Sisters talk about things like that?"

Sheepishly, she said, "Some of us do." After a moment she put her hand on my arm, looked at me and said, "Nick, did she..."

"Did she what?"

"Make advances toward Father Vincent?"

"She did," I said. "The police are suspicious of him."

"Can they really suspect him of...of killing her?" she asked, in shock.

"They can," I said, "and they do."

"Would they really...arrest him?"

"They might."

"Oh, my...I knew there was something wrong, but I didn't know it was this bad. Nick, what can I do to help Father Vincent?"

"You're doing it, Sister," I said, "you're doing it."

27

I spotted Benny the Card as soon as we entered the restaurant. He wasn't hard to spot. He was about eight feet across at the shoulders, dressed in a tux and flashing a pinky ring on each hand. Since he had gone from button man to maître d', he'd put on about fifty pounds, most of it in the gut. His real name was Benvenuto Cardone, and we had gone to high school together.

"Aye, Nicky D," he said, coming over.

He came over and shook my hand, then nodded to Sister Olivia and said, "Good afternoon, Sister."

"Sister Olivia, this is Benny Cardone. Benny, would you tell the Don we're here?"

"Nick, I know the Don's expectin' you, but…"

"Just set another place at the table, Benny. Okay?"

"Sure, Nick," he said, looking confused. "Just let me tell the boss you're here."

While Benny went and told Nicky Barracuda about the extra guest, Sister Olivia looked the place over.

"What do you think?" I asked.

"It looks very nice," she said, "and the smells are heavenly—no pun intended."

"That's the Don's sauce you smell," I said. "It's his own recipe."

"Nick…is this place…"

"Legit? Sure, it's legit. This is Dominick's baby."

"What about Benny?"

"Benny the Card," I said. "Since he's gone legit, he's put on a ton."

"What did he do before he went legit?"

"Sister," I said, "you don't want to know."

Benny came back and said, "All set, paesan. Follow me."

"Sister," I said. She followed Benny, and I followed her. Dominick Barracondi had a table set up in his office, and there were three chairs.

"Nicholas," he said, spreading his arms. "Welcome. I'm glad you came."

There was no denying that Dominick Barracondi was an elegant man. His hair was snow-white, as was his carefully trimmed mustache. He looked like an Italian Cesar Romero.

"Hello, Godfather."

He looked pleased when I called him that, but I did it for Sister Olivia's benefit. I wanted her to remember this afternoon.

"I didn't expect you to bring a friend, though."

He must have been going crazy wondering what I was up to, but I had to hand it to him, he didn't miss a beat.

"I want you to meet my friend, Sister Olivia."

"Sister," Barracondi said, "it's an honor to have you in my restaurant."

"Thank you, Mr. Barracondi."

"Please, sit here," he said, holding a chair out for her. "Nicholas?"

I sat across from Sister Olivia, and he sat between us. "Benny," he said then, "tell Carlo to serve lunch."

Lunch consisted of linguine with white clam sauce, followed by eggplant parmigiana, fried zucchini, and garlic bread. I had to give Dominick Barracondi credit, he had one of the best Italian kitchens in New York City.

"This is wonderful, Mr. Barracondi," Sister Olivia said to him. "This must be the best Italian restaurant in Brooklyn."

"Well, unfortunately, we are not yet considered the best. There is a restaurant just a few blocks from here which has a long history here in Sheepshead Bay, and that one is generally considered the best Italian restaurant in Brooklyn."

"What restaurant is that?"

"It is called Maria's. I have eaten there myself, and the food is excellent. Still, I hope that someday my own humble establishment will be able to match their fine reputation."

We had dessert—fresh peaches soaked in vermouth, something he admitted he had "borrowed" from Maria's—and coffee, and then he said to Sister Olivia, "Sister, if you do not mind, I would like a few moments alone with my godson?"

"Oh, of course," she said, standing up. "I'll wait outside."

"Benny will see to your comfort," Barracondi said, and Benny nodded. He had been standing faithfully by the door throughout lunch, hands clasped in front of him.

"This way, Sister," he said, allowing her to precede him. I had never seen Benny act like such a gentleman before.

My godfather refilled our coffee cups and then sat back in his chair, regarding me with a somewhat critical expression on his face.

"So, Nick?"

"So...what?"

"Why have you and your brother not asked for my help?"

"I beg your pardon?"

"Do not play games with me," he said. "I know that Father Vincent is that much removed from being arrested." He was holding his thumb and forefinger about an inch apart.

"How do you know about it?"

He shrugged.

"How do I know about anything? I hear things."

"*What* do you know about it?"

"Only what I have heard," he said, "that Father Vincent is suspected of killing a woman he may have had an affair with. Both are inconceivable."

"I know that," I said. "What have you done?"

"I? I have done nothing. I have not been asked to intervene. Does your father know?"

"No."

"Ah," he said, as if he understood, "your father would have asked for my help."

"He'll be told tonight."

"And your sister?"

"She, too, but they won't be asking for your help. Neither will I."

"And why not?"

"That will be up to Father Vinnie, and you know how he feels about taking help from you."

Vinnie has been adamant his entire adult like about not taking help from Dominick Barracondi. I've never approved of my godfather, but I have been known to bend the rules from time to time. Not Vinnie, though.

"Your brother is a stubborn man."

"Tell me about it."

"And a proud one."

I knew that, too. That was why I hated seeing what this was doing to him.

"You must tell him, Nicholas, to come to me for help. I cannot help unless he asks."

I'll give the old man credit for that. Even last year, when Maria was on a hijacked plane, as badly as he wanted to help, he did nothing, because we didn't ask him to. He stuck to his guns, or his code, of not interfering unless specifically asked to.

"I don't think we'll be needing your help," I said, "but we appreciate the offer."

"I know an excellent attorney."

"We have an excellent attorney."

"A *Spanish* attorney."

"Heck Delgado is Mexican."

He flinched, as if I'd struck him.

"You must talk to your brother—"

"My brother is his own man. I can't make him do anything he doesn't want to do."

"You underestimate your influence with Father Vincent," he said. "After all, he did come to you, and he has done as you say up to now, hasn't he?"

Damn him. Where was his contact, in the police or in the Church?

"Thank you for lunch, Don Dominick."

"Ah!" he exploded, rising and throwing his napkin down onto the table. Benny must have been right by the door because he was inside in a flash, his hand dipping into his jacket. He still moved well for a big man.

He stared at Barracondi for a sign, and the older man simply waved him away irritably, then turned his attention back to me. Benny backed out of the room.

"I love your family as if it were my own, Nicholas, and yet you spurn me at every turn. Last year I could have helped your sister."

"You would have gotten her killed."

"Do you know what I could have done for your career in the Police Department? You could be a lieutenant by now; all you had to do was ask."

I didn't reply. I had always wondered if he had done something five years ago to keep me out of jail. It would have been against his code, but...

"Do you know what I could have done for your brother over the years?" he went on. "He could be pastor of his own parish right now. A monsignor! In time, I could make him the youngest bishop in the history of the Church, and after that, a cardinal."

"Could you make him Pope?"

He stared at me and then said, "There are limits even to what I can do, Nicholas."

I was a little surprised to hear him admit that.

"Then you've got nothing to offer him," I said. "Thank you for lunch. The Sister and I appreciated it. It was excellent, as usual."

"Nick!"

"Yes?"

I don't know what he was going to say, but instead he said, "Tell your friend, Sister Olivia, that it was a pleasure to meet her."

"I'll tell her."

I left his office and found Sister Olivia sitting at a table nearby. Benny was standing right outside the door, and obviously had been throughout our conversation.

"Hey, Nicky," he said, putting his hand on my arm, "what's with you and the Don?"

"Don't worry about it, Benny."

"He just wants to help."

"I know," I said. "I know he does. Just don't worry about it, all right? It's not your concern."

I started for Sister Olivia and Benny moved his hand from my hand to my chest.

"Nicky," he said slowly, "you hurt the Don and you and me, we're gonna go round and round." He used a sausage-like forefinger on his other hand to make little circles in the air.

I put my hand against his chest, meaning to say something, but then just patted him there and walked to Sister Olivia. She had been watching Benny and me with eyes as big as saucers.

"Come on, Sister," I said, putting my hand out to her. "I'll get you back to the Convent."

28

Sister Olivia was quiet for most of the ride back to the Convent. In fact, she didn't speak again until I had pulled into the parking lot.

"Benny," she said, "he wouldn't actually…hurt you, would he?"

"Benny?" I said, with disdain for the idea. "Benny's a pussycat."

"When you and he were standing there…looking at each other, I thought…"

"Benny and I went to school together, Sister," I said, cutting her off. "I've been dealing with him for years, and he hasn't broken me in half yet." I put my hand on hers on the seat and said, "Don't worry."

I didn't bother telling her about the time, in my junior year, Benny broke my arm to teach me a lesson. I had been looking at his girl. Back then Benny had been a football player and a bodybuilder. Over the years, his body lost the definition it once had, but he never lost his great strength. Even that afternoon, when he put his hand on my chest, I could feel his strength.

"When the two of you were staring at each other, I thought you were going to say something."

"I was," I said, "but Benny was only displaying his loyalty to the Don." I looked up and saw three children at a window watching us. Two girls and a boy. I waved and they giggled. Sister Olivia looked up, craning her neck to see through the windshield, waved, and they giggled some more and waved back.

I think we both realized at the same time that my hand was still on hers. She slowly removed it and said, "Well, thanks for lunch. It was…interesting."

"I hope it was," I said. "I hope you enjoyed it, Sister."

"Well," she said, "it wasn't like anything I've read or seen in the movies. Consequently, yes, I did enjoy it quite a bit."

She opened her door and stepped out, and I opened mine, got out and looked over the roof at her.

"If you think of anything else you might tell me about Gloria Mancuso, please let me know."

"Are you going to talk to her husband?"

"I'd like to," I said. "I've just got to come up with a good enough excuse."

We stared at each other over the roof for a few moments, and I noticed what pretty brown eyes she had. Eyes that were very pretty, even without makeup.

"Well," she said, "I've got to get back."

"I'll see ya."

"Yes," she said. She started to turn, then said, "Oh, wait, wait…"

"What?"

"I just thought of something. Gloria bowled."

"What?"

"She was in a bowling league, at that bowling alley named after the baseball player."

I knew the one she meant, in Mill Basin, on Stillwell Avenue.

"You might be able to find a best friend there."
"Yeah," I said, "I might. Thanks, Sister."
"You're welcome."
"You're a great assistant detective."
"Thanks. Bye."
"Good-bye."
She started to walk away, then stopped and turned back to face me.
"There's something I have to ask you," she said.
"Go ahead." I thought I knew what it was going to be, and I was right.
"Why did you take me with you today, to see Mr. Barracondi?"
I'd been asking myself the same question.
"Would you believe I was just killing two birds with one stone, seeing him and taking you to lunch?"
"I'm afraid I wouldn't."
"I didn't think so."
"Perhaps I can make it easy on you," she said. "It was rather obvious to me that you don't have the feelings for your godfather that he has for you."
"My problem starts right there," I said honestly. "How can he have led the life he did and have feelings for anyone?"
"He obviously thinks highly of you, and is hurt by the fact that you don't return his feelings."
I frowned.
"I think you took me as an act of defiance against him. I mean, it does seem rather odd to take a nun to lunch with a Mafia Don, doesn't it?"
"I suppose you're right," I said. "It is odd, and I do and say a lot of stupid things when it comes to dealing with…him. I'm sorry, Sister."
"Don't apologize," she said. "I'm rather pleased with myself that I figured it out."
"You really are a great assistant detective."
She smiled and turned to walk away.
I watched her walk across the parking lot, and as I watched I saw something beyond her. It was a car…a shiny blue car.
"Sister!"
She stopped and turned, frowning. I trotted after her.
"Do you know whose car that is?" I asked when I reached her.
She turned to look where I was pointing and said, "It belongs to the Church."
"What does that mean?" I asked. "Anybody can drive it?"
"No, not anybody," she said. "There are cars for the use of the Sisters, like that station wagon…and then cars for the use of the priests, and then a car for the monsignor."

"Well, who uses that one?"

"I believe I've seen the priests driving that one."

"What priests?"

"Um, I've seen Father Sullivan drive it, and Father Kelleher, and...Father Delvecchio."

"Vinnie?"

"Nick, I'm sure they've all driven it at one time or another. Is it important?"

"Maybe," I said, "and maybe there are just a lot of shiny blue cars in the city."

She didn't know what I was talking about, and I didn't take the time to fill her in. We said good-bye again and I walked back to my car. When I got in I looked up at the school and those same kids were watching me from the window. I was wondering why they were there and not at their desks when a nun came up behind them and obviously shooed them away, back to their seats. She looked down at me and frowned, and I saw that she was the spitting image of the kind of nun I had when I was in parochial school.

I drove away, feeling that maybe things weren't so different these days, after all.

29

After leaving Sister Olivia I decided to drive right to the bowling alley to check on that lead. I didn't know when Gloria Mancuso's league bowled, during the day or the evening, but it was still early enough for a day league to be in progress. Maybe I could find something out.

The noise in the bowling alley was almost deafening. It seemed that every alley in the place was taken, and my ears were assailed with the sound of rolling balls and falling pins.

I walked up to the desk and the man behind it told me, "No open lanes, Mac."

"I'm not interested in bowling."

"No? Well, you can't be here for the food."

"I'd like to talk to someone about a league."

"Men's league bowls at night."

"I'm interested in the women's leagues."

"Sure you are. You seen some of these women bowlers?"

"Have you?"

"You bet I have. Ain't but one or two of them worth standing behind while they're bowling. I mean, they're nice ladies, but..."

"Maybe you can help me," I said. "You seem to be a man who notices things."

He puffed his chest up and said, "Well, yeah, I keep my eyes open."

"There's a woman who bowls in a league here, but I don't know which one it is."

"What's her name?"

"Mancuso," I said, "Gloria Mancuso. She's a blonde, very attractive—"

He held up his hand to stop me.

"Save it, Mac. Everybody here knows Gloria. She's that exception I was talkin' about. Whoa, is that gal a looker, or what?"

"She's dead."

His jaw dropped and he said, "What?"

"Somebody killed her."

"Aw, no," he said, as if he had been related to her.

"Did you know her well?"

"Naw," he said, "not that I didn't try, but I wasn't her type, you know?"

"You seem pretty upset—"

"Hey, man," he said, "just seeing her walk in here on Thursday night was worth all the shit I got to go through all the other nights and days."

"That's when she bowled? Thursday night?"

"Yeah. Last year she bowled two nights, but this year she cut back to one. Something about the PTA, I think."

"She have many friends?"

"Who knows, man. I watch these women here, and I don't know if they're friends or not. One day they're talkin', another day they ain't. It's easier with the guys, you know? You can tell who hates whose guts, but the women are different. You know what I mean?"

"Yeah, I think I do."

"You a cop?"

"Why didn't you ask me that before?"

"'cause you didn't look like a cop, then."

"And I do now?"

He grinned and said, "There's somethin' about a man who's askin' questions that changes the way he looks."

"I used to be a cop," I said, "I'm private now."

"That explains it."

"Well, thanks for the information."

"It's a shame about that blonde," he said, shaking his head. "I got to find me a new fantasy now."

"Life is hard..."

* * *

I borrowed Hacker's car that night to drive to my father's house. I hadn't heard from Heck or from Vinnie, so I guessed we'd all find out at the same time what had happened at the police station in Staten Island.

I did manage to talk to Sam before leaving.

"How do you look in bowling shoes?"

"What?"

I told her about Gloria Mancuso's Thursday-night bowling league, and explained how I had to go to my father's house with Vinnie to break the news to him and Maria.

"What would I have to do?"

"Ask questions," I said. "Make like you're there looking for her. Get some of the women to talk about her."

"Will they know she's dead?"

"I don't know, but it doesn't matter. Either way, she's the kind of woman who inspires gossip."

"All right," she said, then frowned and asked, "I won't have to bowl, will I?"

"Why?"

"I've never bowled."

"Don't worry about it," I said. "Just wear a short skirt and look athletic. They won't have any open lanes, anyway."

"This is great, Nick. Thanks for giving me another chance to help you. Uh, what about Linda Kellogg?"

"She's being released tomorrow afternoon. I'll try to get in touch with her in the afternoon."

"And how are things going with your brother?"

"I don't know," I said. "I'll find out tonight when I see him."

"Knock on my door when you come home, all right?"

"You might be asleep."

"No, I won't," she said. "Besides, I have the feeling you'll need to talk."

"You might be right," I said. "Okay, I'll knock."

She touched my arm and said, "Good luck..."

On the way to the house I thought about what Barracondi had said to me that afternoon. Maybe I was being too stubborn; after all, it wasn't my neck that hung in the balance, but Vinnie's. If Dominick Barracondi could bail him out of this jam, then why not let him? I decided to talk to Vinnie seriously about asking for help.

When I reached the house I couldn't park right in front because there was already a car there—a shiny blue car. I frowned, drove on ahead about two or three houses and found a spot. When I walked back I examined the car more closely and discovered that it was the same one I had seen earlier in the school parking lot. Vinnie must have driven it here. I didn't know what car Vinnie had driven to Pop's earlier that week, and I didn't know which car he'd driven to my apartment the night we met Heck.

I went up the walk to the front door, found that it was unlocked, and went inside.

"Anybody home?" I called out.

Maria and Vinnie came out of the kitchen.

"It's about time," Maria said, putting her hands on her trim hips. "Maybe now we can find out what's going on."

"Hello, Nick."

"Vinnie," I said. "How're you doing?"

"Okay."

"And why shouldn't he be doing okay?" Maria demanded.

"Is that your sauce I smell?" I asked her.

"It certainly is, and it's left over from the other night."

"That doesn't mean it can't burn."

She turned on her heel and stalked into the kitchen, leaving me and Vinnie alone.

"Where's Pop?" I asked.

"In his room."

"Did you tell him?"

"I was waiting for you."

"What happened in Staten Island?"

"Well," he said, "I'm not under arrest."

"Dinner's ready," Maria said, sticking her head out of the kitchen.

"When should I tell them?" Vinnie asked me.

"After dinner, Vinnie," I said, putting my hand on his arm, "after dinner."

We went in to have dinner, and I didn't envy my brother the task ahead of him.

"That's-a crazy!"

That was my father's reaction to the news. Sometimes when he gets upset, his English acquires just a slight Italian accent. Maria, on the other hand, just sort of sat stunned.

"How could they think that a priest—my son!—could even-a think such a thing?"

"Pop," Vinnie said, "they only see me as a man, not as a priest."

"Well, you didn't know this woman, did you, Father?" It always struck me odd to hear my father call my brother "Father."

"Yes, Pop, I did know her. She was a parent, and a parishioner. She was president of the PTA."

"Yeah, but you know a lot of parents. They gonna arrest you every time one of them gets killed?"

"Pop," Vinnie said, "she was an attractive woman—she was a *beautiful* woman—"

"You ain't supposed to notice things like that!" Pop snapped.

"Pop, I'm a priest, but I'm not dead."

"Don't talk-a like that!"

"Pop," Maria said, "stop it."

My father looked at her in surprise.

"Vinnie, do you have a lawyer?"

"Yes."

"Who?"

"His name is Hector Delgado."

"A Puerto Rican?" my father said. "An Italian lawyer is-a no good enough-a for you?"

"He's not Puerto Rican, Pop," Vinnie said, "he's Mexican."

"That's-a worse."

"Pop—" Vinnie said.

"Pop—" Maria said.

"Stop!" I said, louder than everyone else. "Just stop it!"

They all looked at me.

"Vinnie might be in a lot of trouble," I said, "and he needs some understanding and support from his family."

"But the cops can't be serious about this," Pop said. "He's a priest, for Chrissake, they can't think he killed somebody."

"They do, Pop," I said, "that's why he and the lawyer went to see the detectives today."

"And what happened?" Maria asked.

"Let's give him a chance to tell us."

So we all kept quiet and he told us about it...

30

When Heck and Vinnie reached the one-two-two they announced themselves at the desk. Rather than being sent up on their own, as I was, the desk officer called ahead and Detective Giambone came down to get them. Vinnie described Giambone as medium height but well-built, with his hair perfectly in place and his suit, shirt, and tie perfectly matched. He sounded like a perfect match for his partner.

Upstairs, they spoke to both Detective Lacy and Detective Giambone.

Basically, the detectives wanted to know about Vinnie's relationship with Gloria Mancuso. Heck, who knew the whole story, had instructed Vinnie to tell them everything. Vinnie did, right up to the point where he left the Holiday Inn by the side door and drove back to the Rectory.

"Now let's get this straight," Lacy said when he was done. "You're saying that this woman undressed completely, and you just left the room?"

"That's right."

Lacy looked at his partner, who formed a soundless whistle with his lips.

"I understand Mrs. Mancuso was an extremely beautiful woman," Lacy said. "Of course, I've only seen her corpse, but..."

"Yes," Vinnie said, "she was extremely beautiful."

"And there she was, butt-naked," Giambone said, "and you just walked out?"

"I said that," Vinnie replied. "After all, I am a priest."

"Yes, you did say that," Lacy said. "My partner is just such a pussyhound that he finds it hard to believe even of a priest, Mr. Delvecchio."

"Father," Heck said at that point.

"I beg your pardon?" Lacy said.

"My client is cooperating fully," Heck said. "I would like him afforded the respect he deserves. His name is *Father* Delvecchio."

"Excuse me...Father," Lacy said, "but by cooperating fully that would mean that you were telling us the whole truth, and frankly, we're not all that sure you are."

"What is it you think my client is lying about?" Heck asked.

Lacy and Giambone exchanged a glance and Giambone nodded.

"We think he had sex with Mrs. Mancuso."

"When?" Heck asked.

"Well," Lacy said, "we believe that he had an affair with her, but we also believe that he had sex with her the night she was killed, in the Holiday Inn."

"I didn't," Vinnie said, his heart pounding, "I never did! That would have meant breaking my vows."

"You mean no priest has ever broken his vows?" Giambone asked.

"There have been cases, yes," Vinnie said, "but I have never broken mine."

"Counselor," Lacy said, "we can solve this question easily—at least, the question of whether or not he had sex with her that night."

"What do you suggest?"

"We'd like Father Delvecchio to submit to a blood test, so we can type it to the semen we found in Gloria Mancuso's vagina."

"She had a pussyful," Giambone said, grinning.

Vinnie thought that Giambone was trying to work on his head from the moment he arrived there.

Heck and Vinnie were allowed a few moments to talk over the proposal. Heck took Vinnie out into the hall rather than talk alone in the room. They decided that Vinnie would take the test, because he had nothing to hide. A semen test couldn't prove that he *did* do it, only that he *couldn't* have done it. If the semen didn't type as his, that worked for them, and if it *was* his type, it was still inconclusive. The detectives gave them the name and address of a lab there in Staten Island, where they could stop and have it done before they returned to Brooklyn...

"On the way out," Vinnie said, "we saw Mr. Mancuso and his lawyer."

"Did he say anything to you?" I asked.

"Yes," Vinnie said, "he said he hoped I burned in hell for killing his wife."

"That's-a crazy," my father said, throwing his hands up in the air.

"His being there," I said, "means that he's still a suspect, too."

"There," Pop said, "her husband killed her. It happens all-a the time."

"Nick," Maria said, "what happens if Vinnie's blood type matches the, uh...what happens if it matches?"

"It still won't be conclusive," I said. "There are a lot of people who would match—I would, for instance."

"Yes," Vinnie said, "but you didn't know her. I did."

"Would that be enough to arrest him?" Maria asked.

I hesitated a moment, then looked at Vinnie and asked, "What did Heck say?"

"He said that if there was a match he thought they would talk to the DA about arresting me, but it was still inconclusive."

"Then they wouldn't arrest him? They couldn't," Maria argued.

"Not just on that, Maria," I said, "but they have a lot more. First, Vinnie knew the victim; second, a lot of people know what kind of woman Gloria was. It's no secret that she flirted with Vinnie, among others; third, her husband probably told the police something about Vinnie, but most damaging is that Vinnie admitted he was at the hotel that night, and in her room."

"Thats-a the lawyer's fault," Pop said. "You should-a got an Italian lawyer. Don Dominick could have helped us with that."

"No, Pop," Vinnie said. "We are not going to Dominick Barracondi. That's final."

"Let's not argue about that now," I said, cutting off any reply from my father. "Maria, why don't you clear off the table for coffee."

"Where are you going?" she asked.

"I have to make a call," I said, getting up. "Pop, I'm going to use the phone in your room."

I went into Pop's room to use the phone there, and dialed Heck Delgado's home number.

"I'm glad you called," Heck said when he answered. "I want you to talk to Gloria Mancuso's husband."

"That's what I was calling you about," I said. "Normally I wouldn't do that in an open homicide investigation."

"Your license will be safe, as you are representing me. Technically, we're not investigating the murder, we're simply preparing a defense for our client, in the event he's arrested."

"Fine," I said, "I'll go and see Mancuso tomorrow."

"Keep in touch. Nick, what happened to that information from the desk clerk on the key?"

"I don't know," I said, "but I intend to find out. He might have found himself a better place for the information."

"Let me know what happens."

"You got it."

I hung up and heard the raised voices in the kitchen. I shook my head and walked toward them.

"...have you be so damned stubborn," my father was saying.

"And where do you think I got that from, Pop?"

"Please," Maria said, "don't fight..." I could tell from her voice that she was close to tears.

They all fell silent as I entered the room.

"Vinnie, can we talk?"

"You can't talk in front of us?" Pop demanded.

"I want to talk, Pop, not argue."

Vinnie came with me into the living room.

"What is it, Nick?"

"The car you drove here."

"The Chevy?"

"The shiny blue one out front. How often do you drive it?"

"I don't know," he said. "Whenever it's available, I guess. If no one else is using it."

"What about that night? Did you use it that night?"

"No," he said, "I used the Ford. Why?"

"I told you that the desk clerk said she was dropped off? Well, she got out of a shiny blue car."

"Oh..." he said, realizing what that meant. "All the detectives have to do is check and see what cars we use at the church, and they'll have another nail for my coffin."

"I want you to do something for me," I said. "Find out where that car was that night. If it was being used, find out who was using it."

"I can do that."

"Okay," I said. "Listen, I'm gonna leave now. Why don't you do the same?"

He smiled and said, "I can't do that."

"Pop's gonna stay on you, Vinnie."

"He's worried, Nick, and so is Maria. I'll stay for a while."

"Suit yourself."

"What are you going to do tomorrow?"

"I've got a couple of things to do. I've got to go and see Gloria's husband, and then I've got to find that hotel clerk."

"Stay in touch, okay? If they arrest me, I—I want to be able to find you."

I touched his arm and said, "I'll keep checking in, Vinnie."

31

As promised, I knocked on Sam's door when I returned, even before going to my own apartment. When she opened the door I smelled coffee. She was wearing a T-shirt that said Brooklyn, where the weak are killed and eaten.

"Is that for me?" I asked.

"The coffee is."

"That's what I meant."

"Come on in."

I stepped inside. Sam's apartment is set up exactly the same way mine is, but hers always looks and feels better. The room I use as an office is her bedroom. I use it as an office because mine has a door to the hall. Hers does not. The room that is my bedroom is her office.

"Sit down and tell me how it went at your father's," she said, pouring two cups of coffee.

"Oh, it didn't go well," I said. "Pop *did* react pretty well, but he was pissed."

"What about your sister?"

"She was real quiet."

She put the coffee in front of me and sat across from me. Neither one of us used milk or sugar.

"You know what amazes me?"

"What?" I asked.

"That something like this, and what happened to your sister last year, could happen to the same family."

"Yeah," I said, "well, I guess we haven't had a lot of luck of late."

"That's putting it mildly."

"Never mind that," I said. "Did you go bowling?"

"You shit!" she said, reaching over and punching me in the arm.

"What's that for?"

"You didn't warn me about the lech."

"You must mean my friend behind the desk."

"Greasy-looking guy with dark hair?"

"That's him," I said. "He was real disappointed about Gloria being killed. He said he was gonna have to find a new fantasy."

"Well, I didn't apply for the job."

"Did you talk to the women?"

"I sure did," she said, grinning. "Boy, they had a lot to say about Gloria. Half of them liked her, and the other half hated her but envied her."

"That's the reaction I got from the PTA, too."

In general, the women in the bowling league told Sam just what the women in the PTA had told me.

"You didn't find a best friend?"

"No," she said, "there didn't seem to be any such animal. One woman went so far as to say that Gloria was her own best friend."

"And worst enemy."

"Not much help, huh?"

"You did fine, Sam," I said, touching her knee. "Thanks for going."

"What else did you do today?"

"I had lunch with a nun."

"What?"

I told her about lunch with Sister Olivia and Dominick Barracondi.

"What's with the nun, Nick?"

"She's helping me."

"Is she pretty?"

"Well, yeah, she's pretty."

"Uh-huh."

"Well, the first time I met her she wasn't wearing her habit. How was I supposed to know she was a nun?"

"Uh-huh," she said again.

"Besides, she's given me some information on Gloria Mancuso."

"Like what?"

"Well, she gave me the bowling-alley lead. It's not her fault it didn't pan out."

"Of course not."

I stood up and said, "Cut it out, Sam. She's a nun."

"I didn't say anything," she said, all wide-eyed innocence.

"It's what you were thinking," I said.

"How do you know what I'm thinking?"

"It shows in your eyes," I said. "I'm going home before your dirty mind contaminates me."

"Ha!" she snapped as I made for the door. "Me contaminate *you?*"

I crossed the hall and entered my apartment through my office. My one-eyed friend wasn't blinking any messages at me, so I sat down and dialed the Holiday Inn in Staten Island. I was going to try to bluster my way to the information I wanted.

"I'd like to speak to Riley, please," I said when the phone was answered by a woman.

"Riley's not on tonight."

"Is this the operator?"

"Yes."

"This is Detective Giambone from the one-two-two. I'm investigating the murder that happened there Saturday night."

"Oh yes, that was terrible," she said.

"Yes, it was," I said. "Listen, you could help me out of a jam."

"If I can, I'd like to," she said. She sounded very young, and I was already changing my tactics in mid-stream.

"Riley gave me his home address, and I lost it. I really have to talk to him tomorrow morning. Could you help me?"

"Gee, I don't know," she said. "I don't think I'm allowed to do that."

"Aw, come on," I said. "If you do it for me, I'll send you some flowers."

"Really?"

"When's the last time a man sent you flowers?"

"Oh, a boy has never sent me flowers." Now I knew she was young, because she said "boy" rather than "man."

"What's your name?"

"Tina."

"Tina, nobody's ever sent you flowers?"

"No."

"I can't believe that," I said. "You have such a sexy voice."

"Really? Well, I'm afraid I'm a little overweight."

"Ooh, I like women with meat on their bones," I said. "Listen, Tina, I'll send you a whole bunch of flowers if you help me out just this once."

"Well...I could give you his phone number. Would that be enough?"

"Honey, listen," I said. "I'm a policeman. If you give me his phone number, I can find out his address, but why make me go through all that?"

"Well," she said, coming around, "when you put it that way, it does sort of make sense."

"And nobody'll ever know," I said. "Imagine what your co-workers are gonna think when you get dozens of roses in the mail."

"Dozens?"

"Dozens."

"All right...Detective Giambone, is it?"

"That's right."

"Hold on..."

I held on for a few minutes, and then she came back on. "He lives in Brooklyn," she said, sounding surprised.

"Really? I would have thought he'd live in Staten Island since he works there."

"I know, I live in Staten Island."

"Is that so?"

"Yes."

There was a pause, and I knew she was waiting for "Detective Giambone" to ask for her phone number or address. I wondered just how overweight poor Tina was. "Where in Brooklyn does he lives, Tina?"

"Bay Ridge," she said, "just across the bridge." She gave me his address on Third Avenue, in the Eighties. I knew that area was mostly shops, restaurants and the like, with apartments in the back and over the stores. I was pleased that I wouldn't have to drive out to Staten Island to see him.

"Since you have it there, Tina, how about giving me his phone number, too?"

"Sure," she said, reeling it off.

"Tina, can you tell me one more thing?"

"Sure."

"When was he at work last?"

"I saw him here last night."

"Was he there today?"

"He was off tonight."

"What about tomorrow?"

"He should be off tomorrow, too. I guess he'll be back Saturday night."

"Okay, thanks, honey. You watch for those flowers, okay?"

"I work nights. I start at eleven."

"I'll get them there early, so you can enjoy them all night."

"Thanks," she said. "Oh, if you work nights, maybe we could, you know, have coffee?"

I felt like a heel when I said, "I'll call you, Tina. Okay?"

"Okay," she said happily.

I hung up, making a mental note to remember to send her those flowers, anyway, even if I wasn't Detective Giambone.

32

I still had the list of PTA officers that Sister Olivia had given me, and right at the top was Gloria Mancuso's address. I didn't know what Anthony Mancuso did for a living, so I didn't know when he'd be home. I decided to try and catch him at the school.

At eight-fifteen I was parked in the school parking lot. On other days I had noticed that a good portion of the students entered from the Flatlands Avenue side of the school, and they looked like the older kids. Since Mancuso's daughter was in her last year, I assumed he'd drop her off there.

When Mancuso finally pulled up in front of the school at eight twenty-five, he did so in a shiny blue Monte Carlo. I watched as his beautiful daughter, Lisa, got out of the car. From where I was I could see her clearly. As she lifted her legs out of the car her skirt rode all the way up her thighs, and I didn't think it was an accident. I noticed it, and so did some of the boys who were loitering in front of the school. That wasn't enough, though. She had to lean back into the car to kiss her father good-bye, and again her skirt rode up the back of her thighs, even revealing the fact that she was wearing pink panties.

I started to get out of the car to walk over to Mancuso, but he didn't even wait for his daughter to get into the building. He engaged the Monte Carlo and pulled away quickly. I got back into Hacker's Grand Prix and went after him.

I managed to see him make a left at the next corner, which was Rockaway Parkway. I knew he lived on Avenue M between East Ninety-sixth and East Ninety-fifth Streets, so it was possible that he was going straight home. We passed Avenues J, K, and L, and when he approached M, his turn signal did not go on. He passed M, went on by N and then past Seaview, which meant he had to be heading for the Belt Parkway. If he got on the Belt going east, he'd be going to Long Island. If he went west, he'd be going through Brooklyn toward Manhattan.

As he approached the highway, his right signal went on. He was going west. As we went past the Flatbush Avenue exit I wondered how far we were going to go. I got my answer very quickly, because he got off the very next exit, which was Sheepshead Bay.

As I was following him, keeping a lane and about two or three cars away from him, I wondered if the police knew that Mancuso drove a shiny blue car. He certainly had enough reason to kill his wife, if she was fooling around on him as much as I had heard, but what the hell would he have been doing driving her to the hotel? That just didn't figure at all.

I must have still been half asleep, because it never occurred to me that he might be going where he was going. Even while I was following him down Emmons Avenue it still didn't hit me. He turned his left signal on as we passed Maria's Restaurant, made a U-turn around the island that ran down the center of Emmons Avenue, and then made a right turn into a restaurant parking lot. I stopped my car farther up and watched in the rearview mirror. He came walking out of the parking lot with a dark-colored attaché case in his hand. The place was closed, but when he knocked on the door it was opened to allow him inside. He smiled, laughed, said something and went inside.

I sat in my car, stunned.

What was Anthony Mancuso doing at Dominick Barracondi's restaurant?

I drove farther down Emmons Avenue, found a pay phone in front of a newsstand, and dialed the Rectory. When Mrs. Graf answered I said "Hello, how are you," and asked for Vinnie. She asked me to hold on. She was considerably more pleasant than she had been at first. Flowers can work wonders. It was then I remembered that I was supposed to send flowers to Tina at the hotel. I was just sorry that Giambone was going to get the credit.

"Nick?"

"Quick question, Vinnie," I said. "What does Anthony Mancuso do for a living?"

"Let me think a minute. Um, I think he's—yeah, that's right, he's an accountant."

"An accountant?"

"That's right. Why, what's going on?"

"Did you know that he drove a shiny blue Monte Carlo?"

"No, I didn't."

"Did Gloria have her own car?"

"Yes, she did."

"What kind?"

"A red sports car. I don't know the model."

"So why would she have had to be dropped off at the motel that night?" I asked, talking to myself as much as to him. "And if her husband dropped her off, why? He would have had to know what she was going there for, unless he was totally blind and stupid, and a fool to boot."

"A lot of husbands are," he said. "I can't tell you how many husbands come to me to pour their hearts out about their problems, and they never have an inkling."

"I guess," I said. "Look, I gotta go, but before I do, I just remembered something I wanted to tell you about."

"What's that?"

I told him about my talk the previous morning with Monsignor Genovese, and how I had the distinct impression that the man was very bitter toward Vinnie.

"You know, that's very interesting, Nick," Vinnie said. "Even though he has said that he would back me all the way, he's been very cold toward me. I thought I was imagining it."

"Well, you're not, so watch you back, brother." It seemed odd to have to tell him to watch his back in a Rectory. "Vinnie, what do you know about Father Kelleher?"

"What about him?"

"Did Gloria flirt with him?"

"I imagine so."

"But you never saw them together?"

"What do you mean, together? You don't think that Father Kelleher—Nick, we're talking about a very pious man here."

"Vinnie, I'm just trying to find out if you were the only priest she came on to, and Father Kelleher is the only other one your age."

"She might have...come on to the older ones, too."

"Are you saying—"

"No, I'm not saying she did," he said, "I'm just saying it could have happened."

Sure, I thought, and any one of them could have driven the shiny blue car. My brother was getting worked up, and he had enough on his mind. I decided not to pursue the matter with him any further.

"Did you get those blood-test results yet?"

"No, not yet. I'm waiting for Heck to call. I just hope the detectives don't bring them here in person." He was joking, I knew, but you couldn't have told by the tone of his voice.

"I'll keep in touch, big brother."

"Thanks, Nick."

After I hung up I bought a *Daily News* and a New York *Post* and took them to the car. The *News* headline had to do with a truck hijacking, where a driver had been killed. The *Post* headline had to do with Donald and

Ivana Trump. The things that passed for news these days.

I started the car and pointed it toward Bay Ridge. I needed time to think about the implications of Mancuso's going to Barracondi's restaurant. If he was going on business, that meant that he probably was Nicky Barracuda's accountant.

I didn't like the sound of that.

33

I found a parking spot on Third Avenue, just off Eighty-fourth Street. According to the address Tina had given me, Riley lived on this block, between Eighty-third and Eighty-fourth Streets.

Approaching the building, I realized that I didn't know if Riley was his first or last name. Still, if I had asked her that, even she might have become suspicious.

The address was a Chinese laundry, and next to the laundry was another door. There were two doorbells next to the door, each with a name tag. One said t. hom and the other said r. hornsby. I rang the downstairs bell first, several times. When there was no answer, I rang the upstairs. There was no answer there, either. From the name on the upstairs bell I assumed the occupants were Chinese. That meant that maybe the whole family was working in the laundry.

I went into the laundry and approached the counter. The place had that age-old musty smell of steam and starch. There was a pretty girl there, about sixteen, and an older woman of indeterminate age. She could have been fifty or eighty. She had a mouthful of gold crowns.

Before I could say anything, the older woman said, "You got shirts?"

"Uh, no, no shirts. I want to—"

"You got ticket?"

"No, no ticket." If she said "No tickee, no shirtee," I was going to walk out. I didn't give her a chance. "I'm looking for Riley."

"No Riley," the older woman said, shaking her head. "Shirts or tickets. No Riley." With that she turned and went through a doorway to the back.

The young girl remained where she was, studying me. I smiled.

"Hi," I said. "The whole family work down here?" "Yes," she said. "Why do you want Riley?"

"I want to talk to him," I said. "Does he live here? Downstairs?"

"Riley and me are friends," she said, twirling her beautiful black hair around her finger. "Good friends. I could give him a message."

I wonder if her mother—or grandmother—knew that she and Riley were "good friends." She was very pretty, with long, straight black hair that probably went down to her ass. She had a round, high-cheekboned face and a body that was full for a sixteen-year-old—especially a Chinese sixteen-year-old. I wondered if she had any sisters. I wondered if Riley liked living here.

"What's your name?"

"Helen."

"Helen," I said, taking out a five-dollar bill, "give him this." I handed her the bill and said, "Tell him it's my calling card."

"This?" she said, raising her eyebrows.

"Just that. He'll know what it means. Thanks."

I left the store and started for my car when I thought of something. If the whole family worked in the store, that meant they'd probably be going up and down from time to time. It'd be a bitch to keep unlocking the door.

I hadn't tried the door the first time, and since I didn't have to pass the laundry to get to it, I went back. I didn't stop at the door and look both ways. That would have been a dead giveaway that I didn't belong there. Instead, I simply grasped the door handle and depressed the lock with my thumb. The door opened, and I stepped in.

I was in a hallway. Ahead of me was a steep flight of stairs, and alongside the stairs was a thin hallway leading to a door. I had to slide past a motorcycle to get to the door. The bike was probably Riley's.

When I reached his door I tried it instead of knocking. It was unlocked, and I opened it. As soon as I did, the smell hit me. It was the brackish, metallic smell of blood, and lots of it. I had smelled it enough times when I was a cop. It was the kind of smell you can taste, the kind that stays with you for days afterward.

I was in a living room and could see off to the side a small kitchenette. I went through the living room to the bedroom, and he was there, on the bed. He'd been killed sometime the night before. I knew that because the sheets had soaked up most of his blood, except for what had coagulated around the neck wound. It was a particularly vicious neck wound, so bad that I thought that when they moved him, they'd better be ready to catch his head when it fell off.

I would liked to have a look around, but I didn't have the time to do so thoroughly. It didn't look as if there had been much of a struggle. Either he'd known his killer, or they had gotten the drop on him.

He was wearing a pair of pants and nothing else. I looked around for his Holiday Inn jacket, but didn't see it. I knew my phone number was somewhere around there, but I didn't want to chance being found there. If the young Chinese girl was right about being friendly with him, then she could be coming back here at any moment.

It was bad enough that when the police were called in, she'd be able to describe me as having been there looking for him. Luckily, she couldn't say much more than that.

I went back through the living room and out the front door. Down the hall, past the bike. I got some grease on my shirt. When I reached the front door, I took a deep breath, opened it and stepped out. I headed for my car and didn't look back.

34

I was fitting my key into my door lock when Sam's door opened. I turned to say something and stopped when I saw her face. Her left eye and upper cheek were bruised. The eye was actually puffed and partially closed.

"What the hell—"

"Come inside, Nick," she said. "There's someone here to see you."

"What the hell happened to your eye?" I dropped my newspapers on the floor and walked past her into the apartment. There was a second surprise waiting for me inside. Linda Kellogg was there, and if I was any judge of bruises, the one on the left side of her face was fresh.

"He did it again?" I said in disbelief.

She nodded, and a tear rolled down her freshly bruised cheek.

"He would have killed her this time, Nick," Sam said. "If I hadn't been there, he would have."

"You?" I said. "What were you doing there?"

"I knew he was bringing her home from the hospital," Sam said, "so I went there and followed them home. Nick, they had only just gotten out of the cab when he started hitting her again."

"On the street?"

"I ran across the street to stop him, and he turned and hit me a shot in the face." Sam pointed to her puffed and swollen eye.

"What did you think you were doing?"

"I was keeping that asshole from killing her!" she shot back. "Jesus, her ribs are still taped, for Chrissake!"

"What happened after he hit you?"

"What do you think?" she asked. "I hit him back."

"That must have shocked him."

"It did," Linda said, almost smiling. "God, Nick, she punched him right in the face. She was wonderful!"

"You should have done that to him a long time ago," Sam said.

"And then what happened?"

"Well, I didn't kid myself that I could take him," Sam said, "so while he stood there stunned I kicked him in the nuts." She looked at Linda and said, "You should have done that a long time ago, too." She looked at me again and said, "After that I hustled Linda into my cab and we came here."

"All right," I said, "both of you stay here. I'll be back."

"Where are you going?" Sam asked.

"I think it's time somebody had a serious talk with this asshole."

"Are you going to beat him up?" Linda asked.

"Linda—look, he's hitting my friends now—"

"Nick, please," Linda said, "I love him—"

I nearly blew my top but Sam beat me to it.

"Linda, what are you saying?" she demanded. "The guy's an animal, a serious asshole. He put you in the hospital once, and he would have put you right back there again today."

"If it wasn't for you, I know," Linda said. "Sam, I appreciate what you did; but Nick, I don't want you to hurt him."

"What do you want me to do?"

"I want you to help him."

"*Help* him?"

"Something is seriously wrong, I know it."

"What did he say in the cab on the way home?"

"Nothing," she said. "He had a newspaper and he kept reading it, over and over again, getting angrier and angrier."

"Look," I said, "I'll just go over to your place and talk to him." I doubted I could do that without belting him, but for her sake I was willing to try. Every time I looked at Sam's face, though, I got steamed up all over again.

"He's not home."

"How do you know?"

"I've been calling him. There's no answer."

"Maybe he's just not answering the phone."

"No," she said. "If he's there, he'd have to answer it. It's a phobia with him. He can't not answer a ringing phone. If he's there and not answering, it's because he's passed out drunk. If that's the case, then you won't be able to wake him. He'll have to sleep it off."

I stared at her for a few moments, then said, "All right. I'll talk to him tomorrow. Meanwhile…Sam, can she stay here tonight?"

"Of course she can. I'm not gonna send her home so that animal can kill her." She looked at Linda and said, "I'll sleep on the couch, you take my bed."

"It's comfortable," I assured her before she could protest, "I've used it once or twice."

"I don't want to impose—"

"You're not," Sam said.

"I mean, I don't want to get in the way, if you two, uh..."

"Oh, no," Sam said, smiling, "Nick and I are friends, Linda."

"Best friends," I said. "No hanky-panky."

Linda laughed and stopped drawing in her breath at the pain her ribs caused her.

"All right, I'll stay."

"And don't make her laugh," I scolded Sam.

"That's okay," Linda said. "It hurts whether I laugh or not."

"Nick," Sam said, "come by in the morning and I'll make breakfast."

"Deal," I said, walking to the door. "You guys don't stay up all night comparing shiners."

As I was leaving, Linda said, "I have nothing to sleep in..."

"I have some T-shirts," Sam said, "I always sleep in T-shirts..."

I picked up my newspapers and entered my own apartment. I admired Linda's spunk, but had serious doubts about her judgment. I had heard that most battered wives take it and take it and try to hold on to their marriages. I'd seen it on the job, but this was the first example I'd ever seen in someone I knew.

I went into the kitchen and tossed the newspapers on the table. There was some day-old coffee in a pot on the stove and I heated it up. When it was hot I carried a cup to the table and sat down. The back page of the *Post* was facing up, telling me that the Mets had won on a Strawberry homer, but had not gained any ground on the Pirates. They were still two and a half out.

I pushed the *Post* aside and the *News* was face up, still screaming about the truck hijacking. I frowned at it, then opened it to the story and read it. It said that a Mueller Bros. truck had been hijacked, and a driver killed. They said this was the most recent in a long line of recent hijacks.

I got up, walked quickly to my door and pounded on Sam's.

"Who is it?" Sam called.

"Nick."

"What's wrong?" she asked, opening the door. Linda was still on the sofa, but she was wearing one of Sam's T-shirts. This one was pink and said 122nd belmont stakes on it, with a horse and jockey. All the print didn't hide the fact that she had small but firm breasts. Sam was wearing a shirt that simply said Brooklyn on it. Her breasts were anything but small. Neither of them was wearing anything else but panties. Linda was the only one who tried to hide the fact by pulling the T-shirt down.

"I'm not a Peeping Tom," I assured them. "Linda, what newspaper was Dan reading in the cab?"

"What newspaper? I don't know..."

"Think," I said, "was it the *News* or the *Post*?"

"It was the *News*," she said. "He never reads the *Post*."

"All right," I said. "You girls have a job tomorrow."

"What job?" Sam asked.

"I want you to go to the library and look up some old newspapers." I looked at Linda and asked, "Are you up to it?"

"Will it help Danny?" she asked.

"Sweetheart," I said, "it will help all of us."

35

The next morning a pounding on my door woke me up. I immediately remembered that Sam had told me to come over for breakfast, so I assumed I was late. Since I had gotten a flash of Sam's panties the night before, I decided to give her a look at my boxers. In the morning I often work my way up to "playful" before "lucid."

"Okay, sweetcheeks," I said, swinging the door open, "take a good look—"

"Same to you, sweetbuns," Vito Matucci said, slapping me across the face with a folded piece of paper. I caught a glimpse of it and it looked official. I also caught a glimpse of Sam peeking out her door.

"Matucci," I said, "did I invite you for breakfast?"

"If you did, shithead," Matucci said, "I wouldn't be here. You know what this is?" He was talking about the official-looking piece of paper, which he still hadn't held still long enough for me to get a good look at.

"Well," I said, "I only saw it in passing, but let me guess. Probably the only thing that could bring you up to my penthouse would be a search warrant. How'd I do?"

"Give it to him, Vito," Weinstock said. "Let's get this over with."

"Naw," Vito said, "I wanna make this last."

It was only then that I noticed there was a third man in the hallway.

"You workin' in threes these days, Vito," I asked, "or did they assign someone to teach you manners?"

"Aye," he said, showing me his right index finger. I wasn't impressed. I had one just like it, but a little bigger. Matucci's a bantamweight, and hates it. "I told you, you don't call me by my first name."

"Come on, buddy," I said, "old partners should be able to call each other by their first names."

"Buddy" seemed to bother him even more than his first name, but before he could say anything, the third detective in the hall said, "Can we get on with this? It's crowded out here."

"I'm sorry," I apologized, "I'm being a bad host. Come in."

Matucci took one step forward and I put my hand on his chest to stop him.

"I believe you have a piece of paper for me?"

He frowned and slapped it into my palm. I stepped aside and let them enter. I winked at Sam and closed my door, leaving it ajar. I knew she'd want to listen in.

"Do you mind if I put on a pair of pants?"

"I wouldn't mind if you dropped dead," Matucci said.

"Go ahead," Weinstock said. He was actually a decent guy who had somehow done something to get himself saddled with Matucci as a partner. It had always irked me that Matucci and my father shared the same first name. Weinstock was tall and slender, which was enough of a reason for Matucci to hate him, too. They were both about my age, early thirties or so.

The other detective had already started looking around, which meant he had his mind on business. Matucci had his mind on rubbing my nose in something.

"Who's he?" I asked as Weinstock opened the door to my office and went inside. I probably could have stopped him. I'm sure the search warrant said something about searching my "residence," and the office was my "business" location, but I decided not to be a hard-on about it. There was nothing for them to find in there, anyway. In fact, I couldn't imagine what they would find, but then we're all surprised from time to time.

"Cohen," Matucci said, "six-eight squad. Seems they had a little murder in their precinct, and guess what, shithead? You're on the hot seat."

"Not for murder, I'm not," I said, my mind racing. "That's out of my league."

"Everything's out of your league, scumbag."

"You know, Vito," I said, "more and more you remind me of that detective on *Hill Street Blues*. You know, the one who bit off some guy's nose, and growls at everybody? He's a shrimp too."

"You son of a—"

"Of course, his language was a little more inventive than yours. After all, that's television."

It was obvious to me by this time that they were here about Riley's death in Bay Ridge. Cohen from the six-eight had probably gone to the CO of my local precinct, the seven-eight, for a local escort, and he'd been blessed with Matucci and Weinstock.

Weinstock came out of my office empty-handed, but Cohen came out of the bathroom carrying something. I recognized it as the shirt I'd been wearing yesterday. "What'aya got?" Matucci asked.

Cohen held the shirt open so that we could all see the grease mark across the front. I'd gotten it when I brushed against Riley's bike.

"Found it in the laundry hamper."

Matucci walked up to the shirt and touched it. Then he turned to me, grinning.

"Looks like bike grease to me."

"How would you know?" I asked, my mouth a little dry. "You still haven't outgrown your tricycle."

"You fucker—"

"Never mind," Weinstock said. "Listen, Delvecchio, you were in Bay Ridge yesterday talking to a guy named Riley Hornsby."

"Wrong."

"You deny it?" Matucci asked gleefully.

I spoke directly to Weinstock, ignoring Matucci.

"I went to Bay Ridge yesterday to talk to a guy named Riley Hornsby," I corrected him. "He wasn't home."

"How do you know that?" Cohen asked. He was tall and bulky, older than the rest of us, probably forty-five or thereabouts. Nothing was happening here that he hadn't seen a million times before.

"I rang the bell," I said. "He didn't answer. I'm a detective."

"But you spoke to someone," Cohen said. He was taking charge. I didn't mind talking to him because he seemed to know what he was doing. I could deal with him. In fact, I even relaxed a bit, even though he was holding a nice piece of evidence in his hand. I sat down on my bed. It's at times like this I wished I smoked. Light one up, blow some smoke rings, be cool...

"I talked to two Chinese ladies in the laundry downstairs," I said. "One of them was a pretty thing about sixteen. She told me she and Riley were good friends. I left a message with her."

"Why were you looking for Riley?"

"He's a desk clerk at the Holiday Inn in Staten Island. He was supposed to have some information for me on a client."

"Who's the client?" Matucci asked.

I looked at him and said, "Talk to my lawyer," then looked back at Cohen.

"What's the case?" Cohen asked.

"Runaround wife, using the Holiday Inn for her assignations."

"Assassina—" Matucci said, frowning.

"Trysts," I said, without looking at him.

He made a disgusted sound with his mouth and said, "Keyhole stuff."

I shrugged and said, "Pays the rent."

"Look, Mr. Delvecchio," Cohen said, "I got an ugly murder on my hands.

I got a Chinese girl who's still in hysterics. I got you on the scene, and I got grease on your shirt, which places you inside—"

"I got the grease on my shirt inside the apartment?" I asked.

"There was a motorcycle in the hall," Cohen explained patiently. "You probably got this squeezing by it."

"Can you prove it?" I asked. "You gonna match that grease to one motorcycle?"

"I got enough to haul your ass in now on suspicion," Cohen said, "unless you wanna tell me where you got this grease?"

Sure, I thought, gimme a minute to think.

"Let's take him in," Matucci said. "This asshole ain't got nothin' to—"

The front door opened then and Sam came in, like the Seventh Calvary—only the Seventh never looked like her.

36

She was fucking with their minds. She had knotted her T-shirt tightly under her breasts, leaving herself bare from there to her pink panties. They didn't know where to look first, her tits, her navel, her thighs...I was having the same problem myself.

"Nick, honey," she said, walking right over to me and kissing me. To kiss me she had to bend over and I saw all their eyes go to her ass cheeks in her flimsy panties.

"Oh," she said then, as if just noticing them, "I didn't know you had company. I'm sorry."

"It's...all right," Weinstock said, staring at her.

"I just came to get that shirt," she told me.

"What shirt?" I asked.

"Silly," she said, then walked over to Cohen and said, "yeah, that shirt." She took it from his hands before he could react. "Remember? When you dirtied it fixing my car yesterday I promised to wash it for you?"

"Excuse me, miss," Cohen said, finally finding his tongue.

"Yes?"

"He dirtied that shirt fixing your car?"

"He certainly did, the poor dear," she said. "He got all greasy. We had to—I mean, he had to take a shower."

They all caught her "slip" of the tongue, and I know they were thinking about me and Sam in the shower together. So was I.

"I was gonna tell you that just now," I said to Cohen. "All of it except the shower part. I was gonna keep that between my honey and me."

"You're so sweet, Nicky." She came over and stood next to me. They couldn't see her right hand, which was pinching the flesh on my side.

"Where'd you get the shiner, babe?" Matucci asked.

"I beg your pardon?" she said, her tone dripping ice.

"He means, what happened to your face, miss?" Weinstock said, rephrasing it for Matucci.

"Would you believe it?" she asked, touching her face. "I couldn't even open the hood without hitting myself in the face. That's why I needed Nicky."

"Let's take him in, anyway," Matucci said. "We got enough."

"We got nothing," Cohen said wearily. "He admits being there, he admits talking to the Chinese women, he hasn't lied about anything."

"You say!" Matucci said. "What about prints on the doors?"

"So many people went through those doors before we got there that we got no conclusive prints." Cohen looked at me and Sam and said, "Sorry to have bothered you folks."

"Ain't you gonna ask him if he seen nothing'?" Matucci whined.

"He's a pro," Cohen said, "an ex-cop. If he saw something, he'd tell us."

"Damn straight!" I said.

"Look, you—"

"Weinstock," Cohen said, heading for the door, "bring your partner along."

"Nice of you guys to drop by," I said.

At the door Matucci stopped, said, "Eat shit!" and slammed it.

I stood up, grabbed Sam, hugged her and kissed her soundly on the neck. "You were fabulous!"

She unknotted the T-shirt so that it fell down, covering her up—sort of.

"Don't you ever call me your honey!" she said, poking me in the chest with her forefinger.

"And don't you call me Nicky."

We stared at each for a few moments, and then I took her in my arms again and hugged her warmly. I was very conscious of her breasts pressing against my chest. We were like that when Linda walked in.

"Oh, sorry—" she said, starting to back out.

"Hey, come back here," I said, releasing Sam reluctantly. "I was just thanking Sam for getting me out of a jam."

Linda was still wearing Sam's T-shirt, and now that she was standing up I could see that she had trim, but firm legs.

"What jam?" Sam asked. "What was that about?"

"The desk clerk from the Holiday Inn? The one I was waiting to call me about some keys? He was killed yesterday."

"Murdered?"

"And then some," I said. "Some son of a bitch almost cut off his head—" I stopped short and looked at Linda, who was gaping at us.

"That's horrible," she said. "Is this another case you're working on?"

"Yes," I said, "My brother's a priest and..." I told her the whole story about Vinnie being on the verge of arrest. Maybe I did it to take her mind off her own troubles.

"My God," she said, "you've been trying to clear your brother of murder and I've been bothering you with my troubles—"

"Whoa." I walked up to her and took her by her shoulders. "I'm still gonna help you, Linda. Don't worry about that."

"No, no," she said, shaking her head. She had put her hair into a ponytail and it jumped around as she shook her head. Her face washed totally clean of makeup, she looked eighteen, even with the bruises. "I can't ask you to do that. Jesus, your brother needs you—"

"That's enough of that," I said. "You girls have some work to do today, remember?"

"That's right," Sam said. "We'd better get dressed and get to it."

Linda was staring at me with tears forming in her eyes, and then she threw her arms around my waist and hugged me. It would have hurt her ribs too much to throw them around my neck. For the second time in five minutes I had a firm pair of breasts pressing against my chest—smaller, but still firm.

"He's some guy, huh?" Sam asked from close by.

"I don't know what to say," Linda said, her face pressed against my neck.

"Never mind, honey," Sam said, gently disengaging Linda's arms from around my waist, "let's go get dressed and get to work."

Sam shooed Linda out the door, then turned and gave me a look I couldn't read.

"I'll wash this," she said, still holding the shirt, "so it doesn't get you into any more trouble."

"Thanks."

She nodded and went out, closing the door behind her. Did it bother Sam that Linda had hugged me—and I'd hugged back? Maybe I'd ask her...one of these days.

37

I showered and dressed, scolding myself the entire time for throwing the greasy shirt into my hamper, where the cops could find it. I knew they'd found my phone number in Riley's apartment. They hadn't mentioned that, but I knew that's how they had keyed on me. By telling them I was using the clerk on a wayward-wife case, I explained how he happened to have my phone number.

When I got out of the shower I sat with a cup of coffee and tried to figure out how Riley had managed to get himself killed. I'd gone over it last night over a frozen dinner, but my thoughts had been interrupted by a call from Heck Delgado...

"Did you talk to Mr. Mancuso?"

I hesitated before answering, then said, "No, he wasn't home." That was the truth. He wasn't home, he was at Dominick Barracondi's restaurant. For some reason, I didn't want to mention that to Heck just yet. Not until I checked it out. "Tomorrow's Saturday; I'm hoping to find him home then."

"All right," he said. "Call me at home. I'm very interested in his reaction. Have you found out anything else?"

"Yeah, a few things."

I told him about the clerk seeing Gloria get out of a shiny blue car. I told him that both Mancuso and Vinnie had access to such a car.

"Interesting. Is this the clerk who was supposed to give you the information about the keys?"

"Yeah."

"And did he do that?"

"No."

"Why not?"

"Somebody killed him."

"What?"

I explained about tracking the clerk to his home, and finding him dead.

"It must be related," I said. "It can't be a coincidence. Can you go to the detectives with this?"

"Not without getting both you and Father Vincent in trouble," he said. "You for not reporting it, and Vincent—well, they'll just say that he could have killed the clerk, too."

"Why?"

"Who knows? Maybe the clerk was blackmailing him? Maybe he saw more than just a shiny blue car?"

I thought about that now. It made sense: Riley *had* seen more than just a shiny blue car, and he *had* tried to blackmail someone, and that someone had killed him. It made sense—to me, anyway—that the same person who killed Riley killed Gloria, and tried to pin it on my brother.

I sat up straighter in my chair.

If someone tried to frame my brother for Gloria's murder, and that someone was the one who dropped Gloria off at the hotel, then that meant that Gloria had been in on it. I had that feeling you get when all the puzzle pieces are suddenly dropping into place. If Gloria was in on luring Vinnie out there, then that meant that she was setting him up from the beginning. The only thing she didn't know was that she was setting herself up, as well.

It all made sense to me. The only thing I had to find out now was whom she had been working with. A boyfriend? Her husband? If her husband wanted to kill her, why go through such an elaborate scheme to frame Vinnie? What did he have against Vinnie?

The only one who could shed any light on the subject was Anthony Mancuso himself.

I took about twenty minutes to formulate the approach I was going to take with Mancuso, then called his house. Its being Saturday was no guarantee that he'd be home, but he had a kid, so it was a good bet he wouldn't be working—especially in light of what had happened to his daughter's mother.

"Hello?"

The voice that answered the phone was that of a young girl.

"May I speak to Mr. Mancuso, please?"

"Who may I say is calling?"

"My name is Nick Delvecchio."

"Delvecchio?" she said, surprised. "That's a priest's name."

"Yes," I said, "Father Delvecchio is my brother."

"Hey, Daddy," she shouted, "Father Delvecchio's brother is on the phone." She didn't bother to place her hand over the receiver.

"Give me that phone," I heard a man say, and then there was the sound of his grabbing it from her. "Go to your room, Lisa."

"But, Daddy—"

"Go ahead, do as I tell you."

There was a pause, and then he came on the line. "What do you want, you son of a bitch?"

"Hey, Mancuso," I said, "I don't even know you. Where do you get off calling me names?"

"Your brother killed my wife!"

"What's that got to do with me?"

There was a pause and then he said, "Suppose you tell me that. Why are you calling my house?"

"I want to come over and talk to you."

"About what?"

"About the murder of your wife."

"You wanna try and convince me that he didn't do it?" he asked with a sneer in his voice.

"Yeah, I'd like an opportunity to do that."

"Well, fuck off, Delvecchio—"

"Listen to me, Mancuso," I said, cutting him off, "I'm a private investigator working for my brother's attorney, and if you refuse to talk to me, I'm liable to think you're hiding something."

Now there was a pause on his end before he asked, "What have I got to hide?"

"That's a good question," I said. "I'd like to ask it in person."

There was a longer pause and then he said, "All right, come ahead."

"I'll be there in an hour." I hesitated a moment, then said, "Thanks, Mancuso," trying to build up some goodwill.

"Don't thank me," he said. "I may end up kicking your butt right out of here."

38

Mancuso had a big house on a huge lot on Avenue M in Canarsie. There were only two houses on the block, which was a short one. Mancuso's was the larger of the two, with the most land, and a garage. When I got there I pulled right into his driveway. There were parking spots on the street, but I wanted to pressure him right away.

I walked up to his front door and rang his bell. It was answered in moments by Lisa.

She looked at me through the screen door and cocked her head to one side. The way she was dressed—a halter top and cutoff jeans—she looked sixteen, at least. She had her thumbs hooked in the front of the jeans, pulling them down so that I could see her deep navel.

"Are you Father Delvecchio's brother?"

"That's right."

"I didn't know priests had brothers."

"Well, they do. I'm living proof."

"You're not a priest, too?"

"No."

"How come?"

"I guess I just didn't feel I was right for the job."

"Being a priest is a job?"

"I guess they'd say it was more a calling than a job."

"Lisa," Mancuso's voice called from upstairs, "who's at the door?"

She turned her head for a moment, then looked back at me quickly.

"Did Father Delvecchio really kill my mom?"

"I don't think so, honey."

"I hope not," she said as her father came down the stairs behind her, "I really like him."

"Lisa, damn it," her father said, "I told you not to answer the door."

"Well, you were in the bathroom."

"Go to your room."

"Dadd-eee!" she said, drawing it out. "Johnny's coming over."

"I told you I don't want you seeing him. Now go to your room."

"Oooh!" she said, stamping her foot. "You're ruining my life!"

She ran up the stairs and Mancuso unlocked the screen door.

"Damned eighteen-year-olds sniffing around my daughter. She's just a kid."

"She's a beautiful kid," I said. "Maybe it's got something to do with the way she dresses."

"She's like her mother," he said morosely. "They can smell it on them."

That sounded like a bitter remark directed more at his dead wife than his daughter.

"Smell what on them?"

At that point he just seemed to notice whom he was talking to.

"Never mind! You didn't come here to talk about my daughter." He opened the screen door and said, "Come inside. We'll go into my den."

I entered, he locked the door, and I followed him to the den. We went through an extremely tastefully furnished living room that was primarily light and dark blues. I spotted the dining room, which had a beautiful blond wood table and hutch.

"You have a beautiful home."

"Gloria took care of all the furnishings," he said. "All I did was pay for them."

I followed him into his den, which was spartanly but masculinely furnished. I suspected that he had had more to say about what went in here than Gloria had.

There was a fireplace, and on the mantel was an array of photos. Gloria Mancuso dominated most of them. This was really the first time I had ever seen her, and I could see how men would "smell it" on her. Even in still photographs she reeked of sexuality. It reached out, grabbed you by the throat, and some other parts, as well.

There were a couple of photos of Gloria and Lisa, both laughing. The resemblance was staggering, and looking at the younger girl you could see where she might even surpass the mother, if not in beauty, then in raw sexuality. Unless she went to an all-girls high school, some male students, and teachers, were in for four tough high school years. It was rough having a Lolita in your class.

"She was very beautiful," I said. "I hadn't seen any pictures until now."

"Never mind that." He had seated himself behind his desk. "Say what you have to say. I'm busy."

"You take work home with you?"

"I work at home, Delvecchio," he said. "I'm self-employed...and I have some very important clients."

I wondered if he'd get around to bragging. That was one of the things I wanted. I remembered Harriet Dean pushing her little nose over to the side, implying that Mancuso liked to insinuate that he was Mafia-connected. At the time I thought the remark was nonsense, but knowing what I knew now, he might have had connections. Chances were good, though, that he was just an accountant. Nobody with heavier connections than that is going to brag about them to the PTA.

Mancuso looked to be in his late thirties. He was a tall man with broad shoulders and a sallow complexion. He didn't look Italian, he looked more Jewish. His hair was combed straight back, but it was thinning and came to a widow's peak. He was wearing a light-blue short-sleeved button-down shirt, open at the collar. For all the world he looked like the big executive on his day off. That was probably more true of him than "Mafia insider on his day off."

"Important clients, huh?"

"So you know I don't have much time to spend with you."

"What kind of clients?"

He gave me a level stare and said, "The kind you don't want to mess with, son."

"Really?" I said. "Are we talking...wise guys?"

"You said it," Mancuso said, "not me. Just believe that I'm not someone you want mad at you."

"Top of the ladder, huh?"

"The very top."

"I guess that explains why you went to Nicky Barracuda's restaurant yesterday, huh? Before it was even open?"

"What?" he said. "What'aya mean?"

"I followed you from school, Tony boy."

"You followed me?"

"So tell me, you do Nicky Barracuda's books?"

"Nobody calls him that anymore."

"Oh, I do," I said. "See, you bullshit people by insinuating that you have these big Mafia connections. I, on the other hand, don't talk about it, but Nicky Barracuda is my godfather."

He sat quiet for a moment, then said, "By godfather, you mean..."

"I don't mean Marlon Brando."

"Why are you telling me this?"

"Because I want you to know that you can't shit me, Tony. I'm not in the PTA."

I had him off balance. He knew that he was supposed to be outraged at my presence, since he claimed to believe that my brother killed his wife.

"Now, somebody killed your wife, Tony," I said, "and it wasn't my brother."

"The police think he did it."

"You'll notice that he's not under arrest," I said. "What does that suggest to you?"

"You tell me."

"They have another suspect."

"Who?"

"You know who."

He thought about it for a moment, then said, "Me?"

"Smart man."

"I didn't kill my own wife."

"Convince me."

"I...don't have to convince you of anything."

"Okay, then tell me this. If you didn't kill her, and my brother didn't kill her, who did?"

"You didn't know my wife, or you wouldn't have to ask that."

"What do you mean?"

"Men, Mr. Delvecchio." All of a sudden I was "Mister" Delvecchio. "They couldn't stay away from her, and she couldn't keep her hands off of them."

"And you knew this?"

"Yes."

"Why did you stay with her?"

He spread his hands in a helpless gesture and said, "I loved her."

"Enough to be a willing cuckold?"

"Not willing," he said, "helpless."

Jesus, I thought. I hoped I never loved a woman so much that I'd be helpless. Then again, a woman who looked like Gloria Mancuso, who had her...particular brand of sexual magnetism...

"So you're saying that any one of her boyfriends could have killed her."

"She didn't have boyfriends," he said, "she had men, and she had them once. She never carried on an affair with a man. She had him once, and then came back to me."

"So that's what she was doing at the hotel in Staten Island?" I asked. "Meeting a man?"

"She was meeting your brother. He's admitted as much."

"Yes, I know," I said, "but he didn't stay. He didn't sleep with your wife, Tony. He didn't kill her. He left her alive. He had no motive to kill her."

"If he walked out on her," Mancuso said, "that would have given her a motive to kill him. No man ever turned her down."

"Tony," I said, "did you drive her to the hotel?"

I watched him carefully as I asked the question.

"Drive her?" he asked. "Hell, no, why would I drive her to meet with another man?"

"You've said you were helpless before her."

"Not that helpless," he said. "Believe me, Delvecchio, I didn't pimp for her. She didn't need a pimp. She was better than any whore at what she did."

The last was said bitterly. I wondered if a man could actually be that helpless, and if so, for how long?

I left Mancuso's house assuring him that I intended to find out who killed his wife. Ever since I told him I was Nick Barracuda's godson he had dropped his superior attitude and adopted one of deference. I guess he figured I had no reason to lie about it.

Outside I started down the walk, but stopped when I saw Lisa waiting for me by my car. She was still wearing the halter top, and she had her hands pushed into her back pockets, which thrust her breasts forward. I had never seen a thirteen-year-old with her degree of development.

"I thought you were in your room?"

"I can't stay in my room," she said. "Johnny's coming to get me."

"But your father—"

"Oh, he won't even notice that I'm gone. He doesn't love me, anyway."

"Why do you say that, Lisa?"

"He says I'm too much like my mother, and he hated her."

"Hated her? But he just told me how much he loved her."

"He lied," she said matter-of-factly. "He's glad she's dead."

"Did he say that?"

"No," she said, "but I've heard him tell her that he wished she was dead plenty of times."

"Well, Lisa, sometimes adults say things they don't mean."

"That's stupid," she said. "People should say what they mean. Take Johnny, for instance. He tells me exactly what he wants."

With a degree of sick fascination I asked, "And what's that?"

"He wants to fuck me," she said, as an old car pulled up in front and the boy behind the wheel beeped his horn.

"Lisa, I don't think that's such a good idea—"

"Oh, don't worry about me, Mr. Delvecchio." She spoke to me over her shoulder as she turned to run to the car. "I'm not a virgin, you know."

No, I didn't know, but watching her run to the car, just thirteen years of firm young flesh, I could believe it.

39

I decided to find out what was going on with Mancuso and Dominick Barracondi, so I drove to Sheepshead Bay. They would probably be setting up for lunch about now.

When I got there I parked in the restaurant's parking lot and walked to the front door. It was unlocked, and I walked right in.

"Hey," a man said, blocking my path, "we ain't open yet."

In the old days he would have been called a torpedo. Here he was probably called a headwaiter.

"Benny around?"

"Who's askin'?"

"Nick Delvecchio."

If he recognized my name, he didn't show it.

"Wait here."

I waited while he disappeared, and a few moments later he reappeared with Benny. Benny said something to the guy, who veered off as Benny approached me. Benny was wearing a charcoal three-piece suit, an orange shirt, a light-gray tie, and his pinky rings.

"Hello, Nicky D."

"Benny," I said, nodded. "Is he in?"

"Yeah."

"I'd like to see him."

"I'll have to ask him," Benny said. "Wait here."

"I can do that," I said. "I've had practice."

This time Benny disappeared and when he reappeared he was alone. The torpedo-turned-headwaiter was standing at the bar, and Benny waved to him.

"Come on, Nick."

As I followed Benny, the headwaiter took up his former position by the door.

When I entered Barracondi's office, he was seated behind his desk. I don't know why, but I had the feeling he already knew why I was there. Maybe Mancuso had already called him.

"What can I do for you, Nicholas?"

I sat down, uninvited.

"Tell me about Anthony Mancuso."

"Why should I?"

"Because you're playing games," I said. "You said you wanted to help Father Vinnie, but you were waiting to be asked. All that while you knew that Vinnie was suspected of killing Gloria Mancuso, your accountant's wife."

"What has that got to do with anything?"

"I'll tell you what," I said. "Mancuso's got more motive to kill his wife than Vinnie ever could."

"Maybe he did. I still don't understand—"

"No, I guess you don't, and I don't, either. Who do you want to help, Vinnie, or Tony boy?"

He hesitated a few moments, then said, "Look, Nick, Tony couldn't have killed his wife."

"Why not? Because he's your accountant?"

"Because it's just not in him. He's not a made guy, he's just an accountant."

A "Made Guy" in Mafia parlance is someone who has earned his wings by killing someone.

"Then you better tell him to stop bragging to the PTA about his Mafia connections."

"All right, so he's got a big mouth. That doesn't make him a killer."

"My information is that he hated his wife."

"Still doesn't make him a killer."

"Then you think Vinnie did it?"

He gave me an exasperated look and said, "Of course I don't think Father Vincent killed her."

"Then give me a name," I said.

"Are you asking for my help?"

"I'm asking you to give me some idea who might have killed her if Vinnie and Tony didn't."

"I can't," he said. "She had too many men. She was an embarrassment to Anthony. If he killed her, I couldn't blame him."

"If he killed her and framed Vinnie, I could blame him for that."

"He couldn't have framed Father Vincent," Barracondi said. "He's not smart enough."

"I think he did it," I said. "If not, then I think he knows who did. He knows *something*. I just came from his house and that's the impression I came away with."

"I can't help you there, Nicholas. I have friends in the Police Department, the DA's office. I can help you there."

I stood up and said, "I don't want you pulling strings to get Vinnie off. I want to prove his innocence."

"Did you ask Father Vincent if he wants my help?"

"I did, and he said no."

"And your father?"

"You know my father. Of course he wants to call you, but Vinnie won't let him."

"If my old friend does call me," Barracondi said, "I will help him."

"He won't call," I said, heading for the door.

"Nicholas!"

I turned.

"You reject my help, you treat me with disrespect—"

"I have *never* treated you with disrespect," I said, interrupting him.

He executed a small bow with just his head and said, "I stand corrected. Let us call it *disdain*. You reject me and treat me with disdain, and yet if you come to me later for help, I will give it."

"Just answer me this," I said. "How connected is Mancuso?"

"He is an accountant."

"Whose?"

"Mine," he said. "He is my accountant for this, my legitimate restaurant. That is all I can tell you. I do not know who else he works for."

"All right," I said, feeling frustrated. I had expected to learn a lot more. "All right...if I've treated you with disrespect, I apologize."

"We have determined that what you have for me is disdain."

"I have disdain for what you represent."

"These days I am a restaurateur, Nicholas," Barracondi said, "and nothing more."

"A restaurateur with strings right up to City Hall, huh?"

"I told you, I am not without influence."

"I'm sure," I said. "I'll be leaving now."

"Come back anytime, Nick, for help, for lunch...I would like it if you came back."

"Well," I said, "the food *is* pretty good."

I didn't know what to say further, so I just gave him a half wave and left. As I left I heard him say, almost to himself, "*Pretty* good?"

Outside I found Benny waiting to escort me out. As we walked to the door I figured, what the hell? Benny had always liked to talk.

"Benny, what do you know about Tony Mancuso?"

"He's a pencil pusher." His tone was noncommittal, but I still managed to notice some—Nicky Barracuda had come up with a good word—*disdain*.

"Connected?"

"What's connected?" Benny said, shrugging. "He works for some guys, keeps their books."

"Like who?"

"Like the Don."

At the door I said, "I know he keeps the Don's books, Benny. I want to know who else's books he keeps."

"Didn't you ask the Don?" Benny asked, opening the door and letting the sun in.

"Yes, I asked the Don, and he said he didn't know."

"Well," Benny the Card said, "if he don't know, I don't know."

I patted him on one broad shoulder and said, "Somehow I knew you'd say that, Benny."

40

I wasn't entirely unhappy with the day's findings, so far. I was convinced that Anthony Mancuso knew something, and I was convinced that Nicky Barracuda knew something. Mancuso was hiding it, Barracuda was simply not sharing it. I was also convinced that I was the only one who *didn't* know something.

So why wasn't I unhappy? Simple. Mancuso knew that Vinnie hadn't killed his wife. Barracuda also knew that Vinnie wasn't guilty. That meant that, eventually, I'd be able to prove that Vinnie was innocent. The proof was out there, I just had to keep looking. I just hoped I'd find it before Vinnie was arrested.

I was driving west on the Belt Parkway, toward Manhattan, trying to figure out my next move, when I noticed I was being squeezed. I hadn't noticed it earlier because I'd been paying only partial attention to my driving. That was the reason I had been driving in the right lane in the first place.

Now I noticed that there was a car directly in front of me, driving slowly, and there was a car riding right next to me. There were two men in each car. We were approaching an exit and they weren't giving me any time to think.

The car on my left came over and made contact with me, and the car in front of me slowed almost to a crawl. I had no choice but to go off onto the shoulder. The front car went with me, and stopped, as did the car on my left. It stopped right up against me, pinning the driver's-side door closed. I had one way out, and that was the passenger side. I didn't want to get out, though. At least, not empty-handed. I locked all the doors and started feeling under the seats hoping to find a tire iron, or something...anything. All I found were some computer magazines.

By this time the four thugs were banging on the car doors. One of them went to his car, opened the trunk and took out a baseball bat. It looked like a Don Mattingly model. At least they were going to use a best model to cripple me with.

The other three backed away so the one armed with the bat could get a good swing. He hit the driver's-side front window once, and it starred. The second time, it shattered, and then they were reaching in to unlock the door. The next thing I knew I was being dragged out.

There were four of them. I was hopelessly outnumbered and unarmed, but there was one thing they hadn't counted on.

When I was on the job I once had taken a terrible beating because I had been slow to resort to violence. After months in the hospital I swore that I would never take a vicious beating like that again, from anyone. That was the reason I ultimately had to cut a deal to leave the job so as not to go to jail. I had beaten up a guy who turned out to be a politician's son.

Since then I've always carried that fear inside of me. Last year it had caused me to kill one of two men who were bent on giving me a beating.

Now there were four, and as they dragged me out of the car, I exploded in blind fury...and fear.

They had me by one arm and both legs. I poked one of them in the eyes, digging in with my nails hard. He screamed and released my other arm. I reached out and grabbed two handfuls of hair, pulling with all my might. Hair came loose in my hand and two more screams sounded. My legs were free and I was rolling away, trying to get to my feet. Before I could I felt the bat hit me in the lower back. The pain was numbing, but I kept rolling and finally got to my feet. My back was on fire then, but the adrenaline flow was keeping me from giving into it. If I gave in, I'd be on the ground and they would be free to cripple me, or beat me to death. I'd *make* them kill me before I would allow them to cripple me.

The one whose eyes I had clawed was out of it. Blood was running down his face. I hoped I had blinded the bastard for life.

The other three were advancing on me, the one with the bat in the middle. I charged him, and he swung the bat. It hit me on the shoulder, but I ignored the pain. I charged into his midsection and lifted him up off the ground. I carried him a few feet and then slammed him down on his back. When he hit the ground all of the air rushed out of his lungs, and he released the bat and I grabbed it. Giddy with triumph I started to turn and swing the bat, but the other two were on me, and they were big boys. Their weight bore me to the ground, with them on top. I fought like a wild man, but my arm was pinned and the bat was useless. Finally, I let it go so I could use my hands, my nails, but one of them was kneeling on my arm and it was pinned.

"Hold 'im," someone yelled.

"This motherfucker is crazy!" someone else said.

"I got the bat," another voice said. The third man had probably regained his feet. "Hold him. I'm gonna cripple the bastard."

I screamed then, in fear and frustration and just plain anger, and something hit me in the head. The last thing I remembered seeing was Benny the Card's face over the shoulders of my assailants...or was that a dream?

When I woke up I knew where I was immediately. I could smell it. I knew what a hospital smelled like, because I had spent almost three months in one back when I had been beaten up. For one stark staring mad moment I thought that I was *still* in the hospital from that beating, and that everything that had happened since then was a drug-induced dream.

"Jesus," I said, out loud, "Jesus, Jesus..."

"He's panicking," someone said.

"Oh, Christ," I said, because now I knew I was in the hospital again, and maybe this time I wouldn't get out in one piece.

"Fuck," I said, and then shouted, "Fuck, goddammit!"

"Easy, Nick, easy," someone said, and I felt hands on me, two sets of hands.

I looked to my right and saw Vinnie standing over me. Then I looked to the left and saw Sam.

"Take it easy," she said, smiling and putting her hand on my face, "you're all right."

"God," I said, "am I in one piece?"

"Yes," she said, "you're going to be fine."

"Vinnie?" I said, as if I thought Sam was lying to me. "Vinnie?"

"Nick, you're fine."

"They were gonna cripple me."

"Nick, they didn't..."

I didn't believe them. I couldn't feel anything from the waist down, and suddenly I couldn't catch my breath.

"Vinnie..." I said, but everything started to spin, and the last thing I heard was someone shouting, "Get the doctor."

The next time I woke up I did so slower, and easier. I frowned, took a deep breath, and recognized the hospital smell. The thing that kept me calm was that I could feel pain in my back. If I could feel pain, then I wasn't paralyzed.

I turned my head to the right and realized that I had a bruiser of a headache. That was good, too. Gimme pain, I thought.

I saw Sam sitting in a chair next to my bed, and her eyes were closed. I turned my head the other way and saw Maria on the other side, in the same state.

"Jesus," I said, "can't a guy get any attention around here?"

Vinnie was out in the hall or the lounge with Pop, and Maria went to get them. Sam held a plastic cup of water so I could sip from a straw.

"What hospital?" I asked.

"Methodist."

"How long?"

"Today is Sunday. You've been here overnight, and all day."

"Who brought me in?"

"That guy, Benny, who works for your, uh, godfather?"

"Then it wasn't a dream."

"What wasn't?"

"I thought the last thing I saw when I went out was Benny's face. Jesus, my back is killing me...and my head...and my shoulder..."

"That about covers it," Sam said. "What did they hit you with?"

"A baseball bat."

"That's what the doctor said."

"Did he say a Don Mattingly model?"

"Dave Winfield, I think."

"Nobody's perfect."

The door opened and my family came in. Sam touched my arm, the one with the intravenous tube in it, and then moved away from the bed to make room.

"How you doin', little brother?" Vinnie asked.

"Okay," I said, "I think. Did I, uh, freak out..."

"That was earlier this morning," Vinnie said. "We explained to the doctor about, uh, the last time, and he thought you might be suffering some flashback. You hyperventilated and passed out."

I turned my head and saw my father.

"Hi, Pop."

His eyes were red, and he hadn't shaved.

"How do you feel?" he asked in a soft voice.

"I'm okay," I said. I felt his hand on my other arm and for a moment I had the urge to cry, but it passed. I guess I was glad to see that he was worried, and relieved.

"What's the damage?" I asked.

"The doctor's going to come in and talk to you about that," Vinnie said, "but there doesn't seem to be anything permanent."

"Good news," I said. "Vinnie, why don't you take Pop and Maria home?"

"I wanna stay," Pop said.

"Me, too," Maria said.

"I want you guys to go home," I said. "You look like you been here all night."

"We have," Vinnie said, "all of us. I could use a shower."

"Go home, Pop," I said, "get some rest, and then come back. I don't think I'll be goin' anywhere for a while."

Pop looked at Vinnie, who nodded.

"You do what-a the doctor tells you," Pop said.

"Scout's honor."

"I never could get-a you to join the scouts," he said, putting his hand on my arm again.

"Come on, Pop," Vinnie said. "I'll see you later, Nick."

Maria came close to the bed so she could kiss me on the cheek.

"See you, big brother. I'm glad you're okay."

"Me, too, sis."

"Sam?" Vinnie said. "Can we give you a ride?"

She was standing off to the side with her arms folded. She was wearing a sundress instead of a T-shirt, and it left her arms and shoulders bare.

"I have my car, thanks. I'll be leaving in a few minutes."

"See you later?"

"I'll be here," she said, and Vinnie touched her arm and started for the door.

"Hey, Vin?"

"Yeah?"

"You're not—I mean, they didn't—"

"I'm not under arrest, if that's what you're trying to ask. No changes, Nick. See you later."

I nodded, and he left. Sam came around to the left side of the bed and took hold of my free hand.

"You scared the shit out of us, pal."

"Scared the shit out of *you?*" I said.

She squeezed my hand and we were silent for a moment.

"While we wait for the doctor," I said, breaking the silence, "why don't you tell me what the fuck is going on?"

41

This part Sam got from Vinnie, who got it from Benny, so I was getting it third-hand. Anyway, it went like this:

After I left Nicky Barracuda's office, he called Benny in and told him to follow me. Vinnie asked Benny why, but Benny said he didn't know, and besides, when the Don tells him to do something, he never asks why.

So, Benny got into his Cadillac and started after me on the Belt Parkway. Vinnie asked Benny how he knew I'd be driving west on the Belt, and Benny told him that's what the Don said. Actually, that wasn't hard to figure. Barracuda knew I had come to his place from Mancuso's home in Canarsie, so I wouldn't have had a reason to go back that way.

Benny was driving pretty fast, trying to catch sight of the car I was driving, when he saw three cars pulled off onto the shoulder. It looked like a bunch of guys beating up one guy.

"Actually," Sam said at this point, "Benny said that it looked like you were beating up on a bunch of guys, but he stopped to help you, anyway. Father Vincent said that it sounded to him like Benny was really impressed with the way you were handling yourself."

"That's because I bugged out."

Benny got there just as I was about to be beaten to death, and he pulled the four guys off me.

"Benny said he routed them," Sam said.

"What?"

She laughed and said, "That was Benny's word."

I laughed, and then cringed because laughing made my head hurt.

"I wish I could have seen that."

"What did you do to them?" Sam asked. "Benny told Father Vincent that you ripped the eyes out of one of them."

"Sam," I said, "I honestly don't know what I did."

"Well, Benny put you in his car and drove you straight here. He then called Mr. Barracuda, who in turn called Father Vincent. Your brother made the other notifications, including calling me. I was the first one here, because your brother stopped to pick up your father and sister, but Benny wouldn't talk to me."

"He wouldn't?"

"Oh, he was very polite," she said. "He called me 'ma'am' and said he would rather wait for the family to arrive."

"Well," I said, "I guess I've Nicky Barracuda and Benny the Card to thank for the fact that I'm not crippled, or dead."

"Does that bother you?"

"I hate to admit it, but no."

At that point the door opened and a doctor entered. He was pretty young, probably about thirty-five, and he had a bright smile for Sam. What man wouldn't? He was not tall, but was athletically built. He had brown hair and a bushy brown mustache.

"Nick, this is Dr. Sconzo. Doctor, your patient." She backed away from the bed to allow the doctor to approach.

"How are you feeling, Mr. Delvecchio?"

"How should I be feeling, Doc?" I asked. "What's the damage?"

"Well, we did some X rays while you were unconscious. You have some definite lower-back trauma, and—excuse me, Miss Karson—you might be passing blood for a while, but there isn't any permanent damage. The same goes for your shoulder. You've got a deep bone bruise there, and it will probably bother you for a while, but there were no broken bones. As for your head, you took fifteen stitches just below the hairline, and you have a slight concussion. You'll probably have a small scar as a memento of this incident. I understand there were four men, and a baseball bat?"

"Don Mattingly model," I said. "It's odd that I should have noticed that."

"In a stressful situation," he said, "our senses are very often heightened."

"When can I get out of here?"

"Well, you *could* walk out of here right now, but I'd prefer to keep you a few days for observation."

"I'll split the difference with you," I said. "I'll check out tomorrow."

"Nick—" Sam said.

"I've got to wrap up both of these cases, Sam," I said, "and I think I know how to do it."

"You're free to check yourself out at any time," the doctor said, "but talk to me first. I want to put that arm in a sling."

"Thanks, Doc."

"You're welcome," he said. He turned to Sam and asked, "May I see you in the hall, Miss Karson?"

"Of course." She looked at me and said, "I'll be right back."

They went out into the hall and I wondered what the doctor could be telling her that he didn't want me to hear.

She was back in a couple of minutes, an amused look on her face.

"What was that about?" I asked. "Am I gonna drop dead in a day or two, and he doesn't want me to know?"

"No, nothing like that," she said. "In fact, it didn't have to do with you at all."

"Oh?"

"He asked me out."

"Oh...and what did you say?"

"I said no."

"How come?" I asked. "He's good-looking, and he's a doctor. He must have money."

"Ni-i-ck!" she said, her tone scolding as she drew my name out. "He's also got a wife."

"Oh...well, you wouldn't have liked him, anyway."

"Why not?"

"Never mind," I said. "Where's Linda?"

"Probably outside. She said she didn't want to stay at my place alone, and she's not ready to go home."

"Well, tell her to come in."

"I'll go and get her."

She went out of the room and was back in seconds with Linda.

"I'm sorry you had to wait out there," I said, "but I didn't know you were here."

"That's all right," she said. "I didn't want to get in the way, what with your family here and all."

She came to the left side of the bed and surprised me by bending over and kissing me on the cheek.

"How are you?"

"The doctor says I'm gonna live," I said, "but I feel like shit."

"I think I know how you feel."

"Yeah, you would," I said. "How are the ribs?"

"Sore."

"We'll have to compare bruises."

She surprised me again by smiling and saying, "Sounds like fun."

"Never mind the fun," I said, "you ladies had a job to do today—I mean, yesterday. Did you do it?"

"We did," Linda said, looking at Sam.

"The information is at my place," Sam said. "When you come home I'll give it to you."

"All right," I said, feeling groggy. I must have looked groggy, too, because Linda said maybe she'd wait outside for Sam.

"Be well," she said, kissing me again.

"You're quite a hit with the ladies," Sam said.

"Really? Who besides you and Linda?"

"Sister Olivia," Sam said. "You were right, she is pretty. She wasn't wearing her habit."

"When was she here?"

"Earlier today. I don't know if she'll be back." She put her hand on my arm and said, "You should sleep. I'll be outside until Father Vincent comes back."

"You don't have to stay."

"I want to," she said. "Your father was nice enough to say that I was practically family."

"He's right," I said. "Do me a favor, hand me the phone before you leave? I have to make a call."

"To who?"

"Heck Delgado."

"He was here earlier today."

"He was?"

She nodded.

"Now there's a good-looking man," she said enthusiastically, "and he's not married."

"Don't tell me that he asked you out, too?"

"No," she said, and then added, "not yet."

"Not yet," I said. "Hand me the phone."

"Here," she said, handing me the receiver. "I'll dial it for you."

After my conversation with Heck I tried to go to sleep, but I couldn't. Things were going click! click! click! in my head as puzzle pieces continued to fall into place. He had given me the main piece, and now all the others were slipping right in where they belonged.

I was so excited by having figured it out that I knew I'd never fall asleep. Until I did...

I heard someone speaking, although it was more of a whisper. I opened my eyes and saw Sister Olivia kneeling next to my bed, her hands clasped together, her lips moving. She was wearing her habit, but she still looked pretty. "Why'd you have to be a nun?" I asked.

She lifted her head, looked at me and said, "Shut up and go back to sleep. I'm praying for you."

I shut up and went back to sleep.

42

Tuesday morning, at 10 A.M., I presented myself at the law offices of Walter Koenig. I had checked myself out of the hospital Monday afternoon, after Doctor Sconzo had fitted me with a sling. The sling was a good idea, because the slightest movement of my left arm was impossible. There wasn't even pain, because I didn't have the strength to lift it high enough to make it hurt.

Both Sam and Vinnie were at the hospital when I checked out, and they both had cars. We decided that it made sense for Sam to drive me home, since she lived just across the hall. Vinnie said he was going back to the Rectory to wait for Heck to call him about the lab tests. The lab had been closed for the weekend, but this was Monday and the results should be coming in soon.

When we got home Linda was waiting in my apartment and the two women made me sit down on the sofa and insisted on making me lunch. While they did that, I went through the material they had gotten from the library. Now that I had Gloria Mancuso's murder figured out, Linda Kellogg's problem with her husband Dan began to come together as well.

First, though, I had to keep Vinnie out of jail. Since Linda wasn't anywhere near Dan Kellogg, he could wait.

After lunch I called Koenig's office and made an appointment to see him the next morning at ten. After that I convinced the girls that I wouldn't fall down if left by myself, and after they went back to Sam's apartment, I went to bed. It was only two in the afternoon, but I slept through the night, except for a call I got at 8 P.M.

When the phone rang I tried to reach for it with my injured arm—the left one—but it refused to move, so I grabbed it with my right.

"What?"

"Nick? Vinnie."

"What?"

"Are you awake?"

"What?"

"Nick!"

"*What?*"

"Wake up."

"I'm awake."

"We got the results of the test."

"And?"

"It was inconclusive. My blood type is type O, universal, so they can't prove it was or wasn't me. It could have been anyone. I'm not under arrest...yet."

"That's good, Vinnie."

"Go back to sleep," he said. "You need your rest."

"I was trying to get it."

"I thought you'd want to know."

"I did," I said. "Vinnie?"

"What?"

"I'm gonna wrap this up tomorrow."

"What?"

"Tomorrow," I said. "That's a promise."

"Nick, what are you going to do?"

"I'm gonna go and talk to the son of a bitch who framed you..."

So at 10 A.M. I was in Walter Koenig's reception room. "Mr. Delvecchio to see Mr. Koenig."

His secretary looked at me and said, "Mr. Koenig was called away to court."

"We had an appointment."

"He said he made the arrangements for you," she said. "It's all taken care of. He said you really didn't need to talk to him, anyway."

"You mean he was afraid to talk to me," I said, and added to myself, now that he knew that I knew.

"I beg your pardon?"

"Never mind," I said. "Just tell him that when this is all over, I'll be back for him."

She stared at me and said, "Uh, that sounded like a threat."

I smiled at her and said, "Sweetheart, relay it to him just that way."

Sam refused to let me drive to Attica alone, so instead of taking Hacker's Grand Prix I went in her used, red Nissan Sentra, with her driving. When we got there I made her wait outside the prison while I went in to see the bastard who framed my brother because I wouldn't work for him...

43

A month earlier an attorney named Walter Koenig had called me and asked me if I would come to his office. Since I knew that Koenig represented Salvatore Cabretta, I balked. After all, a little over five years ago my testimony as a police officer played a big part in putting Cabretta behind bars. My high "morals" wouldn't let me work for him. However, my morals didn't stop me from going to Koenig's office after he promised me two hundred and fifty dollars just to listen. After all, you can't eat morals.

Koenig's office was on Court Street, a healthy hike from my apartment on Sackett Street. The front door had gold lettering on cherry oak wood that said Walter koenig, attorney, and I entered without bothering to knock. After I identified myself, his secretary said I could go right in. The other two people in the waiting room didn't like that, but it gave me a feeling of power. I just wished I could do the same thing one time in my doctor's office.

Koenig was behind a cluttered desk that surprised. For one thing, it was small, and that *and* the fact that it was cluttered did not go along with the impression his painfully neat and clean reception area gave. This room—small, sensibly furnished, and anything but neat—seemed to reflect more of the man than the reception room did, which was, of course, only natural. After all, he spent most of his time here.

I might have liked him for that if I hadn't known he was Sal Cabretta's lawyer.

"Ah, Mr. Delvecchio," Walter Koenig said, rising. "I'm so glad you came."

"I'm not sure I am," I said honestly.

"Perhaps if I wrote you a check..."

Not wishing to appear *that* mercenary I said, "You can do that later. Why don't you tell me why you asked me to come here?"

"Please, take a seat."

There was only one to take, a straightbacked wooden chair directly in front of his desk, and I took it.

Koenig was in his mid-forties, a tall, slender, but well-built man with curly brown hair the color of shoe polish. I couldn't help but wonder if he dyed it.

"My client wishes to engage your services."

"By 'client' you mean Sal Cabretta?"

He frowned, as if I was under the impression that he only had one client. "Yes."

I started to stand and said, "We have nothing further to talk about."

"Oddly enough," he said, "you are correct."

"What?" I asked, stopping midway out of my chair, my knees still bent.

"You see," he said sheepishly, "I know that Mr. Cabretta wishes to hire you, but I haven't the faintest idea why."

"He hasn't told you?" I asked. "His own lawyer?"

"Ah, no, he hasn't."

I straightened up and asked, "Isn't that rather odd?"

"I thought so," he said. "I also told him that I had my own investigators. He was quite adamant that he wanted you."

"Why?"

"Alas, I can't answer that," he said. "I've been instructed to pay you for consulting with me, and to ask you to go and see him."

"In prison?"

"Yes."

"I don't understand."

"I have been frank. I don't, either. I'm rather anxious for you to see him so that I can find out what's going on."

"I put him away," I said. "At least, my testimony did. It's ludicrous to think that I'd go up and see him."

Koenig smiled and said, "But it's a fascinating prospect, isn't it?"

He was right, it was fascinating.

"All right, I'll go."

"I'll write your check."

"Double it."

"What?"

"You want me to go to Attica, Counselor, you're going to have to pay my way. Take it or leave it."

He took it.

He pulled a checkbook from his desk drawer, wrote me a check for five hundred dollars, tore it loose, and handed it to me.

"I suppose you'll clear the way for this visit?"

"I'll make some calls, yes."

I stared at him and then said, "You've already made them, haven't you?"

He smiled and said, "How did you guess?"

"I didn't," I said. "I know it, just by looking at you."

"You are a very good detective."

"You're damned right I am," I said. "Just ask your client."

I wasn't a detective when I put Cabretta away, just a patrolman who happened to be in the right place at the right time, but I wasn't about to let that spoil a good exit line.

Sal Cabretta looked every bit as dangerous in prison as he had looked out. The fact that he was wearing prison-issue clothes diminished his stature not one iota. He sat in his plastic chair as if he were sitting in a leather chair behind an oak desk in his luxurious home on Long Island.

"Nick," he said when I walked in.

"I thought I told you a long time ago never to call me that."

Cabretta smiled contemptuously.

"What are you going to do," he asked, "send me to prison?"

I gave way to a small smile and said, "You have a point."

Even here Cabretta was entitled to certain privileges, such as a private meeting room on demand—one that was usually reserved for lawyer/client relationships. I was a private detective, not a lawyer, and Cabretta was certainly not a client. On the contrary, five years ago I had been a cop, and Cabretta was behind bars with my compliments.

That made Cabretta's "summons" even more curious.

"Have a seat," Cabretta said. "I have something I want to talk to you about."

"What makes you think I'm interested in anything you'd have to say to me?"

Cabretta, a good-looking man in his late forties, smiled and said, "The fact that you're here answers that question."

"I'm here because I was paid five hundred dollars to come."

"Five?" Cabretta said, showing mild surprise. "I told my lawyer to offer you two fifty."

"He did," I said, and left it at that.

"I see," Cabretta said. "Will you have that seat?"

I hesitated, then said, "Why not?" and sat across the table from the ex-drug king turned prisoner.

Cabretta turned to the guard who was standing inside the door and said, "Get lost."

"I can't."

"Beat it, screw!"

The guard looked at me and I said, "It's all right."

"I'll be right outside."

"Stay away from the door!" Cabretta called after the guard as he left. "Fuckin' walls have the biggest ears you ever saw in here," he said. "All right, then, let's get to it. I want to hire you."

"That's a laugh."

"Nevertheless," Cabretta said, "it's true."

Warily, I asked, "To do what?"

"Since I've been here my wife has either visited me or written to me at least once a week, sometimes one of each a week."

"So? She's a faithful wife."

Cabretta frowned and said, "That's what I want you to find out."

"Why?"

"I haven't seen her or heard from her in a month."

"Maybe she's sick."

"I don't think so. I think there's something else going on, and I want you to find out what."

"Why not have one of your goons outside do the job?" I asked.

"Because I want it done in the qt," Cabretta said, "and I don't trust anyone else to do it but you."

"Why's that?"

"You put me here," Cabretta said, "that means you're good at what you do. I want to hire the best."

"I'm good, but I'm not the best."

"I'll take my chances with you, Nick."

"I told you—"

Cabretta raised his hand to stay the objection and said, "Sorry...*Mister* Delvecchio."

"Let me get this straight," I said. "You want me to find out why your wife hasn't written or come to see you in a month."

"That's right."

"And then what?"

"And then come back here and tell me."

"You don't want me to report to your attorney?"

"He doesn't know why I'm seeing you today."

"You haven't told your attorney?" I asked in surprise.

"I told you," Cabretta said, "I don't trust anyone on this but you."

I studied Cabretta for a few long moments. His dark hair had begun to show some gray while he'd been inside, but he looked as if he were still keeping himself in shape. He looked fit, with the build of a man ten years his junior. "Why should I do this for you?"

"I knew you'd ask me that," Cabretta said. "You owe me."

I snorted and said, "For what?"

"For putting me here," Cabretta said, showing the first signs of agitation. "For taking away five years of my life, that's why!"

"You deserve to be in here, Cabretta," I replied casually. "You *belong* in here, and for a lot longer than five years."

Cabretta stiffened his jaw and for a moment I thought he was going to explode. I watched as the man brought his fabled temper under control, and thought that at least he had learned something during his stay here.

"All right," Cabretta finally said, "name your fee, then. You work for people for money, right? Well, I've got money. Name your price."

My regular price was two hundred and fifty dollars a day plus expenses. Things had been rough during the past year, and at times the price had come down as low as *one* hundred and fifty.

"Three hundred and fifty a day, plus expenses."

Cabretta never blinked. "Take the case and I'll have my attorney pay you a week's retainer."

"And if I don't catch her doing anything...wrong during that time?"

"Come and tell me, and then we're quits."

"And if I find that she's seeing someone?"

"Same thing."

"And then she ends up dead? Thanks, but no thanks, Sal."

Cabretta looked appalled and said, "My own wife? And even if she wasn't my wife, I don't do business that way. You know that, Ni—Delvecchio."

He was right, he didn't do business that way. He was a businessman—or a hood in businessman's clothing, but he operated his drug empire in Brooklyn just like any CEO would run his business.

I still wasn't about to go to work for him.

I stood up, walked to the door and banged my fist on it.

"Well, what's your answer?" Cabretta asked.

I turned and said, "Me walking out the door is my answer, Sallie."

At that he stood up quickly, knocking his chair over.

His face turned red with anger. At the time something bothered me about his reaction, but I didn't dwell on it then.

"You ain't turning me down, Delvecchio!"

"Watch me," I said, as the door opened.

"You think because you're Dominick Barracondi's god-kid you can turn your back on me? That's the reason you *should* work for me!"

I didn't understand that, but I wasn't about to turn around and ask him to explain it to me—and I didn't need to be reminded that *my* godfather was also *the* godfather of Brooklyn.

"You'll be back, kid," he shouted as I walked down the hall. "You'll be back." And then he started laughing. His laughter followed me all the way down the hall, echoing, bouncing off the walls…

44

Now I was back in that same room with Cabretta, and he looked as if he had never left his plastic chair, like he was waiting for me there all this time, knowing I'd come back.

"You son of a bitch," I said, from the door.

"Walter said you wouldn't figure it out," Salvatore Cabretta said, "but I knew you would. I had confidence in you."

"You low-life scumbag. Once I found out that Koenig was Mancuso's lawyer, it all sort of fell into place. Koenig was the link. He'd never represent a lightweight like Mancuso, not unless you told him to."

He smiled at me.

"Sit down, Nick, and let's talk deal."

"What kind of deal?"

"I can get your brother off the hook."

"He's not on the hook."

"I can do that, too."

"What are you talking about?" I said. "All you've done is heap a bunch of circumstantial evidence against him."

"All I've done so far," he said, "is damage his reputation. There's still one piece of evidence that hasn't been produced yet."

"What's that?"

"You better hope you never have to find out," Cabretta said. "Just believe this, Delvecchio. I can hang him, or I can get him off the hook. It's up to you."

"I can't believe this, Sal," I said. I finally decided to sit down, but only because my lower back was starting to hurt. When I took a piss that morning it had come out red. Luckily, the doctor had warned me about that.

"Is the job still the same?"

"Yes," Cabretta said. "Find out why my wife hasn't come to see me."

I shook my head, not negatively, but in disbelief.

"So to get me to take this job you killed an innocent woman and framed my brother for it."

Cabretta smiled at me and said, "I know you, Nick. You're not wired, so I'm gonna answer your question."

"What makes you think I'm not wired?"

"You'd never have gotten it past the guards."

"Okay," I said, "go ahead and answer my question."

"First of all, I didn't kill anyone. Second of all, Gloria Mancuso was far from innocent. She was an embarrassment to him, and to the family." I knew he wasn't talking about the Mancuso family. "She was a pincushion, Nick. A beautiful pincushion. She'd spread her legs for anything in pants…once."

"That include you?"

"Yeah," Cabretta said, "I had her once."

"So Mancuso's your accountant too, huh? And you fucked his wife behind his back."

"No," Cabretta said, "not behind his back."

"He knew about it?"

"What was he gonna do?" Cabretta asked. "Like you said, he's a lightweight…a lightweight whose dream it was to be a made guy."

"Are you telling me that Tony Mancuso killed his own wife?"

Cabretta missed a beat and then said, "I didn't say that."

No, but that's what he meant. He'd let something slip, and he wasn't happy about it. I decided to be willing to be convinced.

"What did you mean?"

"All I meant was that the man had a beautiful wife and couldn't satisfy her. There's no one man alive who could."

I studied Sal Cabretta for a long moment and things went click! click! click! Cabretta had always been a ladies' man. How would he have reacted to a woman like Gloria Mancuso? Especially if she had slept with him once and wouldn't repeat the performance? A man like Cabretta wouldn't take that lightly. Would that be enough to kill her? For an egomaniac like Sal Cabretta, sure, but add to that the fact that she was his accountant's wife, and knew some things about his businesses...

Click! Click! Click!

What a coup it would be for Cabretta to force Mancuso to kill his own wife, and then pin it on my brother.

But when that was done, why let Vinnie off the hook, just to get me to follow his wife?

Think about it.

Click!

Click!

Click!

Pieces falling into place.

I told Cabretta I'd take his job, but I wanted Vinnie off the hook, *and* I wanted my fee. He agreed, and said that he'd clear my brother when I reported to him about his wife.

I agreed.

He told me I could get all the information I needed on his wife from Koenig.

Just before I left he said, "Welcome to the payroll, Nick."

After I left the prison, before I met with Sam, I found a phone and called Dominick Barracondi. I got Benny, thanked him for what he did, and asked to speak to the Don.

When he came on he said, "Nicholas."

I said, "I need a favor."

45

When I got back to Brooklyn I had Sam drive right to Walter Koenig's office. She waited outside while I went up and presented myself to his secretary again.

"I don't have an appointment this time."

"Yes, you do," she said. "Go right in."

I went into Koenig's office and sat in his visitor's chair. There was a brown 10-by-13 manila envelope on my side of his desk.

"Everything you need to know about Carla Cabretta is in there," he said. "Where she has her hair done, where she has her car serviced, where her health club is—"

"The only thing we don't know," I said, sliding her photo out of the envelope, "is who's fucking her."

"If she is having an affair," he said stiffly. "That is up to you to find out."

I studied the color photo. It looked a studio print, just a head shot—but what a head. If the colors were to be believed her hair was chestnut, her eyes green. She was a beautiful woman, but her photo didn't have the impact of Gloria Mancuso's photo. There was a second picture, a candid shot of her leaving some place, wearing a leotard.

From the looks of her she was tall, with long legs, a tiny waist, small, firm breasts, and wide shoulders.

"Classy-looking," I said.

"Yes, she is."

"All right, Walter," I said, using his first name to his dismay. "I'll get right on it."

"Yes," he said, "you do that." He couldn't wait for me to leave. Now that I was working for Sal Cabretta, he couldn't waste his time on me. I was just another employee.

At the door I turned and said, "Oh, Walter..."

"Yes?"

"I assume Mancuso called you after I left his house, and you sent those four goons after me. That right?"

He hesitated.

"Come on, Wally," I said, "we're on the same team now."

He blanched when I called him Wally.

"That was just business," he finally said.

"Sure," I said, "just business. No hard feelings."

There were plenty of hard feelings, but he wouldn't find out about them until later.

Actually, I had asked Dominick Barracondi for more than one favor.

When we got back to my apartment Sam made coffee while I outlined the whole thing for her, including my plan.

"That's devious," she said afterward. "In fact, it's mean."

"I know," I said. We were in the kitchen, at the table, and I said, "Hand me that phone, will you? And then go check on Linda. Make sure she doesn't go back home until I say so, okay?"

"Okay, but I still don't know what you're going to do about her husband."

"I'll tell you," I said, dialing the phone number that was on the back of Carla Cabretta's photos, "after I get this other thing straightened out."

Sam turned one of the photos around and said, "Ooh, classy dame."

"Dame?" I said. She stuck out her tongue at me and left. Carla answered the phone on the first ring.

"Mrs. Cabretta," I said, "this is Nick Delvecchio."

"Yes, Mr. Delvecchio," she said. "Dominick Barracondi said you would be calling."

"Are you willing to meet with me?"

"I have great respect for Don Dominick," she said. "He tells me you have something to discuss with me that is very important."

"That's true."

"What could that be?"

"Your life, Mrs. Cabretta," I said. "Your life."

Carla Cabretta agreed to meet me in Brooklyn Heights, on the Promenade, a small park that hung over the Brooklyn- Queens Expressway. From it you could look across the East River at the classic Manhattan skyline. The Promenade also boasted the hot-dog vendor with the best hot dogs outside of Nathan's on Coney Island.

I was sitting on a bench when she arrived. I had told her how to recognize me. I knew the sling on my arm and the bandage on my head would come in handy.

She walked to me with a long, athletic, purposeful stride.

"Mr. Delvecchio?" she asked.

"Mrs. Cabretta."

"Did my husband have that done to you?"

"Sort of," I said. "Walter Koenig actually gave the order."

"That figures," she said. "Aren't you the police officer whose testimony sent my husband to prison?"

"I am—or was. I'm not a cop now, I'm a private investigator. Please, Mrs. Cabretta," I said, "sit down. What I have to say might surprise you."

She sat next to me, and I got a strong whiff of her perfume. It was a very nice scent. Up close I could see that she looked older than her pictures. From the photos I had made her thirty-five. Now I could see she was probably forty or more, but wearing it very well. She kept herself in shape, this one.

"Well, Mr. Delvecchio?" she said. "If you've finished checking out the merchandise, I'd like to know why I'm here."

"Mrs. Cabretta—"

"Stop calling me that," she said. "If you must call me something, call me Carla."

"Carla, your husband has hired me to follow you and find out why you haven't come to see him in months."

"Why would he do that?" she asked. "He knows why I haven't come to see him. I want a divorce."

"You told him that?"

"The last time I saw him. I told him I wouldn't be back, either."

"Do you have a lawyer?"

"No," she said, "Sal said that Walter would take care of everything. So tell me, Mr. Delvecchio, why would he send you to follow me to find out something he already knows?"

My answer made even more sense now than it had before.

"Carla," I said, "I'm pretty sure that Sal plans to have you killed, and frame me for it."

She stared at me for a few moments, then said, "That doesn't surprise me, Nick. Can I call you Nick?"

"Sure."

"It worries me, of course, Nick, but it doesn't surprise me," she said. "It also makes sense to me."

"Good," I said. "I thought I was going to have to convince you."

"You don't have to convince me," she said, "but I would like you to tell me what we can do about it."

"I have a plan."

She smiled and said, "I hoped you would."

"Why don't you go and get us a couple of hot dogs, Carla," I suggested, "and I'll tell you all about it."

46

Back to Walter Koenig's office early the next morning. This time I had company in the person of Carla Cabretta and three friends. When I had outlined my plan to her she had reacted much the way Sam had.

"That's mean," she'd said, and then added, "and delicious."

The word "delicious" sounded entirely natural coming out of her mouth.

"It's barely nine," his secretary said to the five of us accusingly.

"That's all right," I said. "Just tell him I'm here, and you won't have to do anything. We won't need you. We can get our own coffee."

"I don't get cof—just a minute. I'll announce you."

"Why don't you go out and get a doughnut or something, honey?" I said, picking up her purse and holding it out to her. "We'll announce ourselves."

She looked at all of us, then took her bag and walked out the door.

"Loyalty," I said, shrugging.

I looked at Carla and said, "Wait here."

"Right."

I went into Koenig's office and left the door ajar.

"What are you doing here?" Koenig demanded. "Where's my secretary?"

"She said something about getting a doughnut."

"I have an early court date, Mr. Delvecchio," he said briskly. He was busy shoving some papers into an attaché case. It looked like an eelskin case, much more expensive than Tony Mancuso's case. Thinking of Mancuso made me look at my watch. "What did you forget yesterday?"

"I didn't forget anything, Walter," I said. "The job's done."

He stiffened, stopped what he was doing and looked at me. "What?"

"I said the job's done," I said. "I know who's been porking Mrs. Cabretta."

"You know..." He stopped and frowned. "Who?"

I smiled at him and said, "You."

He looked stunned.

"That's ridiculous. I've never laid a hand on Carla. What are you trying to pull?"

"What do you think Sal will say when I give him my report, Walter?"

He developed a nervous tick. His mouth kept twitching as if it wanted to smile, but couldn't find anything to smile about.

"You wouldn't—he would never believe you."

"I have a witness."

"A...witness? How could you have a witness? I've never touched her, I tell you."

Only someone who was telling God's honest truth could be that indignant, but it didn't matter that he was telling the truth.

"An unimpeachable witness."

"That's not possible," he said. "Who could this witness be?"

I smiled, walked to the door and opened it. Carla Cabretta walked in and smiled at Koenig. I left the door ajar again.

"I'm sorry, darling," she said, "he beat it out of me."

He gaped at her, then at me, and then understanding dawned in his eyes.

"You're framing me."

"Why not? Cabretta had my brother framed for Gloria Mancuso, and he was going to have me framed for the murder of his own wife. I'd say turnabout is very definitely fair play in this case, Walter, wouldn't you?"

"But...but if you tell him that, he'll have me killed."

He looked at Carla for support and she said, "I'll shed a lover's tears at the funeral, darling."

"You can't—" he said to her; then he looked at me and said, "You can't—"

"Don't worry, Walter," I said, "I'm a reasonable man. We can work something out."

He stared at us for a few moments, and then sighed and said, "What do you want me to do?"

When the phone rang it was almost six o'clock. When Koenig answered the phone, he knew exactly what to say. He put the call on the speaker box so we could all hear it. I also wanted Mancuso to hear that he was on the box.

"Walter? It's Anthony. What are you doing to me, Walter?"

"I don't know what you mean, Anthony."

"Someone tried to kill me tonight."

"That's impossible, Anthony—"

"What'aya mean, impossible? I know when somebody's shooting at me! You gotta tell Sal I won't talk, Walter."

"Anthony," Koenig said, looking at me, "if someone is trying to kill you, we have nothing to do with it."

"What? You gotta help me!"

"Maybe you got someone mad at you, Anthony."

"Mad at me? Why should Sal be mad at me? I did what he wanted. Jesus, Walter, *I killed my* own *wife!*"

I looked at Carla Cabretta and she nodded. She was a witness to Anthony Mancuso's unsolicited confession.

I looked at Koenig, mouthed "Wait," made some noises I was sure Mancuso would hear over the box, and then waved at Koenig to go ahead.

"Look, Anthony," Koenig said slowly, "tell me where you are and I'll send someone to get you."

Now there was a pause at the other end and then Mancuso said, "You'll send someone to kill me, you mean! Jesus, Walter—you got men there now, right? You got me on the damned speaker? Walter, I'm going to Nick Delvecchio. You know him? The priest's brother? He's a private detective. He'll know what to do."

I wasn't sure whether he'd come to me or Barracondi, but I was happy he chose me.

I cued Koenig and he said, "Don't do that, Walter. Look, I'll send someone right over to your house—"

"Fuck you, Walter!" Mancuso screamed. "And fuck Cabretta! I ain't gonna be at my house, Walter. I'm gonna put you both away, you bastards!"

"Anthony, don't—" Koenig started, but Mancuso hung up. Koenig shrugged helplessly and turned off the box.

"Now what?" he asked.

"Now I'd like you to meet a few friends of mine." I walked to the door, opened it and waved my three friends in.

"See this fella here? His name is Detective Weinstock. This well-dressed devil over here is Detective Lacy, from Staten Island. He wants to talk to you about Gloria Mancuso's murder. And this other handsome devil is Detective Cohen. He wants to talk to you about a murder in Bay Ridge." I gave Koenig a tight smile as pain coursed through my arm, shoulder, and lower back and said, "Payback's a bitch, Wally...fuckin' A!"

I took Carla's arm and eased her toward the door. "Now don't fight over him, gents."

"Where are you going?" Weinstock asked.

"When you've settled your jurisdictional disputes, we'll be ready to make statements. Meanwhile, I've got to go home and wait for a call from Anthony Mancuso. When I get it, I'll call Weinstock and let you boys know where you can pick him up." Weinstock was the big reason the other two were there. I had convinced him to accompany me, and he had in turn convinced them. I owed him, which might be why he had done it.

"Delvecchio—" Weinstock started.

"Don't thank me, fellas," I said. "Uh, Detective Lacy, would you like me to notify my brother's attorney that he's no longer a suspect?"

Lacy was fitting the cuffs onto Koenig's wrists.

"Mr. Delvecchio," he said, "you can have that pleasure—unofficially, of course."

"Of course," I said.

On the street Carla Cabretta said, "I'm very impressed, Nick...and grateful."

"I was just clearing my brother, Carla," I said, "but you know what? I don't think you'll have the slightest problem getting a divorce now. In fact, with the extra time this will add to your husband's sentence, you might even be able to get an annulment from the Catholic Church. Hell, I may even be able to help you with that!"

EPILOGUE

Two days later I explained everything to Father Vinnie and Sam. I had a choice of where to do the explaining. I could have done it at my father's house, but I decided against it. I also could have done it at the Rectory, but on second thought, that didn't seem like the place to do it. Besides, Sam wanted to hear it, too, so we finally gathered—just the three of us—at my place, over a take-out pizza and some beer. Yes, priests eat pizza and drink beer—especially my brother, who liked beer, but loved pizza.

He also was not quite ready to wrap up his own case yet. He was still trying to deal with the fact that he was free of all suspicion.

"Before we discuss my case," Vinnie said, "what happened with that woman you were trying to help? What was her name?"

"Linda Kellogg," Sam said.

"Sam helped me with that," I said, "and so did Linda."

"All we did was go to the library." Sam was being modest. They spent *hours* in the library.

"The library?" Vinnie asked. "What for?"

"Newspaper clippings," I said. "They brought me clippings of stories about recent truck hijackings. As it turns out, Dan Kellogg was beating his wife the day after a hijacking."

"What did that tell you?" My brother's a great priest, but a lousy detective.

"Kellogg was a dispatcher for Mueller Trucking, Vinnie. Some of the hijacked trucks were from Mueller."

"He was setting up hijackings inside his own company?" Vinnie asked, looking shocked.

"Outside his company, too," I said. "He was in touch with other dispatchers from other companies, and pumped them for information, as well. Of course, they never suspected what he was doing."

"But why beat his own wife?"

"She was there," I said, "and he had a lot of anger inside of him. He had to take it out on someone."

"He could have gone to church," Vinnie said, "and talked to a priest."

"Well," I said, "now he's talking to the cops. He's going to cooperate and help them catch the hijackers."

"What will that do for him?"

"He'll make a deal with the DA for a reduced sentence, or maybe even probation. He *was* being threatened."

"How?"

"Here's the ironic part," I said. "They threatened to hurt Linda."

"So he goes along with them and instead, *he* hurts his own wife?"

I gave Father Vinnie a helpless look and said, "I can't figure it, Vin."

"There must be more to it than that," Sam said.

"If there was," I said, "he'll tell the cops, eventually."

"What about the wife? Linda? What happens to her?" Vinnie asked.

"She loves him," Sam said, "so she's standing by him."

"She's a brave girl," Vinnie said.

"Stupid," I said.

"Nick!"

"Look at it, Vinnie," I said. "Even if he gets off, he's a walking time bomb. The next time he gets angry enough, he could kill her."

"Have you told her that?"

"I did, on the phone."

"And?"

"She hung up on me."

"You did the best you could, Nick," Sam said. "We all tried to help her, but she just can't see life without a husband."

"Then she should find herself another one."

We fell silent and indulged in pizza and beer for a while—more beer than pizza for me. I had lost my appetite. I was dealing with the fact that there were some real similarities between the Kelloggs and the Mancusos. Of course, in the case of Anthony and Gloria Mancuso, it was actually the wife who was abusing the husband until he couldn't take it anymore, while it was Dan Kellogg who was physically abusing Linda. In both cases, though, the wife ended up the real victim—and it could still get worse for Linda. I just hoped that she wouldn't ultimately end up like Gloria Mancuso.

Finally, Vinnie decided it was time to exorcise the last of his own demons. He wanted to talk about his own case. First, I had to explain what would make a man like Sal Cabretta want to frame a priest for murder. I took the blame for that, but he wouldn't have any of it.

"You did the right thing, Nick." His tone was reassuring. "You put a criminal behind bars. You are not responsible for the form his attempt at revenge took."

"He also wanted to kill his wife," Sam said, and we both looked at her. She continued, ticking them off on her fingers. "Three marriages—Kellogg, Mancuso, Cabretta—and three abused spouses."

"And violence the final result," Vinnie said, shaking his head. "What's happened to the once holy state of matrimony?"

"Don't go sour on me, Father Vinnie," I said. "There are a lot of good marriages in the world. We just happened to run across three bad ones."

"You're right," he said. "That doesn't make them all bad."

"Was Cabretta's wife cheating on him?" Sam asked.

"Maybe," I said, "probably. He was convinced she was, though."

"And that was enough of a reason to want to kill her?" Vinnie asked.

"Maybe that was just another way to get back at me," I said, "to kill her and make it look like I did it."

"This is all…beyond me," my poor brother said.

"You want to hear the rest of it?"

He stared at me for a moment, and then said, "Yes, I suppose I'd better. Tell me what happened after you left Walter Koenig's office that day." He gripped a bottle of St. Pauli Girl very tightly as he waited for my answer.

"I came back here and waited for Anthony Mancuso to call."

"And he did?"

"Yep."

"And?"

"I told him to come right over."

"And did he?"

"He did."

"What finally made up his mind?"

"I arranged for him to think that Cabretta was trying to have him killed."

"How did you do that?"

The last thing I wanted to tell Vinnie was that I called Dominick Barracondi and asked to borrow Benny, so I said, "I just got someone to take a couple of shots at him."

"Nick, you didn't."

"Oh, the shots missed, Vinnie," I said. "They were just supposed to scare him."

"And they did."

"They sure did," I said, "right into my arms."

"And what did you do?"

"I gave him a sympathetic ear."

"Whose?" Sam asked.

"Weinstock's. He was waiting here when Mancuso got here."

"Your old partner's partner?" Vinnie asked.

"That's right."

"Why him?"

"Because I'd shoot Mancuso before I'd give him to Matucci."

"Matucci's going to hate you even more for this," Vinnie said. "First you give Koenig to Weinstock, and then Mancuso."

"And, extending the arm a little further," Sam said, "Cabretta."

"Yeah," I said, smiling, "Vito's probably mad enough to sh—uh, spit, but I don't think he *could* hate me any more than he normally does."

"So what happens to Mancuso?" Vinnie asked.

"He makes a deal with the DA and gives them Cabretta on a conspiracy-to-commit-murder rap."

"He won't get off," Sam said, staring at me over a wilting slice of pizza, "I mean, surely he can't..."

"No," I said, "he won't get off. He'll get life in some country club rather than in a hell hole, but he'll get life."

"But...did Anthony Mancuso really kill his own wife?" Vinnie asked in disbelief.

"I'm afraid so, Vinnie," I said.

"That's...unthinkable!"

"You've never been married," Sam said, and I stared at her. The way she said it made me wonder if *she'd* ever been married and had never told me about it.

"But still..."

"Look, Vinnie," I said, "she was a slut and he was her cuckold. Besides, he wanted to be in the 'family,' he wanted to be a made guy. Cabretta gave him the chance."

"By killing his own wife?"

"Let's not forget," I said, "that he was afraid of Cabretta."

"But why would Cabretta want Gloria Mancuso dead?"

"Gloria wasn't a person to him," I explained, "she was a means to get his revenge on me, to first make me suffer—through *you,* Vin—to then get me to take his case, and then ultimately to have me killed. Put it all together and you've got a motive for murder."

"Terrible," my brother the priest said, shaking his head.

"Hey, that ain't the sick part," I said. "Tony boy screwed her that night."

"Before or after?" Sam asked, and Vinnie gave her a look that asked how she could even ask the question out loud.

"I don't know," I said, "and I don't care."

"And what happens to Lisa Mancuso?" Vinnie asked.

I shrugged. At the mention of her name I remembered her, the way she looked the last time I saw her, running toward "Johnny's" car, cutoff jeans riding up her ass cheeks.

"I don't know, Vinnie. There must be relatives."

"The poor child," she said. "Not only does she lose her mother, but her father, too."

"Her father killed her mother, Vin," I said, "don't forget that."

"I feel sorry for her."

"Don't worry about her too much," I said, "the little Lisa I know will survive. Besides, all I care about is that you're off the hook."

"I owe you a lot, Nick," he said, touching my arm.

"Just buy me a place in heaven, big brother," I said teasingly.

Sam gave me a look across the table that said, "How could you?" just before my brother said, "Nick, what a thing to say!"

His tone was disapproving.

Things were finally back to normal.

THE END OF BROOKLYN

To Marthayn, my beginning.

PROLOGUE

Somewhere in the Midwest, 2010

Brooklynites have no imagination.

For the most part, it's Florida for vacation, and Florida for retirement.

I wasn't on vacation, or retired.

I was hiding out.

And not in Florida.

Actually, that part about no imagination goes for most New Yorkers.

I was a native of Brooklyn, and a lifelong resident, until about fifteen years ago. Since then I'd been moving around, living in different places, doing odd jobs that had some connection to what I did for a living for years—I was a private detective.

These days I did jobs for people that didn't involve paying me with a check, because I didn't have any bank accounts.

I was spending the morning sitting on my deck with a cup of coffee, a forty-five, and looking at the Mississippi, which spread out panoramically below me. At fifty years old, the past fifteen years had not gone the way I might have thought. In my early thirties if you had told me I would live anywhere but Brooklyn I would have told you that you were crazy.

I certainly never would have expected to be living in a house in the Midwest, on a bluff above the most famous river in the world. I liked the isolation. The long driveway that led to the house from the main road was all gravel, which meant vehicles driving on it made a lot of noise. And the only vehicle that drove on it was the mail truck.

The gravel also crunched underfoot—my own security system. So when I heard that crunching sound, being caused by more than one set of feet, I knew they'd found me, and I was in trouble.

I wasn't finished with my coffee.

I tucked the forty-five underneath my left butt cheek, and waited. Running at this point was not an option. Besides, I'd been running for fifteen years. I was getting a little too old for it.

"Nick Delvecchio?"

I turned in the direction of the voice. Three men had come up the steps and onto my deck, which spread the entire width of the house. So at that moment they were about twenty feet from where I sat. I'd once come out on the short end of a shootout at this range.

"Who's asking?"

"I think you know," the spokesman said.

"I like to deal in names."

"Names don't really matter," he said, "but let's go with…John."

"I detect a Brooklyn accent," I said, "so I'll bet as a kid it was Johnny."

He didn't respond. He was about my age, probably grew up in a neighborhood like I did. The other two were younger, maybe late thirties. They weren't talkers. They looked Italian, but the spokesman had a different look to him.

"Are you Delvecchio?" John asked.

"I think you know I am."

"I need confirmation."

I shrugged. "Then I am."

John looked around.

"I can still hear a little of it in your voice."

"Most people can't."

"This is a long way from Brooklyn."

"You said it."

"That coffee?"

I nodded.

"Any more?"

"Inside," I said. "The kitchen. Have one of your…friends go and get it."

"Thanks."

He looked at one of them. The man went inside for a few moments, came out with a mug of coffee. Just one. That established the pecking order for me. I would only be talking to John.

I was sitting in a wrought iron chair, one of a set of four, at a matching table.

"You mind?" he asked, gesturing with the mug.

"Not at all."

He sat to my right, which meant he couldn't see the gun butt sticking out from beneath my ass.

"Nice out here in the fall," he said.

"Lots of bugs in the summer."

"Been here long?"

"Not that long."

"You've led us on a pretty good chase."

"You, personally?" I asked.

"Well, no," he said, "I meant…"

"I know what you meant."

THE END OF BROOKLYN

He sipped his coffee, looked down at the river. The other two leaned against the railing. One watched me, one watched John.

"Parked down at the entrance to your road," John said. "Didn't want you to hear us drive up."

"I probably would've thought it was the mail man."

"Still..." he said, with a shrug.

"So what do we do now?" I asked.

"Well," he said, "there's what we're supposed to do, and then there's what I'd like to do."

"Are they very different?"

"Yeah, they are."

"What would you like to do?"

"Talk."

"And what're you supposed to do?"

"I think you know that, too."

"So," said, "let's talk."

"I'm curious," he said.

"About what?"

"About what happened fifteen years ago."

"Why?"

"Because I was around then," he said. "You wouldn't remember. I wasn't anybody at the time, but I was around. I know a little about what happened, but only the obvious stuff."

"So what do you wanna know?" I asked.

"Nick, I wanna know what happened," he said. "I wanna know what made you do what you did, and then bolt. Leave Brooklyn. Because I can't imagine leavin' Brooklyn. Just bein' out here among all the trees...I mean, it's nice and all...but I'd get the heebie jeebies after a while."

"Takes some gettin' used to," I said.

"So...you mind talkin' for a while?"

"Considerin' the alternative...not at all. Where would you like me to start?"

"Anyplace you feel comfortable startin'."

I looked at him for a minute, then asked, "You ever go to any of your high school reunions?"

1

Brooklyn, 1995

"I'm not going."

"Why not?" my neighbor, Samantha Karson, asked.

"Because it's stupid," I said. "I mean, come on. Eighteen years? Don't they usually have reunions at fifteen, and twenty? But eighteen?"

"Did you go to your fifteenth?" she asked.

"I didn't go to the tenth or the fifteenth," I said. "And I'm not going to the eighteenth—or, for that matter, the twentieth."

"Oh, come on," she said. "Don't you think your high school buddies will find you being a private eye exciting? Or the girl? Didn't you have a girl in high school?"

"I had lots of girls in high school," I admitted. "What I didn't have was a girlfriend."

"Braggart," she said.

She put the invitation down and picked up her turkey club. She was on another diet, which was why we had lunch together a few times a week. She said it helped her. She came across the hall and made us lunch. Today she had a turkey club while I just had a good old turkey sandwich—piled high!

She was a lovely, full-bodied blonde who, as far as I ever knew, was proud of that fact. Why then was she always trying to lose five pounds?

She took a bite of her sandwich and said, "I think you should go."

"Why?"

"Why shouldn't you go? Didn't you have some friends in high school?"

"Sure, I had *some*..."

"But not a lot?"

"A few."

"And no girlfriends?"

"Maybe one or two..."

"And aren't you curious about what's happened to them? What kind of adults they've become?"

"No."

"Why not?"

"I might be disappointed."

She stared at me, then asked, "Or maybe you think they'll be disappointed in you?"

Okay, so I decided to go to the damned thing.

THE END OF BROOKLYN

The reunion was held in Marine Park, at a hall on Avenue N called the Something-or-other Chateau. A chateau in Brooklyn...

I admit to some nervousness as I walked through the front door. Brooklyn was a big place and although not many of us had left, we had spread out across the borough and hardly saw each other over the years. That suited me. High school was not something I thought back on fondly.

But as a huge apparition appeared in front of me, arms spread wide, I also admit to being glad to see him.

"Nicky-D!" he shouted, grabbing me in a bear hug and just about squeezing the life out of me.

"Tony Mitts!" I surprised myself by shouting back at him with almost as much enthusiasm.

It was then I silently thanked Sam for talking me into attending.

It was later that I cursed her for it...

Tony Mitts was just the start of the reunion. In rapid order I met up with Sammy Carter, Joey "the Nose" Bagaletti and Sal "the Ace" Pricci. The five of us used to hang out together in high school, which a lot of people found odd because while the rest of us were Italian, Sammy was black. We used to tell people he was "black" Italian. Among ourselves we also said that if anyone had a problem with him hanging out with us, "Fuck 'em!"

We staked out a place at the bar, watched the girls go by and talked about Gina Gershon making out with Elizabeth Berkley in *Showgirls* and the fact that the Yankees were going to finish second to Boston this year.

"But they're gonna get the wild card spot," Sal said. "Still gonna make the playoffs."

"Boy," Sammy said, "most of these girls have really porked up, huh?"

Showed you the difference between Sammy and Sal, one talking girls, the other baseball.

"What are you bitchin' about?" Tony said. "I thought skinny black guys like you liked your women with big asses."

Sammy fixed Tony with a hard stare. "You gonna start that 'fat-assed black girl' stuff again, Mitts? You were always doin' that in high school and I didn't like it then."

"Yeah, yeah..." Tony said.

It was true. This was an old argument from high school, but the rest of us knew that the two of them always secretly enjoyed the argument.

I examined my four high school friends. What I had told Samantha was close to the truth. In four years of high school I had made four friends. That counted as a few.

Tony had always been big, well over six feet, but he'd never been fat, and he still wasn't. He'd kept himself in remarkable shape, but then as an athlete he would. We called him "Tony Mitts" because he had hands the size of catcher's mitts. His real last name was Bologna, but our nickname was better than what they used to call him in junior high—"Tony Baloney." Ah, junior high kids had no imagination.

Sammy Johnson was as skinny as ever, but his hair had receded to the halfway point of his head. The bald part gleamed the way Lou Gossett's or George Foreman's did. I wondered why he didn't just shave it all off?

Sal had gone to fat, which he had always been leaning to in high school. His arms and shoulders still threatened to burst the seams of his clothes. We would have called him "the Arm" but Tony was "Mitts" and we didn't want another body part in the group. So, because of his affinity for cards—poker, mostly—we called him "the Ace."

Joey's nose was as big as ever, which had made his nickname very easy in high school. It was a family trait, he was always pointing out to us, and all the men in his family were proud of it.

"Anybody seen Mary Ann?" I asked.

Suddenly, Tony smiled.

"She's here," he said.

"Yeah," Sal said, slapping Tony on his broad back. "She came with Tony, the lucky dog."

"Man," Sammy said, "she looks good, even if she don't have an ass on her."

"You wanna see her?" Tony asked me. He was anxious.

"Sure."

I agreed not only because he was apparently so eager to show her off, but because I was curious. Mary Ann had been the best looking girl in our class—maybe in the whole school. I wondered what she looked like eighteen years later.

A couple of girls went by. I didn't recognize them, but they had adopted the new looks of bare, pierced belly buttons, and they shouldn't have.

"Come on." Tony grabbed my arm in an iron grip and dragged me across the floor.

I had never gotten to know Mary Ann Grosso well in high school, although I knew a lot of guys who bragged they had. They all claimed to have scored, too, except for Tony. He not only said he hadn't, but that nobody else had, either.

He pulled me over to a table where a bunch of people were sitting. I was able to pick Mary Ann out with no trouble. She was even more beautiful at thirty-six than she had been at eighteen. She'd grown into her beauty. She had dark hair that hung down to her shoulders. I recalled that she had always had beautiful skin—smooth and creamy and free of acne. She still did.

"Mary Ann, here's Nicky!" Tony said. When she frowned he said, "Come on, you remember, Nicky-D!"

"Of course," she said. "Nicky." I knew she wasn't lying. She remembered me, if not right away. She held out both hands warmly, and I took them. "It's good to see you."

"And you, Mary Ann. You look...great."

"Don't she though?" Tony blustered right over her soft, "Thank you." He was obviously very proud of her, and when he told me that they were to be married, I realized why.

By the following week, Mary Ann was dead.

2

All death is tragic.

Particularly when it's accidental. After all, someone dying as result of a fluke? An accident? Or an act of carelessness? Tragic, to say the least. Now natural causes, that's probably the least tragic of all—if you can use the words "least" and "tragic" in the same sentence. I mean, what can you do about that? A man goes to the doctor one week, is given a clean bill of health, and then drops dead the next week. Happens all the time, right?

So where does murder fit into the equation? Well, in my opinion, murder is just a step below accident. After all, what's tragic about one person taking the life of another? That's not tragic—it's just a damn shame!

And where does suicide fit in?

Who the hell knows.

I stared at the casket from my seat in the back of the chapel. I chose to sit there alone because I was not family. As a matter of fact, I was not even a close friend. I was someone who had known the deceased in high school, and then met her again one evening eighteen years later. And a week later, she's dead.

High school was not a favorite time of my life. I know people of varying ages who claim that, given the opportunity to go back in time, they'd go back to high school and do it all again. Best time of their lives. My opinion of people like that is they can't deal with having grown up.

Given the opportunity to go back to any time of my life, I'd choose to stay right where I am. That either means that this is the happiest time of my life, or I haven't had it, yet. I choose the latter. Why? It means I still have something to look forward to.

To me, looking forward is much better than looking back.

***

From my vantage point in the chapel I could see Tony Bologna's broad back. His shoulders were shaking. Sitting to his right was his mother. Her shoulders were ramrod straight. On his left was Mary Ann's mother. She was alternately patting and rubbing his back, the way I thought his own mother should have been doing.

I looked up toward the casket again, where Mary Ann Grosso was lying, all dressed up and made to look "good" in death. At my mother's funeral I would have throttled anyone who said aloud, "She looks *good*."

Mary Ann Grosso just looked dead.

After the service I decided not to accompany the family and friends to the cemetery. I stopped to tell Tony that and he grabbed my arm tightly.

"Come to Mary Ann's mother's house, Nicky."

"Tony," I said, "I don't want to intrude..."

"Her mother wants you there, Nick. She wants to talk to you."

"I didn't even think she remembered me."

"She doesn't; I told her you're a detective."

"Tony—"

"Please, Nick!" His eyes were as pleading as his tone.

"All right, Tony."

"Thanks, buddy." His relief was palpable. "We should get back to the house by two. Be there, okay? There'll be lots of food."

Of course there would. It was an Italian wake, after all.

"I'll be there."

I stood out in front of the funeral home and watched the procession leave. I became aware that someone was standing next to me.

"It's a damn shame, ain't it?" Sal asked. I hadn't seen him since the reunion, and hadn't noticed him inside.

"Yeah, it is." I looked at him. "I didn't see you inside."

"I didn't go in." He shook his head. "I couldn't. I didn't wanna see her like that."

"Are you going to the house?"

"Nah. You?"

I nodded. "Tony asked me to. Says her mother wants to talk to me."

"They gonna hire you, Nicky?"

"I'm afraid they're gonna try."

"Why afraid? Ain't that what you do? The private eye thing?"

"It's gonna be hard turning them down."

"Why turn them down?"

"I don't investigate suicides, Sal."

"Then there's no problem, Nicky." He slapped me on the back. "She didn't kill herself."

"How do you know that?"

"I knew her—I knew her as long and as well as Tony did. She'd never kill herself."

"Are you sayin' she was murdered?"

"I'm sayin' she wouldn't have killed herself, Nick. And that's *all* I'm sayin'."

"Sal—"

"Gotta go."

He moved away from me abruptly. I watched him walk to the parking lot and get into a new Chevy. I realized I didn't know what he did for a living. I'd pretty much talked to everyone else at the reunion about their jobs, but Sal had always seemed to avoid the subject.

I wondered if he'd meant to imply what I thought he'd been saying when he mentioned knowing Mary Ann as well as Tony did.

3

I got to the house about two-thirty. It was in Bensonhurst, on Sixty-Third Street. Actually, it was walking distance from my father's house, where I grew up. There was a new red '95 Pontiac Firebird in the driveway among some other, older cars.

"Nicky," Tony Mitts said, as I entered. "God." He came to me in the hall and clamped down on my arm again. "I thought maybe you weren't comin'."

"I said I would. Take it easy, Tony."

"I been tryin' to take it easy, Nick, but it ain't that easy. You don't know..."

"Don't know what?"

"Look, lemme tell Mary Ann's mother you're here. Get somethin' to eat and I'll find you. Get a beer. Okay?"

He was talking a mile a minute and was gone before I could reply. I went looking for a beer and found one in the kitchen. I also found a girl crying. It took me a minute, but I recognized her as Catherine, Mary Ann's little sister. Well, maybe not so little, but younger. If I remembered correctly Catherine was about two or three years behind us in high school. She was never as pretty as her sister, but she seemed to have grown into it. She had the same smooth, pale skin.

She was sitting at the kitchen table, clutching a handkerchief and crying softly. I had taken a St. Paulie Girl from the refrigerator when I turned and noticed her.

"Hey, I'm sorry."

She looked up at me, hastily wiping the moisture away from her eyes. She frowned, trying to place me.

"Catherine, I'm Nick—"

"Delvecchio," she said. "I remember. I had a terrible crush on you in high school. But you were a senior and I was a freshman." She blurted it out, then slapped her hand over her mouth.

"Did you?" I said. "I never knew."

She took her hand away from her mouth and said, "Nobody did—except Mary Ann."

There was an awkward silence then, which she broke.

"It's nice of you to come, Nick," she said. "I didn't think you'd remember...us."

"Well," I said, "I was at the reunion...I saw Mary Ann...and the guys."

"Wasn't she beautiful?" she asked, her eyes shining from both tears and pride. "Even more than she was in high school."

"Well, yeah, she was," I said, not really knowing how to answer. What did she want me to say? She seemed sincere, but I had two older brothers, and I wasn't always thrilled about it. Were there times, I wondered, when she didn't idolize her older sister so much?

"I can't believe she's gone," she said, starting to sob into her hanky again. "Not...not like that."

It occurred to me then that I still didn't know exactly how Mary Ann had died.

"Nick, there you are," Tony said bursting into the room. He didn't even seem to notice Catherine. "Come on, Mrs. Grosso wants to talk to you."

"In a minute, Tony. Catherine, are you all right?"

"I'm fine, Nick." She waved her hand. "Go ahead, ma wants you."

"Why don't we talk some more later?" I asked.

"Sure, Nick," she said with a small smile. "Why not?"

"Come on, Nick!" Tony said, impatiently grabbing my arm.

Old friend or not I was tired of having my arm mangled.

"Tony, damn it, take it *easy*, okay? I'm coming."

I jerked my arm away and he released it like it was hot.

"Sorry."

"Lead the way."

I followed him down the hall.

4

Tony took me past a couple of bedrooms to a room at the end of the hall. Inside Mrs. Grosso was sitting on a bed, staring out the window. What she was seeing what anybody's guess.

From the looks of the room it was a girl's—probably Mary Ann's old room. Or did she still live here. I didn't know.

A photo on a nearby dresser, confirmed my suspicion that this had, at least once, been Mary Ann's room. It was her and Tony, arms around each other, laughing. From the looks of the scene behind them it was Coney Island—certainly happier times. It also looked to be an older picture, not one from high school, but certainly not much later.

"Mrs. Grosso?" Tony said.

For a moment she didn't seem to hear him, but then she turned her head and looked at us. I wondered how old she was. Sixty? Sixty-five? She was still an attractive woman, definitely Mary Ann and Catherine's mother. She had the same skin. I remembered Tony telling me she had lost her husband five years before. Now Mary Ann. All she had left was Catherine.

"Tony." Her voice was so hoarse we barely heard her.

"This is Nick Delvecchio, Mrs. Grosso," Tony said, awkwardly. Obviously, even though he was going to marry her daughter, he hadn't gotten around to calling her anything more personal. "He went to school with us."

"Yes," she said, "I know, Tony. I remember Nick. How's your father?"

"He's fine, Mrs. Grosso."

"I see him on the street sometimes," she said. "He's gone through a lot, with the death of your brother, and your sister being on that hijacked plane."

"He's come through it all with flying colors, Mrs. Grosso."

"Good, that's good," she said. "I came through my husband's death, but this...I don't know how I can come through this."

"You still have Catherine, Mrs. Grosso."

"Yes," she said, "I still have Catherine."

"Tell him about Mary Ann, Mrs. Grosso," Tony said, anxiously. "Tell him Mary Ann didn't—"

"Tony." She interrupted him. "Can I talk to Nick alone, please?"

He looked as if she had slapped him in the face.

"But—I thought—"

"Please, Tony?"

"Oh, well...sure, Mrs. Grosso, sure..."

Tony gave me a puzzled glance, then backed out of the room.

"He's a nice boy," she said.

"Yeah, he is."

"Would you close the door please, Nick?"

"Sure."

"And come sit here by me," she said, as I closed it. She patted a spot next to her and I noticed for the first time a folder there. When I sat the folder was between us.

"Mrs. Grosso—"

"Please," she said, "call me Angela. It's actually Angelina, but that's too long, don't you think? And too...old country?"

"It's a very pretty name."

"Yes, well...when I was in high school they called me 'Angel.' Isn't that silly?"

"Mrs.—uh, Angela, can we talk about Mary Ann?"

"Of course. My Mary Ann," she said. "They say she killed herself."

"Who says so, Angela?"

"The police."

"Can you tell me how she died?"

"She died right here," she said, touching the mattress, "on this bed."

"But *how* did she die?"

"Pills," she said. "She took pills...that's what they told me."

"Suicide."

Angela Grosso nodded.

"But Tony doesn't believe it," I said.

"Tony was very much in love with Mary Ann, Nick. He refuses to believe it."

"And you?"

"Mary Ann was...troubled."

"Angela—"

"Here." She picked up the folder and handed it to me.

"What's this?"

"Poems," she said. "My Mary Ann's poems."

"Poems?" I said.

"How well did you know my daughter, Nick?"

"Not well," I admitted. "We went to school together, but after we graduated I sort of lost touch...with everybody..."

"Mary Ann wrote these poems," she said, tapping the folder. "In all these years since high school, she's written these poems. She even had some published in magazines."

"That's, um, nice."

"You don't understand," she said. "You would have to read these poems to understand. The girl who wrote these poems...the *woman*...was troubled."

"Mrs. Grosso, Tony said you wanted to talk to me about—"

"I told him I didn't, Nick. He wants me to hire you to prove that Mary Ann did not commit suicide...but I believe she did. Read the poems, and you'll see."

"All right, Mrs. Grosso. I'll read them."

I left, taking the folder with me. Tony was waiting for me in the hall.

"Did she do it? Did she hire you?"

"No, Tony, she didn't."

He firmed his jaw and said, "Then I want to, Nick. I want you to prove Mary Ann didn't do it. She wouldn't commit suicide. Those are her poems. They're beautiful,. You read them and see."

"I'll read them Tony, and then I'll get back to you."

Angela Grosso thought the poems meant Mary Ann committed suicide. Tony thought they proved otherwise. Now I was curious about them.

5

"So what did you tell him?" Sam asked.

We were in my apartment, sharing a pizza she had shown up at my door with only moments after I had returned from the Grosso funeral. Far be it for me to turn away a beautiful woman *with food*.

"What could I tell him?" I asked. "I took the poems and told him I'd read them."

She looked at the folder on the table, and then looked at me. She had her hair pulled back and secured with a "scrunchie." Scrunchies were all the rage, and I hated them.

"Can I read them, too?"

"Well, duh," I said. "You're the writer. I was hoping you'd read them and tell me what you think."

Samantha "Kit" Karson had been writing Romance novels for a few years, and had only recently turned to writing mysteries. Actually, she says they're called "Romantic Suspense."

"What did they tell you about the poems?" she asked.

"The mother says once I read them I'll know she killed herself. Tony says once I read them I'll know she didn't."

"Well, they're either very depressing," Sam said, "or very uplifting."

"Can they be both?" I asked.

She shrugged and said, "I guess that's what we're going to find out."

There were hundreds of poems—eighteen years' worth, and after reading half a dozen each Sam and I exchanged a look, and then traded.

"Well?" I asked after we'd read those.

"God," she said, "these *are* depressing. The girl who wrote these was so...sad!"

I hated to admit it, but I agreed. Anyone who could write "Angel of Death," "Last Request," and "Midnight Crisis," not to mention something called "Laying Down To Die," *was* more than just sad.

"Listen to this line from 'Midnight Crisis,'" Sam said. "'Raindrops kiss my black lapels, then weep into my chest.'" She looked at me and said, "It's so beautiful...yet sad."

"You're the writer," I said, again. "Are these good?"

We were seated across from each other on the floor with the poems strewn out between us.

"These are...wonderful! I'm no poet, but...I wish I could write with this much beauty and passion."

"But they're sad."

"Well, maybe not all sad. Listen to this. It's from 'Laying Down To Die.' 'She's blind to the jelly bean colors, of balloons on a turquoise sky.'"

"That's great," I said, "but does it all mean she killed herself or not?"

"What if writing it down, writing down all the sadness she felt, was her way of dealing with it, of getting it out. What if she wrote it to keep from committing suicide? It could have been some sort of rite of expiation on her part."

"If you're gonna flaunt something could you make it something other than your writer's vocabulary? Like your body?"

She made a face.

"So, in her own mind, writing this all down would prevent her from having to commit suicide?" I asked.

"Maybe."

"So Tony's not just seeing something he wants to see," I said. "You think that two different people reading these poems could interpret them differently?"

"Well, I think you can always get differing opinions, don't you?"

I looked down at the poems on the floor, shifted them around, then heaved a big sigh.

"What?" she asked.

"I think she took her own life."

"So what are you gonna do?"

"Ask some questions," I said. "Maybe, if I can find out why, I can put her mother's mind at peace."

"I don't know how a woman who has lost a child can be at peace."

"You're probably right."

"So you're not going to treat this like it's a murder?" she asked.

"I can't," I said. "I don't see it that way."

She shrugged. "Maybe somebody poisoned her."

I shook my head. "I think that's your writer's imagination at work."

"All right," she said, getting to her feet. She was wearing a big floppy sweatshirt and a pair of jeans. Her feet were bare, since she'd only had to walk from across the hall. I noticed—not for the first time—that she had pretty feet.

"All right what?"

"Look into it any way you want," she said, "as long as you look into it."

I stood up, too.

"I have to go," she said. "I have twenty pages to do tonight and I've still got to watch Murphy Brown."

"Has all this talk about murder and suicide inspired you?"

"As a matter of fact," she said, as I walked with her to the door, "it has. I'll be up well past midnight if you want to talk more, or get a snack."

"I'll let you know." I looked back at the poems on the floor. "You want to take some of these with you?"

"No," she said, "you better finish reading them. Read as many as you can, Nicky. Maybe it'll help you see something definite."

As she went out the door I thought I already knew something definite. Mary Ann Grosso had been one very depressed girl.

I guess what I needed to find out was why.

I read some more, but at one point I just had to stop. Jesus, I was getting depressed and I'm normally a happy fella. Ask anybody.

I put the poems away in the folder and went to bed around midnight. Let Sam get her own snack.

6

The next morning I got up late and leafed through the poems again while I drank my coffee. I didn't have the heart to start reading again, though, because they would have taken the heart right out of me. I left the folder on my desk and decided to talk to people who knew Mary Ann Grosso a lot better than I did.

I started with Catherine. I called her at home and convinced her to have lunch with me. She agreed, but told me to come to the house at noon and she'd make something. That left me an hour to work with. I decided to talk to the police and see what they had on Mary Ann.

I made some calls, invoked the name of a friend and got the investigating detective to agree to talk to me.

His name was Detective Harry Nolan, and he worked out of the Sixty-Second Precinct.

"What have you got for me, Mr. Delvecchio?" he asked.

"Actually, I was hoping you'd have something for me, detective," I said. "I have two people trying to hire me. One thinks Mary Ann committed suicide, and one thinks she didn't."

"Well, all I've got for you is this: The M.E. says she died from a massive ingestion of sleeping pills. There were no signs of violence on the body, no signs that she'd been held down and fed the pills."

"What about the presence of other drugs?"

"Nada," he said, "not even aspirin, or birth control. She appeared to have simply taken all the pills, and then laid down to die."

The irony of that statement did not escape me.

"Did you find the pill container?"

"Yes. There was one in the upstairs master bathroom. They were the mother's pills. The daughter must have taken the pills, left the bottle in the sink, and then walked to bed. And then there was the note."

"What?" That was the first I'd heard of it. "What note?"

"The one they found clutched in her hand."

"What did it say?"

"I don't know," the detective admitted, "the title had something to do with suicide."

"Title?" I grabbed the folder, went through it.

There were several with suicide in the title. I read them off to him.

"That's the one. She had it in her hand."

"I'd like to see it."

"It's in evidence," he said.

"If I come in can you show it to me?"

"I suppose so."

"I'll call first," I said, "let you know I'm coming."

"Okay."

"I might not be in till later today."

"I'll be here."

"Is the case still open?" I asked.

He hesitated, then said, "Technically. We're just tying up loose ends, but..."

"You're buying suicide."

"Yes."

"Okay, Detective," I said. "Thanks."

Why hadn't Mary Ann's mom or Tony told me about the note?

I was reading the poem when there was a knock on the door. I opened it;

Sam was standing there.

"What are you doing up?" I asked. "I thought you worked till late."

"I did, but I wanted to see if you read any more of the poems."

"I'm reading one now," I said, waving it. "Listen to this. 'Eyelids covering forever her pain, beating heart eternally resting.' She had this, or something like it, in her hand."

"Which one is it?"

"It's called 'Suicidal Daydream,'" I said. "What do you think about that?"

7

When I got to the Grosso house Catherine had made some soup and sandwiches. She also looked as if she had dressed for a date. She had her midriff showing, belly button pierced with a gold stud. I hoped I hadn't given her the wrong idea. Actually, she looked very pretty...

"Nick," she said, when we were seated at the table, "Tony told me he hired you."

"He thinks he hired me," I said. She looked puzzled. "I'm not going to bill him, Catherine."

"Well...that's very nice of you...but what can you do for him...us?"

"I don't know," I said, honestly. "Do you feel the way he does about Mary Ann's death, or do you agree with your mother?"

She opened her mouth to answer, but her voice seemed to fail her. There were two glasses of water on the table. She took a sip from one, either because her mouth was dry, or she was buying time to think.

"I don't know how I feel, Nick," she said, finally. "I mean, sometimes I'm absolutely numb."

"Do you think that someone might have killed your sister?"

"My God," she said, shaking her head. She held her hands up, as if she was going to cup her head between them, but instead she just held them there. "It sounds so ludicrous when you say it out loud like that. Who'd want to kill Mary Ann? And why?"

She reached out suddenly and grabbed my hand.

"Nick, do you actually think somebody killed my sister?"

"No, Catherine, I don't," I said. "I'm sorry, but I believe she committed suicide."

I took "Suicidal Daydreams" from my pocket and held it out to her.

"What's this?"

"This is the poem they found in her hand. The police consider it a suicide note."

She unfolded the page and read it, then let her hand drop to the table, holding the poem loosely.

"Do you know when she wrote that?" I asked.

Her face reddened.

"Catherine..."

"Yes."

"When?"

She touched her forehead with her left hand, as if she had a headache.

"Catherine?" I made my voice firmer.

"A couple of years ago," she said, finally.

"Did she talk about suicide then?"

She lifted her eyes to look at me. They were shiny with tears.

"It's not about suicide, Nick."

"Come on," I said, "look at the title. What else could it be about?"

"Look at the last line of the first stanza." She smoothed the page out on the table.

"'Damaged goods denied final blessing,'" I read.

"And the second stanza."

I looked at the last line of the second stanza and read, 'Remains of a deadly assault.'"

"Don't you see?" she asked. "'Damaged goods?' 'Deadly Assault?'"

"What are you trying to tell me, Catherine?"

"Nick..."

Suddenly it came to me.

"Catherine...are you telling me Mary Ann was raped?"

She nodded, tears streaming down her face.

"When? By who?"

"She never told anyone," she said. "Anyone but me."

"Why not?" I asked. "Why didn't she tell your mother?"

Her eyes widened. "Oh God, Nick, she would never have told Ma. She would have thought...Mary Ann was dirty."

"No," I said, "your mother would have helped her—"

"You don't know my mother, Nick," she said. "If she ever found out about this it would disgrace her. She would...would..."

She'd what, I wondered. Whatever she was thinking she couldn't say it out loud.

"Nick, haven't you wondered why Tony and Mary Ann are getting married—*were* just getting married now, after all these years?"

"Well...yeah, I wondered...a little."

"Mary Ann's led kind of a wild life, Nick," Catherine said. "She's not—wasn't—the nice little Catholic girl that...well, she's not..."

Was she going to say, "...the nice little Catholic girl that I am?"

"She's been...promiscuous in the past, but now she was ready to settle down, and Tony—he's loved her all these years, and he was ready to marry her."

"Who was it, Catherine?" I asked. "Who raped her?"

"She told me," Catherine said, "but...do you think he killed her? I mean, it was two years ago and she...she forgave him, Nick. Can you imagine? So why would he kill her now?"

"I don't know, Catherine," I said. "Why don't you let me go and ask him?"

8

Sal Pricci lived in the old neighborhood, not far from where Mary Ann grew up and died, and where my father now lived. I walked a block of identical two-family, brick, semi-attached homes, and then a block filled with a couple of pizzerias, a donut shop, travel agent's office, Chinese takeout, deli/grocery store, and newsstand. A couple of kids with dirty knees, elbows and faces almost ran into me, then ducked between parked and double-parked cars, chasing each other. Two teenagers shouted remarks at a pretty, big-boobed blonde who came out of one of the pizza places and got into her double-parked car while ignoring them. A couple of old pensioners ran into each other and stopped to shoot the shit. These were normal Brooklyn blocks, but I bet none of these normal neighborhood people knew what had been going on in Mary Ann Grosso's life.

Sal actually lived in his father's house, since both parents had passed away. He had no brothers or sisters, which was unusual for someone of our generation. When I was a kid I didn't have many friends who were only children. That's what happens when you grow up Catholic and Italian.

I didn't know if Sal was home or not, but I hoped he was. I wanted to be able to wrap this case up quickly. I just found the whole thing too depressing.

So I was hopeful when I rang the doorbell.

Sal came to the door.

"Nick," he said, surprised. He stared at me through the storm door, didn't unlock it. "What are you—it's good to see you."

"Can I talk to you, Sal?"

"Well...well, sure, come on in." He unlocked the door, backed away to allow me to enter.

He closed the door behind us and led me into the living room. The house was very much like Mary Ann's, very much like my father's. It's funny, I grew up in my father's house. It was my home for almost twenty years, but I always thought of it as my father's house.

"Can I get you a beer?" he asked. "Or...somethin'? I was watchin' ESPN. Fuckin' Mets are twenty games out."

"Braves are hard to beat," I said.

"Damn near impossible."

"No, drink, Sal. I just wanna talk."

"Sure. About what?"

"Mary Ann."

He frowned. "What about her? Did you find out anything about her suicide?"

"No," I said, "but I found out some other things."

He shuffled his feet uncomfortable and said, "Uh, what other things?"

"Come on, Sal," I said. "I think you know."

He shook his head slightly and said, "Uh, Nick, sorry, but I don't know—"

"I know about the rape, Sal."

"What?" he asked, his eyes widening. "No, whoa, wait a minute, there wasn't no rape, Nick. I don't know who you been talkin' to but—"

"I've been talking to someone Mary Ann confided in, Sal," I said, cutting him off.

"Jesus," he said, touching his face, "she didn't tell Tony that, did she?"

"I think if she had told Tony you'd know about it, Sal—you would have known two years ago, when it happened. He would've killed you."

"Nick," he said, "wait, let me show you something. All right? Before you say anything else."

Sal went into the dining room without waiting for an answer. He went to a hutch and opened a drawer. Just for a moment I wondered if he was going to come out of there with a gun, but instead he took a folded-up piece of paper and carried it back to me, leaving the drawer open.

"Here."

"What is it?"

"A poem," he said. "Mary Ann wrote it...for me. Read it."

I unfolded the paper and read the title: "You." I read the first stanza And saw that it was Mary Ann's voice, all right. I was starting to recognize her style.

"'Disappointments in life are many,'" it started. It was three stanzas, and the third finished with the line, "'Now I will be forever changed, refreshed, from loving you.'"

I looked at him. "Did she write this before the rape, or after, Sal?"

Sal stared at me for a few moments, and his eyes widened again. He said, horrified—and if he was acting he was damned good—"Jesus, you think I killed her!"

"Tell me what happened, Sal."

"Nick...look...I've been in love with Mary Ann for years, man. You know those stories we useta hear, about guys who scored with her?"

"Tony said they weren't true."

"Well, they were. I mean, I loved her, too, but I wasn't as blind as Tony was. He refused to believe those stories, but I knew they were true."

I didn't know what to say. If what Catherine said about her sister's promiscuity was true, it must have started in high school.

"So what does that mean, Sal, that she deserved—"

"No, you don't understand," he said. "Just listen." There was a look of desperation on his face, and in his eyes. "Tony wanted to marry her right out of high school, but she wasn't ready for that. She wanted to live her life, ya know? She traveled, she had affairs, one-night stands, but she always came back home. Tony and her mother, they kept treating her like she was a saint, but I knew different.

"I was always here, too, Nick, and always in love with her. Then, about three years ago, she came home and she was different. It was like she found God, or something. After all these years? It was like suddenly she *was* the saint Tony and her mother thought she was—but not quite. Even though she started to see Tony regularly, and they talked about marriage, all of a sudden she noticed me ya know? It was like a high school dream come true for me. We talked, we went places together, we did things...but we never had sex. She just wouldn't have sex with me. I couldn't understand that. She always told me I was the one keeping her sane, who knew her for what she was and still loved her. Tony, she said, loved who he thought she was. And her mother—well, Angela would never believe anything bad about her precious Mary Ann."

"So she wouldn't come across, huh?"

"It wasn't like that." He wiped away the sweat on his forehead with his palm. "I didn't want a quick fuck, Nick. I wanted to marry her, take care of her. I couldn't understand why she wouldn't make love with me."

"So you got tired of waiting?"

"Damn it, why won't you understand?" he shouted. "She came over here one day and gave me that poem, said she'd written it for me. I was blown away. Nobody'd ever done anything like that for me before. She...she let me kiss her, and then...then when things really started to heat up, she pushed me away...but she didn't push very hard ya know? I felt if I pressed her, if I insisted...and before you knew it we were on the floor...okay, so I tore her clothes a little...but I wouldn't call it rape, Nick. I'd never call it rape!"

"But she did, right?"

"Yeah," he said. Suddenly, it was as if all the strength had gone out of him. He sank into a chair and said, "Yeah, she did...but you know what? She said she forgave me. She understood."

"And?"

"And she said she never wanted to see me again...not like that. She said we were finished, even as friends."

"And you took that?"

"Sure, I took it," he said. "I loved her. I'd never hurt her."

I stared at him. I didn't know exactly what had happened between them that day. She called it rape. He didn't. Who knew? She told her sister it was rape, but was too ashamed to tell her mother.

He looked at me with anguished eyes. He wouldn't wait two years and then become angry enough to kill her, would he?

He hung his head and said, "I didn't kill her, Nick. I swear, I didn't...I didn't..."

I believed him.

By the time I left Sal's all I had was another reason Mary Ann might have committed suicide. Maybe the "rape" was weighing heavily on her mind, even after two years.

I went home, entered my place by the office door, rather than my living quarters. I had the biggest unit on the floor, so it had two entrances.

From the door I could see the message machine on my desk flashing. Odd, but when I think back to that moment later on it would seem to me that the light was flashing more urgently than usual. The red readout said there were six messages.

I pressed play, and my life changed.

9

When I went through the emergency room doors Benny was right there waiting for me. His face was covered with tears. I had never seen Big Benvenuto Carbone—Benny "the Card"—cry.

"They was havin' lunch, Nicky," he said, "at an outside table, ya know? And then it just happened. I was inside. When I come runnin' out they was just...lying there."

I put my hand on his big shoulder and said, "How are they, Benny?"

"They're workin' on them," he said. "Jeez, Nick, there was so much blood. I'm so sorry..."

"You've got nothing to be sorry about, bro," I said. I patted his shoulder and dropped my hand. "I'm gonna talk to somebody."

"Yeah, okay," he said, "they won't tell me nothin' 'cause I ain't related."

"Well, I am," I said, "so let's see what I can find out."

I left him there looking lost and went to the desk. The nurse was fifty-something, plain, and harried looking. There are two places in New York you never want to end up—Motor Vehicle, and any hospital emergency room. Both places are usually crowded, and that night was no exception.

I had to wait while a couple of people in front of me finished their business before I could step up to the counter.

"Yes?"

"My name is Delvecchio," I said. "My father and, uh, uncle were brought in, victims of gunshot wounds."

"Oh, yeah," she said. "They're being attended to right now."

"I'd like to talk to the doctor."

"The doctor will be with you as soon as he can."

"Well, at least you can tell me how they are?" I asked. "I really don't know anything."

"Actually, sir," she said, "there's nothing I can tell you. The doctor will be out—"

"Yes, I know," I said, "as soon as he can."

She gave me an exasperated look.

"Wouldn't you rather he do what he can for your father instead of coming out here and talk to you?"

"Okay, fine," I said, "you succeeded in making me feel this big." I held my forefinger and thumb an inch apart.

Her face softened.

"That wasn't my intention, sir. I'm sure the doctor will be out soon."

"Can you at least tell me…if they're alive?" I asked.

She looked around, then said, "They're alive, sir."

"Thanks."

I walked back to where Benny was still standing.

"Let's sit down, Benny."

We went over to a couple of orange plastic chairs and sat down. Benny's bulk threatened to flatten his chair, but it held. Because of how big he was I had to leave an empty chair between our two. There were a few other chairs empty, but those were the only ones where we could sit together.

"Benny?"

"I'm sorry, Nick," he said. "I just…can't get it together."

He was right. I'd never seen the big man so out of it. I was wondering why I was so calm, but I had a feeling it was because Benny was falling apart. I probably had him to thank for the fact that I wasn't a basket case. Especially since I didn't know how close or far from death my old man was.

"Benny," I said, "come on, man. Just tell me what happened."

"I tol' you," Benny said, shaking his head, "They were having lunch at Rizzo'd in the Bay, sittin' outside, when I heard the shots."

"Where were you?"

"Inside," Benny said, "I was sittin' inside. I shoulda been outside, but the Don said they wanted to talk."

"You gotta do what the Don says, Benny," I reminded him. "Then what?"

"I ran outside and there was a car speedin' away. It was a drive-by, Nick. A goddamned drive-by."

"How bad were they hit, Benny?"

"They was each hit a few times," he said. "I tried to put pressure on the wounds with napkins." He looked straight at me then, his eyes shining with tears. "I'm sorry, Nick. I—I went to the Don first."

I patted him on the shoulder and said, "It's okay, Benny. I understand."

"When the ambulance came and they were loaded in they was both breathin', Nick. I swear. Your old man was breathin'."

"I believe you, Benny."

He put his elbows on his knees, and his head in his hands.

"Benny, I have to go and call my brother and my sister," I said. "Will you be okay?"

"Yeah, yeah, I'll be okay."

"Okay," I said. "I'll be right back."

I got up and walked to the pay phones. I dialed my brother's church first.

"Nick?" Vinnie said. "What're you doing? I'm supposed to be hearing confessions."

"It's Dad, Father Vinnie," I said. "He was havin' lunch with the Barracuda and somebody shot them."

"What?"

"They're in emergency at Victory Memorial Hospital," I said. "Better get over here fast, Vinnie. He needs his oldest son, and his priest."

"Damn it...have you called Maria?"

"No, I was gonna do that next—"

"I'll go and get her, and bring her with me," Vinnie said. "We'll be there as soon as we can."

"Okay, Vin."

"Nick...how is he?"

"Alive, Vinnie," I said, "they're both alive...so far."

"See you soon."

We hung up, and I went back out to sit with Benny.

10

Vinnie and Maria got there within half-an-hour. Benny and I both stood when they came in, but Benny held back as I went to greet them. I had to duck, bob and weave to keep from being flattened in the crowded E.R.

"Nicky!" my sister said, coming into my arms and crying.
"How are they?" Vinnie asked.
"Still no word," I said. "Vinnie, I hate to ask, but..."
"What?"
"You've got your collar on."
He knew what I meant immediately.
"I'll go and see what I can find out."

I'd tried to get my older brother to use his white collar before to get us better seats at a game, or a restaurant, but he always refused. This time was totally different.

He went to the front desk and spoke with the same nurse, then came back to us.

"They're gonna let me in, just in case one of them needs last rites."
"Oh, Vinnie..." my sister sobbed.
"They're still working on them, Maria," Vinnie said. "I'll just go and find out how bad they are."
"Go ahead," I said, still holding Maria. "Hurry, Vin."

He went and I took Maria to the chair between me and Benny, which she could use because she was so small.

She asked me what happened and I told her while Benny sat there looking miserable and guilty.

A few minutes later, when she went to the ladies room, I said to Benny, "What's goin' on, Benny?"
"Whastaya mean?"
"There's no soldiers here," I said. "I thought when a Don got hit—even a retired Don—the soldiers turned out to protect him."
"I ain't called anybody," he admitted.
"Why not?"
"Because I don't know who to trust," Benny said, keeping his voice low. "I only called you Nicky, 'cause I trust you. You and me, we'll keep 'im safe."

I had grabbed my thirty-eight out of the safe in my office floor before heading for the hospital. After all, Benny had just told me that both my father and godfather had been shot. And I knew Benny was heeled. He always was.

"What about the cops?" I asked. "Why aren't they here?"
"I didn't call for 'em," he said. "I just called for an ambulance."
"Well, they'll be here, as soon as the hospital reports they have two gun-

shot wounds here."

As if on cue flashing lights reflected from outside, and when the automatic doors opened, two uniformed cops came walking in.

"I'll take this," I said to Benny, and rose to meet them.

The cops were from the Sixty-Eighth Precinct in Bay Ridge, where the hospital was located. Before long we also had detectives from the Sixty-Eighth and then detectives from the Sixty-First. The Sixty-First were representing Sheepshead Bay, where the shooting took place.

I had to talk to all of them, while trying to keep them away from Benny. He was wound up so tight there was no telling what he'd say or do when pressed about why he hadn't called the cops immediately. If they searched him and found his gun they might use it as an excuse to haul him in.

Meanwhile, I had to keep one eye on Maria, and another one out for Vinnie. I was running out of eyes.

Eventually, we were all just waiting for a doctor to come out and tell us what was going on.

Finally, one did.

The detectives charged him immediately, but he brushed them off and came to me.

"Are you Mr. Delvecchio's son?" he asked. He had on a name tag that said Doctor Ramirez. He was in his forties, gray hair and mustache, and just the slightest Spanish accent.

"I am."

"And I'm his daughter," Maria said, rushing up to my side. "How is he?"

"We're still working on him," he said, "but he has a very rare blood type. We're getting some now from Father Vincent, but we're going to need more."

"We're ready," Maria said.

Ramirez looked at her.

"I think we'll be able to get what we need from your two brothers."

"But—"

"Gimme a minute, Doc."

He nodded. I took Maria by the shoulders and pulled her away to where nobody would be able to hear us. It wasn't easy, but there was one corner we were able to use.

"Maria, I need you to stay and look after Benny," I said.

"But Nick—"

"If we leave him alone with these cops he's gonna end up in trouble. I need him out of jail if I'm gonna find out who shot Pop."

"Nicky, you're not gonna—"

354

"Hell, yeah, I am," I said. "You don't think I'm gonna leave this to the cops, do you? Come on, Maria. I need you now."

"All right," she said, "all right." She took two fists full of my shirt. "But you let me know if something happens!"

"I will. I swear."

I walked over to Ramirez and said, "Let's go, Doc."

11

He took me through a set of double doors, into the back, to where Vinnie was lying down on a gurney with a tube in his arm. I looked around for the Don, and for my Pop.

"Where are they?" I asked.

"We have them in operating rooms upstairs," Ramirez said. "We'll take your blood down here."

"Okay."

"But first I have to test and make sure you have the same type."

"I'm his son," I said.

"Do you know your blood type? Or his?"

I had to admit I didn't.

"It's just a formality," he said. "I'll check for your type, and then we'll pump you dry."

"What?"

"Just kidding. Lie down over here."

I laid down on a table next to Vinnie. There was a curtain between us, but it was open. The doctor found a good vein in my arm, swabbed me and took a vial of blood.

"I'll be right back."

I turned my head to look at Vinnie.

"Did you see them?" I asked.

"Yeah, they took me upstairs."

"How are they?"

"Still alive."

"Vinnie," I asked, "do you have that thing…"

"What thing?"

"You know," I said, "that purple scarf thing you put around your neck when you give last rites. Do you have it with you?"

"My stole?"

"Yeah, that thing."

"Yes, Nick," he said, "I always have it with me. It's folded up in my jacket pocket."

"Okay," I said. "I just wanted to make sure."

A nurse came and removed the tube from his arm. She told Vinnie to stay there a while.

Doctor Ramirez reappeared after about ten minutes—I don't remember how long exactly—and looked at both of us.

"Father, perhaps you should come upstairs with me."

"What's wrong?" I asked.

Vinnie sat up, and I did, too. I helped him off his table.

"What is it?" Vinnie asked.

"I think you should come up," Ramirez said, again.

"Is he—" I started to ask.

"Not yet," the doctor said, "but soon."

"All right," Vinnie said.

"I'm comin', too," I said.

"Nick—"

"You might get lightheaded, Vin," I said. "I'm comin'."

Vinnie looked at the doctor.

"All right," he said, "but please hurry."

They took us up in an elevator to the floor where the operating room was. We were quiet on the ride up. I felt cold, inside. I hadn't come close to shedding a tear yet, maybe because I'd been taking care of Benny, and then Maria. Now, knowing that my father might be dead by the time we got to the right floor, I still felt calm. Maybe I'd been ready to hear the news from the moment I'd gotten there.

When we entered the operating room there were people standing around in blue scrubs, many of them soaked through with sweat, covered with blood.

Another doctor approached us, took off his mask.

"I'm sorry," he said. "We did all we could, there was just too much damage. The arteries leading to his heart were shredded. We tried to take some from his leg to graft, but we didn't have enough time…"

Vinnie took his stole from his pocket and put it around his neck. We both approached the operating table, he on Pop's right and me on the left. Pop's face looked gray, even though he had probably only died in the last few minutes. He was covered to the neck with a bloody sheet.

Vinnie made the sign of the cross, started to speak, giving him last rites, but I wasn't listening. I reached between the sheets to take my father's hand and hold it tightly.

"I'm sorry, Pop," I said. "I'm so sorry."

12

They covered my father's face with a sheet and we left the room. I was numb, and there were still no tears. I'd seen lots of death before, but what was wrong with me? This was my Pop.

I turned to a doctor and asked, "Where's Don—where's Mr. Barracondi?"

"In the next operating room," the doctor said. "His wounds are serious, but I believe we're going to be able to save him."

"Can we see him?" I asked.

"I'm sorry," the doctor said, "I can't—"

"Mr. Barracondi is my brother's godfather, Doctor," Vinnie said. "Do you know what that means in an Italian family?"

I don't know which meaning the doctor was thinking of but he said, "Well, all right. But just for a moment."

We walked to the door of the next room. The doctor went in first, me behind him. Somebody tied a mask around my mouth from behind, and then they let me approach the table.

The old man's blue eyes looked as bright as ever as he saw me. There was an oxygen mask over his face, which was pale, but not gray. He reached a heavily veined hand out to me and I took it. His grip was weak. There were tubes in his arm.

He started to say something but the mask muffled the sound. Knowing him, I was sure he was trying to ask about my father. It was better that he didn't know yet.

I released his hand and allowed the doctor to steer me out of the room.

"How is he?" I asked. "Why aren't they workin' on him?"

"He needs more surgery," the doctor said. "We're waiting for him to stabilize, first. It will be some time before we're finished with him."

"I see."

Doctor Ramirez said, "I'll take you both back down."

"Are you sure you won't need me—" Vinnie started to ask.

"No," the other doctor said. "I think we've got this one, Father."

Ramirez took Vinnie and me back down. On the way in the elevator Vinnie took off the stole, folded it lovingly and put it back in his pocket. We didn't speak. One of us was going to have to tell Maria that Pop was dead.

When we reentered the emergency room it was full of people. There were still uniformed cops, but now there were two sergeants and a lieutenant. The detectives from both squads were still there, too.

Maria was sitting next to Benny, holding his big hands in hers. When they saw us they both got to their feet.

"Mr. Delvecchio—" the lieutenant said.

"Lieutenant," my brother said, "in a minute, please."

"Father, I understand what's going on, but we need to talk—"

"Talk to me, then," Vinnie said. "My brother has to give some bad news to our sister."

I nodded to Vinnie and went to talk to Benny and Maria.

"Nick?" she said, studying my face.

"I'm so sorry, Maria," I said. "He's gone."

Her eyes overflowed with tears and as they streamed down her face her mouth opened, but no sound came out. I grabbed her and pulled her to me so that when she did scream it would be muffled by my chest.

"I'm sorry, Nick," Benny said, putting a big hand on my shoulder.

"Benny," I said, "the Don's gonna be okay."

His eyes went wide.

"Can I see 'im? I should be with him."

"It's gonna be a while," I said. "He still needs some more surgery."

"But Nick, I gotta—"

"Benny," I said, "there are probably gonna be a lot of cops up there soon. Don't do anything silly, okay? It won't do the Don any good for you to get yourself tossed in jail."

"Yeah," he said, "yeah, okay, Nick. Geez, I'm really sorry about your dad. He was a good guy."

Rubbing my sister's back while she sobbed I said, "Yeah, he was a good guy."

Vinnie came over. "Nick, I think you ought to talk to the police. That's more your department."

"Yeah, okay," I said. I handed Maria over to him and turned to talk to the police.

13

I ended up in a small room with the detectives from the Six-One, since that's where the shooting took place.

They were a mismatched pair, the older on—Detective Blaine—in his early fifties with a receding hairline and granite jaw. His partner, Detective Hart, was in his thirties, with a weak jaw that worked furiously on a piece of gum.

THE END OF BROOKLYN

The room was an examining room, filled mostly with Blaine's bulk. Luckily, Hart and I together barely took up the same amount of space as he did.

"We've already questioned your friend, Benny," Blaine said.

"You did?" That was news to me.

"He told us what happened," Hart said.

"Then what do you need me for?" I asked. "I just lost my father. I've got things to do."

"We understand," Blaine said. "We'll only keep you a few minutes."

"Okay, whatever," I said.

"Did you talk to Nick Barracuda when you were upstairs?" Blaine asked.

"That's what you want to know?"

"We figure Barracuda maybe told you who the shooters were."

"First of all his name is Mr. Barracondi," I said. "Have a little respect. The man's lying upstairs with holes in him."

"You're pretty defensive of a man who probably got your father killed," Hart said. "The shooters must've been after him, and your old man got in the way."

"That means the shooters are at fault, not the D—not my godfather."

"Godfather," Blaine said. "That's rich."

"He happens to *be* my godfather," I said.

"Look," Blaine said, "we all know who Nicky Barracuda is, Delvecchio. Somebody tried to take out the Don, and got your father at the same time. Seems to me you'd be wantin' to help us find out who it was."

"What did the Barracuda say to you upstairs?" Hart asked.

"Nothin'," I said. "He can't talk, yet. He still needs some more surgery."

"Look," Blaine said, "we're just doing the preliminary on this. Your dad died, that means Brooklyn South Homicide is gonna get this case. So if you don't help us, you'll have to help them."

"Detective," I said, "believe me, there's nothin' I want more than to find out who did this."

"Don't think you're gonna be able to go lone wolf on this, Delvecchio," Blaine said. "This was a Mafia hit. You can't take them on alone, no matter how far they've fallen in the past few years."

Since John Gotti, supposedly the Last Don, was sentenced to life in prison in 1992 the Mafia had fallen on hard times. They were no longer the crime power they had once been. Other so called "mafias" had popped up, most notably the Russians.

"Maybe it wasn't the Italian Mafia who did this," I said.

"You mean the Russians?"

"Or the South Americans. Or the Koreans," I said. "Who knows?"

"Well," Blaine said, closing his notebook, "let Homicide worry about it.

They'll question Barracuda when he's ready to talk."

"Well it ain't gonna be tonight," I said. "Can I go? I've got arrangements to make."

"Sure, go ahead," Blaine said. "You're not bein' any help to us. If we patted you and your buddy down would we find you both heeled?"

"I don't know," I said. "Would you?"

Hart stood up but Blaine put his hands on his partner's chest.

"I'm givin' you a pass, Delvecchio, because your dad was killed tonight. Don't count on the same pass from Homicide. Those guys are a little more hard ass than I am."

"I'll keep that in mind," I said, then as an afterthought said, "Thanks."

I wasn't being any help to them because I couldn't be. I didn't know squat. The Don hadn't told me anything, and Benny didn't know anything helpful. Once I could talk to the Don, and ask some questions around Sheepshead Bay, maybe I'd get some answers.

But right at that moment all I could really do was try to deal with the death of my father.

14

Hours later it was just us in the emergency room. Me, Vinnie, Maria and Benny. There was nothing else the police could do until the Don was able to talk. There was one cop upstairs, waiting to take a statement.

Other emergencies had come in, been taken care of, and either admitted or released. There were still a few people sitting and either waiting to be seen, or waiting for someone being treated. One person was cradling an arm, another was holding a handkerchief to his nose. Even though the E.R. had been crowded for a while, it had been a relatively slow night for Victory Memorial's emergency room. And for Brooklyn. Odd.

An odd night, all around.

"Can we take him home?" Maria asked.

"What?"

"Dad," she said. "Can we take him home?"

"I doubt it," I said. "They'll want an autopsy."

"Autopsy? What for? He was shot."

"Mandatory for homicides," I said.

"What about the Don?" Benny asked. "Are they gonna let me go up and see him?"

"Probably when they put him in a room."

"Private room," Benny said. "It has to be a private room."

"We can arrange that."

Father Vinnie was quiet, head bowed. I thought he was praying.

"Sir?"

I looked up. It was the reception nurse—a different one from before. I hadn't seen her or spoken to her, yet. This one was older, gray-haired, very businesslike.

"Yes?"

"I'm sorry, but I need to have you fill out some papers."

"Papers?"

"Yes, for billing?"

"Billing?" Maria asked, appalled. "You want to talk to us about billing... now?"

"I'm sorry," the woman said, "but it's my job."

"Listen, lady—"

"Nick," Benny said. "I'll take care of it. The Don would want to take care of it."

"Benny—"

"I got it," Benny said. He stood up, towering over the woman, who stared up at him in awe. "Come on, dear."

He took her elbow and led her back to her desk. Another oddity. Benny, being gentle, and even charming.

"The Church has medical insurance," Vinnie said.

"Uncle Dom will take care of it," I said.

"I haven't heard you call him that in a long time," Maria said.

"I know."

The double doors opened and Doctor Ramirez came out. I stood up and went to meet him.

"Can we talk?" he asked.

"Sure."

He looked past me at Maria and Father Vinnie, and said, "Away from the others."

"Anything you want to say to me you can say in front of my brother and sister."

"I think maybe I'll leave it up to you, if you want to tell them later," he said.

I studied his face for a few moments, not really getting anything from him. I turned and said, "I'll be right back."

I followed him through the double doors and into a treatment room.

"What's goin' on, Doc?"

"Your blood."

"What about it."

"When I took the sample I checked it for compatibility."

"Yeah, so?" I stared at him. "Oh great, you're gonna tell me you found something in my blood. Am I sick?"

"No, no," he said, "you're not sick. But I did find something."

"What?"

"I gave it a lot of thought before deciding to tell you," he said.

"Tell me what, Doc?"

"Well...your blood type."

"Yeah?"

"It, uh, doesn't match."

"Match what?"

"Your father's blood type—you weren't a match. We would not have been able to use your blood on him, just your—just Father Vincent's."

"Doc," I said, "you're gonna have to spit this out in plain English for me."

"Well," he said, "simply put...your father is—was—not your father."

15

Was it odd that of everything that had happened that night, this was what hit me the hardest? I felt like I'd been hit square in the belly. I couldn't take a breath.

"Mr. Delvecchio?" Doctor Ramirez said. "Are you all right?"

I couldn't answer.

"Come over here, sit down." He led me to a chair and lowered me into it.

I looked up at him and said, "Wha—what?"

"I'm sorry," the doctor said. "Obviously, you didn't know you were... adopted? Some parents don't ever tell the child..."

"Adopted?" I said.

"That's the only explanation I can think of."

Of course, given the business I was in, I could think of another possibility.

"Your blood type is O positive. It's the most common type. Your father was B positive, not the rarest, but still rare."

"And...my brother?"

"Father Vincent is also B positive. Do you know what your mother's blood type was?"

"N-no." If I didn't know mine before that night, how would I know my mother's?

"I'm sorry…"

I stared at the floor, my mind racing. I didn't like where it was going, though, so I tried to shake it off.

"Can I…get you anything?" he asked.

"No," I said, "no, I'm fine. How's the Don—how's my godfather?"

"He resting easy," Ramirez said. "We moved him to Critical Care."

"Can we go up?"

"Sure," Ramirez said, "it's the eighth floor, but there's a policeman up there."

"I'll talk to him," I said. "Thanks, Doctor."

"Mr. Delvecchio," he said, "you had more than one shock tonight. Perhaps you should go home, get some rest."

"I will, Doctor," I said, "soon."

"I…I hope I did the right thing in telling you," he said, with concern.

"You did, Doctor," I assured him, "you did."

"Everything okay?" Father Vinnie asked when I returned to the emergency waiting room. People were moving around us very quickly.

"Yeah, what's happening?"

"Some kind of accident. They're bringing in a lot of casualties."

"Then we better get out of here."

Benny came over.

"What's going on, Nick?"

"The Don is in Critical Care," I said. "We can go up. When we get there I'll have to talk to the police officer."

"Let's go!" Benny said.

"Get Maria, Benny."

He went to where she was sitting and helped her to her feet.

"Is everything okay, Nick?"

"Nothing's okay, Vinnie."

"No, of course not. I know that. I just meant…with you. Are you all right?"

"I don't think I'll know until I get home," I said. "All of this has to… process."

"I don't think any of us should be alone tonight, Nick. We can all go to Maria's."

"Or Pop's," I said.

We all had keys to my father's house. After all, we used to live there.

"Let's go," Benny said, with Maria looking on.

***

When we got out of the elevator we came face-to-face with the police officer, a young guy with "Deaver" on his chest.

"Officer Deaver."

"Who are you people?"

"Delvecchio," I said. "I'm Nick, this is Maria, and...Father Vincent."

"Oh, hello, Father," Deaver said.

Good, I thought, a Catholic.

"And this is Benny. We'd like to see Mr. Barracondi."

"Are you family?"

"Yes," I said. "He's our uncle. Our father was killed in the attack on both of them."

"I'm supposed to take a statement when he comes to," the cop said.

"No problem," I said. "We just want to see him, and one of us will be staying all night."

"I'll have to okay that with my boss."

"Talk to Detective Blaine, Six-One Squad."

"Six-One?" He looked confused. "But we're in the Six-Eight."

"Talk to Dr. Ramirez," Vinnie said.

"Dr. Ramirez?"

Another elevator opened and Ramirez stepped out.

"I'm sorry," he said to me. "I was delayed."

"Hey, Doc, these folks wanna see Mr. Barracondi—"

"Yes, yes, it's all right," the doctor said. "They won't stay long."

"They say one of them will be staying all night."

Ramirez frowned.

"Is that right?"

"Vinnie," I said, "take Benny and Maria in to see...Uncle Dom."

"Oh, I'm afraid that won't be—" Ramirez started, but I cut him off.

"Doctor, do you know who you have in there?"

"Uh, Mr. Barracondi? Your uncle."

"Let me tell you a little about Dominick Barracondi," I said.

16

When I entered the room, Vinnie turned to look at me.

"All right?" he asked.

"The doctor now knows who he has here," I said. "He said 'oh, that Godfather.' He understands the need for Benny to stay. He also thinks that a bunch of mafia foot soldiers are gonna storm the hospital at any moment."

"Did he see *The Godfather*?" Vinnie asked.

"Yeah, he did," I said. "He also saw *Casino* this year. But I assured him that Uncle Dom is not Marlon Brando and Benny's not Al Pacino and there are no Joe Pesci's on the way. But I also convinced him that there was a need for Benny to stay, even if it was Benny's need."

"I wouldn't want to be the one to tell Benny he couldn't stay," Vinnie said.

"Me, neither," I said, "and the doctor doesn't want to be that man, either."

"What about the cop?"

"I think the doctor convinced him for us," I said. "Of course, when the detectives come back in the morning that'll change, but until then…"

"I talked to Maria about all of us going back to Pop's, and she agreed. She doesn't want to be alone tonight."

"Okay."

"There's somethin' else on your mind, isn't there, Nick?"

"Yeah, there is, Vin," I said, "but we'll talk about it later. I've got to talk to Benny. Why don't you take Maria out into the hall?"

"Okay."

Vinnie steered Maria out and I went to stand next to Benny.

"Ben."

"He don't look too good, Nicky," he said.

"The doctor says he'll be fine, barring complications."

"Don't they always say that?"

"Yeah," I said, "it kinda covers them. Look, you can stay tonight."

"Damn right, I'm stayin'!"

"No, I mean I got you permission," I said. "Don't get into it with the cop outside. If the Don wakes up it's his job to write down whatever he says. You gotta let him, you hear?"

"I hear ya, Nick."

"And if the detectives come back early and kick you out, don't argue," I said. "It won't do the Don any good for you to get yourself tossed in jail. Got it?"

"I got it," he said, "but what do I do then? If they kick me out?"

"Go back downstairs and wait for me," I said. "I'll be back in the morning."

"Okay."

"I'll bring you some breakfast."

"Thanks, Nick. Hey, about your dad—"

"It's okay, Benny," I said. "I know, okay?"

"Sure."

"I'll see you in the morning," I said. "And look, don't pull that gun unless you absolutely have to, okay?"

"I ain't stupid, Nick."

"I know that, Benny," I said. "Believe me, I know it."

I slapped him on his broad back, took one more look down at the Don—who was still hooked up to tubes and monitors—and then went out to grieve with my brother and sister.

Or whoever they were.

17

My Dad's house—the house I grew up in—was in Bensonhurst on Ovington Avenue, between Fourteenth and Fifteenth Streets. The thing I really enjoyed about my childhood—apart from my mother's cooking—was that we were walking distance from pizza, bagels and Chinese food.

As we entered the house Maria went into mother mode, which was good for her.

"I'll make coffee."

She went into the kitchen with the bag of bagels we had stopped to pick up around the corner at the 24-hour shop.

Vinnie and I stood for a moment in the hall. I knew we were both thinking the same thing: What do we do now?

Only I was wrong. That wasn't what Vinnie was thinking.

"What's wrong, Nick?"

"What do you mean?"

"Something happened tonight. Something other than Pop and Uncle Dom being shot. What is it?"

I peered down the hall to the kitchen, where Maria was keeping herself busy.

"Come into the living room."

He followed me there. I turned to him and kept my voice down.

"Did you know what your blood type was when they asked you?"

"Not really," Vinnie said. "I guess I should have but—"

"Never mind," I said. "Here's my point. The doctor told me my blood was the wrong type for Pop."

"Well," Vinnie said, "they had mine, and given what happened I guess it really didn't matter—"

"You don't understand," I said. "The doctor said there's no way I could be related to Pop."

"What?" Vinnie looked puzzled.

"We don't have the same father, Vin."

He stared at me with his mouth open, then said, "That can't be."

"That's what I said."

"It's gotta be a mistake, Nick."

"The doctor said he double-checked it."

Vinnie sat down heavily on the sofa. Maria startled the hell out of both of us by appearing and asking, "You guys want the bagels in here."

"Yeah, that's good," I said.

She nodded and went back to the kitchen.

I sat down on the sofa with Vinnie.

"What does this mean, Nick?"

"The doctor thought it meant I was adopted."

"Adopted? Why would you be adopted? Mom and Pop had Joe, then me. Why adopt you, and then have Maria?"

"Didn't make sense to me, either."

"Then what's the explanation?"

I hesitated, then said, "You won't like it."

"What?"

I shrugged. "Maybe Pop didn't know."

Vinnie stared at me for a few moments until the meaning of what I was suggesting set in.

"Oh, no...Mom?"

I shrugged again. "The doctor's got no reason to lie, Vin."

"I know, but...Mom? And somebody else?"

"I know," I said.

"I don't believe it," Vinnie said.

"Don't believe what?" Maria asked. She entered the room carrying a tray with coffee cups and a platter of bagels and butter.

I looked at Vinnie, who just stared back at me. How would Maria react to this after everything that had happened that night?

She walked to the coffee table and put the tray down on it.

"The coffee will be ready soon," she said. "What's goin' on? You don't believe what, Vinnie?"

Maria hadn't had an easy time of it for the past few years. She had gotten divorced, was on a hijacked plane, and had to live through—as we all did—the time that Father Vinnie was suspected of having an affair with a parishioner, and murder.

Now this. Pop was dead, and apparently, he wasn't my real father.

"Nick? Vinnie? What's goin' on?"

"Sit down, Maria."

She sat in one of the armchairs, staring at both of us warily.

"You guys are scarin' me," she said. "What could be as bad, or worse, than what happened to Pop?"

"Well," I said, "Apparently—the doctors were taking blood from Vinnie, and wanted to take some from me, except..."

"Except what?"

"I didn't match."

"Can that be?" she asked. "How could that be?"

"That's what we were wondering," Vinnie said.

"And...what's that mean?"

"Well..." I said. "According to the doctor...Pop wasn't my real father."

She stared at me for a few seconds, then buried her face in her hands and started crying.

18

Vinnie went to the kitchen to get the coffee. Maria had had enough. The news I'd just given her was the last straw, and she just dissolved. I crouched next to her while Vinnie went to the kitchen.

"Take it easy, Maria..." I said.

"I can't take it, Nick," she said. "Pop's dead, and now you're tryin' to tell me you're not...not my brother, anymore?"

"I'm always gonna be your brother," I assured her. "That's not gonna change."

"But...but what's this mean?"

"That's what Vinnie and I were tryin' to figure out."

I didn't tell her about the possibilities we'd come up with. No point in upsetting her even more.

Vinnie came in with the coffee pot, filled all our cups, and we took the time to butter our bagels and take bites. Never let it be said that an Italian family allowed adversity to effect its appetite.

Vinnie and I started to turn the subject away from the blood types. We talked about who would do what—make calls to family, talk to the funeral home, talk to the cops—me, of course—and so on.

"What about Uncle Dom?" Maria asked. "Who's gonna take care of him?"

"I guess that'll be Benny," I said.

"Benny?" Maria asked. "And who's gonna take care of *him*?"

We finished our bagels and coffee and I said to Vinnie, "How about a beer?"

He gave me a wry look and said, "I'm sure Pop has some in the refrigerator."

"I'll take this tray back into the kitchen," Maria said, "and get three beers."

"Three?"

"Sure," she said. "Why can't I have a beer with my...brothers?" She looked right at me when she said it, defiantly, then took the tray and left the room.

"She's gonna be okay," Vinnie said.

"Until the funeral."

"We just have to let her take care of us," Vinnie said. "That'll keep her busy."

"Yeah," I said, "us, and maybe Benny."

"That's a good idea," he said. "Make her feel really needed."

"I'll talk to Benny later."

"He'll be at the hospital."

"I know," I said. "He won't go home. I should bring him some fresh clothes."

"How will you know his size?" Vinnie asked.

"He's been the same size since high school," I said, holding my hands as far apart as I could. "Size Benny."

Vinnie laughed.

"He wasn't at the reunion, was he?"

"No," I said. "Man, the reunion, that seems years away, now."

And so did Mary Ann's death, and agreeing to look into it. Now I had my own death in the family to look into.

Maria came back with three bottles of Rolling Rock, the caps already removed.

"What are you gonna do, Nick?" she asked.

"Whataya mean?"

"I know you," she said, "and Father Vinnie knows you."

"She's right," Vinnie said. "We know you're not gonna take this laying down. You're not about to sit back and let the police handle this."

"What are your plans?" Maria asked.

"What makes you think I have any plans, yet?"

"Like she said, Nicky," Vinnie said. "We know you."

I took a swig from the cold green bottle in my hand and looked at both of them.

"Okay," I said. "First I have to go back to the hospital, talk to Benny and to the Don. After that I'm gonna have to talk to the Homicide dicks. Weinstock is still assigned there. We get along."

"Then what?" Maria asked. "Will they work with you?"

"Oh, no," I said, "they'll warn me off. Threaten me. Blah-blah-blah."

"But you said you got along with them," Maria said.

"That doesn't mean they'll want me in their business."

"But...this is our business. Family business."

"You're right, Maria, it is."

"I don't know…" Vinnie said.

Maria and I both looked at him.

"Pop's dead, Vinnie," I said. "That makes it our business."

"But this is what the police do."

"Don't forget," I told him, "it's what I do, too."

He took a sip of his beer and looked dubious.

"Okay," he said, "what else?"

"I'll have to go to Sheepshead Bay and ask questions," I said. "See if anyone saw anything."

"Can I come and help?" Maria asked.

"Oh," I said, "oh, no, Maria. You and Vinnie will have to stay out of it."

"But…you just said it's family business."

"Yeah, but I'll handle it," I said. "We're dealing with people with guns, who aren't afraid to use them. You and Vinnie have to just stay out of it. Besides, it'll be up to the two of you to plan Pop's funeral."

I looked at Vinnie and jerked my head, hoping he'd get the message and leave me alone with Maria.

"Be right back," he said. putting down his beer bottle. "Stuff goes right through me."

As he left the room I moved closer to Maria.

"Listen," I said, "I'm gonna need your help, after all."

"Good," she said. "What can I do?"

"I need you to take care of Vinnie," I said.

"But…he's a priest."

"I know," I said. "That means everyone will expect him to take care of everything. And like you said about Benny, who'll take care of Vinnie? He's gonna need you, Maria."

"Okay, yeah," she said. "I understand."

"You and Vinnie will have to notify the rest of the family, such as they are."

"Oh," she said, "right. uncles, aunts, cousins…"

There were a lot of them, but we hadn't seen them in some time. Still, they deserved to know.

"And then there's Benny," I continued, "like you said, he'll need somebody to talk to."

"But he has you."

"That's true, but he may need you, too."

"I can't imagine Benny needing a woman," she said, "I mean, other than… you know…"

"I know." Most of Benny's relationships with women had been professional.

When he needed companionship, he called a whore.

"Isn't Benny gonna want to help you investigate?" she asked.

"I'm sure he will, and I'll let him," I said. "I'm gonna need his contacts to get me to the other families."

We were talking about different family, now.

"God," she said, shaking her head, "this is gonna get all Mario Puzo on us, isn't it?"

I hugged her and said, "I'm afraid it is."

19

I decided to go home to get myself ready to look into the shooting. Vinnie and Maria were going to spend the rest of the day at my father's house, calling family. I walked past my office door to enter through the other one. As I walked in, my foot encountered something on the floor. A 3x5 envelope. I picked it up and unfolded the note inside.

"Where have you been?" it asked. Signed SAM.

Jesus, I'd forgotten to tell Sam what happened with my dad and the Don. Normally I would have banged on her door when something unusual happened. She was pretty much the only person I talked to other than my brother the Father. I didn't have drinking buddies.

She was going to be pissed!

I decided to get it over with. I went across the hall and knocked on her door. It was late afternoon, but I knew she'd be up.

"There you are!" she said, as she opened her door. She had her straw colored hair pulled back in a ponytail, which she only did when she was working. She was wearing a tank top that was stretched tight across her breasts, and short shorts. She never went out on the street like that, but in the privacy of her own home I was surprised she didn't go naked most of the time. Actually, I was glad she didn't. I'd be across the hall thinking about it all the time.

"Where have you been? I've been waitin' for you."

"Come across the hall," I said, "and I'll tell you."

She stared at my face. "Nick? What happened?"

She followed me into my apartment, closed the door behind her, then turned, a serious look on her face.

"Nick?"

"My dad's dead."

"What?"

"He was shot to death yesterday."

"Omigod!"

She grabbed me immediately and pulled me close. I buried my face in her neck and almost cried. I breathed her in, comforted by her scent, and her touch.

"I'm so sorry!" she said, rubbing my back.

We stood like that for a while, then stepped apart with no hint of awkwardness. There was always sexual tension between us, but at the end of the day we were friends.

"God, you've been up all night, haven't you?" she asked.

"Yeah, I have. I just came from my father's house, left Vinnie and Maria there."

"Nick, what happened?"

"Sit down, Sam," I said. "I just need to get some coffee first."

"I'll make it" she said. "You sit down and relax, because if I know you, you've got all sorts of reasons why you shouldn't go right to bed now and get a few hours' sleep."

Yeah, she knew me.

I sat on the sofa and Sam had to wake me up to hand me a mug of coffee.

"How long was I asleep?"

"Five minutes."

She sat next to me on the sofa, also holding a mug of coffee.

"Okay," she said, "tell me."

I told her everything that had happened, saving the part about the blood tests. As far as I was concerned that was completely separate from the shooting, and would have to spend some time on the back burner.

"Oh, my God," she said. "What can you do about it, Nick. You've got to leave this to the police."

"The police can't go where I can go, Sam," I said. "They don't know the people I know."

"That may be, but this is the Mafia, Nick."

"Sam, they're not as scary as they make out in the movies," I said, then added to myself, well, not anymore.

"Scary enough to shoot down two men in broad daylight," she said. "Besides, isn't it obvious who did it? And who they were after?"

"Whoever did it," I said, "and whoever they were after, they still managed to kill my dad. I'm not gonna walk away from that."

"That's your ego talking, Nick."

"Maybe," I said. "Maybe it is." I put the coffee mug down and rubbed my face vigorously with both hands.

"I'm gonna take a shower, see if that wakes me up," I said.

"Sure," she said. "I'll wait here."

I went into the bathroom, got undressed and under the shower. I meant for it to be quick, because to tell you the truth, I hate showers.

20

"Jesus," Sam said, when I came walking out dressed in sweats, "were you in there two minutes?"

"Just long enough."

"If your hair wasn't wet..."

"You want a beer?" I asked.

"Sure."

I went to the kitchen, came back with two bottles of Brooklyn Brown Ale for me and an India Pale Ale for her. Both came from the Brooklyn Brewery.

"What else is going on, Nick?"

"Whataya mean?"

"I mean we've been neighbors and friends for a few years," she said. "I know when something's bothering you."

"You don't think what I've told you is enough?"

"It's plenty," she said, "but there's more, isn't there?"

I sipped my beer and asked, "What are you, a witch?"

"When it comes to you, yeah."

"Okay," I said, "sit down for this one."

We sat, and I told her about the blood tests.

"And you believe this?" she asked.

"What's not to believe?" I asked. "What reason would the doctor have to lie? He double-checked the results."

"I still think you should get a second opinion," she said.

"Yeah, well, you're probably right," I said, "but I don't think it's as important as finding out who killed him."

"You know," she said, "he's the man who raised you. No matter what happens, he was your father."

"Yeah," I said, "but if it's true, what does it say about my mother?"

She stared at me for a minute, then said, "Oh."

"Yeah, right."

"Have you told your brother and sister?"

"I told them."

"How'd they take it?"

"Vinnie was okay," I said. "Maria didn't take it well, but she's all right. I've given her some things to keep her busy."

"That's good."

"She and Vinnie are notifying the rest of the family."

"Are there a lot?"

"It's an Italian family," I said. "We have so many relatives we think it's okay not to be talking to half of them. But they'll all have to be notified."

"What about…Don Barracondi?"

"Benny will notify whoever needs to be."

"I'm not up on my Mafia etiquette," she said. "He's retired, right? So does this start some kind of war?"

"I'm not sure," I said. "I'm sure along the way someone will tell me, though."

"Isn't this gonna be dangerous?" she asked. "I mean, getting involved in their business."

"This is my family business, Sam," I said. "If anyone will understand that, they will."

"I guess so."

I finished my beer and asked, "Want another one?"

"No," she said. "In fact, I'll take this one with me back to my apartment. I've still got three chapters to write."

"I'm sorry I interrupted your work," I said.

"Don't be dumb," she said. "I wish you'd told me yesterday. I could've been at the hospital with you."

And I knew she would have been, too.

I walked her to the door and she kissed me on the cheek.

"Let me know if I can do anything," she said. "You know, help with the funeral, or at the house? Whatever."

"I will, Sam," I said. "Thanks."

I closed my door behind her, heard her door open and close. I got myself another beer and took it to my office.

The message machine was like a Christmas tree. There were several calls from Tony Mitts, a couple from Catherine, and one from Catherine's mother. There were still some old ones from a frantic Benny. I deleted them all. I was going to have to let them know I couldn't work on Mary Ann's death, not today.

I had other things to do.

I changed out of my sweats into jeans and a T-shirt and a pair of Rockports. Before leaving the office I put my gun back in the safe. I was going to be talking to the Homicide boys, probably in their office. Not a good idea to wear a gun into the police station.

But first, I had to go back to the hospital.

21

I stopped off at a Duane Reade and a big man's shop so I could bring Benny a change of clothes and some other stuff he'd need to clean up—toothpaste, deodorant, a comb.

"Thanks, Nicky," he said, when I handed him the bags.

The cop outside the door didn't know me, but apparently had my name on a list, because he allowed me to enter the Don's room.

"How is he?"

"He opened his eyes a few times," Benny said. "I think he's just checkin' ta see if I'm here, because he just nods at me and goes back to sleep."

"Probably give you hell if you weren't here."

"Yeah, don't I know it."

"Doctor been in?"

"This mornin'," Benny said.

"What'd he say?"

"That I should go home and get some rest."

"He's probably right."

"You don't look like you got no rest."

"No, I didn't. Why don't you go into the bathroom and get changed."

"Yeah, okay."

"And I got some cologne, too," I called after him as he closed the door.

Alone with the Don I started down at him. He was pale as a ghost, but his chest seemed to be rising and falling evenly. The machine he was hooked up to was scrolling numbers and an uneven line kept beeping along.

I didn't realize I had my hand on the bed until I suddenly felt his hand close around my wrist. When I looked down he was staring up at me.

"Hey," I said, "you're okay."

He reached with a hand that looked more like a claw and dragged the oxygen mask away from his mouth.

"Vito," he said, "Vito…"

"He's dead, Godfather," I said. "Pop's dead."

He closed his eyes for a moment, then opened them, looked at me and said, "*Mea culpa…Mea culpa…*"

"No," I said, putting the oxygen mask back in place, "it's not your fault. It's the fault of whoever shot you, or whoever sent the shooters. Do you know who that was?"

He didn't answer.

"Just shake your head or nod, Godfather," I said. "Do you know who shot you and killed Pop?"

His eyes closed, and didn't reopen. But his chest was still moving up and down, so I knew he'd simply fallen asleep.

Benny came out of the bathroom with a clean shirt, combed hair and too much of the cologne I'd bought him splashed on. He was still wearing the same pants and shoes, of course. He obviously had his dirty laundry in the plastic Duane Reade bag.

"Did he wake up?"

"For a minute."

"What did he say?"

"He said Pop's name, and then he said it was his fault Pop's dead."

"It ain't his fault, Nicky."

"I know, Benny," I said. "I told him that."

"Good," Benny said. "It's important to him that you don't blame him."

"Have you and he talked?"

"Briefly," Benny said. "He ain't made much sense—not as much as he just made to you, anyway."

"Have the Homicide guys been here?"

"This mornin'," Benny said.

"Give you a hard time?"

"Yeah," Benny said. "They took my gun, Nick. I could use another one."

"I'll look into it," I said. "I left mine home for just that reason. I didn't want them taking it off me when I go see them."

"You gonna do that next?"

"Yeah, and then I'm goin' to Sheepshead Bay to have a look around."

Benny nodded, looked down at Nicky Barracuda.

"Benny," I said, "do we know who to trust?"

He looked at me sadly and said, "Not really, Nick. I mean, there's one or two guys I could tell you to depend on, but nobody who knows anything." He looked down at the Don again. "This coulda been ordered by anybody."

"Is there a power struggle goin' on?" I asked.

Benny shrugged. "The Don's retired, Nick."

"Come on, Benny," I said. "If there's a fight for power and he put his name behind somebody, it would mean somethin'."

"In the old days, maybe," Benny said. "Not so much now, Nick."

I frowned, looked down at the old man in the bed. If that was true, then who'd have reason to try and kill him?

22

The offices of the Brooklyn South Homicide Squad were in the Sixty-Seventh Precinct, on the second floor. I'd been there before, could have ducked into a staircase or elevator and gone up, but I decided to stop at the front desk and let them announce me.

"Delvecchio?" the salt-and-pepper haired sergeant asked.

"That's right."

"You a cop?"

"Used to be," I said. "Now I'm private."

"And who do you wanna see?"

"Detective Weinstock, Homicide."

"Hold on."

I didn't know if Weinstock would be catching this case, but he was the one I knew up there—actually, he was the one I knew would *talk* to me.

The sergeant got on the phone, said a few words, listened, then hung up.

"You know the way?" he asked.

"Unless you moved it."

"Naw," he said, "same place. Go ahead."

"Thanks, Sarge."

I took the stairs rather than wait for the elevator for one floor. When I entered the squad room I got some strange looks from the detectives but I walked through like I belonged there.

At the end of a row of desks sat Detective Weinstock. He was my age, seemed to give me more respect than most cops did. That included his asshole partner, Vito Matucci, who I knew from my seven years on the job.

Weinstock saw me coming, while Matucci had his back to me. He was echoing Matucci's sentiments and bitchin' about the Mets being twenty games out, even though they were in second place.

"Nick," Weinstock said, by way of greeting. "Sorry about your dad."

Matucci—who shared my father's first name—turned to look at me and said, grudgingly, "Yeah, sorry."

"Thanks, Vito," I said to Matucci. I looked at Weinstock. "You guys catch this?"

"No," Weinstock said, "we didn't. The whole case—your dad, Nicky Barracuda—is being handled by Sergeant Hicks and Detective Del Costa."

"I don't know them."

"They don't know you, either," Weinstock said. "I don't know if that's gonna work for you or against you, Nick."

"Why a sergeant?" I asked. "They don't usually catch cases."

"Because it's the Don," Matucci said.

"Is Hicks around? Or Del Costa?"

"Both," Weinstock said. "You want me to introduce you?"

"I'd appreciate it."

"I don't know if that'll help, either," Weinstock said. "He's not too fond of Jews." Weinstock pointed to himself.

"Or Italians," Matucci said.

"How's he feel about Mexicans?" I asked.

"He lumps us all in together," Weinstock said, standing up. "This guy's a pip, Nick. A throwback. I'd tell you to watch you p's and q's, but I know you too well for that. Come on."

Once again I walked the length of the squad room, but this time I was walking with Weinstock, so nobody paid me any mind.

As we approached a desk I saw the name plate with "Sgt. Andrew Hicks" written on it.

"Sarge, this is Nick Delvecchio," Weinstock said. "It was his dad who was killed yesterday in that Sheepshead Bay shooting."

Hicks looked up at Weinstock, then at me, with no expression. He had a bloated, drinker's face, making him look fifty when he was probably forty.

"Have a seat," he said to me.

I pulled over a chair.

"You can go back to your desk, Detective," Hicks said to Weinstock.

"I thought I'd sit in—" Weinstock said.

"I don't think so," Hicks said. "I'm sure you got your own case load."

Weinstock stood there a moment, then turned and walked back to his desk. I noticed all the other detectives in the room studiously avoided watching him.

"Mr. Delvecchio," Hicks said, "needless to say we're very sorry about your father—"

"Thank you."

"—personally, it woulda been no skin off my nose if Nick Barracuda had bought it instead."

"You'd have to investigate either way, though, right?" I asked.

"That's right," he said, "I would. And the outcome will probably be the same. I'll catch the bastards and they'll go down for murder."

"I'm glad to hear it," I said. "You mind me asking what you've got so far?"

Hicks sat back in his chair and took a long look at me.

"Look, I understand you used to be on the job, now you're private. I'm not obligated to fill you in on my investigation."

"No, you're not," I said. "I understand that."

"Good."

"I'm just here as a courtesy," I said. "First, to keep you from having to look for me and second, to arrange some sort of quid pro quo."

"Quid pro quo," Hicks said. "That means you're gonna be doin' some investigatin' of your own? On an active police investigation? That's a good way to risk losin' your license, you know."

"I'm aware of that," I said. "I didn't say I was going to investigate, but I might hear somethin' useful."

"Which you would naturally turn over to me, because you wanna see your father's killer caught. I don't see any quid pro quo in that, Mr. Delvecchio."

He had a point. I did want my father's killer caught, and if I heard anything at all I'd turn it over to him, even though I'd work the info myself. That didn't obligate him to me, at all. And he was also right that I would be putting my license at risk by working an active homicide case.

"Well then," I said, starting to stand, "I guess we don't have anything—"

"Hold on," Hicks said. "We do have some questions for you before you leave, if you don't mind."

I sat back in the chair.

"I don't mind."

"This is Detective Del Costa," he said, looking at somebody behind me. "We're workin' this case together."

I smelled her before I saw her. When I turned my head and saw the woman behind me I immediately stood up. She had thick black hair, dark eyebrows, red lipstick, tailored jacket and pants that did nothing to hide the fact that God had blessed her. I put her at about thirty-five.

"Angie," Hicks said, "this is Nick Delvecchio. It was his father who was killed in the Sheepshead Bay killin'."

"I'm sorry for your loss," she said, holding my eyes.

"Thanks."

"He was kind enough to come in so we wouldn't hafta go lookin' for him. Do a quick interview, will ya? Get what you can?"

"Sure, Sarge. Would you come this way to my desk, please?"

"Sure."

"Thanks for comin' in, Delvecchio," Hicks said.

I followed her to her desk, initially eyeing her from behind like any man would do, until I noticed that—once again—all the other men in the room were making a concerted effort not to watch her.

23

Detective Angie Del Costa was a looker, and nobody was looking. It was odd, unless she and the sergeant had something going and everybody knew it. Most women in the department had to deal with that kind of unfair supposition, but I'm a firm believer that where there's smoke there's fire. In some cases, it had to be more than just supposition. Maybe this was one of them.

I risked a look over at Weinstock, who I thought was trying to send me some kind of message with a look. Unfortunately, I couldn't figure it out at that moment.

I ignored the fact that Detective Del Costa was a good-looking woman and treated her like just another detective.

She asked me a series of questions about my dad. What did he do for a living? Did he have any enemies? Did he associate with Nick Barracuda on a regular basis?

I said he was a longshoreman for years, he was retired, and yes.

"Did he do anything else?" she asked. "I mean, other than working the docks?"

"For a long time he was a union rep."

"Ah." She furiously made a note.

"Detective, you are acting on the assumption that Nicky Barracuda was the target, aren't you?"

She looked at me and smiled. One of her front teeth had a smear of red lipstick on it.

"We're looking at every option, Mr. Delvecchio."

"You're not from Brooklyn," I said.

"No," she said, "I'm not originally from New York. I'm from Connecticut."

"There's no chance my dad was the target, here," I told her.

"As I said, sir, we're looking at every option."

She asked if I had seen my father yesterday, before he went to Sheepshead Bay for lunch? Had I spoken to him? Had I spoken to Mr. Barracondi lately?

I said no, no, and no.

I noticed during the interview that Weinstock got up and left the squad room. By the time Del Costa was done with me he hadn't come back.

"Okay, Mr. Delvecchio," she said, handing me an embossed business card, "if you hear anything useful we'd appreciate a call."

"Sure," I said, taking the card.

I ceased to exist for her, then, so I stood up and left.

I found Weinstock waiting for me outside the building.

"Just a word to the wise," he said. "Del Costa is Hicks's private stock."

"What's that mean, exactly?"

"Protégé, punchboard, whatever you want it to mean."

"You know this for a fact?"

"Yep," he said. "Word is she got tired of fighting her way to the top."

"So she decided to sleep her way?" I asked. "With a sergeant?"

"Hicks knows where a lot of bodies are buried," Weinstock said. "And he likes being a sergeant."

"So he's a user."

"Don't kid yourself," Weinstock said. "So is she."

"You sayin' they deserve each other."

"I'm saying watch your step. I saw you watching her step."

"I'm not lookin' to get laid, Weinstock," I said. "I'm lookin' for my dad's killer."

"Well, just watch yourself around those two."

"What's your lieutenant got to say about all this?"

He laughed and said, "Wake me when it's time for my pension," and went back inside.

24

Sheepshead Bay was next. Fishing boats, restaurants, diners, a few shops here and there.

What confused me was why were Nicky Barracuda and my father eating at Rizzo's—at a sidewalk table while the Don owned a restaurant called On The Barge, and usually ate his meals at his own place.

Both the Barge and Rizzo's were on the Bay's main drag, Emmons Avenue, but on opposite sides of the street, and several blocks apart.

I went to Rizzo's, which was serving lunch. The shooting must have made a mess of the windows, but they had already been replaced. Business must go on. I went inside and was approached by a maître d'.

"One, sir?"

"I'm not here to eat," I said. "I have some questions about the shooting yesterday." I figured let him think I was either a cop or a hood. Either one worked for me. "Were you working yesterday?"

"Oh, yes, sir."

"So you were here during the shooting?"

"Such a terrible tragedy," he said. "Those poor men."

"What's your name?"

"Salvatore."

"Did you know the two men?"

"No, sir."

Salvatore was sweating. His bald head was gleaming with it, and one drop ran down from his temple to his cheek. It was hot for spring, but not that hot.

"Come on, Sal," I said. "You know who one of them was. I know you do."

"Sir..." he said, nervously, "I'm not lookin' for any trouble."
"Are you the owner?"
"No, sir."
"Is he here?"
"He's in his office."
"Was he here yesterday, when the shooting took place?" I asked.
"No, sir."
"Okay, stop calling me 'sir,'" I said.
"Yes, s—"
"I'm not a cop," I said.
"I didn't think you were."
Oh, I got it.
"I'm not a wise guy, either," I said. "Look, let's go inside so you can relax. I only have a few questions."
"I don't understand," he said, "if you're not a cop and you're not..."
"One of the men who was shot was my father," I said. "He died."
"Oh..."
"Inside, Sal."

We went inside where it was cooler. It was not a heavy lunch crowd. I directed him to the bar and called the bartender over.

"Get Sal some cold water, please."
"Something for you, sir?" the bartender asked.
"No—yeah, bring me a Peroni."
"Yes, sir."
"Now Sal," I said, "you know very well who one of the men was."
"Yes, s—yes," he said. "Mr. Barracondi. We were very surprised to see him here."
"Why's that?"
"Because he always eats at his own restaurant."
"Good," I said, "you know that much. Now, tell me what you saw."

The bartender came over with his water, and my bottle of beer. Sal drank half the water down. I sipped the beer.

"I didn't see anything. I was inside when the windows shattered. I didn't even know there was shooting until later."
"Did you go outside at all?"
He looked embarrassed.
"I ducked behind the bar and stayed there until the police came."
Great.
"What about their waiter?"
"That was Frankie."
"And where's Frankie right now?"

"H-he didn't come in today."

"Did he call in sick?"

"No, he just didn't show up."

"Did he talk to the police yesterday?"

"Yeah," Sal said. "We all did."

"Then I'm gonna need Frankie's address."

"Excuse me, but if you're not the police…"

"I'm a private investigator," I said. "The man killed was my father. I need that address. I can pay you for it, or I can threaten you."

"Just a minute."

He left me at the bar for ten minutes, but instead of reappearing, another man came over to me.

"Mr. Delvecchio?"

"Yes?"

"My name is Rizzo, Joseph Rizzo. Would you be kind enough to come unto my office?"

"Can you help me?" I asked. "I assume Sal told you what I'm looking for."

"Yes, of course," Rizzo said. He was slick, but with hair gel, not sweat. "Please?"

"Lead the way."

I followed his wide back, tailored suit and bald spot, taking my beer with me. He led me into the back to an office, closing the door after we entered.

"Have a seat, Mr. Delvecchio," he said. He sat behind his desk. He picked up an index card from his desk top. In fact, other than a lamp it was the only thing on his desk. There was a computer on another table next to him.

"I have here the address you're looking for," he said. "Our waiter, Frankie?"

"Frankie who?"

"Frankie…" he frowned at the card. "…DiGuardi."

"And how much is it gonna cost me?"

"Not a thing. Well, not money."

"What, then?"

He sat forward.

"All I want you to do," he said, "is tell Nicky Barracuda that Joey Rizzo was…helpful to you in a time of need."

"That's it?"

"That's it." He sat back.

"I can do that."

He smiled, and handed me the card.

"And the beer's on the house," he said, as I went out the door.

25

Frankie the waiter lived in the basement of a two-family house in Marine Park, which was only about a fifteen-minute ride to work for him.

I parked a few doors down from Frankie's address and walked back. I went through a freshly painted wrought-iron gate and down four concrete steps to the doorway that was beneath the front steps of the house. This time of day the block was quiet, no kids at play because they were still in school. I passed one young mother pushing a baby carriage, but she didn't pay any attention to me. She only had eyes for her little angel, who was screaming his or her lungs out.

I rang the doorbell and waited. There was one window that I could see, but it had an air-conditioner in it, so I couldn't see into the basement apartment.

I rang the doorbell a second time, then opened the screen door and knocked on a wooden door that had no peephole in it.

With a bad feeling I tried the doorknob. It turned. The door was unlocked. Since the police had already spoken with Frankie at the scene the day before, there would have been no reason for them to come and talk to him today.

"Crap," I said. Anybody who watched TV or movies would know I was gonna find a body inside. I knew it. I also knew I should probably call the police, but I decided to make sure first.

"Crapcrapcrap," I muttered, and opened the door.

When I stepped inside I was immediately chilled. The air-conditioner in the window must have been set on high, because it was freezing.

"Hello?" I called. "Frankie?"

No answer.

"Come on, man," I pleaded, "don't be dead."

Nothing.

There was a second door, but it was already wide open. I stepped through into the basement apartment. It looked like it had been partitioned off into three rooms, shotgun style. I was in the living room with a sofa and some bookshelves, but not much else. No sign of Frankie there. There were some posters on the wall, one of lady bodybuilding champion Cory Everson. Another was a poster of New York Yankee great Don Mattingly, who was probably playing his last season due to back problems.

I could see through to the small kitchen.

It was the room in between I was concerned with. I took four steps across the room, spotted the single bed against the wall and the body on it, tangled in the sheets.

He hadn't been dead long or I would have smelled him, or the blood, when I came in. He was lying face down on the bed, a single bullet hole in the back of his head. Maybe somebody who dealt with gunshot deaths more than I had would have smelled the residue in the air from the gunpowder. Or felt the body and figured out how long he'd been dead. Standing this close to him I could smell the blood, but the rest was beyond me.

Obviously, Frankie knew something that had gotten him killed. He either saw something yesterday, or he'd been involved from the start. Maybe he'd made a phone call when Pop and the Barracuda first sat down.

I did a quick search of the apartment, knowing I wouldn't find anything. The shooter must have removed anything incriminating. He was good at his job.

Now I had to get myself out of there without being seen.

There was a bathroom, and next to it another door. I opened it and found myself in a boiler room that led to a back door. I used my shirt tail and wiped off anything I might have touched, then pulled the apartment door closed behind me.

I went out the building's back door, found myself in a backyard, climbed a couple of fences and came out on a street around the corner. I got back to my car and drove away. I prayed there were no busybodies peering out their windows, taking down license numbers. Hoped I hadn't contaminated the crime scene.

Either thing would leave me a lot of 'splainin' to do.

26

I had a decision to make: Place an anonymous call to the cops, or let somebody else find the body.

By the time I got to the hospital I'd decided not to make a call. I parked, went inside and took the elevator to the Don's floor. When I came out I could see down the hall that there was still a cop on the door. Once again I had to identify myself to be let in. The guard studied me for a long minute and I wondered if I'd gotten blood on my nose or something. My heart started to pound, and then he let me pass.

Benny turned and looked. I could see the tension in his face and body, but he relaxed when he saw me.

"You react that way every time somebody comes in?" I asked.

"Yeah," he said. "The Don's life is in my hands."

"Must scare the hell out of the nurses."

He shrugged his massive shoulders.

"How is he?" I said.

"In and out."

"Say anything?"

"No."

"The detectives been by?"

"Yeah, some sergeant named Hicks and a hot-lookin' lady detective." He frowned for a moment, then said, "I think he's doin' her."

"So the Don hasn't made a statement to anybody yet?"

"No. Where you been?"

"Sheepshead Bay."

"Find out anythin'?"

I turned and looked at the door, lowered my voice, and told him about Frankie the waiter.

"You call the cops?"

"No," I said. "I'm gonna let somebody else find the body."

"That's cool. Better to stay out of it. You talk to Joey Rizzo?" he asked.

"Yeah. He gave me the address."

"What'd he want for it?"

"Nothin', except for me to put a good word in for him with the Don."

"That figures."

"Rizzo connected?"

"No. He just runs a restaurant. He ain't a wise guy, no matter how much he wants ta be."

"Tell me somethin', Benny," I said. "Why were the Don and Pop eatin' at Rizzo's and not on the Barge?"

"I don't know," Benny said with a shrug. "The Don just told me he was goin' to Rizzo's to meet your dad."

"To meet?" I asked. "So they didn't go there together?"

"No. Me and the Don walked. Your dad was already there."

"How did he get there?"

"I don't know. I figured he drove."

"No, he doesn't—didn't—have a license, anymore. He had cataracts."

"Can't they fix that, these days?"

"He wouldn't go for the operation," I said. "Stubborn. Said he didn't trust doctors to go pokin' around in his eyes."

"I can understand that," Benny said, looking around the room. "I don't like doctors or hospitals, myself."

"Why did you and the Don walk? Doesn't he still have a driver?"

"Yeah, but he said it was a nice day and he wanted to walk."

"So anybody could've taken a shot at him during the walk," I said.

"The shooters might have been watchin' the restaurant," Benny suggested.

"How would they know he was gonna be there? Did he make a reservation?" We were speaking in the plural, even though we didn't know if there had been more than one shooter.

"No, no reservation."

"I figure the dead waiter must've fingered him," I said.

"But why?"

"Why else? Money."

"That would mean the word went out on the hit," Benny said. "Money was offered for somebody to finger the Don." Benny was getting mad.

"Can you find out about that?"

"I can try," he said. "Nobody's gonna tell me they was willin' to finger the Don. They know I'd kill 'em. But somebody might talk and give somebody else up. Unless they're too scared to."

"You're right," I said. "We need somebody else to do the asking."

"Lemme give it some thought."

I nodded.

"You sure nobody saw you at the waiter's place?" he asked.

"As sure as I can be," I said. "I didn't see anybody, so I'm hopin' the vice is versa."

"Huh?"

"I hope nobody saw me."

"Oh."

"Have you eaten today?"

"No," Benny said. "I ain't left this room."

"I'll go get you somethin'," I said.

He grabbed my arm as I turned.

"Nicky, not from the cafeteria," he said, almost pleadingly.

"Okay. Burger King?" I asked. "I saw one down the street."

"That's good. A whopper. With fries, and a large coke. Oh, and a shake."

"What flavor?"

He looked at me like I was crazy and said, "Chocolate."

"And do you want the burger your way or theirs?" I asked.

27

I came back with a Whopper and fries for Benny, and a chicken sandwich and fries for me. I had asked the cop on the door if he wanted anything, so I brought him a Whopper meal, too.

Benny and I sat on either side of the Don's bed and ate. A nurse came in at one point, a young one. She steered away from Benny, giving him a frightened look, and came around to my side of the bed to check on the Don's readings.

"Fry?" I asked, offering the box.

She giggled, took two and ate them.

"Don't tell anyone," she said.

"I won't."

"Neither will I," Benny said.

She looked at him, gave him a tentative smile, said, "Thanks," and left.

"She won't be so scared of you now," I said.

Around a mouthful of fries he asked, "She's scared of me?"

"Most people are, Benny."

Before he could say anything the Don moaned, moved his head, then reached for the oxygen mask.

"Hey, don't—" Benny said, but the old man was determined.

"W-when..." he managed.

"Yesterday," I told him.

He looked at me, then back at Benny, then almost smiled. "My boys." Then Benny put the mask back over the Don's nose and mouth.

"That's all he does," Benny told me. "In and out."

"How many bullets hit him?"

"Three."

"They said four hit my dad," I said. "It was either a car full of guys with guns..."

"...or one guy with a machine gun."

"The cops know and aren't telling us," I said.

"That Hicks is an asshole."

"Give you a hard time?"

"He tried."

"What about the woman? Del Costa?"

"Didn't say much," he said. "I think she only talks when he says somethin' to her, or gives her the okay. She could be a hot piece of ass if she dressed different. What's she doin' with him?"

"Makin' a career move, I've been told."

"Some career."

I put my Burger King garbage in the bag and dropped it in the trash. Benny did the same.

"I better get movin'," I said.

"Where ya goin' next?"

"That depends on you," I said. "Give me a name. Somebody who's got their ear to the ground and isn't afraid to talk about what he hears."

He thought a minute, and then said, "There's a guy named Winky Manzo."

"Winky?"

"Yeah, don't worry about that. If there's word on the street, this guy'll know it."

"Where do I find him?"

"You'll have to let him find you."

"And how do I do that?"

"I got a couple of places you can go and say you're lookin' for him," he said. "After that you'll just hafta wait."

"How long, Benny?" I asked. "I don't want this trail goin' cold."

"Don't worry," he said. "He'll get back to ya. Meantime, ain't there somethin' else you can do?"

Actually, there was.

28

I went back to my office. Sam must have heard my door close because just moments later she entered. When I'm at my desk I don't keep the office door locked.

"You okay?" she asked, sticking her head in.

"I'm fine," I said, then added, "for now."

She entered, closed the door behind her.

"How's your, uh, uncle?"

"The same," I said. "Hasn't fully woke up, yet, so the cops haven't gotten a statement from him. Neither have I."

"Have you found out anything?"

I decided not to let her in on the dead waiter.

"Not much. I'm waitin' for some calls."

"What are you going to do while you wait?" she asked.

"Actually, I'm also gonna make some calls. I've got to find out how my dad got to the restaurant."

"His cataracts wouldn't let him drive," she said.

"You've got a good memory. That's right, so I've got to find a car service that took him. That means callin' all the ones who serve that area."

"You need my phone?"

"No, I have two lines here."

"How about something to eat?"

"I just had some Burger King with Benny."

She made a face.

"If you're still here at dinner time I'll make something."

"That'd be great."

"Nick, can you give me a phone number for your brother and your sister. I'd like to give them my condolences."

"Sure." I wrote down a bunch of numbers. "Try my dad's number first. They might still be there."

"Thanks. I'll see you later."

"Thanks, Sam."

As she left I looked at my message machine. It was blinking convulsively. I pressed play.

First one was from Tony Mitts: "Nick, I ain't heard from you. What's goin' on?"

Second from Mary Ann's mother: "Nick, I just heard about your father. I'm so sorry. Listen, you don't have to continue looking into Mary Ann's death. Y-you have enough to worry about. I'll understand."

Third was my sister, Maria: "Nick? We're still at Pop's. Call us and let us know you're okay."

Tony again: "Aw, jeez, Nick, I just heard. I'm really sorry...but d'ya think you can still work on Mary Ann's death? I know, I sound like an asshole, but...aw, jeez—" Click.

Then Benny: "I put the word out to Winky, Nick. Give him a chance to call ya, then go and check out those places I todja about. The Don's okay, he's breathin' good."

Finally, one from an anonymous voice: "Delvecchio, I might have somethin' for ya about Nicky Barracuda's shootin'. I'll call ya again, but we gotta meet if you want my info. And it won't be free."

If that had been Benny's guy, Winky, he would've said so. That meant somebody out there thought he had something to sell. I'd have to wait and see.

I called Maria, caught her and Father Vinnie at my dad's. I told her I was okay and that I was working on the shooting.

"Don't do anything stupid, Nicky. You hear me?" she said.

"I hear you, Maria," I said. "Nothin' stupid. I promise."

I hung up, pulled out a Yellow Pages and started looking up car services.

A couple of hours later I closed the phone book. I'd run out of companies to call. None had made a pickup at Pop's address. It was too far for him to walk to Sheepshead Bay. That left two possibilities.

He took the bus.

Or somebody picked him up and drove him there.

***

"Delvecchio?"

"That's me."

I was about to check with Sam on her promise to cook when the phone rang. It was the same anonymous voice.

"You investigatin' the shootin' of Nicky Barracuda?" he asked.

"How would you know that?" I asked.

"I asked around. I got some info for ya."

"Why don't you give it to the cops?"

"I don't talk to no scumbag cops."

"And they wouldn't pay you."

"You got that right."

"Well, I've got to tell you I don't have much money. I'm just a hard workin' P.I."

"Yeah, but you can get it."

"What makes you think that?"

"Because you and the Don, you gotta—whatayacallit—a bond."

"Who've you been talkin' to?" I asked.

"Look, if ya don't want the info it's no skin offa my nose. I'm just tryin' to make a few bucks, here. And help you out at the same time."

"Okay, okay," I said, "when can we meet?"

"Can you get the money by tonight?"

"How much are we talkin' about?"

"Five G's oughtta do it."

I was suspicious. Five thousand dollars did not seem like enough for somebody who was trying to squeeze me.

"I'll get it," I said. "Where do we meet?"

"I'll call ya tonight around nine," he said. "If you got the money, I'll tell ya where ta meet me."

That gave me a few hours to come up with the five grand.

"Okay," I said. "I'll wait for your call."

He hung up without saying another word.

I went next door to see what Sam had cooking.

29

Sam made a pot roast, which was fine with me. I'd had her cooking before, and it was great. This was no different.

Over dinner I told her about the call.

"You're going to meet him tonight?"

"Yeah."

"Alone?"

"Not necessarily."

"And where are you going to get five thousand dollars?"

"That's already been taken care of," I said. "It's being delivered here in a couple of hours."

"You made a call and got five thousand dollars in two hours?"

I nodded and said, "I've got connections."

Yeah, connections named Benny. The five grand was the Don's money, and Benny was sending it over with the Don's driver.

Now the question was, who was gonna watch my back?

I was in my office, waiting for the money to be delivered—hopefully, before the phone call. When the phone rang it was too soon.

"Nicky? Hey, it's Tony."

Great.

"Hello, Tony."

"How you doin', buddy?"

"I'm doin' okay."

"I was really sorry to hear about your dad. I feel really bad about the messages I left."

"That's okay, Tony. You didn't know."

"Yeah, thanks. Uh, so what's goin' on? The cops lookin' into your dad's death?"

"Yeah, they are," I said, "but so am I."

"Oh." He sounded disappointed.

"Tony...look..."

"Nicky, man...I was countin' on you...so was Mary Ann's mom."

"Yeah," I said, "that was kinda before my dad got killed, Tony."

"Look," he said, "I feel like a shit, okay?"

"Mary Ann's mom called me, Tony. She told me to forget it. She'd understand."

"Yeah, she would," he said, "she's like that. She's definitely a better person than me."

Jesus.

"Look, Tony," I said, "I may have some time tomorrow to do...something. I want to talk to Mary Ann's mom again, about the rape."

"Rape?" he asked. "What rape?"

I couldn't believe I did that. I forgot that Tony didn't know about the rape.

"Nick? Whataya talkin' about?"

"I heard that Mary Anna was raped, Tony."

"I never—she never said—who told you that?"

"I'm not gonna tell you that right now."

"Then who did it?"

"I'm not tellin' you that, either, Tony," I said. "You'll go off half-cocked."

"I won't go off half-cocked," he said. "I'll just kill the bastard! My Mary Ann was raped? Are you shittin' me, Nick?"

There was a knock on my door at that moment.

"Tony I gotta go. Somebody's at the door."

"Nick! Don't you hang up—"

I hung up.

Then opened the door.

The Don's driver was standing there with a brown envelope.

"Five G's," he said, handing it to me.

"Okay, thanks."

He didn't move.

"Somethin' else?"

"Benny said I was to drive you wherever you wanna go," he said.

He was dressed all in black, with dark glasses and a black chauffer's cap. If I hadn't recognized him I might've acted differently.

"What's your name?"

"Carlo."

"Okay, Carlo. I'm not quite ready to go yet. You wanna come in and wait?"

"If it's okay, I'll wait in the car."

"It's fine with me," I said. I looked at my watch. It was almost eight. "I'll see you in a while."

He nodded and walked down the hall. I took the money back to my desk. The phone rang and I had a feeling it was Tony, so I let the machine pick up.

"Nicky, you prick," Tony said. "You can't tell me my Mary Ann was raped and then hang—"

I disconnected. I didn't have time to deal with Tony's outrage.

The phone rang again.

30

I got into the back of the Don's limo and said, "Canarsie."

"Canarsie?"

I nodded.

"Where?"

"East a hundred and eighth street and Avenue N," I said.

"What's there?" he asked.

"We'll find out when we get there."

He shrugged and said, "Okay."

He started the car and off we went to South Brooklyn.

"You got a gun?" I asked from the back seat as we drove.

"I'm just a driver."

"Yeah, but you drive the Don," I said. "You do that unarmed?"

"Well...Benny's always with us."

And Benny was always armed.

Carlo pulled the car to a stop at our destination. It was a pool club for the locals to bring their kids, spend their summer days sunning, swimming and—for all anyone knew—swapping.

Carlo turned in his seat and looked at me.

"This ain't it," he said.

"I know," I said. "How do *you* know?"

He pointed his gun at me.

"Cut the crap," he said. "How'd you know it was me? I disguised my voice."

"Not very well. Rich Little you ain't."

I figured after he handed me the money and went down to his car he'd gone to a pay phone and called me. I know the sounds of my own neighborhood, and they had come to me in the background. Also, it made sense. Who else would know something but somebody close to the Don?

But I wasn't dead sure, so I gave Carlo a different location than the one he'd given me on the phone.

And he'd lied about his gun.

"Why not just take the five grand when Benny gave it to you?" I asked.

"Then he'd know I took it," Carlo said. "This way..."

"How were you gonna do it?"

"Let you out, wait until you were out of sight, then get out of the car and meet you."

"Wearing a mask?"

He held up a ski mask in his other hand, then dropped it.

"Okay, then," I said, "what've you got, Carlo?"

"The money first."

I took the envelope out of my windbreaker jacket and handed it over the seat. He riffled the contents with his thumb.

"It's all there," I said.

"Didn't slip one or two bills out for yourself?"

"No."

He studied me, then said, "Yeah, you wouldn't." Without the dark glasses I could see he was in his early thirties, with startling blue eyes. Trying to build himself a nest egg, maybe.

"Okay, Carlo, so talk to me."

"The Barge."

"What about it?"

"I can let you on it," he said. "Let you into the Don's office."

"Why would I want to go there?"

"Check it out," he said. "The Don got a call that day. I was in the room. He got a call, then told me to step out. After that he told me he didn't need me to drive him."

"And you think that was because of the call?"

"Yeah."

"And you're thinkin' maybe he wrote somethin' down?" I asked.

"He don't remember things so good no more," Carlo said. "He makes notes."

I thought about it. It made sense. If he went to the restaurant to meet somebody, though, why was my dad there, too?

"Okay," I said. "Take me."

"What, now?"

"Why not?"

"Well...it's late."

"You got a date?"

"No."

"Somethin' else to do?"

"Well, no but—"

"So let's go, Carlo," I said, sitting back. "Drive."

"What about Benny?" he asked. "You won't tell him about this, will you?"

"No," I said, "no reason to tell him."

"Okay, then."

He lowered his gun, turned and started the car. Sheepshead Bay was only a couple of exits away on the Belt Parkway.

I released my gun and took my hand out of my jacket pocket.

31

Carlo unlocked the door of the Barge and we entered.

"Does Benny know you have a key?"

"No," he said. "The Don gave it to me the last time he forgot his. He's been gettin' forgetful."

We walked through the restaurant part, where the chairs were stacked on top of the tables. I knew the way to the Don's office. Carlo followed me. It occurred to me that I was letting a guy with a gun get behind me, but I didn't think he was in on the Don's shooting…and I had my own piece.

When we got to the office we entered and turned on the light. The Don's desk was immaculate. I wasn't going to find any notes on top of it, that was for sure.

I went around and sat down. Benny would have been appalled.

Carlo sat across from me and watched while I went through the desk drawers. The middle one was filled with slips of paper, the Don's scrawl all over them.

"I see what you mean by notes," I said. I scooped them out and laid them on the desk. Yellow and blue post it notes, torn scraps of paper, even pages torn from magazines and newspapers. All with scribbling on them.

"Gonna read them here?" Carlo asked.

"Too many."

I went through the other drawers. Apparently the Don kept all his notes in one. I found an empty 8x11 brown envelope and swept all the scraps into it.

I did a quick scan of his desk top but there was nothing there.

"What about his files?" Carlo said.

I looked over at the single file cabinet in the room. I stood up and tried the drawer, found it locked.

"You got a key for this, too?" I asked.

"Naw," he said. "Pick it."

It would have taken me a while without lock picks.

"Benny should have a key," I said. "If I got in here now I wouldn't know what I was lookin' for. I can get into it later if I have to."

Carlo shrugged. He didn't care. He had his five grand.

"Let's blow," I said. "Drive me back home?"

"Sure, why not?"

Moments later, as we left the Barge and walked back onto the dock, I found out why not.

There was a shot, and Carlo went down.

32

Carlo made a sound as he went down, but the way he hit the ground I knew he was dead. There was a finality about it.

I hit the concrete of the dock and rolled, trying to get my gun out of my jacket. The hammer snagged and I ended up ripping the pocket.

There wasn't much cover for me. I either had to go into the water, try to get back on the Barge, or use Carlo's body. But for the moment I was a clear target and nobody was shooting at me. Was Carlo the intended target? If so the shooter was very good at his job. Took Carlo out with a single shot, and then got out quick.

I took a chance, stood up and moved back toward the Barge. There was no shot, so I stopped at the base of the gangway, where Carlo was lying. I bent down to take a look at him. He'd been shot in the heart, the bullet going right through the envelope of money.

Another dead body for me to deal with. I'd left the waiter for someone else to find, but this was different. We were out in the open, the shot had been loud. Even though I couldn't see anyone it didn't mean there wasn't someone out in the dark looking at me. Plus, to get away from there I'd have to lift Carlo's keys and use the limo.

I decided to get to a phone and call the cops. Not 911, though. I was going to call Sergeant Hicks directly. Or Detective Del Costa.

I walked up the dock to the street to find a pay phone, feeling like I had a bullseye painted on me.

It turned out to be Del Costa. Although she'd been dragged out of bed she looked perfect, hair and make-up expertly applied, wearing another tailored suit. She arrived with the precinct sector car for that area. They got out and left their turret lights flashing.

"Where's your boss?" I asked.

"I called him," she said. "Whataya got?"

"Shooting," I said. "Over here."

As we walked up the dock, the two uniforms in tow, she asked, "What are you doing here this late?"

"Just checking the place out," I said. "The Don's in the hospital, and so's his man. I was just checking to make sure the place was secure."

"You get inside?"

"We were inside, and when we came out there was a shot."

"Who's we?"

"The Don's driver, Carlo. Came to pick me up and take me over."

"A little bodyguarding, too?"

"If he was he didn't do a very good job, did he?"

"He's the one who's dead, right?"

She had a point.

When we reached the body she called for the uniforms to shine their maglights on the body. She checked him, heard the rustling inside his coat and pulled out the envelope.

"Looks like a wad of cash," she said to me. "You know anything about it?"

"He didn't take it from inside," I said. "We were together the whole time."

She looked me up and down. I had stashed my envelope full of scribbled notes in the back seat of the limo.

I raised my hands.

"Wanna check?"

"No," she said, handing the bloody envelope to one of the cops. "Tell me again what happened?"

I did, exactly the way it had happened. There was nothing for me to hide.

"One shot?" she asked. "He got it in the heart. That was good shooting."

"I know."

"You armed, Delvecchio?"

I took my gun out, using two fingers so the cops didn't get nervous, and handed it to her. She sniffed it, then handed it back.

"What about him?" she asked.

"I didn't ask, but it looked like he had a piece under his arm."

She squatted again, reached in and pulled his gun out. It was a .38, much like mine. She stood, smelled it, then handed it to one of the cops, who used his pen through the trigger guard to take it from her.

We all noticed headlights as another car joined the flashing lights at the front of the dock.

"Sergeant's here," one of the cops said.

"Wait here," she said. "All of you."

She walked to meet Hicks halfway. The two cops were watching her ass, so I joined in. She spoke with her partner, then they walked over to us together.

"Delvecchio," he said, "we're gonna need you to come in and make a statement."

"No problem."

He looked down at the body with his hands in his jacket pockets. He was wearing a windbreaker similar to mine. Unlike his partner, he looked like he'd rolled out of bed and dressed in a hurry.

"One shot, huh?" he asked. He turned to look at me. "And you didn't see anythin'?"

"Not even a muzzle flash."

"Why didn't you call it in to nine-one-one?" he asked.

"You're workin' the Don's shooting," I said. "I figured you'd want in on this."

"Okay, come on," he said. "You'll ride in with us. Where's your car?"

"He drove the Don's limo," I said, indicating Carlo's body. "It's parked."

"Okay, we'll leave it. Anythin' in there you need?"

"Nope," I lied, "I've got everything I need on me."

Hicks looked at his partner.

"Take him in," he said. "I'll wait for the M.E. and see you there."

She nodded and said to me, "This way."

33

Two hours later I was sitting at Del Costa's desk, signing my statement. Hicks had still not returned from Sheepshead Bay. The evidence—Carlo's gun, and the bloody envelope of money—would have been taken to the Sixty-Second Precinct, so maybe he was trying to get it from them. Or the M.E. may have taken a long time to respond. In addition, Hicks would have had to wait for a boss to arrive, most likely a Captain.

I signed the statement and pushed it across the desk to Del Costa.

"Okay, thanks." She looked it over briefly, then said, "You can go."

"That's it?"

"That's it."

"I've got a question," I said.

She stared at me and said, "What?" I had a feeling she thought she knew what I was going to ask.

She was wrong.

"It's about my father," I said. "Have you found out how he got to that restaurant?"

"No," she said. "He didn't drive, and we haven't found a car service that took him. We're checking cabs, now, but we're not hopeful. He may have gotten a ride from someone."

"That's what I was thinkin'," I said.

"Any idea who?"

"Normally, he'd ask me or my brother or my sister," I said. "But none of us took him."

"What's that like?" she asked.

"What?"

"Your brother," she said. "What's it like having a priest in the family?"

"Are you Catholic?"

"Yes, I am."

"Well, it ain't all it's cracked up to be," I said. "I don't go to Mass, so I always have to defend myself to him."

"What do you have against Mass?" she asked. "Or is it God?"

"I don't have a problem with God," I said. "I'm not real crazy about the Church."

"Aren't they the same thing?"

"Not to me."

"Hmm," she said.

"You go to Mass regularly?"

"No."

"Confession?"

She colored and said, "No."

"Me, neither. It's been years."

"How'd your dad feel about that?"

"We didn't discuss it," I said. "Not for a long, long time."

I stood up.

"You want a ride home?"

I didn't. I wanted to go back to Sheepshead Bay and get that envelope out of the limo, but it was probably too soon for that.

"Sure."

"I'll take you myself," she said.

"Hey, you're busy—"

"Don't worry about it," she said. "I'll probably go right home after that."

"You won't have to come back here?"

"Hicks will be handling things," she said.

We walked down the stairs to the main floor, and out the door.

"Sorry I had to wake you," I said.

"That's the job," she said. "You know, you did it for a while."

"A while."

We walked to her car. It was dark and quiet, I could hear her heels on the ground. She was tall, and her stride was equal to mine.

"My parents would've loved it if my brother became a priest," she said, out of the blue as we approached her car.

"Oh? What did he become, instead?"

"Dead," she said.

She drove in silence for a while, then said, "He was murdered when I was a teenager."

"Cops find out who did it?"

"No," she said. "I guess maybe that's why I became a cop."

"How'd it happen?"

"He was playing basketball in a schoolyard and a couple of guys came up and shot him."

"Witnesses?"

"The other players, but they claimed they didn't know the shooters."

My first thought was drugs, but I kept my opinion to myself.

"That's too bad," I said. "I know what it's like to lose a brother."

"You, too?"

"My oldest was killed in Viet Nam."

"That must have been tough."

"It was," I said, nodding. "My mother died a few years later, but it's my brother that my father has a small shrine to."

"That could be...creepy."

"Tell me about it."

"So Father Vincent is older than you?"

I nodded. "And Maria is the youngest."

"I have a younger sister, but Robert was my only brother."

We drove a while longer in silence. I was sure she didn't have time to put on perfume, but the car smelled like her, anyway.

"When did you get your shield?"

"A couple of years ago," she said. "It took me eight years."

"That's an accomplishment."

"Is it?" she asked, sounding almost bitter. "That depends on how you got it, doesn't it?"

"I just assumed you'd earned it."

She gave me a quick look before turning her attention back to the road.

"That's not the general opinion."

"What's it matter what anybody thinks as long as you know you earned it?"

She was quiet again until we pulled up in front of my place.

"I want to tell you something," she said.

"What?"

"I'm not sleeping with Hicks."

"It's no skin off my nose if you are."

"I know," she said. "That's why I wanted to tell you."

"But he is your rabbi, right?" When you had somebody in the department who was superior to you, and they helped your career, they were your "rabbi."

"We have an agreement," she said. "We let people think what they're going to think, and he helps me."

"Hey," I said, "you gotta do what you gotta do."

My reply didn't seem to be what she wanted. She turned and stared out the windshield.

"Look, I'm sorry," I said. "But if you want to know the truth, I really never thought you were sleepin' with him."

"What?" She looked at me and blinked.

"You're way too classy for him," I said. "Anybody who can't see that is an idiot."

"I—well—thank you."

"Thanks for the ride."

I started to get out, then paused and looked at her.

"What?" she said.

"Can I ask somethin' else about the case?"

"Sure, why not?" she asked. "We're bonding here, right?"

"Yeah, uh, right," I said. "Did you determine what kind of a gun was used on my dad?"

She hesitated, then said, "From the shells we recovered we figure they were shot with an Uzi."

"An Uzi?"

"Yeah, why?"

"Nothin,'" I said. "Thanks."

"Look—" she said, then stopped.

"What?"

"Never mind. Keep in touch…about the case, I mean."

"I'm not looking into it, you know," I said.

"Yeah," she said, "sure. Just let us know if you hear anything."

"Will do."

34

The message light was going like crazy.

I had a feeling most of the calls were going to be from an incensed Tony Mitts. And I figured he had a right to be mad. I was going to have to do something, since I had opened my big mouth. But I still needed to get back to Sheepshead Bay to get those notes from the limo. And I needed to let Benny know what had happened at the Barge. But I also needed to get a few hours' sleep or I'd be no good to anybody.

I fell into bed without even getting undressed…

I woke as daylight came through my window. I could have used a few more hours, but I got up and showered and made myself a quick breakfast of coffee and toast. I got dressed, switched to my other windbreaker, once again stuck my .38 in the pocket. There was just too much lead flying around for me to go unarmed.

I left my apartment as quietly as possible. I didn't want Sam to hear me because I didn't want to take the time to explain everything to her. I could do that later.

I got my car, a five-year-old Toyota I'd picked up cheap, out of the parking lot where I kept it and aimed it at Sheepshead Bay. I still had Carlo's keys in my pocket, which was the only thing I'd lifted from his body before the cops arrived.

I drove down Emmons Avenue once without stopping, just to make sure there were no cops around. Second time I pulled in behind the limo, got out and quickly retrieved the envelope from the back seat. I locked the car, got back in mine and drove to Victory Memorial to see Benny and let him know what had happened.

"Carlo's dead?" he asked.

"Yeah," I said, "and that's not all. He was the one who called me about the five grand."

"I never liked him," the big man said. He was munching an Egg McMuffin I'd brought him. In fact, I'd brought him three.

We were standing in the Don's room, talking across his bed. He was still out.

The cop outside the door was gone. Benny said the detectives asked him to call when the Don could talk and they'd come by for a statement.

"There's some stuff happening, Benny," I said. "Let's sit down and talk about it."

We pulled two chairs together and sat at the foot of the Don's bed.

"What was Carlo up to?" Benny asked.

"He said you told him to drive me to deliver the five grand."

"I never did."

"I know. He did that himself. I figured out it was him, and we made the exchange."

"What was he sellin'?"

"He told me the Don got a phone call the day he was shot."

"The Don gets a lot of phone calls."

"Well, he got this one while Carlo was in the room. He told Carlo to leave, that he was walkin' to the restaurant."

"So what's that mean?"

"I don't know, but I had Carlo drive me to the Barge and let me in."

"How'd he do that? He ain't got no key."

"Yeah, he did. He said the Don gave him one to carry because he was startin' to forget his."

Benny frowned.

"Why didn't he tell me that?"

"Because the old man doesn't want you to know he's gettin' forgetful."

Benny shook his head and said, "Stupid," then looked at the Don quickly, checking to see if he'd heard him. "So what'd you find?"

"I went through the Don's desk and found a bunch of scribbled notes."

"What'd they say?"

"I don't know. There was too many to read right there and then, so I took them with me. When we got outside, somebody put one in Carlo's heart."

"One shot? From where?"

"I don't know," I said. "A ways off."

"A pro," Benny said. "Only a pro would be that good at night. Probably had an infrared scope."

"Why not plug me, too?"

"If he was a pro working on a contract he wouldn't," Benny said. "He's only gettin' paid for one."

I looked at the old man in the bed.

"They could be comin' for him next," I said.

"They gotta come through me to get him," Benny said.

"They might do that," I said. "You need somebody you can trust here with you."

"You're the only one I trust, Nicky."

"I can't stay here with you, Ben. But I can make a call and get somebody."

"Who?"

"Friend of mine," I said. "Maybe two. You can trust them."

"If you say so, Nicky."

"Okay," I said. "Let me make the calls, and then I'll get back to you. Have somebody here by this afternoon."

"Okay. You hear from Winky?"

"No. I'll go and check those addresses you gave me, askin' about him. And I've got to go through the Don's notes."

"Leave 'em with me," Benny said. "I'll go through 'em."

I hesitated.

"What?" he asked. "You think I ain't smart enough to find somethin'?"

"I think you're plenty smart, Benny," I said. "It's a good idea, because I'm gonna be on the move for a while. I'll go down to my car and get 'em. Oh, speakin' of the car." I took Carlo's keys out of my pocket. "Here's the keys to the limo, and whatever other keys Carlo had."

Benny took them. "These are for the limo, this one for the front door of the Barge. The rest must be his private keys."

"I'll be right back."

I went down to the car and got the envelope with the notes. Benny wasn't the sharpest knife in the drawer, but he knew the Don, and he could read his handwriting. If there was something there to find, he'd find it.

I brought it back up to the room and handed it to him.

"You went through the Don's drawer," he said.

"Yeah."

"He won't like that."

"Maybe," I said, "we won't have to tell him."

He looked at me for a few moments, then said, "Yeah, maybe."

"I'll call you about who I'm sendin' to back you up, Benny. You'll be able to trust them."

"Okay, Nicky," he said. He held up the envelope. "I'll start readin'."

"Let me know what you find out."

35

I went back to my place and used the phone to make arrangements to back Benny up at the hospital. I called two P.I. buddies I know, Miles Jacoby and Henry Po, and asked them each if they'd do it.

"Cash money?" Jacoby asked.

"A payin' gig, Jack," I said.

"I'll take the Don's money, Nick, but not yours," he said.

"That can be arranged."

Hank Po said the same thing. The three of us used to hire out to each other for special jobs, but as we became friends we did it more as a favor. But there was risk, here, and I wanted them to be compensated. So the Don would pay them both.

I called Benny and told him to expect Jacoby and Po at the hospital.

"I ain't found nothin' in these notes yet, Nick," he said.

"Keep lookin', Benny."

With that taken care of I was ready to go looking for Benny's contact, Winky. Benny had given me two addresses in Brooklyn. I grabbed my windbreaker, hanging heavy with my gun in the pocket, and my keys and headed for the door. When I opened it to step out I ran into a brick wall.

Otherwise known as Tony Mitts.

As I bounced off him he advanced on me and grabbed me with both hands.

"What the fuck, Nick?" he shouted. "What the fuck?"

He started to shake me, his eyes blazing with rage. My toes were barely touching the floor.

"Let me go, Tony."

"What the—"

"Don't make me shoot you."

He stopped short. I put my hand in my pocket, then pressed the barrel of my gun to his belly. His eyes cleared a bit as he felt the metal.

"Nick—"

"Let me go and calm down," I said. "Then we can talk."

Slowly, he released the front of my shirt and my feet touched down. I backed away, took my hand out of my pocket.

"I'm sorry," I said to him. "I'm all involved in my dad's death and I let the business about the rape slip."

"Jesus, Nick, what rape?" he asked. Now he looked anguished rather than enraged.

"Mary Ann told her sister that years ago she was raped."

"Years?"

"Two years, before you were engaged."

"That's before we started goin' out again."

"There's even some question as to whether or not it was rape," I said.

"If Mary Ann said it was rape, then it was." He clenched his big mitts into fists. "Did she go to the police?"

"She didn't."

"Who was it, Nick?"

"I'm not tellin' you that, Tony, because you'd go out and commit murder. That wouldn't help anyone."

"So he gets away with it?"

"Well...she forgave him, Tony."

"So it was somebody she knew?"

"I didn't say that."

"Why else would she forgive him?"

"I don't know," I said. "I can't get the answers from her, Tony, she's dead."

"Then I'll go ask Catherine," Tony said. "I'll wring her neck until she tells me."

"No you won't," I said. "you're gonna come with me now."

"Where?"

"I'm lookin' for a man named Winky. He might be able to tell me who shot my father. I need somebody to watch my back. If you help me, I'll help you. I'll keep working on Mary Ann's case and find out the truth, about the rape, and about her death. Deal?"

He stood there for a few moments, going over it in his head, and then said, "Deal."

"Let's go."

Tony had driven his car, but we left it parked in front of my building. It would be ticketed by the time we got back, but probably not towed. I didn't tell him that. No point in getting him even more upset.

The first place Benny told me to ask for Winky was a bar in Bay Ridge, on Eighty-Seventh Street and Fourth Avenue. It was about three doors down from an OTB office.

We parked down the street and walked to the bar. There were neon signs in the windows advertising "Budweiser" in red and "Heineken" in green. Above the door was printed "Rafe's."

Naturally, it was a dive, but I'd spent many a pleasant evening in dives. I felt at home in them.

The bar ran along one wall, almost the entire length of the place, which was impressive. Couldn't say that about the width of it, though. It was almost unable to accommodate Tony's wing span.

"This place stinks," he said.

"What kind of bars have you been hangin' out in?" I asked. "They all smell like this. It's a well-earned odor."

Beer, whiskey, sweat and despair. They had all soaked into the walls, and the grain of the wooden bar.

We went to the bar and added our elbows to the ones already leaning there. A few of the patrons gave us a look, but most of them were too busy nursing their beer.

"What'll it be?" the bartender asked. Or maybe he asked, "What'll ya have?" Either one sounded the same to me.

"Beer."

"What kind?"

"Whatever's on tap."

He drew two frothy mugs and set them down in front of us. Tony looked at his dubiously, and I wondered when he'd gotten so finicky. I picked mine up and took a sip. Pretty much made me finicky, too.

"I'm lookin' for Winky," I said to the bartender. "He been around, lately?"

"No."

"You sure?" I asked. "Benny told me I might find him here."

"Benny?"

"That's right."

The bartender squinted at me from beneath big, bushy black eyebrows that were shot through with gray. If he had any hair it would have been the same, but he was as bald as an egg.

"This about the Barracuda shootin'?"

"That's right," I said. "Benny told me I could find Winky here, or at a bar out on Pennsylvania Avenue."

"Naw, he don't go out there anymore," the bartender said. "He does his drinkin' here—when he's drinkin'."

"And when is that?"

"When he ain't gamblin'."

"And is that what he's doin' now?"

"Yup."

"Where?"

The bartender stroked the hard, black bristles on his cheeks and jaw.

"If I tell you, you'll let the Don know I helped?" he asked.

"I'll tell 'im."

"You can find him down the street."

"OTB?"

"That's right. As long as they're runnin', or they're open. Then he'll come back here until his poker game starts."

"What's he looks like."

"Tall, thin. Looks like he could use a good meal. But...you'll know him when you see him."

"Okay, thanks."

"If I was you I'd wait till he comes back here, then buy him a drink," the bartender said. "That'll make him more talkative."

"I don't have the time to waste."

"He ain't gonna be happy to be interrupted when he's playin' the horses."

"I'll have to take that chance," I said. "Thanks for the info."

I walked out of the bar with Tony behind me.

36

Just the short time we'd spent in Rafe's made the sun outside seem ten times brighter.

"Now what?" Tony asked.

"OTB."

"We gonna interrupt the guy?"

"Oh, yeah."

"You know anythin' about him?"

"Like what?"

"Like how big he is?" Tony asked. "Or if he carries a gun?"

"No," I said, "but you're plenty big, and I carry a gun."

"I ain't fought much since high school, Nick."

I looked him up and down.

"But you kept in shape."

"So?"

"Just stand behind me," I said, "and look mean. You can do that, can't you?"

"Sure," he said. "I can do that."

We entered the OTB and went unnoticed. That's because there was a race going on, showing on the monitors around the place. All eyes were on the race and half the place was shouting while the other half—the half that was probably already out of the race—were watching in silence.

The loud one were yelling things like "Oh, come on!" or "Get up, get up, get up!", and the horse player's lament, "One time! One time!" They were either punching the air, pounding the back of the person next to them, or snapping their fingers.

But they all had one thing in common. They were all standing with their heads at the same angle, chins up, watching the monitors which were bolted to the ceiling. There was very little elbow room in the place.

Tony and I were the only ones not looking at the race. We were checking everybody out, looking for a tall, thin, hungry-looking race fan. Ultimately, we didn't find him until it was over and everybody's chins came down.

"There he is," I said.

"Where?"

"Black hair, dirty white T-shirt…and that blink."

That was why they called him "Winky." He had one eye that was constantly blinking, so he looked like he was always winking.

I knew there were horseplayers—real degenerates—who sold their blood for money they could bet with, and that's what Winky looked like.

"Now what?" Tony asked.

"Let's get him out of here before the next race," I said.

We approached him, and I signaled Tony to move to his other side.

"Winky!" I said. "Good to see ya. How're you doin' with the nags?"

"Huh?" He looked at me, frowned, his right eye going wink-wink-wink. "I know you?"

"Sure, you do," I said. "Nick Delvecchio. I'm friends with Benny Carbone."

"Benny?" Winky turned his head and looked at Tony, who did his best to appear menacing.

"Didn't you hear he was lookin' for you?" I asked.

"Uh, I might've, but I been on a hot streak."

"Let's step outside for a few minutes."

"I got a longshot in the next race," Winky complained.

"The quicker we make this, the quicker you'll get back in to play it."

I looked at Tony, and he got my message. He grabbed Winky's upper arm and squeezed.

"Yeah, yeah, okay," Winky said. "He don't hafta mangle me."

I nodded to Tony, who released the arm. We walked outside.

"Okay, whataya want?"

"What do you know about the Don's shooting?" I asked.

"What makes ya think I know anythin'?" he asked.

"Benny says you keep your ear to the ground," I said. "He says you're his friend and he can usually count on you."

"Yeah," Winky said. "Benny's my friend."

Which meant that I wasn't. Big surprise. I already knew that.

"Come on, Winky," I said. "Who put the hit out on the Don?"

"Like I know?"

"If you knew would you tell me?"

"If I knew I'd sell you the info."

"Would you sell it to Benny?"

He paused, then said, "Benny scares me, but yeah, because he'd pay me."

"Then he will pay you."

"Look," he said. "I don't know who put the hit out, but I'll try to find out. Gimme your number."

I gave him one of my cards.

"One more thing," I said.

"What?"

"Somebody shot Carlo, who drives the Don, last night," I said. "I was with him, but there was one shot and it hit him in the heart."

"A pro," Winky said.

"That's right. And how many pros would be working the city at one time? Last night whoever he was used a rifle. The shooting of the Don and my dad was done with an Uzi."

"Uzi?" Winky frowned. "That don't make sense. That sounds like the Jamaicans or South Americans."

"I know," I said. "That's what I was thinkin'."

"Those fuckers are crazy," Winky said.

"Then you better make sure they don't hear about you," I said.

"Yeah, uh, yeah," Winky said, rubbing his nose vigorously with the palm of his hand. "Look I gotta make this bet, and it'd be better if I had, uh, more money."

"What's the name of the horse?" I asked.

"Aroma Girl. She's been beaten fifty lengths in her last two races, but they're puttin' her on turf today. I been waitin' for this one."

I took out my wallet. I had two fifties, a ten and some singles. I took out the two fifties.

"One is for you," I said. "Put the other one on the horse to win, for me."

"Uh, okay, sure."

"Hey, I'll get in on that," Tony said. "Put twenty on the nose for me."

Winky took the twenty and stared at Tony. Mitts finally took out another twenty and handed it to him.

"We'll collect next time we see you," I said. "Where's it running?"

"Third at Belmont."

"Okay," I said. "Remember, call me as soon as you know anything."

"Yeah, okay. Oh, hey."

"What?"

"The other guy with the Don. That was your dad?"

"Yeah," I said. "They were friends. The Don is actually my Godfather."

"Sorry about your old man," Winky said. "I'll find out what I can."

"Thanks."

37

We walked back to my car.

"So that's what you do every day?" Tony asked, as we got inside.

"What?"

"Pay for information. Or scare it outta people. And then wait?"

"Not every day, Tony," I said, "but yeah, a lot of waiting."

"Now what?" he asked.

"Now I'll keep my word," I said. "You helped me out, so now we go and talk to Mary Ann's mother and sister again."

"Okay."

"And on the way, Tony," I said, glancing at him, "you can talk to me again."

"About what?"

"About everything, Tony," I said, turning the key. "About everything."

We were closer to the Grosso house than to my place, so we still left Tony's car where it was, on Sackett Street.

I used part of the drive to get my head back into the case. I went over my visit to Sal, our talk about the rape. I remembered I'd left his house believing him about two things. He didn't think it was rape, and he didn't kill her.

"Tony, if you want me to help you, you'll have to tell me the truth," I said.

"About what?"

"You and Mary Ann were engaged, right?"

"Right."

"And she never told you she was raped?"

"She never said a word to me, Nick," he said. "I swear."

"Why not, Tony?"

"I—I don't know," he said. "Maybe for the same reason you weren't gonna tell me."

"Because you'd kill the guy?"

"Yeah."

Tony was always a big baby to me. Women called him a teddy bear. If he ever hurt anybody it would have been by accident. But in my office his eyes had been filled with enough rage to kill.

"You don't believe me?" he asked.

"No, I do," I said. "I don't think you can fake the shock you showed when I told you. You're not that good an actor."

We drove in silence for a while, then Tony asked, "What did you mean there was a question whether it was a rape or not?"

"Mary Ann said it was, but the guy said it wasn't."

"And you believed him?"

"Yeah, I did."

"Why?"

"He was convincing," I said, "and it's very easy for a girl to yell rape."

"Easy?"

"Don't get me wrong," I said. "A woman has a right to say no, and lots of them get raped, but there are those who misuse the word."

"And you think Mary Ann was one of those?"

"I don't know," I said. "Let's see if we can find out."

38

I parked in front of Angela Grosso's house and we got out.

"What are you gonna do?" Tony asked, facing me across the top of my car.

"I'm gonna do what I do," I said. "Ask questions. Seems to me somebody has to know what the hell was goin' on with Mary Ann. Somebody has to know who the real Mary Ann was."

"Yeah," Tony said, "I did."

"I don't think so, Tony. I don't think you did."

"Who then?"

"Her mother?" I asked.

Tony shook his head.

"She didn't get along that good with her mother."

"Then how about her sister?" I asked. "After all, it was Catherine she told about the rape."

"What if there wasn't any rape?" Tony asked. "What if Catherine lied?"

"And why would she do that?"

Tony shrugged. "Maybe she was jealous of Mary Ann."

"Well, why don't we go inside and find out," I said.

We went up the walk to the front door and rang the bell. After a few moments I rang it again.

"Catherine might be at work," Tony said. "I don't know if she was ready to go back."

"Where else might she be?"

Tony shrugged.

"Where does she work?"

"The Brooklyn Museum."

"And her mother?"

"I don't know where she might be. Maybe the cemetery."

"Okay," I said. "I might as well take you back to your car."

"Museum's on the way," Tony said.

"Depending on how we go," I said.

The Museum was on Eastern Parkway, and we could have gone that way, but I didn't want him with me when I talked to Catherine again. So I jumped on the Belt Parkway and took that to downtown Brooklyn.

"Whataya want me to do now?" Tony asked when I dropped him by his car.

"Nothing," I said. "Just stay out of it. I don't want you to lose your head and do somethin' stupid."

"You're gonna tell me everythin', right?" he asked.

"I'll tell you whatever I find out," I promised.

I drove away, leaving him standing there. I took Flatbush Avenue to Grand Army Plaza, drove around it and veered off onto Eastern Parkway. It might have been a good day to turn into Prospect Park, but I didn't have the time.

There was a Grand Army Plaza in Manhattan, too, across from the Plaza Hotel. I always wondered why nobody had the imagination to come up with another name.

The Museum had on-premise parking, so I didn't have to go looking for a space on the street. The shittiest man who ever lived invented parking meters. If I didn't have to use one, that suited me.

I entered the Museum. The day was about ten degrees hotter than usual, which put it in the mid to high 80s. The chill of the Museum air-conditioning was welcome.

I stopped at the first rent-a-cop I saw—staring off into space—and asked him for Catherine Grosso.

"She works in the office," he said, and directed me.

"You mind tellin' me what her job is?"

The guard shrugged and said, "I think she's a secretary or somethin'."

He was probably a retired cop just playin' out the string.

"Thanks."

He nodded, went back to staring.

I made my way up some marble steps to the second floor, found a string of offices. Catherine was sitting at a desk in the third one.

"Catherine."

Her head jerked up and she frowned when she saw me standing in the doorway. She was wearing a pair of wire-rimmed glasses, took them off so she could see me better.

"Nick? What are you doin' here?"

"I needed to talk to you," I said. "I tried your house, and then Tony told me where you worked."

"Tony told you?"

"Your mother wasn't home."

"She—she's probably at the cemetery."

"Can we walk and talk?" I asked.

"Oh, sure. Just wait for me out in the hall."

I nodded, and stepped out.

39

She joined me after a few moments. She had her glasses in her hand, kept them folded there.

"You get somebody to cover for you?" I asked.

"For a few minutes."

"Are you important here?"

She laughed.

"Oh, no," she said. "I'm just an assistant."

"To who?"

She shrugged.

"To a lot of people. I'm hoping for a promotion, soon."

"I'm sure you'll get it," I said.

"I hope you're right," she said. "What was it you wanted to talk about?"

"Well, if it's okay, I'd like to talk about Mary Ann, and the rape."

"Oh, that." She folded her arms, hugging herself. "Did you talk to Sal?"

"I did," I said. "He says it wasn't rape. He said he and Mary Ann had a relationship."

"They never—"

"Oh, not a sexual one," I said. "He just said they were friends."

She didn't reply.

"Does that sound like Mary Ann to you, Catherine?" I asked. "Did she make friends with men?"

"Mary Ann—" she said, then stopped short. "Nick, Mary Ann wasn't what everybody thought she was."

"And what was that, Catherine?" I asked. "What did everybody think she was?"

She hesitated. "A good girl."

I'd heard the talk in high school, the talk that Tony had chosen not to believe. I never took steps to find out if it was true or not. I wasn't friends with the guys who claimed to have been with her.

"Are you talkin' about high school?" I asked. "Or are we not goin' back that far?"

"Yes," she said, "high school—and after."

"And how about when she went away?"

Catherine shrugged and hugged herself tighter. "I only know that when she came back she was different. Something had changed her."

"And that was before Sal?"

"Yes."

"So, changed her how?"

"Well, all of a sudden she didn't even like to talk about sex," Catherine said. "It was as if she'd taken a pledge or somethin'."

"So she was off sex after being promiscuous for…what? Years?"

"I guess."

"And did your mother know about Mary Ann's promiscuity?"

"Oh, yes, she knew," Catherine said, "but she went on pretending that Mary Ann was this saint, you know? She couldn't face the truth."

"And what about you? Could you face the truth?"

"Me? What did I care? It didn't matter to me if she slept around or not."

"Come on, Catherine," I said. "You were the younger sister. Weren't you jealous? Weren't you angry about the way your mother treated Mary Ann, ignoring the fact that she was a slut?"

"I didn't say that!" Catherine said, loudly. So loudly that it echoed. She looked around quickly, then pulled me down on a nearby bench.

"I didn't say she was a slut," she said.

"Did you ever hear your mother say that?"

She squirmed.

"Catherine?"

"I heard them having an argument," she said. "During it my mother did call her a slut, but Mary Ann told her that was all over now. She said she was going to marry Tony. My mother told her to make sure Tony never found out about her past."

"And what did Mary Ann say to that advice?"

"She said she was gonna tell Tony everythin'," Catherine said, "That they could only have a good marriage if they were honest with each other."

"What did your mother think of that?"

"She thought Mary Ann was bein' foolish. She even said she was crazy. There was no way Tony would still marry her if she told him. Mary Ann said he would, that Tony loved her no matter what."

"Then what?"

"That was it. Mary Ann left the room. I…hid."

"Did you and your mother ever talk about the argument?"

"No."

"When did it happen?"

"The day before."

"The day before what?" I asked, to be clear. "The reunion?"

"N-no," Catherine said. "The day before Mary Ann died."

I asked a few more questions while I walked her back to her office.

"Catherine, did Mary Ann have trouble sleeping?"

"No. She slept like a baby." She sounded almost envious.

"But she died of an overdose of sleeping pills. They were your mother's How did she get them?"

"I—I didn't give them to her. If they were my mother's they were in her bathroom. We were never allowed in mother's bathroom. Never!"

Some aspects of childhood—like certain rules—died hard.

"I'm not accusin' you of anything," I said. "I'm just tryin' to get some answers."

Before we got to the door I turned and took her by the shoulders.

"I don't think Mary Ann ever told Tony anything, Catherine," I said.

"I've spoken to him a couple of times. I let it slip about the rape and he exploded."

"Did you tell him who did it?"

"No," I said. "I don't want him to know."

"So is Sal gonna get away with rape?"

"I'm not convinced it as rape," I said.

"But Mary Ann said—"

"Maybe she convinced herself it was," I said. "You said she took the pledge. Maybe she was ashamed...Sal didn't act like a rapist, Catherine. He acted like he was in love with Mary Ann."

Catherine bit her lip and asked, "Weren't they all?"

40

I kept my answer to myself until I got back to my car.

No, I wasn't in love with Mary Ann Grosso, and good for me. I had enough problems without being part of that club. But with Tony and Sal as members, I wondered how many others there were? What about Sammy? And Joey the Nose?

But despite what Catherine told me, I could hear in her voice that she was envious or jealous of her older sister. Was she still jealous of Mary Ann, even after her death? And would she say anything to Tony about his Mary Ann not being so perfect?

And what about their mother, Angela? What did she know that she was keeping to herself?

I was going to have to talk to my old school buddies, and to Mary Ann's mother again, but first I had to check in with Benny on the Don's condition.

I went back to my office to use the phone. Mobile phones were getting to be all the rage, but they were expensive and I didn't think they'd last. Who needed them with pay phones on every corner? And I was very happy with the phone on my desk.

Now, if I could figure out a way to exist without the damn answering machine. Once again as I entered it was winking its red eye at me.

I sat behind my desk and stared at the machine. I really toyed with the idea of not listening to the messages. However, if I did that I'd end up sitting in my office alone, thinking about...things. Things like how the man who raised me wasn't actually my father. And if he wasn't, who was?

I pressed the play button.

First it was Maria: "Nick, call me at Pop's. I need to know when to schedule the funeral."

Next, Father Vinnie: "Nick, we need to hear from you. We want to know what's going on."

The third was a surprise: "Mr. Delvecchio, this is Detective Del Costa. Please give me a call at my office. I need to, um, I would like to talk to you about something."

The fourth, fifth and sixth calls were from Benny: "Nick, the Don is awake. He's askin' for ya."

I ignored all the other messages, left the office and headed for the hospital.

41

When I got to the hospital Po and Jacoby were outside the door.

"Who kicked you out?" I asked.

"The Don woke up and got agitated because he didn't know us," Jacoby said.

"We thought it was better if we stepped out," Po said.

Jacoby had been a middleweight boxer in his youth and still looked in shape. Hank Po and I could also have been middleweights at some time. When the three of us were together it could have looked like we were created by the same person.

"Thanks. I'll see what I can do."

"It's okay," Hank said. "We're probably better off out here, anyway."

"Benny?"

"He's real protective of the Don," Jack said. "I'd hate to be in the ring with him. He's a big guy."

"But with us out here," Po said, "nobody's gonna get inside."

"Good," I said. "Benny call the cops yet, about the Don bein' awake?"

"Not yet," Po said. "We all agreed you should talk to him first."

"Okay, thanks." I went inside.

Benny turned quickly, his hand going inside his jacket. He relaxed when he saw it was me.

"I told you that you could trust those guys, Benny," I said.

"I only trust you, Nick," he said, "and so does the Don."

I looked down at the bed and the old man looked back at me. He had blue eyes, clear as could be, and he smiled at me.

"Ciao, Nicholas."

"Uncle."

I usually called him "Mr. Barracondi." Once I wasn't a kid anymore

"Godfather" seemed dramatic. Thank you Mr. Puzo.

"How are you feelin'?" I asked.

"Worn out," he said. "Shot up. I am sorry about your Papa."

"I know," I said. "What did you see, Uncle?"

"What did I see?" he asked. "I am an old man, with old eyes. I saw nothing. What I heard, that is different. I heard the chatter of the gun. Boom-boom-boom-boom. Glass everywhere. And blood. Your Papa, he pushed me down. Probably why he is dead and I am alive."

"He's dead because he caught a few more bullets than you did," I said. "In worse places."

"Ah," he said, and a tear formed in his eye. "My oldest friend, you know?"

"Who were they, Uncle?" I asked. "Who killed Pop? And tried to kill you?"

"If I knew," he said, "I would tell you. And you and Benny would kill them."

"Uncle, the cops are lookin', I'm lookin', we've put the word out. If someone put a contract out on you we'll find out. But if you know—"

"A contract?" He laughed until he choked and Benny put his hand on the old man's chest until the coughing stopped.

"That was the old days," he rasped, then. "There was no contract. It was probably somebody with an old grudge."

"So who has a grudge?"

"Lots of people. Benny can make you a list."

I looked at Benny and he shrugged.

"Uncle, did Benny tell you that Carlo is dead?"

"Si."

"If it was a grudge why'd they kill Carlo?"

"I do not know. Maybe because they missed me, and now they can't get to me or Benny, so that was the only way. Too bad. Carlo was a good boy."

"Carlo told me you got a call before you went to Rizzo's," I said. "Who called?"

He closed his eyes.

"I don't remember."

"He said after the call you told him you'd walk to the restaurant. You don't walk anywhere, Uncle."

"I must've felt like a walk that day."

"Must have?"

"I told you, Nicholas, I don't remember." He closed his eyes again and turned his head away. "I am tired."

"Uncle, we have to call the detectives and tell them you're awake."

"So call them."

"If you have somethin' you want to tell us before they get here, you have to do it now."

He didn't respond. I looked at Benny and he shrugged again.

"Okay," I said.

I started away and the Don said, "Nicholas."

"Yes, Uncle?"

He turned his head and looked at me.

"Those two boys, you brought them?"

"Yes."

"You trust them?"

"With my life."

"They would die for you?"

"Yes," I said, although I wasn't sure.

"Would they die for me?"

Before I could answer he drifted off again.

42

I pulled Benny over to the door with me.

"Why's he lyin', Ben?"

"The Don don't lie, Nicky."

"Yeah, he does," I said. "And he is."

"Nick, don't say that."

I could see that if I argued further I'd be banging my head against a stone wall. I'd also risk getting Benny really angry with me. I moved on.

"Ben, you're gonna have to call the detectives," I said, "and don't tell them I was here."

"Okay. Which one should I call?"

"Did they both leave you cards?"

"Yes."

"Call the sergeant, Hicks," I said.

"Okay, Nick."

"Just give me twenty minutes to get out of here."

Benny nodded.

I stepped outside.

"Anythin'?" Jacoby asked.

"The Don's lying to me."

"Why?"

"I don't know."

"What'd he say?" Po asked.

"He doesn't know who fired the shots," I said. "He rejects the idea that it might be a contract. Instead he said it was probably somebody with a grudge, but he didn't give me any names."

"Could he still be...confused?" Po asked.

"In shock?" Jacoby said.

"I don't think so," I said. "I think he knows exactly what he's doin'. I just have to figure out what the hell it is."

"And what about Benny?" Hank Po asked.

"When I suggested the Don was lyin' he got mad."

"He's incredibly loyal, isn't he?" Jacoby asked.

"Yes, he is. Sometimes it's scary."

"Sometimes?" Po asked.

"You guys better stay out here," I said. "I told Benny to call Sergeant Hicks. He and Detective Del Costa will probably be here soon."

"Okay," Po said. "What do we tell them when they ask us why we're here?"

"Tell the truth," I said. "You're bein' paid."

"What if they ask by who?" Jacoby asked.

"Don't tell 'em unless you have to."

"And if we have to?"

I took a breath. They couldn't say the Don was paying them. He was out of it. Benny? I don't think they'd believe he was smart enough.

"Okay," I said, "tell 'em you work for me."

They nodded.

"What are you gonna do now?" Jack asked.

"I've got to find out what the Don is lyin' about," I said, "and why."

I made sure I got away from the hospital before Hicks arrived. And since Del Costa would probably be with Hicks, I'd have to put off calling her until later.

That meant I had to go to Pop's house to see Maria and Vinnie.

When I got to Pop's I let myself in. There were cars out front, and lots of people in the living room.

Great.

Maria spotted me and came rushing over.

"What's goin' on?" I asked.

"When the neighborhood heard that Pop was dead they just...started turning up."

"How are you feedin' all of them? Gettin' them stuff to drink?"

"They're showin' up with food and drinks, Nick," she said. "I can't believe it. Wait, here's Mrs. Trombetta. Vinnie's in the kitchen."

Some of the people I knew and exchanged greetings with on the way to the kitchen. Other people I had no clue who they were.

In the kitchen Vinnie was standing at the sink, talking to a man and a woman. When he saw me he excused himself, came over and slapped a bottle of Rolling Rock into my hand.

"They even knew Pop's brand," he said.

"This is weird."

"I know. A wake without a body. Do you know when we'll be able to—"

"Not for a while, Vinnie. There's still an investigation goin' on. The detectives are still waitin' to talk to the Don."

"How is he? When's that gonna happen?"

"He woke up today. The detectives are probably talkin' to him now."

"Did you talk to him?"

"He told Benny he wanted to see me," I said. "I spoke to him before the cops, but he didn't tell me anything. Claims he didn't see anything, and doesn't know anything."

"What's he say about Pop?"

"That he saved his life," I answered. "He says Pop pulled him to the ground. It's probably why Pop took more bullets than the Don did."

"Pop's a hero."

"A dead hero, Vinnie."

"Nick—"

"Well, you can be proud of him," I went on. "Apparently he's your dad, not mine."

"Nick," Vinnie said, putting his hand on my shoulder. He was wearing an open neck polo shirt, no collar, but his manner was still that of a priest. "Blood tests can be wrong. We can do it all again after this is over."

"Sure," I said. "Look, I'm sorry. Really, I haven't even been thinkin' about that. All I've been thinkin' about is findin' out who the shooters were."

"What about the thing with Mary Ann Grosso? You told her mother you'd look into it."

"And I am," I said, "when I have the time. I talked to both Tony and Catherine today."

"Catherine?"

"Mary Ann's sister."

"Oh, yeah. I was out of high school when she came in. Maybe I should pay her mother a visit? In my official capacity, I mean."

"Sure, Father Vinnie," I said. "Maybe she'd like that."

"Father?" someone said, coming over.

"Oh, hi," he said. "This is my brother Nick. Nick, Mr. Voulo, Pop's neighbor."

"Your dad was a very nice man," Voulo said. He was tall, gray haired, and well-tanned, and I didn't remember ever having seen him in the neighborhood.

"Where do you live?"

"Two doors down," he said. "My wife and I moved in last year. Your dad was very welcoming." He looked at Vinnie. "We have to leave, Father."

"I'll come and say goodbye to your wife. Nick?"

"Go ahead, Vin," I said. "I'll stay here and finish this."

He nodded, took Voulo out of the kitchen.

I was thinking the house was full of people, a lot of whom I didn't know. How was I to know there wasn't a shooter in there, somewhere?

43

Was I being paranoid?

Hell, somebody had shot my old man. Maybe they were after the Don, but they'd managed to kill Vito Delvecchio. Who was to say there wasn't somebody here in the house…nah, I was being paranoid. Whoever had killed Pop—the Mafia, the Russians, the Jamaicans—what reason could they have for putting somebody in Pop's house? None at all. They'd be concentrating on getting to the Don, again.

Maria came into the kitchen with a tray of food.

"Mrs. Delgado made lasagna."

"Good," I said. "Save it for us for later, when everybody leaves."

She giggled, and said, "Help me make room in the fridge."

There were already a bunch of plates and Tupperware in there, but we managed to shove the lasagna in. I knew Mrs. Delgado from the neighborhood and knew she could cook. For a Spanish woman she made a hell of a lasagna.

Maria pushed it all the way in the back, then covered it. When she came out of the fridge she grinned at me and said, "Our secret."

Then she started to cry.

When the crowd thinned out Maria, Father Vinnie and I got the kitchen to ourselves.

"What's goin' on, Nick?" Maria asked.

I gave her a quick rundown so she knew what Vinnie knew, then filled in some blanks. Finally, I told them what I thought I was going to have to do.

"But why would Uncle Dom lie?" Maria asked, for the third time.

"That's what I have to find out, Maria," I said. "I'm at a disadvantage until I do."

"What about the shooter?" Father Vinnie asked.

"Shooter?" I asked. "You gettin' the lingo down, Father?"

"Get stuffed," Vinnie said. "Do you think the same people who shot Pop and the Don shot at you? And killed Carlo?"

"I'm not sure they were shootin' at me," I said. "They killed Carlo clean, with one shot. Also, the people who killed Pop fired off I don't know how many rounds. Maybe hundreds."

"So, two different…shooters?" Maria asked.

"See what you started?" I said to Vinnie. "Look, guys, I can't stop what I'm doin' to check in with you."

"We're worried about you," Vinnie said.

"When's the last time you slept?"

I had probably gotten three hours since the first shooting.

"I've slept."

"For how long?" she asked.

"Don't worry about me," I said.

"Can you just call in from time to time so we know you're alive?" Vinnie asked.

"Why don't you just pray for me to stay alive? Then you won't have to worry."

"Nick!" Maria said.

"Sorry, Vinnie," I said. "I didn't mean—"

"Don't worry about it, Nick," he said. "Where are you headin' after here?"

"Believe it or not," I said, "I have a date with a lady detective."

"A date?" Maria asked.

"Well…sort of…"

44

I left the house without calling Detective Del Costa. I figured she'd still be at the hospital trying to get something out of the Don that I couldn't get. I doubted he'd give it to them. He'd use that "I'm tired" excuse on them, too.

It was getting dark. Since I had nowhere else to go at the moment, I drove back to my place.

THE END OF BROOKLYN

***

I stopped at Sam's door and knocked. When she opened it she smiled. Her door was the only one I felt I could always knock on and find a smile.

"You look tired. Hungry, too?"

"I am," I said. "I was supposed to have some lasagna, but it didn't work out." When I left the house a new group of people were just arriving. Maria and I would have to break into our private stash another time.

"Come on in," she said. "I have some leftovers."

"Take out?" I asked, closing her door behind me.

"Home-cooked."

"Good."

Her apartment was like mine, minus the office.

"Here." Her arm came out of the kitchen door clutching a beer. I grabbed it. A cold Killian's Red, the top already popped. I carried it over to her desk, took a peek at the computer screen. It was black, even though the power was on. I studied the keyboard, saw a key marked SLEEP MODE.

"What's been happening?" she asked. "Come on into the kitchen and tell me."

I went in, sipped my beer and told her everything I had told my brother and sister while she heated up some leftover chicken and potatoes.

I finished my story at the table while I ate and washed it down with a second beer.

"When are you going to call the lady detective?" she asked.

"When I get back to my desk."

"What do you think she wants?"

"I don't know," I said. "Maybe an exchange of information."

"Why would she be that cooperative?"

"I don't know," I said. "Maybe she's got a crush on me."

"Well, you said she was good looking."

"I said she was hot."

"Oh, yeah."

"How's your book goin'?"

"Changing the subject?"

"Oh, yeah."

She grinned.

"It's goin' fine. Nick."

"Yes?"

"Okay if I go and see your sister tomorrow?" she asked. "Maybe she needs somebody to talk to. You said she was upset today."

"She's got Father Vinnie."

"That's a man."

"A priest."

"Her brother," she said. "She probably needs a woman to talk to."

"Then maybe it's a good idea," I said. "Thanks, Sam."

"I just want to help."

"This was really good," I said, pushing the empty plate away. "Thanks."

I stood up. She walked me to the door. I took the rest of my second beer with me.

"I'll go see Maria after breakfast," she said. "Ham and eggs?"

"If I'm around," I said. "Gimme a knock in the mornin'."

45

Alone in my office I once again thought back to the question of the blood tests. What was I supposed to do with the fact that my whole heritage—or lineage—was a lie? The answer was, at the present time, nothing. There were other things going on that were more important, such as people's lives. I could cry about my own problems later.

I checked my watch. If the Don was as unresponsive to the cops as he was to me, Detective Del Costa might be at her desk. I dialed the precinct and asked for her. Moments later, she picked up.

"Del Costa, Squad."

"You get anythin' out of the Don?" I asked.

"No," she said. "Did you?"

I remained silent.

"Come on," she said, "I know Big Benny called you first."

"I got nothin'," I said. "He claims he doesn't remember anythin'."

"He's lying," she said.

"I know he is," I said, "the question is, why? And why lie to me?"

She hesitated, then said, "You're serious, aren't you?"

"Hell yeah," I said. "I've been waitin' for him to wake up because I was sure he'd tell me somethin' important."

"You think maybe he's trying to protect you?" she asked.

I paused, then said, "I didn't think of that."

"You are family, right?" she asked. "I mean, real family?"

"Yeah," I said, "sort of."

"So maybe he doesn't want you getting shot."

I got a cold, fluttery feeling in my stomach and tried to ignore it.

"So Detective," I said, "what was it you wanted me to call you about?"

"I just thought maybe you'd like to meet for a drink," she replied.

"Meet?" I asked. "Like…a date?"

"I was thinking more of an exchange of information."

"Sounds good," I said. "When?"

"Half an hour?"

"Where?"

"Why don't you pick," she said, "as long as it's not a cop bar."

Okay, so she didn't want to be seen with me. Probably didn't want word getting back to Hicks.

"Let's go someplace no self-respecting cop would ever go," I said.

"A coffee bar?"

"A singles bar," I said. "A place called Last Exit, on Atlantic Avenue."

"A singles bar?"

"During the day it's a neighborhood bar, at night it gets kind of trendy and caters to singles. No cops, though."

"Well," she said. "Atlantic Avenue is far enough away. Okay, I'll meet you there in half an hour."

"If you're hungry I'll order some appetizers."

"Suits me," she said. "See you there."

I hung up, stood up to leave, decided to change my clothes and maybe put on some cologne. If I was going to Last Exit I figured I might as well look like a single on the prowl.

46

Last Exit was just down the block from Pete's Ale House, but you were more likely to run into cops at Pete's because of their beer selection.

The front of Last Exit was not fancy. In fact, it kind of looked like a dive. Over the door was a neon sign that read "Last Exit" with a neon arrow pointing to the door. It was the kind of place you might see Pete Gunn walking into.

The bar was long, very shiny mahogany. The inside had a little more class than the outside had.

The singles were in full swing. It looked like an under-thirty crowd and I was starting to think I'd picked the wrong place. The bar was crowded, and so were most of the tables. Even if we got a table, talking might be a problem. Especially if we had to yell at each other about shooting and blood.

I found a place at the end of the bar nearest the door so I'd see Del Costa when she arrived.

I ordered a Brooklyn Lager, fended off the feelers put out by a couple of thirtyish singles who were probably as out of place as I was.

One of the ladies was just walking away from me when I saw Del Costa step inside the door.

I almost didn't recognize her. She was wearing dark blue jeans, a red belt and a maroon silk blouse. She wasn't big breasted but the silk hugged what she had, which was very nice indeed. It was air-conditioned inside Last Exit and the silk made it easy to see that she reacted to the chill. Her hair was different, too. She had pulled it back into a ponytail that was worn sort of high up. Her mass of black hair was pulled back so tightly it gave her face and head a whole different look. Very unbusinesslike.

"Breaking hearts?" she asked, as she approached me.

"I think they're desperate," I said.

"It's kind of crowded in here."

"There's a little courtyard in the back with tables and chairs," I said. "I haven't been out there to see if it's also full. Would you like a drink?"

"Beer's good," she said. "You live near here, right?"

"Oh, yeah, right. I do. I mean, I drove, I didn't walk, but yeah, I live on—"

"And you have beer in your fridge?"

"Um, sure."

"Then why don't we just go there?" she suggested. "I mean, it'll be a lot quieter."

I looked around while I tried to think of an answer. The guys were admiring her, probably wondering what she was doing with me.

Of course, if she walked out with me they'd all be crushed, wouldn't they?

"Sure," I said. "Let's go."

Losers! I thought as we walked out.

47

I hoped Sam didn't hear us coming down the hall. I mean, we were just neighbors...well, no, we were friends, but not more than that...but still...I breathed a sigh of relief when we got inside and I locked the door behind Del Costa.

"Beer?" I asked.

"Sure."

"Bottle or glass?"

"Let's go with the bottle and see what happens," she said.

I went to the kitchen and came back with two opened bottles of Newcastle. Might as well break out the good stuff.

She had dropped her purse on the sofa and sat down next to it. Keeping her gun close, I thought, as I handed her the beer.

"Thanks."

I hadn't had time to notice in the bar, but her make-up was different. It seemed softer, and her lipstick was not as harsh a red as it had been the other times I'd seen her. She licked her lips and sipped from the bottle.

The way she smelled was also different. Less of a work scent and more of a...what? Play scent? Social?

The sofa had three cushions. I sat down and left the one between us empty.

"You look great tonight," I said. "Different."

"I don't get out much," she said. "I'm usually either dressed for work, or I'm at home in sweats."

I had a quick flash of her in sweats, then tried to push the thought away. There was something in the air, here, unless I was reading it wrong.

I sipped my beer and then asked, "What's on your mind, Detective?"

"We got back a complete report on ballistics," she said.

"And?"

"There's something there I thought you'd find interesting."

"And what was that?"

"Well, all of the rounds we found were fired from an Uzi—except one."

"One round different? What kind of gun was that from?" I asked.

"A sniper's rifle," she said. "A Dragunov SVD."

"A Russian gun?"

She nodded.

"Very popular in the seventies, very accurate from up to six hundred meters. I can give you all the specs if you like."

"I don't care about the specs," I said. "Uzis can be bought by anybody, but a Russian sniper rifle? Wouldn't that be a specialized weapon? You wouldn't see a bunch of Jamaicans buying a Russian sniper rifle from the trunk of a car, like they would an Uzi."

"You're right."

"So what the hell—some Russian sniper took a shot while somebody else was firing hundreds of rounds from an Uzi?"

"Maybe they were using the Uzi fire for cover. There's something else."

"What?"

"The same rifle was used to kill the driver, Carlo."

"Okay," I said, putting my bottle down so I could gesture with both hands while agitated. You can't take the Italian out of the boy. "So this connects both shootings. Somebody with a Russian rifle shot at Pop and the Don, and killed Carlo. The question is, was it somebody from the Russian *Mafiya*, or is it somebody trying to pin it on the Russians?"

"That's what I'm wondering."
"What's your partner wonderin'?"
"He's thinking a little differently than I am."
"Like how?"
"He's still looking into the first shooting as an attempt on the Don."
"And you?"
"I'm kinda wondering who might have had a reason to shoot your dad?"
"Nobody," I said.
"You sure?"
"I'm positive," I said. "Sure, my dad worked on the docks and he was a union rep for a long time, but he's been retired for years. He hasn't done anythin' to get shot over."
"So he was just in the wrong place at the wrong time?"
"That's what I was thinkin'."
"And that's what Hicks is thinking."
"But you're thinkin' different. Why?"
"Well," she said. "That's one of the reasons I called you."
"What?"
"The Russian 7.62 slug was found in your father."

48

I grabbed my bottle as I stood up quickly from the sofa. I took a swig while I paced. I just felt the need to move.

"You're sayin' my father was the target?"

"*I'm* saying that," she was quick to point out. "Nobody else is. Hicks even has our boss convinced the Don was the target. The fact that his driver was also killed supports that."

"The Don said my father jumped up and dragged him to the ground, tryin' to save him," I pointed out. "Could the bullet have struck him then?"

"The bullet hit him in the heart," she said. "Dead center. Just like the driver. If it hit him by accident, but took him in the heart, that'd have to be a helluva coincidence."

"If Hicks is right," I said, "then the Don is still a target."

"Right."

"Are you covering the hospital?"

"We've got a couple of men watching it, but they're not in plain sight."

"So you're hoping to catch the killer in the act," I said. "You don't care if it's while he's killing the Don."

"Not me," she said.

"Okay, Hicks and your boss."

"Right."

"But if my Pop was the target, why kill Carlo?"

"Maybe they were trying to kill you," she said. "That'd make more sense."

"But we're talkin' about another heart shot," I said. "They couldn't have missed me and hit Carlo in the heart. We were a good six feet apart. That's not a miss."

"No. That's a good shot."

"Two good shots, straight to the heart. We're dealin' with a pro, a crack shot. A sniper."

"For hire, maybe," she said. "Not a member of the Italian Mafia, and not a member of the Russian Red *Mafiya*, or any other gang. A hired pro."

"With a fondness for Russian rifles?"

"That might still be a ploy to blame the Russians," she said.

I kept pacing. She got up and walked over to me. She put her hand on my arm.

"Stop. Stand still."

I did. She stood very close to me. In her heels she was about an inch taller than me.

"There's nothing we can do about this tonight," she said. "This was just something I felt I had to tell you."

"I appreciate it."

"I can't begin to understand how you feel about losing your father. Both my parents are still alive. But to lose him the way you did, and now this."

I laughed, shook my head.

"What?"

"You don't know the half of it."

"What do you mean?"

"It's not important—"

"Maybe it is," she said.

So I told her about the blood tests.

"Oh my God," she said. "With everything you have to deal with, you don't need that, too. What have you done about it?"

"Nothin'," I said. "I've been tryin' not to think about it so I can concentrate on everythin' else. Plus I'm workin' another case." I told her about Mary Ann Grosso's apparent suicide.

"And you're still working that?"

"I took the case on first," I said. "I feel an obligation..."

She shook her head.

"You must be going crazy right now," she said. "I should leave..."

But she didn't. Instead she leaned forward and kissed me on the mouth, a soft, tentative kiss.

"Too forward?" she asked.

"No, I'm just...surprised."

"Well...this is the other reason I called you."

"Are you serious?"

"I don't date cops, Nick," she said. "And I don't like going to bars and picking up men for one night stands—although I'm not proud to say, I have done it."

"And me?"

"I thought we had something...in common," she said. "The last time we talked I felt that you might be somebody I could...relax with."

"Detective Del Costa," I asked, "are you tellin' me this is a booty call?"

She grinned sheepishly and asked, "Would that be so bad?"

"No," I said, pulling her to me, "no, that wouldn't be so bad, at all."

49

I woke up the next morning with a lady cop in bed with me. That was a first.

Del Costa's first name was Lydia. She was lying on her side with her back to me and I had to admire the view. She had a very toned body that she kept that way with jogging and volley ball. Long, strong legs, a rounded, solid butt, mid-sized firm tits with brown nipples that were hidden from me now, but I had spent a lot of time on them during the night.

I tore my eyes from her body—did I say how smooth and creamy her skin was?—and stared at the ceiling. I thought about everything I had learned from her last night. She had kept me so busy during the night, so this was my first chance to go over it, but I found it was all too much and too early. I needed more diversion.

I reached out and stroked her buttocks, ran my middle finger along her butt crack. She must have been awake because she rolled toward me right away.

She smiled and said, "I was wondering how you'd feel about all this in the morning."

"Well, about all this," I said, running my hands over her, "I feel pretty damn lucky. About the other stuff? I haven't had time to process it, yet."

"Mmm," she said, putting her arms around my neck, "well, maybe I can keep you from having to do that, yet."

We came together but before anything could develop there was a knock

on the front door.
"Oops," I said, suddenly remembering.
"Who's that so early?" she wondered aloud.
"My neighbor," I said. "Checkin' to see if I want breakfast."
More knocking.
"Your neighbor?"
I nodded.
"A girl?"
I nodded again.
"Does she make you breakfast often?"
"Sometimes," I said. "Last night she said she'd knock and see if I want breakfast this morning."
"And do you?"
"Well, yeah," I said, "but not right now."
"This neighbor," she said. "Is she a neighbor with benefits?"
"Not for a long time," I said. "Right now we're just friends."
"Uh-huh. I'm not stepping into the middle of anything, am I?"
"No, no," I said.
Knocking...
"But you're not going to answer the door, are you?" she asked.
"Ah, no."
"Because you don't want to have to explain?"
"Well," I said, looking down at our naked bodies, pressed up against each other, "I'm kinda comfortable, right now."
"You know," she said, "I'm not even gonna get involved in this. You'll just have to explain yourself later. Right now I want some attention."
"I have no problem with that," I said.
She pushed me onto my back so she could lie on top of me, trapping my hard cock between us. She rubbed her black pubic hair over me while we kissed and pretty soon had gotten so worked up she was getting me wet. Finally, she lifted her hips and just slid me into her, and then started working her butt up and down, biting her lip and squeezing her eyes shut...
The knocking at the door stopped.

50

Later, I watched her get up and trot over to the bathroom to take a shower. Her hair had come down from its ponytail pretty quick last night, and now was a mass of curls running down her back.
When I heard the shower go on I got up and pulled on a pair of boxer

shorts. I took my terry cloth robe from the closet and laid it on the bed for her. Next, I went out to the kitchen and got a pot of coffee started. I really didn't have anything to make for breakfast, but then I wasn't all that sure she'd be staying.

I went to where we'd left our clothes on the floor and started picking them up. I felt bad about letting Sam knock on the door so long. It was true we had slept together in the past, and that we were more friends now than anything, but I still hadn't wanted to have to answer the door and make an excuse, and I certainly didn't want to have to explain anything to her later on.

I left our clothes on the sofa and went back to the kitchen. By the time she came in wearing the robe, her hair wet from the shower, the coffee was ready.

"That smells good," she said.

"I don't make the best coffee," I told her, "and I have nothing for breakfast. We can go out—"

"Coffee will be enough," she said, accepting a cup from me. "I have to get home, get dressed and go into the office."

"Listen," I said, as we stood there drinking coffee, "thanks for bringin' me the info about the sniper rifle."

"I don't have to tell you how much trouble I'll be in if Hicks finds out I told you," she said.

"Of if he finds out about…this?" I asked, indicating our present state of undress.

"This is none of his business," she said. "What I do on my own time, and who I do it with, is up to me."

"As long as you don't do it with a cop."

"No cops is my choice," she said, "but yes, you're right. As long as I want him to be my rabbi, no cops. So it wasn't a very hard choice to make."

"I hope you get what you want out of that partnership," I said.

"And I hope I didn't spoil anything between you and your neighbor."

"Don't worry about that."

"I better get dressed and get going." She put the coffee cup down on the counter. "Nick, listen, about this…"

"I know," I said. "It may never happen again."

"Then again," she said, "it may. Is that okay with you?"

"I'm fine with booty calls, Lydia," I said.

"Well," she said, "I really wasn't thinking of it as a booty call—"

"Yeah, you were."

"Yes," she said ruefully, "you're right, I was."

She kissed me quickly, then went and got her clothes from the sofa and went to the bedroom to put them on.

***

When she came out of the bedroom she looked perfect, make-up in place, ponytail back.

"How do I look?" she asked.

"Unruffled."

"I just have to look decent enough to get back home," she said.

We'd both driven our cars back from Last Exit, so there was no need for me to give her a lift.

"Is there a back way?" she asked.

"There's another door, through the office, but you don't have to do that—"

"Hey," she said, "if I come out of the office door it might look better for both of us."

I shrugged and said, "Okay."

I walked her into the office, then let her out that door. As she stepped into the hallway she looked both ways and said to me, "Empty."

She gave me another quick kiss, then wiped lipstick from my mouth with her thumb.

"Call me," she said, "if you come up with anything."

"Yeah," I said "you, too."

"Wait." She took out her card, wrote on the back, and handed it to me. "My home number's on the back. You don't necessarily have to call me at the precinct."

"What about Hicks?" I asked. "Is he gonna want to talk to me again?"

"He's pretty pissed about not getting anything from the Don," she said. "He's not convinced that The Barracuda didn't tell you something."

"He didn't," I said. "I was tellin' the truth. But I'm gonna go and talk to him again. Maybe I can get somethin' out of him with this news that you gave me."

"Okay," she said. "Let me know. And you might run into me and Hicks at the hospital."

"I'll be properly respectful, Detective Del Costa."

She smiled, said, "Bite me," and walked down the hall.

51

I managed to get dressed and out without running into Sam. That was a situation I didn't want to handle until I had to. I was going to have to decide whether or not to lie to her.

I drove directly to Victory Memorial Hospital. I wanted to see if the information Del Costa had given me would shake the Don up at all. Or maybe he could just explain it to me.

As I got out of the elevator and approached the door I saw Jacoby in front of the room, but not Po.

"Where's Hank?"

"He went to get breakfast for us and Benny."

"Burger King?"

"For Benny," Jacoby said. "Bagels or somethin' for us. How you doin'?"

"Okay," I said.

"You look…agitated."

"I learned somethin' new last night."

I told him about the sniper rifle round being found in my father.

"Shit, that sort of changes things," he said.

"Doesn't make sense to me that my father was the target, and then Carlo would be killed."

"So somebody tryin' to pin this on the Russians, and hit your dad by mistake?"

"I don't know," I said. "I wanna see how the Don reacts to this news. He knows somethin', I'm sure of it."

"Those detectives were pretty steamed when they didn't get anything out of him," Jacoby said. "Well, that guy, Hicks. He was pissed. The woman… she was hot when she got here."

"Yeah, I know," I said.

"I mean, she gave us the cold shoulder, but—"

"I know," I said, again, cutting him off. "I'm gonna go in and see what I can get from the old man."

"Good luck. I'll send Benny's breakfast in when Hank gets back."

"You guys are gonna need to clean up and get some clothes."

"We've been takin' whore's baths in the sink in the Don's bathroom," Jack said. "When the nurse's aren't lookin', you know? And we both have some fresh underwear. We're okay."

"Okay," I said. "See you when I come out."

I went inside as Benny was coming out of the bathroom.

"Just freshenin' up," he said. I could smell the excess of cologne he'd used.

"How's he doin'?" I asked.

"In and out, but when he's awake he's pretty alert. And he wants to go home."

"He's got too many holes in him for that," I said.

"I keep tellin' him that. Hey, Nick, he's real upset about your dad."

"If that's true then maybe he should help me find out who did this."

I saw Benny's ears get red.

"You still think he's lyin'?"

"About somethin', Benny," I said. "Maybe he's lyin' because he's tryin' to keep us safe, huh?"

That seemed to mollify him a bit. "You think so?"

"He thinks a lot of you," I said. "He wouldn't want you to go out and get yourself killed tryin' to avenge him."

"No, no," Benny said, "you neither, Nick."

"So I'm gonna ask him some questions, Benny," I said, "and it may sound like I'm bein' harsh, you know? But I'm really just tryin' to get to the truth. You okay with that?"

"Yeah, yeah, Nicky, I'm okay with that."

"Okay." I slapped him on the arm. "Let's do this."

52

We approached the bed and the old man opened his eyes. I could see how alert he was.

"Can you get me out of here, Nick?" he asked.

"Sure," I said. "As soon as the doctors say you can leave without dying."

He made a rude sound with his mouth and said, "Doctors. They been tellin' me for years I'm gonna die. I'm still here."

"You're still here, Uncle," I said, "but my dad isn't."

"Do not remind me," he said, putting one hand over his eyes. I saw tears roll down his face. "Vito, my old friend."

"Uncle," I said, "my dad was shot with a different weapon."

"What?"

"You were both strafed with Uzis," I explained to him. "The cops aren't sure how many. But Pop was shot with a Russian sniper rifle. One bullet through the heart. Had to be fired by a pro."

"Russians?" he said, frowning.

"Not Russians," I said. "A Russian weapon."

"You mean," Benny asked, "somebody's tryin' to make it look like it was Russians?"

I looked at him. "Maybe." I looked back at the Don. "You have to tell me what you're holdin' back, Uncle. I need the whole story."

"I am holding nothing back."

"Who would want to kill Pop?"

"They were after me," he said, slowly, "not your father."

"Then why don't you have a bullet from a Russian sniper rifle in your heart?"

He didn't answer.

"You either know who did this," I said, "or you thought you knew, and now you're not so sure. So which is it?"

He gave that some thought.

"If you're tryin' to protect me, or Benny, or anybody else, forget it," I told him. "They already killed Carlo. If they're goin' after everyone close to you, that puts us on a hit list and there's nothin' you can do about it." I leaned in closer to him. "Except help us catch 'em before they kill us all."

Now he covered his face with both hands. There were tubes sticking in both arms.

"Let's start with the phone call," I suggested. "Who was it?"

For a moment I thought he wasn't going to answer, but then he dropped his hands away from his face.

"A voice," the Don said.

"Whose voice?"

"I don't know."

"What did it say?"

"One word."

Benny and I waited.

"*Vendetta.*" He said it in Italian.

"And then?"

"And then they hung up."

"Vendetta?"

"Blood feud," Benny said.

"I know what a Vendetta is," I said. "Who was it, Uncle?"

"They did not say."

"Who could it be?" I asked. "Vendetta is usually involved family against family, isn't it? What family would call Vendetta against you? And why now?"

"It could be many families from over the years," he said. "To choose one would be like..."

"...a needle in a haystack?" I asked.

"*Si.*"

"That can't be," I said. "This must go back many years. You are—well, you're..."

"Old," he said.

"Well, yeah. So someone with a Vendetta against you would also be... old."

"Vendetta is handed down from generation to generation," he said.

"So it could be someone's children?" I asked. "Or grandchildren?"
"Yes."
"And you?" I said. "Who is left in your family, Uncle? I mean, not Carlo, or Benny, or Pop, but an actual blood relative."

He stared up at me from the bed.

"There is only one."

I was afraid to ask.

"Who?"

"You," he said, "*figlio mio.*"

My son.

53

I stared at Dominick Barracondi, then looked at Benny, who was in turn staring at me with a dumfounded look on his face.

"Nick..." the Don said, reaching a hand out to me. "Forgive me."

"Not now," I said, backing away from the bed. "This is too much. On top of everythin' else, this is too much."

"Nick—" he called from the bed.

"Hey, Nicky—" Benny said.

But I wasn't listening to either of them. I was heading for the door. I had to get out of that room.

I burst out into the hall, surprising both Jacoby and Po.

"Nick—" Jacoby said.

"What the hell—" Hank Po said.

"I need a few minutes, guys," I said, holding my hands out to them. "I need to clear my head. That old bastard just told me I'm his son!"

I headed off down the hall, leaving them both stunned. But maybe not as stunned as me.

I found the cafeteria, got myself a bad cup of coffee and sat down at a table.

Okay, it made sense.

If Vito Delvecchio wasn't my father, who else was around back then that my mother might have been with? When we were kids Uncle Dom was always around. Who else would my mother go to if she had a problem?

We knew my parents had some problems in their marriage from time to time. Their relationship was...tempestuous. But the death of my older brother seemed to fix that. After he died they got closer. But by then the damage had been done. I had already been born. According to the doctor I wasn't Vito's son, and according to Dominick Barracondi, I was his.

I guess if I needed a second opinion, I'd gotten it from the horse's mouth.

I felt the floor vibrating and when I looked up saw Benny stalking towards me with a determined look on his face.

"Nicky—" he said.

"Take it easy, Benny."

"The Don just told you you're his son," Benny said. "You can't just walk out on him."

"How would you like it if you found out your dead father wasn't your father," I asked. "And then you find out that the Don is."

"If the Don told me I was his son, I'd be proud," Benny said.

"Benny, this means the Don bedded my mother."

Benny looked as if I'd slapped him. He'd never really talked about his mother, not even when we were in high school. But that had stopped him.

"Sit down, Ben," I said.

He sat.

"I'm dealin' with a lot here, man," I said. "I just need time to make some sense of it."

"Okay," Benny said, "I guess I understand that."

"If this is a Vendetta against the Don, that still doesn't explain why a sniper put a bullet in my dad's heart."

Benny remained silent.

"And if this is a Vendetta against the Don and I'm his only blood relative, then I've got a huge target on my back."

"I guess—"

"Then why was Carlo killed that night, and not me?" I asked. "You see? There's so much about this that doesn't make sense."

"Uh-oh," Benny said, looking past me.

"What?"

"More trouble."

I turned and saw Detective Sergeant Hicks heading toward me.

Benny stood up.

54

"Beat it, Guido," Hicks said, pointing at Benny. "I'm here to talk to Delvecchio."

Benny's ears reddened.

"It's okay, Benny," I said. "Go back to the Don's room."

Benny gave Hicks a hard look, then turned and stalked away.

"Is that coffee any good?" he asked, indicating the cup on the table in front of me.

"No," I said. "It's terrible."

"It's gotta be better than the crap at the office," he said. "I'll be right back."

"Where's your partner?" I asked.

"She was late this mornin'," Hicks said. "But she should be along soon. I left a message tellin' her to meet me here. You're right. I'll get her one, too."

Well, it looked like I wasn't going to get any time to myself to process my new information. It was just as well. If I'd had any spare time at all over the past couple of days I probably would have curled up into a little ball.

"Okay," Hicks said, appearing across from me. He put down a pastry and two cups of coffee, one black and one with milk, then proceeded to dump a few pounds of sugar into the milky coffee from the holder on the table.

"You ever heard of diabetes?" I asked.

"Yeah, my whole family has it," he said. "If I'm gonna get it, I'm gonna enjoy sugar while I can. Pastry? I'm not sure what kind it is, but—"

"No, not for me," I said. "What's on your mind, Sergeant?"

"Probably the same thing that's on yours," he said. "That is, if you've been tellin' the truth."

"About what?"

"About what Nicky Barracuda told you."

"He hasn't told me anything."

"And that's what he's told us," Hicks said. He bit into his pastry, licked icing from his upper lip, then sipped his coffee. "Nothin'. Only I think he knows more than he's tellin'."

"You know," I said, "that's what I think."

"Good," he said. "Then you can help us."

"How?"

"Get him to tell you what he knows, and then you tell us."

I sat back in my chair and looked at him.

"Do you have any new information?" I asked. "About my father, for instance?"

"Your father? No, nothin' new. Why?"

"I was just wonderin'."

"Look, it's the old Don who was the target, not your father," he said. "That's what we have to concentrate on. Oh, there she is."

I turned in my seat and saw Detective Del Costa coming towards us. Suit, red lipstick, hair down, very businesslike.

"Good morning," she said.

"Mornin'," we both said.

"I got you a coffee," Hicks said.

"Thanks."

"There was a pastry, but I ate it."

"That's okay."

She sat with us, removed her purse from her shoulder and hung it on the back of the chair.

"What've we got?" she asked Hicks.

"Nothin'" he said, "which is what I was tellin' Mr. Delvecchio here. We've got nothin', and he's got nothin', so maybe he can help us get somethin'."

She looked at me as if she had never seen me before.

"Oh, yes?" she said. "Going to be helpful?"

I shrugged. "If he tells me anythin', I'll let you know."

"We're gonna go talk to him while we're here," Hicks said. "You still got those two friends of yours on the door?"

"Yep."

"We've got men watching the place, you know."

"I can't see them."

"That's the point," Hicks said.

"So you're staking the Don out?"

"The Don," Hicks repeated. "You say that with such respect. He's a fuckin' gangster, for Chrissake!"

"Doesn't mean you can stake him out like a goat," I said.

"Don't worry," he said. "We'd get them before they got him."

"Or after," I said. "Wouldn't make much difference to you, would it?"

"Look—" Hicks started.

"Mr. Delvecchio," Del Costa said, "why don't you go and talk to the Don, tell him that we'll be in to see him and that he should cooperate."

"And you think he'll listen to me?"

"He'll listen to you more than he will to us," Del Costa said. I had the feeling she was trying to tell me something with her eyes.

"Okay," I said. "I'll go and talk to him, while you two finish your coffee."

"Thank you," she said.

I stood up and headed back to the Don's room.

55

"The detectives are right behind me," I said to Jacoby and Po.

"Tough," Jacoby said. "No more bagels left."

I laughed and went inside.

"Nick?" the Don said.

I went to his bedside.

"You came back—"

"No time to talk...Uncle. The detectives are on their way to question you again."

"I will tell them nothing," the old man said.

"That's up to you if you want to be stubborn," I said. "Just don't tell them what you told me about...us."

A hurt look came into his eyes. "You are...ashamed."

"I don't know what I am," I said, "but I need time to figure it out. So let's just keep that little piece of information between the three of us, okay?"

He nodded and said, "As you wish."

I looked at Benny and he said, "Okay."

"I gotta go," I said. "I'll see you both later."

As I left the room I saw Hicks and Del Costa coming up the hall towards us.

"Man, she is hot," Jacoby said.

"Uh-huh," Po agreed.

I kept quiet.

As Hicks reached us he ignored Jacoby and Po and gave me a knowing look. Behind his back Del Costa gave me a whole different kind of look.

"Jesus," Po said.

"What?" Jacoby asked.

"He hit that," Po said. He looked at me. "You hit that, didn't you?"

"I'll never tell."

"He did!" Jacoby said.

"I gotta go," I said.

"What'd he tell you, Nick?" Jacoby asked. "I mean, about...you know."

"Nothin' yet," I said. "I haven't had a chance to talk to him about it. Hell, I haven't even had a minute alone to think about it."

"Maybe that's for the best," Po said.

"Yeah," I said, "I'll deal with it all after this is over."

"Is he gonna tell them anythin'?" Po asked, jerking his head toward the door.

"I doubt it."

"Then you better get out of here before they come lookin' for you."

"Good advice," I said, stating down the hall. "I'll be in touch."

I got out of the hospital. Now where to? I was armed with new information—the Russian sniper rifle, and the little fact that the Don was claiming to be my father. I decided to drive over to Pop's house and see if Maria and Father Vinnie were still there. I wanted to talk to Vinnie but wondered if I was going to be able to do it without Maria around?

I parked out front and hoped there wouldn't be such a crowd in the house today. I know they liked my dad, but couldn't they wait for his wake?

As I entered I realized I hadn't asked either Hicks or Del Costa when we could have the body for a funeral. I knew their case was still ongoing, but if Hicks was so sure that the shooters were after the Don, why not release Vito's body?

Vito! When had I ever thought of my dad as Vito? Already I was starting to think of him differently.

I entered the house with my key. "Hello?" I called. "Anybody home?"

"In the kitchen!" Maria shouted.

I joined her there. She had containers and bowls out and seemed to be consolidating food to make more room in the refrigerator.

"Hey, where's Vinnie?"

"He had to go to work," she said.

"They're pushing him to come back?"

"No, no," she said, "they'll give him as much time as he wants, but one of the priests got sick, so he's covering. Why?" She looked up from the Tupperware she was closing. "Is there something you can talk to him about and not me?"

"What? No. What makes you think that?"

"Because now that you know he's not here you're edging towards the door."

Suddenly, my stomach was growling and I remembered all I'd had so far was my own bad coffee and the hospital's worse.

"I tell you what," I said. "You make me somethin' to eat and I'll tell you what I was gonna tell Vinnie."

56

"He said *what*?"

We decided to keep Mrs. Delgado's lasagna for dinner, so Maria heated up somebody's tuna casserole for me.

"He told me he's my father."

"You mean Uncle Dom and Mom..."

"That's what it means."

She took a moment to try to digest what I'd told her, then asked, "Do you believe him?"

I dropped my fork, letting it clink into my plate and put my elbows on the table.

"I don't know what to believe, Maria," I said. "I've got things comin' at me from all sides."

And I included in that Detective Del Costa's booty call—as if I didn't have enough to think about.

"But Ma, cheatin' on Pop?" she asked.

"We know they had some trouble," I said. "They never made a secret of that."

"Yeah, but they got over it."

"Well, maybe she was with Uncle Dom during that time."

She hesitated, then asked, "So, does this mean you're in the Mafia?"

"Yeah, probably," I said. "I'll probably have to kill somebody so I can be a made man."

"Nick!"

"Of course I'm not in the Mafia, Maria." I picked my fork up again.

"I was just asking."

I decided not to tell Maria about the "Vendetta" talk. For one thing, why push everything that was burdening me onto her shoulders? For another, it sounded so fucking dramatic.

"What are you going to do when you finish eatin'?" she asked.

I shrugged. "I guess I'll go and see Vinnie," I said.

And tell him the rest that I didn't tell her, like the stuff about the Russian sniper rifle.

"Nick, do you want me to go to the hospital and give Benny some time to go home and change?"

"You could try," I said. "I don't think Benny's gonna leave the Don's side for a second."

"Maybe I should go and just give him someone to talk to, huh?"

"That sounds good," I said. It would also get her out of the house. Vito's house. My father's—*her* father's house.

Ah, shit.

Vinnie worked at the Church of the Holy Family, in Canarsie. The church was on the corner of Flatlands Avenue and Rockaway Parkway, the school at the other end of the block. The Rectory was positioned between them.

At one time this was considered one of the well-to-do parishes in Brooklyn, but things had begun to change. The original owners of many of the homes in the area had started to sell and move away. How to put this without sounding like a bigot? Less desirable types had begun to move in.

I stopped at the front door of the Rectory and rang the bell. A priest I didn't know, white-haired and slightly bent, answered.

"I'm here to see Father Vincent."

"Do you have an appointment?"

"I'm his brother, Nick." Unless I suddenly found out that we didn't even have the same mother!

"Oh, of course," he said. "Come in. I'll tell him you're here."

I waited just inside the door. There wasn't a sound in the place. As a kid the Rectory had always felt more eerie to me than even the big churches had.

Vinnie came down the hall and said, "Hey, Nick, come on up."

He took me up to his room on the second floor. It was not large and was very simply furnished. The only sign that it was my brother's was a bookshelf full of paperbacks. Agatha Christie, Andrew Greeley, and G.K. Chesterton's Father Brown, among others.

"I had to come in and cover for Father Paul—" he started to explain, but I cut him off.

"Maria told me."

"Why are you here?"

"Well, you guys both told me you wanted me to check in."

"And you said you couldn't be checking in with us all the time, so somethin's wrong. What is it?"

"More...weird news."

"Like what?"

He sat quietly while I told him about the Russian sniper, what the implications of that could be, and then hit him with the *"figlio mio"* stuff last.

57

Vinnie sat there, stunned.

"I don't know what shocks me the most," he said, "that the Don is your father, or that Pop might've been the target."

"Yeah, well...it's all been kind of shockin', hasn't it?"

"Nicky..." He reached out and put a hand on my knee. He was sitting on the edge of his bed, and I was in the room's only chair.

"I know, I know," I said, "you're still my brother, Maria's still my sister."

"And the Russians killed Pop?"

"I think the Uzis are supposed to make us suspect the Jamaicans, and the rifle is supposed to make us suspect the Russians."

"Then who did it?"

"Well," I said, slowly, "I haven't told you about the Vendetta."

Just the word "Vendetta" conjures up a gray-haired old Italian woman flicking her thumb off her gold front teeth.

"What?" Vinnie said.

I told him how I knew the Don was holding something back and was finally able to drag it out of him.

"Was he serious, Nick?"

"Looked pretty serious to me."

"So is he gonna tell the cops?"

"I don't know what he's gonna tell them, but I asked him not to tell them that I'm his son. When I told Maria she asked me if that meant I was in the Mafia. What are the cops gonna think?"

"They'll never believe you didn't know, will they?"

"No," I said, "suddenly, I'll be Michael Corleone in their eyes."

"Nick," Vinnie said, "maybe you should just back off and let the police handle it. All of it."

"I could do that, Vin," I said, "but if the Don is right, if I'm his son and this is a Vendetta, then I won't be allowed to do that. They'll come after me."

I'd tried to figure this out six ways from Sunday, talked it out with a few people. What I hadn't done was sit in a room by myself and give it all some good, hard, analytical thought.

Like Father Vinnie said.

All of it.

Vinnie walked me down to the door with his arm around my shoulder.

"What a mess," he said.

"Yeah," I said, "a confusing mess."

"I don't know how you can concentrate. I guess it's that detective's brain of yours. What Hercule Poirot calls 'the little gray cells.'"

"I think I need a drink," I said. "Or lots of drinks. What does Poirot say about that?"

"I think he's a teetotaler."

"Yeah, well, tea ain't gonna do it," I said. "I'm sure even Father Brown went into the sacrificial wine, sometimes."

He slapped me on the back as I opened the door. He said, "Let me know what happens—and when we can get Pop's body and plan the funeral."

"Okay, Vin," I said. "I'll be in touch."

58

I drove back to my place. This time I was hoping my message machine would be flashing, and that it would be Winky with some information. But if there wasn't a hit out on the Don, what could Winky even find out for me?

For a change the red light was off. I slammed my door, then realized this would probably attract Sam's attention. I still had to explain to her why I wasn't around for breakfast.

I waited, listening for her door to open, and when it didn't I assumed I lucked out and she wasn't home.

I took off my windbreaker, still weighed down by the gun in my pocket. I was sure Hicks had noticed, but he hadn't said a word. I might not be so lucky next time, but I did have a permit so it would just be a matter of whether or not he wanted to give me a hard time. The cops could always pull my license and confiscate my gun while they examined my qualifications. It had been tried before, but I had hardly any shooting incidents on my record.

I went into the bathroom to wash up, found the terry cloth robe Del Costa had worn hanging on the door, still smelling like her. I knew my sheets would smell of her, too, so I'd have to change them or try to sleep with blue balls all night.

Not that I'd been getting much sleep.

Suddenly, as I was drying my hands, sleep seemed like a damned good idea. I didn't even bother with the sheets. I shucked my clothes, wrapped myself in the Del Costa sheets, and was asleep in moments, despite the daylight.

It was dark when I woke up. I was confused. I didn't know what time of day it was. I looked at my window and saw that the shade was up. After a few moments my eyes got used to the darkness and I realized it wasn't *that* late.

I turned onto my back and then stopped. Something had woke me up. What was it? I'd had a thought, but now I couldn't retrieve it. I listened, and then I heard it.

Somebody was in the office.

Sam?

Or somebody with Vendetta on their mind?

Jeez, where was my gun? Oh yeah, in my jacket pocket. Where was my jacket?

I got off the bed.

To get to the office I had to walk through the entire apartment. It was dark, but not pitch black. I was wearing only my boxers, and no shoes. I managed not to stub my toe anywhere.

Behind my front door I always kept a Mickey Mantle baseball bat for emergencies. I got my hands on it, and then crept toward the office, holding it ready.

And at that moment there was a knock at the door.

I stopped. Not a sound came from the office. Then I heard the office door opening. I'd been meaning to oil those hinges.

I turned and ran for my front door. To get off the floor the intruder had to go by there. I heard noise in the hall, the sound of somebody hitting the floor. I swung the door open with the bat ready.

Sam looked up at me from the floor, and pointed down the hall.

"He went that way!"

"You all right?"

"Go!"

I ran down the hall, into the stairwell. I could hear him pounding down the stairs, but it wasn't easy to chase somebody when I was only wearing boxer shorts and no shoes.

I made it as far as the main floor, but he was out the door and gone. I stopped at the front door, looking both ways, saw somebody hotfooting it down the street.

I put the bat on my shoulder and walked back upstairs. Sam was still in the hallway, leaning against the wall and rubbing her left foot.

"You okay?" I asked.

"He stomped on my foot," she said.

"Come on." I grabbed her arm and helped her into my place.

I put her on the sofa and said, "Let me get dressed."

"Go ahead."

I was in the bedroom pulling on my pants when she yelled, "So you were in the bedroom and he was creepin' around your office?"

"Yeah," I called out. "Believe it or not, I finally fell asleep."

"So what was he lookin' for?"

"I don't know." I stepped back into the room, dressed. "Why don't we find out? Can you walk?"

"Yeah."

She got up and we walked to the office. I turned on the light.

"So it was a he?"

"Definitely a he," she said. "Tall guy, but not husky."

"Fast, too," I said. "I saw him running down the street. Even if I'd been dressed I don't think I could've caught him."

I went to my desk, stood behind it, and surveyed the room for anything out of place.

"And if he had a gun, what were you gonna do with your bat?"

"Hit a home run, hopefully," I said, still scanning the room.

"Anything missing?" she asked.

"Nothing missing," I said, "nothing disturbed."

"You can tell?"

She looked around. Maybe it was a little messy, but I knew where things went.

"I can tell."

"So then who was it? A burglar? Or a killer, lying in wait?"

"'Lying in wait?'" I asked. "Have you ever really written that line?"

"Just last night, actually," she said. "Beer?"

"Let's go."

We left the office and went to the kitchen. She went into the fridge, came out with two Rolling Rocks. "So how did it go with your lady detective?" she asked.

I froze.

59

"Come on, Nick," she said. "The good stuff's gone. Your Newcastle? You only pull those out for special situations. I knocked this morning, you didn't answer, but I knew you were home. And then she came walking out of your office. What'd she do, show up on your doorstep at dawn?"

I studied her, to see if she was playing games. She wasn't, but I thought she was giving me an out. After all, who has Newcastle for breakfast?

"No," I said, "she spent the night."

She sipped her beer.

"She wanted to meet the night before, so I picked Last Exit, only it was too crowded to talk."

"Could've went down the street to Pete's."

"She didn't want to go anywhere we might be seen by other cops."

"Don't tell me, let me guess," Sam said. "She doesn't do cops."

"No, she doesn't."

"So you ended up here?"

"Right."

"And you couldn't answer the doctor and tell me to go away?"

"Uh, no."

She sipped her beer again.

"So what'd you find out?"

"The killing shot on my dad didn't come from an Uzi, it came from a Russian Dragunov."

"A Russian sniper rifle?"

I stared at her.

"What? I do my research."

"I'm impressed."

"So what's it all mean?"

"A heart shot, just like the driver, Carlo."

"That doesn't make sense," she said. "I could see Carlo and the Don, but this…"

"I know," I said. "I've hashed and rehashed it."

"There's something else, isn't there?"

"Yeah," I said. "The Don says it's some kind of Vendetta."

"For real?"

"Yeah, for real."

"So anyone close to him or related to him, is in danger?"

"Blood relatives."

"Does he have any?"

"Just one."

She stared at me, then put her hand over her mouth and took a deep breath.

"Oh, Nick."

"Yeah."

"Do the cops know?"

"No," I said. "Not from me, anyway. They went in to talk to the old man today."

"Do you think he told them?"

"We agreed he wouldn't, but who knows?"

"How sharp is he?"

"Very sharp."

"Then he won't blurt it out by accident?"

"No."

"So this, tonight, a killer?"

"Probably."

"Nick, you need to be careful."

"Yeah," I said, "better locks."

"More than that," she said. "You need to hide."

"Hide?" I asked. "That's one alternative I didn't think of."

"No, you wouldn't. Let me ask you this. If you're included in this Vendetta because you're a blood relation to Dominick Barracondi, are Maria and Father Vinnie at risk because they're your blood relatives?"

I stared at her over my green bottle and then said, "Oh, shit."

60

"You want me to what?" Father Vinnie asked.

I was sitting on my sofa watching Sam drink beer from a bottle—always a pleasure—talking to Vinnie, who I called on the phone at the Rectory.

"Take Maria and go on a vacation," I said. "Maybe Florida."

Sam shook her head violently.

"What?" I asked.

"Everybody goes there. Tell him to go someplace else."

"There's a monastery," Vinnie said, "a retreat. We could—"

"No," I said. "Vin, that's too obvious."

"Not for Maria."

"She's Catholic, isn't she?"

"Well, yeah…"

"Well, yeah…and what do you mean, not for her?" I asked.

"Well, I assume you're worried about us."

"Good guess."

"So I agree that Maria should go away."

"But not you."

"I'm needed here, Nick."

"Vinnie—"

"Father Vincent."

"Don't pull rank with me."

"Maine," Sam said. "That's where I'd go."

"Great," I said. "Nobody in my family would ever think of that."

"Of what?" Vinnie asked.

"Maine."

"What about Maine?"

"Go…to…Maine!" I shouted into the phone.

"Nick," he said, "what happened tonight?"

I told him.

"What the hell—sorry—heck were you gonna do with a baseball bat against a gun?" he asked.

"You're not the first person to ask me that," I said, "and it was a Mickey Mantle."

"And because somebody broke into your office you want me and Maria to go into hiding?"

"Look, Vinnie, it's this Vendetta thing."

"What about it?"

I laid it out for him the way Sam had laid it out for me.

He was quiet. Then he said, "You just worked that out tonight?"

"Um, well, Sam asked me the question."

"Well...it's a good one," he said. "But maybe before we go into hiding you should ask someone if that's really what happened to him."

"Like who?"

"Like the Don."

That was probably a good idea.

"So you're gonna go to the hospital and talk it all over with...the Don?" Sam asked.

"If I get this part cleared up, I can stop thinking about it. Then maybe I can solve the shooting."

"So you're gonna go tonight?"

I checked my watch.

"Visiting hours are over," I said, "but the two men on the door *are* workin' for me."

"Nick?" she said. "Let's get something to eat, then you can go back to bed, get some more rest and go see the Don in the morning."

"I should do it tonight..."

I realized I was hungry.

"You think this guy's going right from here to Father Vinnie's? Or Maria's?"

"Maria," I said. "I should go and see Maria." I looked at her. "Did you go see her?"

"I was going to," she said, squirming, "but I got involved in my book, and—"

"It doesn't matter," I said. "Come with me now."

"Nick, I have to—"

"Wait."

I called my father's house. The phone rang five times and I was just starting to get worried when Maria answered.

"Where were you?"

"I went to the hospital to see Benny," she said. "I just got back."

"Okay, stay there. I'm comin' over and I'm bringin' company."

"To eat?"

"Yes."

"Good," she said. "I'll pull out the lasagna."

I hung up and looked at Sam.

"There's food," I said. "Lots of it. The whole neighborhood turned out."

"You're inviting me to dinner with you and your family?" she asked.

"Yes."

I dialed the Rectory, got Vinnie again.

"Now what?"

"Food, at Pop's, tonight," I said.

"Yeah, sure," he said. "I'm hungry. Is there still some of Mrs. Delgado's lasagna?"

"We haven't touched it yet."

"See you there."

We hung up.

"Ready?" I asked Sam.

"Sure, why not?"

61

We went downstairs and got in my car.

"What were you comin' to see me about tonight?" I asked.

"You mean when I interrupted your plan to go up against a killer with a Louisville Slugger?"

"A Special Mickey Mantle Louisville Slugger."

"Okay!"

"You know who Mickey Mantle was, right?"

"Yes," she said, "I've been in New York that long. And I was just coming to see if you wanted to eat. I was going to heat something up, but I like this better." We drove in silence for a while and then she said, "You're too honest sometimes, you know."

"Am I? Oh, you mean tellin' Vinnie that it was your idea that he and Maria—"

"No," she said, "I didn't mean that. I gave you every out with your lady detective."

"Oh, that," I said.

"Yes, that."

"We're friends, Sam," I said. "Close friends. I didn't want to lie to you."

"Nick...what you do in your own apartment is your business."

"Yeah, I know..."

"But?"

"I didn't plan it," I said.

"I know," she said, staring straight ahead. "It just happened."

"It just happened," I repeated, and then there it was. The thought I'd woken up with, and lost.

I turned the car around.

"What are you doing?"

"One stop," I said.

THE END OF BROOKLYN

***

When Catherine opened the door she looked at Sam, and then me, and asked, "Was there something else you wanted to talk to me about, Nick?"

"The last time we talked you said Mary Ann slept well, that she didn't take sleeping pills."

"That's right."

"Is your mother home? I'd like to talk to her."

"Come on in," she said. "She's in Mary Ann's room."

I looked at Sam.

I'll wait here," she said.

"I went down the hall and found Mary Ann's mother sitting alone the way I had left her when I saw her last.

"Angela?"

For a moment it seemed as if she hadn't heard me, then she suddenly looked up.

"Nick?" she said. "What are you doing here? You have your own family to think of—"

"It's okay," I said. "I just have some things to ask you."

"Oh, well, all right. Come, sit."

I moved into the room, sat at the foot of the bed, leaving some space between us.

"Tell me about Mary Ann, Angela."

"What about her?"

"What kind of child was she?"

She got a faraway look in her eyes. "She was a beautiful child, so beautiful. Obedient, when she was younger..."

"And when did she change?"

"Change?"

"You know what I mean. Was it in high school? When she got boy crazy?"

"Boy crazy? What do you mean?"

"I've read her poetry, Angela. I've talked with Catherine...and with Sal."

"Sal..."

"You know Sal, Angela. You know a lot of things."

She remained silent.

I moved closer to her. "Come on, Angela. Tell me about Mary Ann. Tell me what she was really like."

She waited a long time to answer me, and I waited with her. I didn't want to hear any more of that "beautiful child" stuff and if the truth was going to come out, I was willing to wait.

Finally she looked at me and her expression was totally different. No longer was she the mother in mourning. Now she was the dissatisfied mother, the long-suffering mother.

"She was disrespectful," she said. "She was...bad...a trial, Nick, believe me. She was...wild. Everyone thought she was such a saint, but—"

"Who's everyone, Angela?"

"My friends, our relatives," she said. "Tony. She had him totally fooled. She had them all fooled. That don't know what she was like when she discovered boys and...sex!" She said the word as if it had four letters, not three. "She had sex for the first time in junior high school. Did you know that?"

I didn't know that, but what could I say?

"She was...uncontrollable! But she was smart."

"Smart enough to fool everybody but you, huh, Angela?" I asked. "And Sal. She couldn't fool Sal."

"Sal," she said, shaking her head. "What she did to that poor boy."

"You mean...the rape?"

"Rape!" she spat. "There was no rape. I think Sal may have been the only boy to give her exactly what she wanted."

"Why was she marrying Tony, then?"

"Why? Because she said she had changed, that's why. Saw the *light*. That after she had spent her life doing things no Catholic girl should ever do."

She averted her eyes. She didn't look at me, or out the window, but at the crucifix that was on the wall.

"She said God forgave her, and she wanted me to forgive her."

"But you couldn't?"

"I knew she hadn't changed. I knew she'd go back to making my life miserable, and she'd do it to Tony."

"So you killed her."

"I did not!" she said, her head snapping toward me, her eyes flashing. "She was my daughter, for God's sake."

"Angela, the police found a bottle of sleeping pills in her room. They were yours."

"She must have...taken them."

"But they were in your bathroom, Angela. Your daughters never went into your bathroom. Never."

"She was bad," Angela said. "She'd do...anything."

"But why go upstairs to get the pills and then downstairs to take them? And why leave the container on the sink?"

"I...I don't know. She must have taken them."

"Did she, Angela?" I asked. "Did she do that? O did you give them to her?"

"I did not *force* her to take them."

"Maybe you didn't force her," I said, "but you gave them to her, didn't you?"

She looked at me, then away, back at the crucifix.

"I—I didn't know what to do. I prayed for guidance. If she stayed here...got married...eventually people would find out...what she was really like."

"What if she really had changed? How about that?" I asked. "What if she married Tony, made him a good wife, and had grandchildren?"

"She wouldn't..." she said, shaking her head. "She wouldn't..."

"Well, you'll never know, Angela," I said, "because you badgered her into taking those pills."

"I told her, if she had really changed there was only one way to get right with God."

"Suicide?" I asked. "Suicide is a mortal sin, Angela. Not exactly the way to get right with God, is it? No, you wanted her to get right with you, and dead she could never disgrace you again."

She remained silent.

"Did you sit with her, Angela? Watch her take them? Or did you leave her alone? Let her die alone." I got in her face, so she couldn't turn away. "Did you actually tell your own daughter she'd be better off dead?"

"I did the right thing," she said. "I know I did."

I left the room. She was still saying it, over and over, trying to convince herself.

62

"So what are you going to do?" Sam asked in the car. "Tell the police?"

"I can tell them," I said, "but I can't prove anything. Angela would have to admit it. And even if she did, she's right. She didn't *force* those pills down Mary Ann's throat."

"But...she was responsible."

"For what?" I asked. "She gave her pills. She didn't mean to kill her daughter. It just...happened."

When we got to the house Vinnie hadn't arrived yet. Sam and Maria hugged and then went to the kitchen together. I stayed in the living room, waiting for Vinnie. I was tired of hashing and rehashing things out in a half-assed fashion because I was actually trying *not* to think about who my father was. Maybe with these three people—the people I felt closest to—I could work things out and clear my head.

When Vinnie arrived I had to admit it had a calming effect on me to see him wearing his collar. On other men the white collar affected me the way a red flag affects a bull.

We embraced briefly then he went into the kitchen and came back with two Rolling Rocks.

"The girls said dinner will be ready in a few minutes," he said. "It's nice to see Sam here."

"Yeah," I said.

"What did you do?" he asked.

"What do you mean?"

"That look on your face, it's the same one you had when they caught you in a closet in fifth grade with Bernadette McDonald."

"You're crazy—"

"Come on," he said, lowering his voice, "who were you in the closet with this time?"

I took a swig from my bottle and then said, "Detective Del Costa."

"With all the black hair?" he said, eyes wide. "Jesus. I thought you said she was a ballbuster—"

"Father Vinnie!"

"I'm just quoting you."

"I don't think I ever said that."

"Well, you insinuated it."

"Maybe that's her reputation in the department, but..."

"Jeez, Nick," he said, "what's wrong with you? Well, I hope you had the good sense not to go to your own apartment."

I kept quiet.

"You did it right across the hall from Sam?"

"Look, Vinnie," I said, "Sam and I are friends—"

"Are you gonna be this dense all your life?"

"Vinnie," I said, bringing my voice even lower, "I didn't come here to talk about me and Sam, okay? I've got enough on my mind."

"Okay, okay..."

Sam and Maria came out of the kitchen carrying bowls and plates and Maria said, "It would be nice if someone went into the kitchen and brought out the drinks..."

"...and the silverware," Sam said.

"On it!" I said and Vinnie and I ran and obeyed.

Over Mrs. Delgado's lasagna and Mrs. Benedetti's antipasto I tried to work everything out in front of a captive audience.

I hashed, rehashed and re-rehashed it while they ate and listened. When I was done they all stared at me.

"I got nothin'," Vinnie finally said. "I'm a priest, not a detective. I still say you've got to ask the Don about the blood thing. If we're not in danger there's no reason for us to go anywhere."

He looked at Maria, who simply shrugged and said, "I'm just a girl."

That didn't sit well with Sam. She hated women who adopted that attitude and I admired her for not smacking my sister in the back of the head.

"Okay," she said, "I know I'm the one who brought up the question of Vinnie and Maria being in danger, but now I don't think it's true."

"Why not?" I asked.

"Well," she said, "even if you are related to the Don, who knows that? Just you, him and Benny, right?"

"Right."

"So why would the Vendetta extend to them?"

We all looked at her.

"She's right," Vinnie said. "We're safe if nobody knows."

"So basically," I commented, "if you hadn't said a word about this we wouldn't have spent all this time talkin' about it."

She stared at me and asked, "Are you saying I should've just kept my mouth shut?"

"No, no," Vinnie said, "he's not saying that."

"No," I said, "that's not what I meant..."

"More lasagna, anyone?" Maria asked.

63

The biggest question we could come up with was: If Pop was the target, why?

"If the Don's right," Vinnie said, "and it's Vendetta, maybe they hit Pop because he was Dominick's closest friend."

"I'm his godson," I said. "Why kill Carlo when I was right there, out in the open? Or why not Benny? The Don is closer to Benny than he was to Carlo."

"Can I speak?" Sam asked.

"Of course you can," I said, wishing I hadn't said a word, earlier.

"Maybe they haven't been able to get a shot at Benny, especially since he's been inside the hospital all this time. And where was he when the first shooting took place?"

"Inside the restaurant."

"There you go."
"And me?" I asked.
"Maybe," she said, "they're just saving you for the end."

I called the hospital and got them to put me through to the Don's room by telling them it was a life-or-death emergency.

Benny answered. Instead of telling him everything and having him relay it to Jacoby or Po I did it the other way around. I told him to put one of them on the phone.

Jacoby came on.

"What's up, Nick?"

"I caught somebody creeping around my office tonight, Jack," I said.

"You thinking they were gonna make a try at you?"

"Maybe," I said. "He got scared away before we could find out. But nothin' was missin', so I think he was just waitin' in there for me."

"Okay, well, we'll keep on our toes. You gettin' any sleep?"

"Maybe too much. I'll talk to you later."

"Okay."

"Look, stay together, okay? You, Hank and Benny, don't let anybody catch one of you alone."

"We got it, Nick. Later."

I hung up, looked at Sam, who was standing in the kitchen doorway looking at me. Behind her Vinnie and Maria were cleaning the kitchen.

"Ready to go?" she asked.

"Yep," I said, standing up.

We hugged and kissed Vinnie and Maria, and left.

"I'm sorry," I said, as I drove.

"About what?"

"I didn't mean—"

"I know you didn't mean it," she said, "but you were right. If I hadn't brought it up you wouldn't have had to deal with it, at all."

"But you didn't know that at the time. You were tryin' to help."

"I'll always try to help you, Nick."

All my life I was either "Nicky" or "Nicky D" to people, but to Sam it was always "Nick."

"I know you will, Sam, and I appreciate it."

"So what's happening with you and the lady detective?" she asked.

"Nothing, as far as I can tell."

I explained the situation to her and she started laughing.
"What's so funny?"
"You were her booty call."
"I came to that conclusion all by myself."
"And do you feel...used?"
"Actually, no," I said.
She laughed again.
"Just like a man," she said, "and you're all man, Nick."
I didn't know if she meant that was good or bad.

64

The red light, blinking, blinking.
"Nick," Benny's voice said, "the Don wants to talk to you. He wants you to come and see him in the mornin'."
The second message was from Winky: "Delvecchio, I've got some information for you. I'll call you at eight a.m. and tell you where to meet me."
The third was from Lydia Del Costa: "Call me."
The red light stopped blinking.
It occurred to me that this case was probably going to have to be solved without benefit of real detective work. If Winky could tell me something, and the Don could tell me something, it would just be a matter of putting the information together. Information that the police would not have.
Unless I shared it.
If this was a Vendetta being pursued by one man I could probably handle it, but if it was being perpetrated by a group, I would need help. And if I needed help I'd go to Del Costa.
There was a time when I had a friend high up in the department, but Inspector Ed Gorman had retired several years ago. The older I got, the less valuable my time on the job became, because the men I had worked for, or with, had moved on, or had not moved up very far in the Department—or had died.
My connection to Lydia Del Costa, at the moment, was my most valuable Department asset. The only other one I might have called on was Detective Weinstock, who was also in Homicide.
I had said goodnight to Sam at her door. No promise of breakfast in the morning. No arrangement for a knock at the door.
I could have gone to bed without acting on any of the three calls. I couldn't call Winky because I didn't have a number. Could have called Benny and gotten the call put through as another emergency, but it wasn't necessary.

I certainly could have called Del Costa back, but what if it was another booty call? As Sam had said, I was all man, and probably wouldn't have been able to resist.

I decided to do nothing until the morning. I got myself ready for bed, put fresh sheets on the mattress, and turned in for the night.

The phone jarred me awake. I grabbed it before it could ring a second time. I checked the clock. It was 7:58 a.m.

"What?"

"Delvecchio?"

"Yeah."

"It's Winky, man. I got somethin' for ya."

"Hey, Winky," I said, rubbing my eyes. "Wait a minute." I held the phone against my chest while I hacked until my throat was clear. How bad would it have been if I smoked?

"Whataya got, Winky?"

"I got two Jamaicans braggin' that they took out a Mafia Don."

I sat up straight in bed.

"Where are they?" I asked. "Who are they?"

"They're a couple of would-be drug lords who take on work like this," Winky said. "But they have big mouths, so nobody's been usin' them lately."

But somebody did, I thought, maybe *because* they have big mouths. Somebody set them up for this.

"Where do I find them, Winky?"

"East Flatbush. They hang out in a bar on Utica Avenue and East Fifty-First Street. Place called Kingston's."

"A dive?"

"Definitely. Don't go near it without a gun."

"You got names for me, right, Winky?"

"One's called Huntley," Winky said, "the other one is Dalton."

"No last names?"

"Last names ain't special, Delvecchio," he said. "'cept maybe for Dagos You're lookin' for Huntley and Dalton. I don't know if they're your men, but they're sure braggin' like they are."

"Thanks, Winky."

"This worth somethin'?"

"It's worth a lot. Don't worry, you'll get paid. Especially if you come up with the name of the sniper."

"Yeah, well, I'm still workin' on that. If it was a Russian it'll be a little harder. If it was somebody tryin' ta frame the Russians, I might be able ta do somethin'."

"Okay," I said, "I'll be waiting."

I hung up, called the hospital and managed to get put through to the Don's room. Benny answered on the first ring.

"Where the hell are ya, Nicky?" he asked. "The Don wants ya."

"And I want to talk to him, too, Benny," I said, calmly, still giving him the benefit of the doubt because he was upset, "but I just got a tip on the guys with the Uzis."

"You gonna check it out?"

"Yeah, but later," I said "It's a dive called Kingston's in East Flatbush, won't be open this early."

"Then what's the hold-up?"

"The cops want to talk to me, too," I said, "so I'm probably gonna have to go see them before I come to the hospital."

"Yeah, okay, but then hurry."

"Is he okay?"

"Who know? He's still hooked up to machines and the beepin' is drivin' me crazy."

"Benny, I think the trouble starts when the beeping stops."

"Yeah, yeah, I know. See ya, Nicky."

I hung up and decided to get myself showered, dressed and coffeed before I called anyone else.

65

I had a second cup of coffee before I fished out Detective Del Costa's number and dialed it.

"You're up and around early," she said.

"The phone woke me," I said. "What's goin' on?"

"Hicks wanted me to bounce this off you," she said.

"What?"

"Your friend Benny."

"What about him?"

"We're looking at him for this."

"Wait," I said. "You're lookin' at Benny for the attempt on the Don? And the shootin' of my father?"

"Yes, what do you think?"

"No way," I said. "Benny would cut off his left arm before he hurt the Don. And he'd never do anything to hurt my dad."

"You're sure?"

"I'd bet my life on it," I said. "Benny has been loyal to the Don for twelve years, or so. He loves the Don."

"Okay," she said. "I'll tell Hicks."

"What put you on this track?"

"Hicks is running the investigation," she said, "and he doesn't always clue me in. Anyway, thanks."

"Wait, that's all you wanted?"

"Yes," she said. "Why? Was there something else?"

"Nope," I said. "Not for me."

"Okay, then," she said, and hung up.

The kind of girl every guy wants, right? Booty call the night before, attitude like nothing ever happened the next day.

Okay, sure. Why not?

When I got to the hospital Jacoby was alone at the Don's door.

"We decided to work in shifts," he told me. "Hank will relieve me in about an hour."

"Sure, fine," I said. "Whatever works. I'm hoping I won't have to keep you here much longer."

"You got a solid lead?"

"I do," I said, and told him about my 8 a.m. call.

"Want me to go with you?" Jacoby asked.

"No," I said. "I might take Benny, though."

"Why?"

"Because I might not have a choice. I don't know that I'll be able to stop him."

I went into the room. Benny was standing at the Don's bed, staring down at the old man. I moved closer just as the Don's eyes opened. They were sunken and bloodshot, his face shiny with perspiration, jaw covered by gray stubble.

"He's been askin' for you," Benny said, backing away from the bed.

I took his place, stared down at the man who claimed to be my real father.

"Nicky," he said, grabbing for my hand, "Vendetta, Vendetta..."

I stared into his eyes. They didn't seem to be focusing. He knew who I was, but beyond that he only seemed able to say that one word.

"Benny, what—" I started, turning, but Benny was not in the room. "Benny?"

I ran to the bathroom, but he wasn't there, either. He was gone.

I opened the door and asked Jack, "Where's Benny?"

"He just left. Said something about fixing things."

"Great."
"Where could he be going?" Jacoby asked.
"Only one place that I know of," I said. "Jack..."
"I know," he said. "Stay here."
"Thanks."

If Benny had gone off halfcocked he was on his way to East Flatbush to find those two Jamaicans. I had served them up to him on a platter.

I drove as fast as I could to Utica and Fifty-First. The area, right near Linden Boulevard, had a large Jamaican population. I pulled up in front of the Kingston Bar, parked illegally. I wasn't the only one. Benny's Fleetwood was half on the sidewalk.

I was heading for the door when I heard the shots—definitely an Uzi.

I rushed inside with my gun in my hand as more shots rang out, but singles. When I got inside it was over. Benny was standing there with his .45 in his hand. The two Jamaicans were down.

"Benny! What the hell?"

He turned and looked at me.

"When I walked in they went for their Uzis," he said, pointing.

Beneath the table the Jamaicans must have been seated at was a gym bag—big enough to hold the two Uzis that were on the floor. The ceiling had holes in it, stitched by an Uzi. The bartender who had been crouched behind the bar, stood up slowly.

"What hoppen, Mon?" he demanded, glancing up. "Look at me ceilin'."

"Did you call the cops?"

"Yeah, I call dem—"

"Just relax."

"Relax, Mon?" the man asked. "He kill two of me best customers." He pointed at Benny.

"You always let customers in carrying Uzis?"

"I don't know what me customers are carryin', Mon."

"Yeah, well, tell it to the cops." I could hear the sirens. "Benny, give me the gun before they get here."

"What for?" he asked. "All I did was defend myself."

"Yeah, but you came here to kill them," I said.

"No...I didn't, Nick..."

"Yeah, you did. Come on, give it to me before they come through the door." I put my gun away and held my hand out for his. The sirens pulled up out front. He handed me the gun.

66

"Why didn't you tell me this morning on the phone?" Detective Del Costa asked.

"I didn't know, then," I lied. "I got the call after we talked, and then I was in a hurry."

"No," she said, "that won't wash. You told me that the phone woke you up. You got the tip before we spoke."

"Okay, look," I said. "I just wanted to make sure the tip was good, then I would have called you."

"So instead, you told Benny?"

"That," I said, "was bad judgment on my part, I admit."

We were in an interview room at her headquarters. I'd convinced the patrol cops not to shoot us, and to call Hicks and Del Costa. I was sure Benny was in another room in the building, probably with Hicks.

"Once I blabbed I was gonna take Benny with me, so I could control him. But he jumped the gun. Got there ahead of me."

"And executed two men he thought shot the Don."

"He didn't execute them," I said. "When he went in they went for their Uzis."

"You say."

"What's the bartender say?"

"He ducked behind the bar when Benny came in with a gun."

"Benny says he pulled his gun when the two Jamaicans went for theirs."

"Of course that's what he'd say."

"Look," I said, "they had Uzis, and they'd been braggin' about takin' out a Mafia Don."

"We're checking on that," she said. "Talking to the bartender, other customers. Meanwhile..."

"You've got to let us go."

"I can let you go," she said. "I don't know about Benny."

"While you investigate," I said. "He's not goin' anywhere. Not with the Don in the hospital."

She stood up.

"Take his gun, sure," I said. "But he's got a permit for it."

"It's up to Hicks," she said. "I'll talk to him about it."

As she left I wondered where the girl I had met with at Last Exit had gone—or if she had ever really existed?

***

About a half hour later Hicks came in. He had two containers of coffee. He set one in front of me, then sat across from me with the other one. I removed the plastic lid, found it black. The way I liked it.

"Thanks."

"Sure."

I sipped.

"You're not gettin' the treatment you expected from Del Costa, are you?"

"I'm getting what I'd expect from a cop."

He leaned forward.

"But not from a cop you slept with, huh?"

I didn't say anything. He sat back.

"You're surprised I know about it? I know about all her fuck buddies. Did you think you were special?"

"No," I said. "Not special."

"The bartender says you came after the shootin'," Hicks said. "That means I'm gonna let you go."

"And Benny?"

"I can hold him a while longer," Hicks said. "I'm gonna do that, just to be a nutbuster." He laughed.

"When do I get out?" I asked.

"As soon as you finish your coffee," Hicks said. "And sign your statement."

"What statement?"

"It's bein' typed up."

"I didn't write a statement."

"Del Costa's writin' it up from what you said," Hicks said. "If you don't like it, you don't have to sign it."

I nodded, drank some more coffee.

"I thought we were gonna work together on this, Delvecchio."

"I thought I was gonna stay out of it."

He laughed again.

"I never expected that," he said. "Not from you, Nick. Del Costa thinks you knew where those Jamaicans were and didn't tell us."

"I told her—"

"I know what you told her," Hicks said. "If you hear any other news, you'll let us know first, right?"

"Yes."

"Yeah, you will."

We drank our coffee.

"I'll let your friend Benny out tomorrow," Hicks said, "unless I hear somethin' in the meantime from witnesses."

"The bartender was the only witness," I reminded him, "and he ducked down behind the bar."

"Well, we're still canvassing the area," Hicks said. "We might find somebody else who saw somethin'. If not, I'll let him out."

I finished my coffee, put the empty container on the table. At that moment Del Costa walked in and put my statement down in front of me. Amazingly, what she'd written sounded as if I'd written it myself. I signed it.

"Okay, Nick," Hicks said, "you can go."

Del Costa had nothing to say.

"You goin' to the hospital?" Hicks asked.

"That's right."

"In case you're interested," he said, "the Don is still hangin' on."

"Thanks."

"Of course," Hicks said, "he could move on to his eternal reward before Benny gets out."

At the door I said, "For your sake, I hope not."

67

When I got back to the hospital both Jacoby and Po were there.

"What happened to working in shifts?" I asked.

Jacoby shrugged. "We figured with you and Benny gone we might as well both stay."

"What happened?" Po asked.

I told them.

"What the fuck," Po said. "The big guy blew it."

"You think he went there planning to kill them?" Jacoby asked.

"I hope not," I said. "I hope it went the way he said it did."

"What did the Don have to say to you this morning?" Jacoby asked.

"Nothin'," I said. "He called my name, and then said that word again."

"Vendetta?" Po asked.

I nodded.

"It's like that's all he can think of."

"Maybe it is," Po said.

"I'm gonna go in for a minute," I said. "In case he can understand, I want to tell him that Benny'll be back."

They nodded.

Inside was quiet, except for the beep of the machines. I walked to his bed and looked down at him. My feelings were mixed. I didn't want him to die, but I wanted to yell at him, "Why didn't you ever tell me!"

I've never been one of those sons who doesn't look at his parents as people. And especially given the business I'm in, I could understand if my parents had marital problems at one time and my mother went looking for solace in the Don's arms. After all, he was always around. Maybe they felt they were protecting me as a child, but once I reached my adulthood, I would like to have known who my real father was.

"Benny should be back tomorrow," I told the unconscious man. "He's out...checking on somethin' for me. We're workin' together to find out who shot you. You're probably happy to hear me and the big guy are working' together. Funny, I always thought you probably looked at Benny like a son. And maybe you did. Maybe you saw us both as your sons. I don't know. I'm still kinda confused by the whole thing. Maybe you could do me a favor and pull out of this so you can tell me the real story? Is that too much to ask? Just don't die, because I don't know how I'd be able to handle losing two fathers at the same time."

Okay, so much for talking to an unconscious man. They say people can still hear you when they're like that, or in a coma. I didn't know if that was true, but maybe something of what I'd said had gotten through.

I left the room, was saying goodbye to Po and Jacoby when I saw Sam running down the hall towards me. She had obviously dressed in a hurry. Her hair was in tangle and tears were streaming down her face.

"Nick, Nick" she said, breathlessly. She reached and gripped my upper arms with surprising strength. "I didn't know where else to look for you."

"What's wrong?" I asked.

"It's...it's...something's happened at your father's house. Vinnie called. He said...he said...Nick, it's Maria."

"What?"

"Something happened to your sister."

"Watch him," I said to my two friends. "Watch him like a hawk!"

I grabbed Sam's arm and we ran.

We couldn't get near the house. The street was blocked off not only by police vehicles, but by fire trucks and cars.

The sky was filled with black smoke.

"Jesus," I said, as we got out of the car.

I started running, avoiding cops, firemen, vehicles, barricades, until two uniformed cops grabbed me and stopped me before I could get to the house, which was ablaze.

"Hold on, fella," one of them said.

"That's my house," I said. "My father's house."

"It's okay," somebody said. "Let him go."

I turned my head, saw Vinnie coming toward me. He was covered with soot, which made his white collar stand out.

"He's my brother," he said to the two cops.

They let go, but one of them—the older one—said, "Take it easy, pal. You can't go runnin' in there."

Vinnie grabbed my arm.

"He's right, Nick," Vinnie said. "I tried...I tried to get inside."

"Vinnie," I said, "Maria, where's Maria?"

He looked at me, eyes streaming with tears and said, "Inside, Nick. Maria was inside."

68

Father Vinnie wanted me to pray, but I refused. After all, what kind of God takes my father, and then my sister?

We stayed as long as we could. They managed to extinguish the fire, but it was going to take some time for things to cool down enough for them to go in and look for bodies. Until then, I could hold out hope that maybe Maria wasn't inside the house.

According to the cops and the witnesses, they heard an explosion, and then the house just went up.

"Could be a lot of things," the Fire Chief said. "Could've been the hot water heater, or a gas explosion..."

Yeah, I thought, or a Molotov cocktail tossed in a window.

I had just one word running through my mind at that moment.

Vendetta!

I told Vinnie what had happened that morning with Benny and the Jamaicans.

"That sounds crazy," he said. "Why would Benny go there to kill them? You needed at least one of them alive to find out who put them up to it."

"He says he had no choice."

"Do you believe him?"

I shrugged.

"When I pulled up in front I heard the Uzi fire, and then single shots, probably from Benny's forty-five. So yeah, I think they fired first."

"But?"

"But...I don't know. He says he didn't pull his gun until they fired, but if he rushed in with his gun in his hand..."

"...then he instigated the exchange."

"Yeah."

"Well, Nick, going all the way back to high school Benny was never the sharpest knife in the drawer."

"I know that, Vin."

It was a surreal scene. My father's house reduced to rubble, the two of us standing there, discussing the case while waiting for our sister's body to be carried out.

Sam was standing off to the side, arms folded, probably unsure what to do. Should she stay, should she go? Should she try to talk to us? Vinnie had called her when he couldn't get me, and she'd promised she'd find me.

I walked over to her, took her by the upper arms.

"You should go home."

"No," she said. "I'll stay."

"Vinnie and I are gonna stay until…until they bring her out."

"Maybe," she said, "maybe she's not in there."

I took her hand.

"That's what we're hoping."

She squeezed my hand and said, "I'll stay."

It was hours later, dark out, the street lit by portable lights, when two firemen wheeled her body out on a stretcher. She was zipped into a body bag.

"Stay here," I said to Vinnie.

"I have to give her last rites," he said. He took his stole from his pocket.

"Okay." I turned to Sam. "Wait here."

She hugged herself and nodded.

We walked over.

"Are you sure you want to do this?" the Fire Chief asked.

"I'm sure we have to," I said.

He nodded to his men and they unzipped the body bag.

She was too burned for us to tell it was her, but there was a ring on her finger that we both knew.

"Is it her?" the Chief asked.

"Looks like it," I said. "That's her ring. But the M.E. will have to tell us."

Vinnie put the stole around his neck and gave her the last rites, then nodded for them to take her away.

"Come on, Vin," I said. "Let's go."

We turned, and I saw Sergeant Hicks and Detective Del Costa standing by Sam. Vinnie and I walked over.

"We heard about it over the air," Hicks said. "We're sorry for your loss."

"Thanks."

"Do you think this has any connection to your father's death?"

I shrugged. I was shaking inside, and trying to hold it together.

"No way to tell now," I said. "We'll have to let everybody do their jobs, tell us how the fire started, tell us if it's really her."

"Then maybe you should all go home," Hicks said, "and let us do our jobs."

"Yeah," I said, "maybe we should."

I looked at Del Costa, whose face was expressionless.

"Come on, Sam," I said. "Let's take Vinnie back with us."

"I'll talk to the local detectives," Hicks said.

I looked at him, wondering why he was being so helpful.

"Okay," I said. "If they want to talk to me later just let me know."

"Go on," he said, "take your brother home."

The three of us walked back to my car. I didn't know if Vinnie had driven himself or not, but he wasn't talking. Ever since he completed the last rites he hadn't said a word. In fact, his stole was still around his neck.

Sam got in the back seat with him and I drove away from the site.

"Nick," he said, finally.

"Yeah?"

"Take me to the Rectory."

"Are you sure, Vin? Maybe you should come home with me—"

"No," he said, "you have work to do. You have to find out who did this. And I have arrangements to make. And my own job to do."

"Vinnie—"

"The Rectory," he said.

"Okay, Vinnie," I said, "Okay."

69

We dropped Vinnie at the Rectory. Before he went inside he turned and gripped my hand.

"Do what you have to do, Nick," he said. "And be who you have to be."

Then he ran down the steps to the front door.

"What did he mean by that?" Sam asked.

"I'm not sure," I said.

I drove us home.

* * *

We walked down the hall to our apartment doors. At least, I thought we were, but Sam didn't stop at hers. She walked with me to mine.

"I'm coming in with you," she said. "You shouldn't be alone tonight."

I didn't argue with her. I was too damned drained. I unlocked the door and we went inside. I walked to the sofa and sat down. Sam went to the kitchen and came back with two beers.

"Unless you want whiskey?" she asked.

"No," I said, taking the green bottle from her, "this is fine."

She sat down next to me.

"Maybe it's not her, Nick," she said.

"We'll find out tomorrow," I said, "but who else could it be?"

"A neighbor, maybe?" she asked. "Somebody who came over to talk to Maria. Maybe your sister went out to the grocery store?"

"There was still plenty of food in the frig," I said. "besides, if she went shopping where is she now?"

Sam shrugged helplessly.

"Look, Sam, I appreciate the company," I said, "but I really do need to be alone, to think."

"You're going to work tonight?"

"I need to find out if this has anything to do with my dad bein' shot, and the Don."

"Are you going out?"

"I don't know," I said. "I just need some time."

She put her hand on my back.

"You'll call me if you need me?"

"You can count on it."

"Nick—" she said, putting her arms around me. I buried my face in her hair and breathed her in. It would have been very easy for me to just stay like that, but I reluctantly pulled away.

"Thanks for goin' with me, Sam."

She nodded, put down her beer, and stood up. Maybe I was a fool to let her walk out, but I did, and then I was alone. I finished my beer, and hers, while I sat there and tried to figure out my next move.

Vendetta.

That was all I could think about. It was pretty much all the Don was able to say from his hospital bed. If there was someone out there who knew I was the Don's blood, then I was included in the Vendetta. And if I was included, then anyone related to me by blood was, too.

They had killed my father, and Maria.

And that left Vinnie.

And I had dropped him at the Rectory, alone.

I couldn't afford to wait for an autopsy to tell me if the dead girl in the fire actually was my sister. I had to save my brother.

70

I drove through the streets of Brooklyn like a madman, taking the shortest route I knew, ignoring traffic lights and stop signs. Rehearsing my story for when I got stopped by cops.

But I never did.

At that moment, if Vinnie was right and there was a God, he was looking over me, helping me to get to Father Vinnie in time.

I had tried calling the Rectory, but at that time of night no one answered.

I stopped my car in front of the Rectory and rushed to the door. It was locked, so I pounded on it, and rang the bell. Eventually, a sleepy Priest answered the door with a less than priestly look on his face.

"What in God's name—" he said.

"Father Vincent, where is he?"

"Now look here—"

"I'm his brother," I said. "I need to see him…now!"

I pushed past him to the stairway, up to Vinnie's room. The door was locked.

The Priest came in behind me.

"It's locked," I said. "Do you have a key?"

"What are you doing?" he demanded.

"What's going on?" another man asked, coming down the hall.

"Monsignor, this man burst through the door—"

The priest was white-haired, in his sixties. The Monsignor was a younger man by at least ten years, his head bald with a fringe of gray around. They were both wearing robes—expensive robes. That fact was one of the reasons I didn't like the Church.

"I need to get into Father Vinnie's room," I said. "I'm his brother, Nick."

"Yes, I recognize you," the Monsignor said, "but why are you here this late—"

"Monsignor," I said. "My brother is in danger. I need to get inside." I threw my shoulder into the door, but it was solid and hardly budged.

"I need a key!" I shouted at them.

"Yes, yes, all right," the Monsignor said. "Just a minute."

He went to his room, I assumed to get his keys. I tried the door again with my shoulder, but it was thick and well built. Expensive, damn it. Carvings on the outside.

"How do these doors lock?" I asked the old priest. "From the inside."

"Or the outside," he said. "You just have to pull it closed behind you when you leave."

The Monsignor reappeared.

"Hurry!"

He turned on the light in the hall, started going through the keys on his ring.

"Hurry up!"

"I've got it," he said. "I've got it."

He leaned over the door and slid the key into the lock. When he turned it he stepped back and I pushed through, into the room.

Vinnie was on the floor.

Bleeding.

Dying.

He had his hands over his belly, ribbons of blood flowing from between them. He looked up at me.

"Nick," he said, "oh Nick."

"Vinnie!"

I ran to him, got on the floor, took him into my arms, trying not to jar him.

"Call nine-one-one!" I shouted at the two stunned priests. "Call an ambulance!"

The old priest withdrew from the room. The Monsignor continued to stare for a few second, then also backed out. He returned with his stole around his neck, and knelt by us.

"No!" I said.

"I must give him last rites."

"No! You can't!" I looked down at Vinnie's face. He was pale, so pale. "Vinnie, who did it? Who did this to you?"

The Monsignor started to drone on, praying, gesturing.

"Come on, Vinnie," I said, clutching him to me. "Hang on."

He moved one of his hands and I took it, sticky with his blood. He squeezed my hand tightly.

"That's it," I said, "that's it. Squeeze, and keep squeezing." I looked up. "Damn it, where's that ambulance."

I reached up to the bed, pulled a pillow from it and tried to press it over his belly, tried to staunch the flow of blood. I didn't know how bad the wound was, but if I could just stop the bleeding.

"Vinnie," I said, "Vin, who did it?"

"Nick," he whispered.

"What? What is it?"

I lowered my head so that my ear was almost to his mouth.

"Nick," he whispered, "Nicky."

And he stopped squeezing my hand.

71

I watched as they carried my brother's body out of the Rectory on a stretcher. The ambulance had arrived, too late, and then the police.

And then Hicks and Del Costa.

I was sitting in a small room of the Rectory, where couples waited for their counseling appointments, or to arrange a wedding, a baptism—or a funeral mass. Where they waited to hear words of comfort from the men who served God—or claimed to.

God!

I had thought God was protecting me as I drove through those red lights and stop signs. Protecting me so I could get to my brother and save him. But no. He was protecting me so I could get there in time for my brother to die in my arms.

God damn you, I thought, and then started to laugh because I realized how silly that was. God wasn't about to damn himself. Not when he could have his fun damning all of us.

I looked up, saw Hicks and Del Costa staring at me, probably wondering if I had lost my mind. At least this time the lady detective who had shared my bed one night had the good grace to look sad.

"You're the last one in your family left, Delvecchio," Hicks said. "Maybe you should tell us what the hell is goin' on?"

"I thought he was out of his head," I said. "It seemed like the only word he could remember."

"What are you talkin' about?" Hicks demanded.

"The Don," I said. "Every time he wakes up he says the same word—'Vendetta.'"

"You're tellin' me all these killings are the result of some wacky Italian Vendetta?"

"I'm not tellin' you that," I said. "The Don told me, and now..." I stopped, shook my head, too choked up to finish.

"And now what?" Hicks said. "Come on, Delvecchio. Spit it out! Mourn on your own time."

I glared at him through tears and said, "Just before my brother died in my arms he looked at me and said 'Vendetta.'"

"Goddamit!" Hicks said. "This ain't a damned Godfather movie!"

"Look, what can I tell you?" I asked. "My father, sister and brother are dead. If you think there's another connection, find it. Do your job!"

Hicks pointed his index finger at me.

"I been coddlin' you because you been losin' family," he said, "and my partner's been pushin' me, but no more."

"Well, I've got no more family to give, Sergeant Hicks," I said. "All I've got left are the Don, and probably Benny."

And maybe Sam, but I didn't even want to say that out loud.

"You tellin' me you're related to Benny Carbone?" he asked.

"No, I'm not related to him. Just do him a favor and keep him in your jail."

"Too late for that," Hicks said. "I cut him loose hours ago."

Was Benny in danger? I wondered. He was close to the Don, but he wasn't blood.

"Why would a Vendetta against the Barracuda include you and your family?" he demanded. "What the hell are you hidin'?"

I bit my tongue.

"Is he more than your godfather?" Hicks demanded. "Your uncle, maybe?"

I still wasn't ready to admit that the Don was my father. Not to Hicks, anyway.

"I should take you in," Hicks said.

I looked down at my hands.

"For what?" I asked. "For being covered in my brother's blood?"

He didn't take me in, not that I cared much, at that moment. He and Del Costa left and I sat there a few more minutes, trying to process everything that had happened that night, until the Monsignor and the old priest came up to me.

"Is there something we can do for you, my son?" the Monsignor asked, solicitously.

"Yeah," I said, standing up, "get the fuck away from me."

He flinched like I'd slapped him.

"You and your God," I added. "Just stay the hell away from me!"

72

They were all gone.

My whole family.

If the Don was my father, then he was the last one left—but he was also the reason they were all dead.

I headed for the hospital.

Visiting hours were long over, but I didn't let that stop me. I walked into the place like I belonged there and took the elevator to the Don's floor. When I saw the crowd, I knew I was too late. It had all gone down in one night.

I hurried down the hall, was met by both Po and Jacoby.

"We're sorry, Nick," Jacoby said.

"What happened?"

"He just...died," Po said.

"What?"

"They're saying it happens," Jacoby said. "A patient seems to be doing okay, and then..."

"He wasn't killed?"

"No, Nick," Po said. "He just died. Why? What's going on?"

I told them.

"Jesus," Jacoby said, "my God, I'm so sorry."

"Yeah," Po said. "What the hell is going on, Nick?"

"Vendetta," I said.

"That again?" Jacoby asked.

"It's the only explanation," I said. "It's what my brother said before he died. Whether I really am the Don's son or not, somebody obviously thinks so. And my blood is his blood."

"And you're the last one left," Jacoby said.

"Nick," Po said, "you've got to get out of town."

"I can't—"

"You have to," Jacoby said. "Whoever's doing this is determined. Hell, they got your brother *in* the Rectory!"

I couldn't think about leaving town and running. I had to find out for sure what happened to the Don.

I moved past Po and Jacoby and headed for the room. As I reached the door it opened and Benny came out.

"Benny, what the hell—" I said.

"He's gone, Nick," he said. "The Don's gone."

I talked with the doctor. He repeated what Jacoby had told me. "Sometimes it happens."

"Doctor, he couldn't have been killed?"

The Doctor frowned.

"He was a very sick man, Mr. Delvecchio," he said. "This is not an unusual situation. I feel no compulsion to notify the police that his death may be suspicious."

"That's okay, Doc," I said. "There'll be an autopsy, anyway, just because of who he was, and why he was in here."

"That may be," the doctor said, "but my job is done."

He walked away. I thought about going into the Don's room to look at him, then thought, why bother? Dead is dead. He may have been my real father, but my whole family was dead because of something he had done in his past.

And I might still die as a result of it.

I walked down the hall to where Benny was seated, and Po and Jacoby were standing. I told them to go home.

"You need us to watch your back, Nick," Jacoby said.

"Go home," I said. "You're done. I appreciate your help, but I can't have you around me. I don't want to be responsible for any more deaths."

"Nick," Po said, "you're not responsible for any of this."

"I appreciate that, Hank," I said. "Go home, both of you...please."

Po turned and headed for the elevator. Jacoby put his hand on my arm and said. "Get out of town, Nick. Run. At least until this all blows over."

As he joined Po in the elevator I wondered if Vendettas ever really blew over? Didn't they just go on until everybody was dead?

I walked over to Benny, who looked up at me through bloodshot eyes.

"There was nothin' I could do, Nick," he said. "I mean, I'm a strong guy, and I can shoot, but...there was nothin'..."

"I know, Benny," I said, patting him on the shoulder. "I know."

"The dicks told me about your family," he said. "I'm so sorry."

"Yeah, thanks."

"I don't know what to do now, Nick," he said. "What're you gonna do?"

"I don't know, Benny."

"Maybe," Benny said, "we should work together, find the people who killed your family."

I thought about what he'd done to the two Jamaicans. And who would we look for? Italians, or a Russian killer working for Italians?

"I don't think you should be near me, Benny," I said. "I don't think anybody should be near me."

"Nick—"

"You've got the Don's business to take care of, Benny," I said.

"But you," he said, "you're his—"

"Nobody was more his son than you, Benny," I said. "You take care of it. And take care of yourself."

"Nicky—" he said, but I walked to the elevator which—thankfully—opened at that moment. I stepped in and rode down.

EPILOGUE

Somewhere in the Midwest, 2010

1

"I ran, and ended up here," I finished.

The three men had listened to my story, two of them with bored looks on their faces, but the spokesman, he looked very interested the whole time.

"That's some story," the spokesman said.

"Answer your questions?" I asked.

"Most of 'em."

"Why so interested?"

Before he could answer he cocked his head, put the fingers of his left hand to his ear. Obviously he had an earpiece there.

"Yep, we're in. Yes, you can come up."

"Somebody else arrived?" I asked.

"My boss."

"You guys aren't cops," I said. "Not Feds. Mafia?"

They all snorted.

"There's no more Mafia, Mr. Delvecchio," the spokesman said.

We all waited and I heard the gravel crunch again beneath the tires of a vehicle. I could see enough of it to tell it was a stretch Hummer. But I couldn't see who was getting out, so I leaned forward, careful not to let the gun I was sitting on slip to the floor.

I caught my breath.

Benny.

And it all clicked into place, fifteen years later.

Benny, in the restaurant when the Uzi strafed the Don and Vito Delvecchio;

Benny, rushing ahead of me to gun down the two Jamaicans;
Benny, not in custody when Maria and Vinnie were killed;
Benny, alone with the Don when he died.
Benny...not as dumb as he made out to be.

The driver stayed by the car while Benny walked up onto the deck. I sat back in my chair, comforted by the gun under my left buttocks.

"Hey, Nicky."

"Benny."

There was a look in his eyes I had never seen. Benny had always had street smarts, but now he looked...almost intelligent. Also, he'd gone to fat over the years, was a lot wider than he used to be. His hair was gray and thinning.

"You look good, Nick," he said. "Ain't aged much. Still got your hair."

"Can't say the same for you," I said. "You're fat and bald."

He didn't like that, but he shook it off.

"You don't look surprised to see me."

"I was surprised when the door opened and you stepped out," I said, "but then it all made sense."

"It did, huh?"

"You were alone with the Don," I said. "What'd you do, pinch off his oxygen?"

"Actually, that made it easy. They had just put him on oxygen that morning, because his breathing started to labor."

"So let me guess," I said. "There was no Vendetta."

Benny made a rude sound with his mouth.

"That's goombah stuff, Nicky. But all I had to do was keep whisperin' that word in the Don's ear while he was unconscious. Every time he woke up, he said it."

"And killin' Maria and Father Vinnie?"

"Supported the idea of a Vendetta," Benny said. "Kept the cops—and you—off balance. Nobody ever looked at me."

"And why kill the Don in the first place?" I asked.

"He let it slip a couple of years before that you were his son," Benny said. "Right then I knew I wasn't gettin' nothin'. You would get it all. So I started to plan."

"The Jamaicans?"

"A couple of idiots I had use for. The one thing I'm sorry about was your dad. I mean Vito. I never wanted him to get killed."

"But you did," I said. "Your sniper hit him right in the heart."

He chuckled, which made me want to choke him with my bare hands.

"Yeah well, in the end I figured that'd confuse the cops, too. Who was the target? The Don? Vito?"

"It was a good plan, Benny," I said. "Confused everybody. Frustrated the hell out of me. Tell me something."

"What?"

"You didn't somehow mess with the blood test results, did you?"

"Nope," he said. "I had nothin' to do with that. You really were the Don's son."

"And that's really why you're here, fifteen years later?" I asked.

"I never thought you'd run, Nicky," he said. "I thought we had time to kill you. But you disappeared."

"And you've been lookin' for me all these years?"

"On and off. When I'd hear somethin' about a job bein' done that sounded like you, I'd send somebody to have a look."

"This guy?" I asked, indicating the spokesman.

"Usually. He's my number one."

"He's not Italian."

"There's no more family, Nick," Benny said. "I run my own shop."

"But you started with everything the Don had, right?"

"True. His cash, he had some investments, I sold the Barge…he left me everything, but only in the event you weren't around."

"So now what?"

"Well," Benny said, "I can't have you ever comin' back and claimin' your birthright."

"I don't want it, Benny."

"So you say," Benny said. "But I'm makin' sure. That's how I got where I am—makin' sure."

"So where's your shooter?" I asked. "He out in the trees with a Russian sniper rifle?"

"I don't need shooter for this, Nick," he said. "I never liked you. Did you know that?"

"You know, Benny," I said. "I always thought you were even dumber than you seemed."

Benny chuckled, shook his head, and reached leisurely into his jacket for his gun. Still a .45. I saw that just before I raised my left hand and shot him in the chest.

Talk about surprised.

2

Following my shot the sound of the hammer being cocked above their head attracted the other three men. As Benny slumped to the deck they looked up at Sam, pointing a 9-mm Glock at them. She was holding it with both hands, the way I taught her. The three men paused with their hands chest high, ready to reach into their jackets.

The spokesman looked at me.

"What's it gonna be?" I asked. "Your boss is dead. The empire is up for grabs."

"He really wasn't very smart."

I shrugged.

"You really aren't going to come back?" he asked.

"No."

"Is she any good with that Glock?"

"Very good."

He waved at the other two men to put their hands down.

"Take him with you," I said. "There's an ordinance around here about burying dead animals on your own property."

"Pick him up," he said to the others.

"He's heavy, Alexei."

Alexei made an annoyed face as the man spoke his name.

"Get Harry to help you."

They waved to the driver, who came warily up the steps, took stock of the situation, and then helped the two men carry Benny off the deck.

"Good luck to you," Alexei said, and started to turn.

"Alexei."

He stopped.

I stood up.

"That's Russian, right?"

"I was hoping you wouldn't catch that."

"The sniper," I said. "You killed my father. And Carlo."

"It was my job."

"And my sister and brother?"

"Still my job. Benny paid me."

"And that made you his number one."

He was half turned. I couldn't see his hand, but Sam could.

"Tell me something, Mr. Delvecchio," Alexei said.

"What?"

"That horse you gave Winky money to bet for you?" he asked. "What did it do?"

"It won," I said. "Paid Fifty-five dollars. I picked up the money from him before we left town. I needed every cent I had."

"Guess you're pretty good with longshots."

"Not typically."

"I don't suppose you'll let me walk off this deck."

"Not likely."

"I didn't think so. You know, it was nothing personal."

"Sorry I can't say the same."

He nodded and went into his jacket for his gun. Sam and I fired at the same time. Alexei went down, his gun flying out of his hand and off the deck.

The three men carrying Benny dropped him and ran up the stairs. Sam and I had them covered.

"Put Benny in the car, come back for Alexei," I said. "Then leave."

They looked at me, then Sam, then at each other. In the end they put Benny in the back seat, and Alexei in the trunk. Then they sent one last look our way before getting into the car and leaving.

Sam came down from the upper deck, the gun hanging limply from her shaking hands. I took it from her, and gave her a hug.

"Did I hit him?" she asked.

"I killed him," I said. "But you probably saved us."

"Should I pack?" she asked. "Again?"

"Afraid so."

"Shit," she said. "I liked it here."

"Me, too."

"Another new address for my agent."

After leaving Brooklyn with me Sam had been writing her books under all different names, depending on her agent to sell them on their merit. We couldn't afford for her to keep using the same name.

She probably shouldn't have been writing at all, but once she agreed to leave Brooklyn with me I couldn't ask her to give up what she loved.

"Someday," I said, "you'll be able to come out from behind all the pen names."

She squeezed me around the waist and said, "Oh, I complain, but I don't care. As long as we're together."

"Better get packed," I said, kissing her.

She went to the door, then stopped.

"Nick?"

"Yeah?"

"With Benny dead, and the Russian who killed your family, what about…"

"We can't go back to Brooklyn, Sam," I said. "It was the end of Brooklyn for us a long time ago. We can't change now."

"I know," she said. "I know."

I didn't really care about Brooklyn, anymore. There was nothing there for me. All the family I had left was Sam, and as long as she was with me, I was home.

ROBERT J. RANDISI is the author of the "Miles Jacoby," "Nick Delvecchio," "Gil & Claire Hunt," "Dennis McQueen," "Joe Keough," and "The Rat Pack" mystery series. He is the editor of over 30 anthologies. All told he is the author of over 600 novels.

Randisi is the founder of the Private Eye Writers of America, the creator of the Shamus Award, the co-founder of Mystery Scene Magazine.

On the following pages are a few
more great titles from the
Down & Out Books publishing family.

For a complete list of books and to
sign up for our newsletter,
go to DownAndOutBooks.com.

Driving Reign
The De La Cruz Case Files
TG Wolff

Down & Out Books
April 2020
978-1-64396-087-6

The woman in the stingy hospital bed wasn't dead. The question for Detective Jesus De La Cruz: did the comatose patient narrowly survive suicide or murder?

Faithful friends paint a picture of a guileless young woman, a victim of both crime and society. Others describe a cold woman with a proclivity for icing interested men with a single look.

Beneath the rhetoric, Cruz unearths a twisted knot of reality and perception. A sex scandal, a jilted lover, a callous director, a rainmaker, and a quid pro quo have Cruz questioning if there is such a thing as an innocent man.

Catawba Point
A Jim Grant Thriller
Colin Campbell

Down & Out Books
June 2020
978-1-64396-105-7

When Jim Grant's flight home to give evidence about Snake Pass is cancelled he is diverted via Charlotte NC where he is forced to spend a 3-day layover at a seedy motel on the outskirts of town.

All Grant wants is a good night's sleep, but with a skinny hooker and her pimp causing trouble along the hall that isn't going to happen. Maybe throwing the pimp over the balcony wasn't such a good idea but that's just the start of Grant's problems, which lead him to a gang of white supremacists and their training camp at Catawba Point.

Man of the World
Paul D. Brazill

All Due Respect, an imprint of
Down & Out Books
April 2020
978-1-64396-099-9

Ageing hit-man Tommy Bennett left London and returned to his hometown of Seatown, hoping for respite from the ghosts of the violent past that haunted him. However, things don't go to plan and trouble and violence soon follow Tommy to Seatown.

Tommy is soon embroiled in Seatown's underworld and his hopes of a peaceful retirement are dashed. Tommy deliberates whether or not to leave Seatown and return to London. Or even leave Great Britain altogether. So, he heads back to London where violence and mayhem await him.

Kraj the Enforcer: Stories
Rusty Barnes

Shotgun Honey, an imprint of
Down & Out Books
October 2019
978-1-64396-059-3

Meet Kraj, low-level errand boy and hitman for Tricky Ricky Gutierrez. In upstate New York Kraj strongarms his way through the ranks of Ricky's shabby organization until he is ultimately committing murder for the man in charge.

Follow him in his adventures with his girlfriend Cami and night club manager Mikael on a trail of equal parts savage lechery and even more savage murder.

www.ingramcontent.com/pod-product-compliance
Lightning Source LLC
Chambersburg PA
CBHW020238030426
42336CB00010B/520